DevOps Security and Automation

Building, deploying, and scaling modern software systems

Nishant Singh

bpb

www.bpbonline.com

First Edition 2025

Copyright © BPB Publications, India

ISBN: 978-93-65895-544

To View Complete
BPB Publications Catalogue
Scan the QR Code:

Dedicated to

My son Avyaan Singh, who at 2 years old would innocently ask what u doing papa? in his sweet baby voice, while I wrote late into the night. Your curious spirit inspires me every day.

My wife Mahek, whose unwavering support and encouragement made this book possible. Thank you for understanding the long hours and believing in this dream.

My parents, whose constant guidance and help have been the foundation of everything I achieve. Your sacrifices and wisdom continue to light my path.

About the Author

Nishant Singh is a senior software engineer at LinkedIn, where he specializes in building large-scale observability infrastructure using cutting-edge technologies including Azure Data Explorer, Go, Python, and Azure OpenAI. With over 9 years of experience spanning software engineering and DevOps, Nishant architects and codes solutions that serve millions of users while ensuring optimal performance and reliability.

At LinkedIn, Nishant has evolved through multiple senior engineering roles, developing next-generation log and events platforms that process data at massive scale. His software engineering background enables him to build robust, performance-optimized applications while implementing sophisticated automation, disaster recovery systems, and visualization tools. His dual expertise in software development and operations provides him with a unique perspective on building reliable, scalable systems from the ground up.

Prior to LinkedIn, Nishant developed infrastructure-as-code solutions and data-ML pipelines at Paytm and designed high-availability software systems with comprehensive security implementations at Gemalto (now Thales Digital Identity and Security). His hands-on experience across the complete software delivery lifecycle, from coding applications to managing production infrastructure, gives him practical insights into the challenges and solutions that modern DevOps teams face daily.

Nishant holds a master's degree in computer engineering from Amity University Delhi and has published research in areas including algorithmic optimization and cloud automation. His technical expertise encompasses the full DevOps ecosystem, from containerization and orchestration to observability and security. As both a software engineer and DevOps practitioner, he understands the critical importance of bridging development and operations teams to achieve successful software delivery in today's fast-paced digital landscape.

About the Reviewers

❖ **Akhilesh Pandey** is a freelance cloud, Kubernetes, DevOps, and solution architect with deep expertise in cloud-native technologies across AWS, GCP, and OCI. He engineers robust, automated infrastructure solutions using Terraform, Ansible, and Kubernetes, prioritizing infrastructure as code practices and operational efficiency. Akhilesh emphasizes monitoring the right signals through tools like Grafana, Nagios, and the ELK Stack to ensure reliability and observability. He is also an avid reader and technical reviewer for books on DevOps, CI/CD, and Kubernetes, actively contributing to the engineering community.

❖ **Thiago** specializes in designing, architecting, and automating mission-critical deployments across expansive infrastructures. Boasting over fifteen years of dynamic experience in the information technology sector, his expertise lies in crafting robust CI/CD pipelines and configuring management tools with a strong focus on infrastructure as code principles.

He is highly proficient in fostering seamless communication, nurturing collaborative environments, and excelling both in team settings and independent projects. With advanced English proficiency and a hands-on approach, Thiago is driven by a passion for problem-solving and delivering impactful results.

Renowned for his analytical acumen, he consistently drives innovation by envisioning and implementing forward-thinking strategies and solutions.

Acknowledgement

I would like to express my sincere gratitude to all those who contributed to the completion of this book.

First and foremost, I extend my heartfelt appreciation to my family and friends for their unwavering support and encouragement throughout this journey. Their understanding during long writing sessions and their constant motivation have been invaluable.

I would like to extend special thanks to my ex-colleagues and engineers I worked with, for their insights and real-world experiences that shaped many of the practical examples in this book. Your daily collaboration and problem-solving approaches have enriched the content significantly.

I am immensely grateful to the DevOps community at large, the open-source contributors whose tools we rely on daily, and the thought leaders who continue to push the boundaries of what's possible in software delivery.

I would also like to acknowledge BPB Publications for their guidance and expertise in bringing this book to fruition. Their support and assistance were invaluable in navigating the complexities of the publishing process.

Special recognition goes the editors and technical reviewers who provided valuable feedback and contributed to the refinement of this manuscript. Their insights and suggestions have significantly enhanced the quality and accuracy of the technical content.

Lastly, I want to express my gratitude to the readers who have shown interest in mastering DevOps practices. Your eagerness to learn and improve the software delivery process is what drives the continuous evolution of our field.

Thank you to everyone who has played a part in making this book a reality.

Preface

In today's rapidly evolving software landscape, the ability to deliver high-quality applications quickly and reliably has become a competitive necessity. DevOps has emerged as the transformative methodology that bridges the traditional gap between development and operations, enabling organizations to achieve unprecedented speed, stability, and scalability in their software delivery processes.

This book is designed as a comprehensive guide for software engineers, system administrators, and IT professionals who want to master the complete DevOps ecosystem. Through fifteen carefully structured chapters, this bootcamp covers everything from foundational cultural principles to advanced automation techniques, providing both theoretical knowledge and hands-on practical experience.

Chapter 1: Understanding DevOps Culture and Principles - This chapter introduces the fundamental concepts and cultural shift required for successful DevOps adoption, exploring the evolution from traditional silos to collaborative, automated workflows.

Chapter 2: Setting up Development Environments - This chapter focuses on creating consistent, reproducible environments using Docker, Vagrant, and Docker Compose, establishing the foundation for reliable software delivery.

Chapter 3: Version Control and Git Workflows - This chapter dives deep into Git workflows and best practices, covering branching strategies, code review processes, and collaboration techniques essential for modern development teams.

Chapter 4: Continuous Integration Fundamentals - This chapter explores Continuous Integration using Jenkins, GitHub Actions, and GitLab CI, teaching readers to build automated pipelines that catch issues early and maintain code quality.

Chapter 5: Introduction to Infrastructure as Code - This chapter introduces Terraform, CloudFormation, and Ansible, enabling readers to manage and provision infrastructure through code, ensuring consistency and repeatability.

Chapter 6: Continuous Delivery and Deployment - This chapter covers advanced deployment strategies including Blue/Green and Canary deployments, automated rollbacks, and feature flags for safe, reliable releases.

Chapter 7: Configuration Management - This chapter explores Ansible, Puppet, and Chef for maintaining consistency across environments and managing configuration at scale.

Chapter 8: Observability with TEMPLE- This chapter introduces a comprehensive framework covering Tracing, Events, Metrics, Profiling, Logs, and Exceptions using tools like Prometheus, Grafana, and the ELK Stack.

Chapter 9: Containerization and Docker Best Practices - This chapter focuses on containerization best practices, security, and optimization techniques for building efficient, secure container images.

Chapter 10: Kubernetes Essentials - This chapter covers container orchestration, auto-scaling, and Helm for managing complex applications in production environments.

Chapter 11: DevSecOps: This chapter integrates security into DevOps workflows, covering automated security testing, secrets management, and compliance automation.

Chapter 12: Continuous Testing and Quality Assurance - This chapter explores comprehensive testing strategies including TDD, BDD, and automation frameworks for maintaining quality throughout the delivery pipeline.

Chapter 13: Site Reliability Engineering - This chapter introduces SRE principles, error budgets, and reliability practices for building and maintaining resilient systems at scale.

Chapter 14: Advanced DevOps Automation - This chapter covers advanced patterns including microservices, GitOps, and platform engineering for scaling DevOps practices across large organizations.

Chapter 15: Platform Engineering - This chapter explores emerging technologies like AI in DevOps, edge computing, and next-generation automation tools that will shape the future of software delivery.

Each chapter includes practical exercises designed to reinforce learning through hands-on experience with industry-standard tools and real-world scenarios. Whether you're a developer looking to understand the complete software lifecycle or an operations professional wanting to embrace automation and collaboration, this bootcamp will equip you with the knowledge and skills needed to excel in today's DevOps-driven world.

By the end of this journey, readers will have gained not only comprehensive theoretical knowledge but also practical experience in implementing DevOps practices, enabling them to drive digital transformation within their organizations and advance their careers in this critical field.

Code Bundle and Coloured Images

Please follow the link to download the
Code Bundle and the *Coloured Images* of the book:

https://rebrand.ly/16d547

The code bundle for the book is also hosted on GitHub at
https://github.com/bpbpublications/DevOps-Security-and-Automation.
In case there's an update to the code, it will be updated on the existing GitHub repository.

We have code bundles from our rich catalogue of books and videos available at
https://github.com/bpbpublications. Check them out!

Errata

We take immense pride in our work at BPB Publications and follow best practices to ensure the accuracy of our content to provide with an indulging reading experience to our subscribers. Our readers are our mirrors, and we use their inputs to reflect and improve upon human errors, if any, that may have occurred during the publishing processes involved. To let us maintain the quality and help us reach out to any readers who might be having difficulties due to any unforeseen errors, please write to us at :

errata@bpbonline.com

Your support, suggestions and feedbacks are highly appreciated by the BPB Publications' Family.

Did you know that BPB offers eBook versions of every book published, with PDF and ePub files available? You can upgrade to the eBook version at www.bpbonline. com and as a print book customer, you are entitled to a discount on the eBook copy. Get in touch with us at :

business@bpbonline.com for more details.

At www.bpbonline.com, you can also read a collection of free technical articles, sign up for a range of free newsletters, and receive exclusive discounts and offers on BPB books and eBooks.

Piracy

If you come across any illegal copies of our works in any form on the internet, we would be grateful if you would provide us with the location address or website name. Please contact us at business@bpbonline.com with a link to the material.

If you are interested in becoming an author

If there is a topic that you have expertise in, and you are interested in either writing or contributing to a book, please visit www.bpbonline.com. We have worked with thousands of developers and tech professionals, just like you, to help them share their insights with the global tech community. You can make a general application, apply for a specific hot topic that we are recruiting an author for, or submit your own idea.

Reviews

Please leave a review. Once you have read and used this book, why not leave a review on the site that you purchased it from? Potential readers can then see and use your unbiased opinion to make purchase decisions. We at BPB can understand what you think about our products, and our authors can see your feedback on their book. Thank you!

For more information about BPB, please visit www.bpbonline.com.

Join our Discord space

Join our Discord workspace for latest updates, offers, tech happenings around the world, new releases, and sessions with the authors:

https://discord.bpbonline.com

Table of Contents

CHAPTER 1
Understanding DevOps Culture and Principles

Introduction

In this chapter, we will discuss DevOps, a transformative approach that has redefined software development and IT operations. We will start by understanding DevOps' origins and evolution, tracing its journey from bridging the gap between **development** (**dev**) and **operations** (**ops**) to becoming a global movement shaping modern software delivery.

We will then explore the core principles of DevOps, like collaboration, automation, and continuous improvement. These principles foster a culture of shared responsibility, customer-centricity, and rapid feedback loops, enabling faster, more reliable software releases.

We will also cover DevOps maturity models and assessment frameworks. These provide organizations with structured ways to measure their DevOps practices, set target maturity levels, and establish roadmaps for continuous improvement. By assessing their current state, companies can identify areas to enhance their DevOps alignment with business objectives and technical goals.

Structure

In this chapter, we will cover the following topics:

- History and evolution of DevOps

- Core principles of DevOps

- DevOps culture and mindset

- Benefits of adopting DevOps practices

- Relationship between DevOps, Agile, and Lean methodologies

- Overcoming organizational resistance to DevOps

- Key DevOps roles and responsibilities

- DevOps maturity models and assessment frameworks

Objectives

By the end of this chapter, you will be able to explain the origins and significance of the DevOps movement, describe its core principles of collaboration, automation, and continuous improvement, discuss the cultural shift required to adopt a DevOps mindset and understand the role of DevOps maturity models in helping organizations measure and enhance their DevOps practices. These practices enable faster, more reliable software delivery.

History and evolution of DevOps

As we discuss the fascinating origins of DevOps, it is essential to share how this methodology has transformed the landscape of software development. DevOps is defined as a set of practices, tools, and a cultural philosophy that automates and integrates the processes between software development and IT teams. It emphasizes collaboration, communication, and automation to improve the speed and quality of software delivery.

The story of DevOps begins with *Patrick Debois*, who is often referred to as *the father of DevOps*. In 2007, *Patrick* started exploring the complexities of IT from multiple perspectives. He quickly realized the pain points where software projects required constant switching between development and operations, highlighting a significant gap in collaboration. This realization laid the groundwork for what would eventually become DevOps.

Fast forward to 2008, when *Patrick* met *Andrew Shafer* at the Agile Infrastructure conference in *Toronto*; their conversation centered on the limitations of Agile methodologies, particularly in addressing the friction between development and operations teams. This dialogue sparked the idea of DevOps, aiming to resolve these ongoing issues and create a more integrated approach.

In 2009, the concept of DevOps began to gain traction. A pivotal moment occurred with a presentation titled *10+ Deploys a Day: Dev and Ops Cooperation at Flickr*, delivered by *John Allspaw* and *Paul Hammond*. This talk not only introduced more IT industry methods into the DevOps dialogue but also generated considerable interest, culminating in the establishment of the first *DevOpsDays* conference in *Ghent, Belgium*. This event marked a turning point, as the term *DevOps* became a buzzword.

As we moved into the 2010s, DevOps continued to grow. The *DevOpsDays* conference made its way to the *United States* in *Mountain View, California,* bringing together thought leaders and practitioners eager to share insights. By 2012-2013, *Alanna Brown* at Puppet produced the inaugural *State of DevOps Report,* providing valuable data and insights into the adoption of DevOps practices.

In 2013, the release of *The Phoenix Project,* authored by *Gene Kim, Kevin Behr, and George Spafford,* became a landmark moment for the DevOps movement. This book not only popularized the concept but also illustrated it through the story of *Bill Palmer,* who navigated the challenges of managing IT within a struggling organization.

The momentum continued, with *Forrester Research* declaring 2017 as *the year of DevOps,* noting that up to 50% of organizations were starting to implement these practices. By 2018, the *DevOpsDays* conferences had expanded, with up to 30 events scheduled across the *United States,* reflecting the growing interest in the methodology.

Figure 1.1 shows a timeline of this journey as follows:

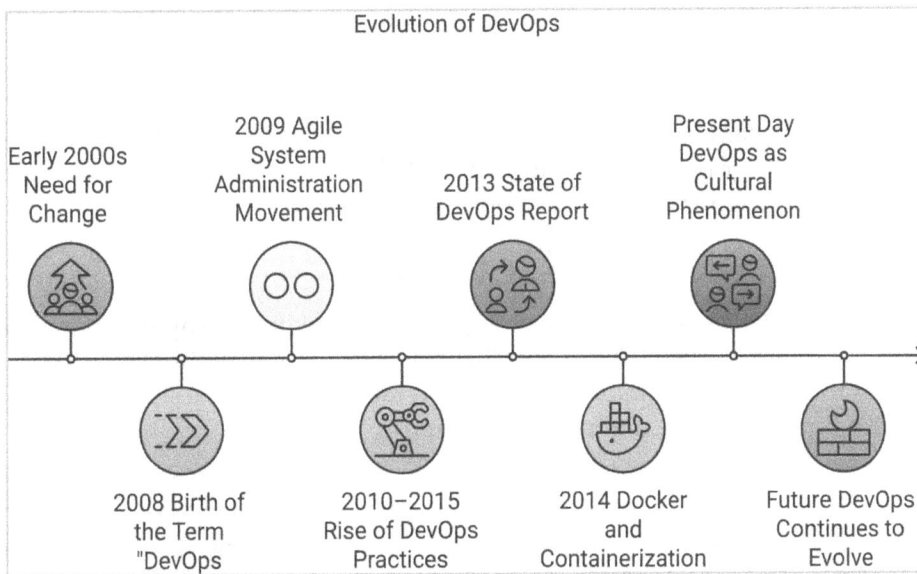

Figure 1.1: *Evolution of DevOps*

Despite this rapid evolution, challenges remained. In 2019, *Gartner* reported that while infrastructure and operations leaders were still pursuing DevOps initiatives, many organizations struggled with the necessary cultural and operational changes.

This journey illustrates how DevOps has not only transformed the way we develop and deliver software but has also emphasized the importance of collaboration, automation, and continuous improvement. By understanding this evolution, we can better appreciate the principles and practices that make DevOps an essential part of today's technology landscape.

Moreover, the significance of DevOps extends beyond its origins and principles, offering a range of compelling benefits that organizations can leverage for success as follows:

- **Enhanced collaboration:** DevOps promotes collaboration by breaking down silos between development, operations, and stakeholders, leading to improved communication and unified software delivery goals.

- **Accelerated delivery:** By automating repetitive tasks and streamlining processes, DevOps enables organizations to quickly and reliably deliver software updates and new features.

- **Improved software quality: Continuous integration and continuous deployment (CI/CD)** practices ensure that code changes are frequently tested and deployed, reducing defects and enhancing software quality.

- **Increased customer satisfaction:** Rapid delivery of features and bug fixes, combined with a strong emphasis on customer feedback, results in higher satisfaction and loyalty.

- **Scalable infrastructure:** DevOps practices and tools support a flexible infrastructure, allowing organizations to easily adapt to changing business needs and market conditions.

With a solid understanding of the history and evolution of DevOps, let us now explore its core principles to grasp how they drive the collaboration, automation, and continuous improvement essential for modern development and operational practices.

Core principles of DevOps

DevOps is not just about development and operations working side by side; it is a mindset and a cultural transformation that encourages teams to adopt new, more effective ways of working. At the heart of this transformation is the idea that everyone shares responsibility for delivering quality, speed, and user satisfaction.

In a DevOps culture, we aim to break down the silos between development and operations, allowing each team to better understand and respond to the needs of the other. This shift empowers developers to gain a deeper understanding of user requirements while operations teams actively participate in the development process, ensuring that maintenance and customer requirements are integrated from the start.

The following principles guide DevOps teams to consistently deliver applications and services at a faster pace and with greater reliability than traditional development models.

Let us explore the principles of DevOps using *Figure 1.2:*

- **Collaboration:** At its core, DevOps is about collaboration. It is more than just bringing teams together; it is about fostering a true partnership where development, operations, and other stakeholders work as one. Instead of being isolated groups, we form a cohesive team that communicates openly, shares feedback and collaborates throughout the entire product lifecycle.

When we collaborate effectively, the lines between development and operations blur, and everyone shares responsibility for delivering a high-quality product. We also see more full-stack development, where teams take ownership from the backend to the frontend, ensuring every part of the product is delivered with care. This holistic approach leads to stronger accountability and, ultimately, a better product.

- **Automation:** Automation is one of the pillars that enable DevOps teams to move quickly and efficiently. By automating repetitive tasks, we free up time for more meaningful work, such as writing code or implementing new features. Automation is particularly critical in CI/CD, where it helps streamline testing, deployment, and monitoring.

When we automate the software development lifecycle, we reduce human error, speed up processes, and increase productivity. This allows us to deliver updates and new features to users more quickly while maintaining high-quality standards. Through automation, we can consistently iterate, improve, and adapt in response to user feedback, as follows:

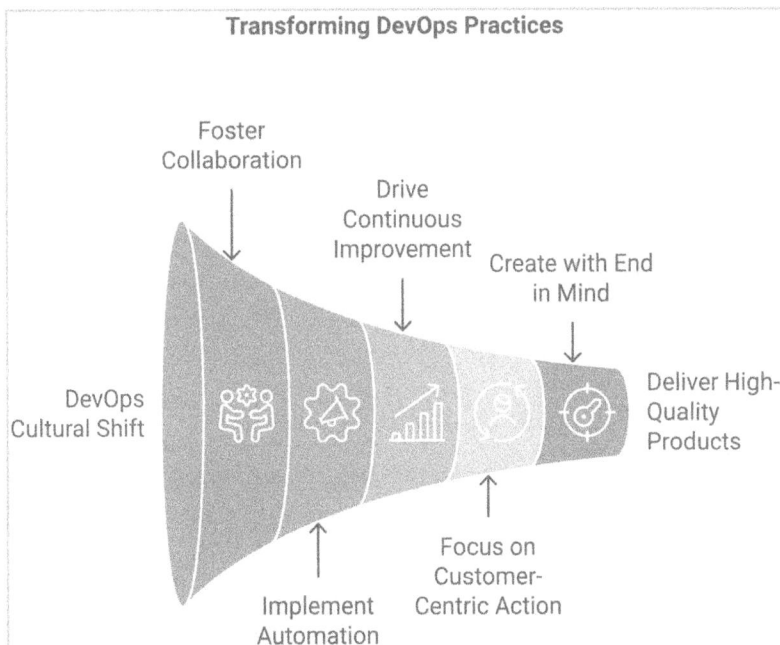

Figure 1.2: DevOps practices and principles

When we automate the software development lifecycle, we reduce human error, speed up processes, and increase productivity. This allows us to deliver updates and new features to users more quickly while maintaining high-quality standards. Through automation, we can consistently iterate, improve, and adapt in response to user feedback.

Modern automation tools like GitHub Actions, Jenkins, and GitLab CI enable teams to implement CI/CD pipelines with minimal configuration. For example, a simple GitHub Actions workflow can automate testing on every code push, as shown:

```
name: Run Tests
on:
  push:
    branches: [ main ]
  pull_request:
    branches: [ main ]
jobs:
  test:
    runs-on: ubuntu-latest
    steps:
    - uses: actions/checkout@v3
    - name: Set up Python
      uses: actions/setup-python@v4
      with:
        python-version: '3.10'
    - name: Install dependencies
      run: |
        python -m pip install --upgrade pip
        pip install -r requirements.txt
    - name: Run tests
      run: pytest
```

This workflow automatically runs tests whenever code is pushed to the main branch, providing immediate feedback to developers.

- **Continuous improvement:** In DevOps, we continuously seek ways to improve our processes. This focus on improvement is rooted in Agile and Lean methodologies, where minimizing waste and optimizing for speed, cost, and efficiency is key. The goal is to create a constant loop of feedback, experimentation, and iteration to ensure that our product evolves to meet both technical and user needs.

  Continuous improvement is closely tied to continuous delivery, allowing us to push updates in small, frequent increments. This approach helps eliminate inefficiencies, improve team performance, and deliver more value to our customers with each release.

- **Customer-centric:** DevOps places a strong emphasis on keeping the customer at the center of everything we do. By using short feedback loops, we are able to quickly gather insights from real users and adapt accordingly. Tools like real-time monitoring and rapid deployment allow us to see how users are interacting with our product and respond to their needs in near real-time.

In this way, we do not have to rely on assumptions about what our users want. Instead, we build based on their actual behavior and feedback, making our software more valuable and user-friendly.

- **Creating with the end in mind:** This principle reminds us to keep our focus on the end goal, solving real problems for our users. As DevOps teams, we should not build software in isolation or based on what we think users might need. Instead, we need to ensure that we have a holistic understanding of the entire product lifecycle, from initial conception to final delivery, and how each piece serves the user's needs.

  By creating with the end in mind, we build solutions that are not only functional but also meaningful to our users. This approach reduces the risk of wasted effort and increases the value of the product we deliver.

These principles form the foundation of DevOps and help guide teams as they work towards delivering faster, more reliable software with a focus on collaboration, automation, and continuous improvement. By keeping the customer at the center and fostering a culture of teamwork, we create an environment where innovation thrives, and quality is never compromised.

DevOps culture and mindset

DevOps, at its core, represents a fundamental shift in culture and mindset. It transforms the way teams collaborate, how work is delivered, and how ownership and accountability are distributed. It is this shift that allows organizations to continuously improve, innovate, and deliver higher-quality software at greater speed.

In this section, we will explore what makes the DevOps mindset unique, why it matters, and how it fosters an environment of continuous learning and improvement as follows:

- **Collaboration over silos:** In many traditional organizations, development and operations teams are siloed. Developers write code, and once it is ready, they hand it over to operations, which then deploys and maintains the software. This separation often leads to communication barriers, delays, and misunderstandings. DevOps breaks down these silos by promoting collaboration between all teams involved in the software lifecycle. Developers, operations, **quality analyst (QA)**, security, and others come together to work as a single, cohesive unit.

  This shift means that everyone shares responsibility for the product's success, from initial development to deployment and beyond. It fosters a culture of shared ownership, where teams do not just blindly build software but also take accountability for its performance in production. This sense of ownership is what drives teams to deliver higher-quality code more quickly.

- **Importance of loosely coupled architectures:** One of the key enablers of DevOps success is adopting a loosely coupled architecture. In tightly coupled systems, changes to one part of the system often require changes in multiple areas, making deployments slow and risky. However, with loosely coupled architectures, components can be developed, tested, and deployed independently. This allows teams to move faster and reduces the risk of one change negatively affecting other parts of the system.

  Loosely coupled architectures also encourage team autonomy. Each team can take full ownership of their part of the system without constantly waiting on other teams to make progress. This autonomy is critical in enabling faster iteration, better decision-making, and, ultimately, quicker delivery of value to the customer.

- **Iterating and evolving roles:** Another critical aspect of the DevOps mindset is the importance of iteration. Instead of trying to overhaul an entire organization or product in one go, DevOps encourages starting small, running pilot programs, and learning from those experiments before scaling up. By iterating on processes and continuously improving, organizations can make steady progress without overwhelming teams or introducing too much risk at once.

  This iterative approach also applies to how roles evolve within DevOps teams. In many traditional organizations, roles are clearly defined and siloed. Developers write code, QA tests it, and operations deploys it. But in a DevOps culture, roles start to blend. Developers take on more responsibility for quality, security, and performance. Business analysts may evolve into product owners, making day-to-day decisions about what the team works on and ensuring alignment with business goals.

  These evolving roles require teams to adopt a more holistic view of the software they build. Developers no longer just focus on writing code; they must think about the entire product lifecycle, from development to deployment to ongoing maintenance. This broader perspective fosters more thoughtful, higher-quality work.

- **Managing risk in a DevOps environment:** One common myth about DevOps is that giving teams more control over deployments increases risk. However, the opposite is often true when DevOps practices are implemented correctly. Traditional change management processes can sometimes feel like risk management theatre, where organizations go through the motions of managing risk without actually reducing it. DevOps takes a different approach by focusing on continuous delivery and building resilience in the system.

  By automating the delivery pipeline and ensuring that teams can quickly detect and fix issues, DevOps reduces the risk of major failures. Instead of relying on lengthy, manual processes to review and approve changes, teams use automated testing, monitoring, and deployment processes to catch issues early and fix them fast. Reducing **mean time to recovery (MTTR)** becomes a more effective way to manage risk than simply trying to prevent any and all failures.

- **Workload management and feedback loops:** Effective workload management is essential in a DevOps environment. Teams need to track not just features but also technical debt, operational work, and unplanned work. By having visibility into these categories, teams can better prioritize and ensure they focus on the right tasks at the right time.

  Another key to managing workload is creating feedback loops. When teams receive rapid feedback on the work they are doing, whether it is through customer input, operational performance data, or internal metrics, they can quickly adjust and improve. Shorter feedback loops mean faster learning, quicker fixes, and a more agile response to changing needs.

- **Employee engagement and organizational health:** Finally, a DevOps culture emphasizes the well-being and engagement of the team itself. **Employee Voice Score/Survey (EVS)** is a valuable metric that tracks how likely team members are to recommend their organization as a place to work. High EVS scores are often correlated with high-performing teams that feel a sense of ownership and connection to the business outcomes they are driving.

DevOps is fundamentally about fostering a culture of collaboration, continuous improvement, and shared ownership. It requires a shift in mindset, where teams embrace autonomy, iterate on their processes, and take responsibility for the product's success from development to deployment and beyond. By focusing on these principles, organizations can not only deliver software faster and with higher quality but also build happier, more engaged teams.

Benefits of adopting DevOps practices

Some of the major benefits of DevOps are as follows:

- **Enhances collaboration and communication:** DevOps breaks down traditional silos between development, operations, and other teams, creating a unified environment where cross-functional teams work together seamlessly. This promotes transparent communication, rapid knowledge sharing, and a collective sense of ownership over the product lifecycle.

- **Drives efficiency gains:** By automating repetitive tasks and complex workflows across the development pipeline, DevOps eliminates time-consuming manual work, reduces human error, and increases consistency in deliverables. This frees up valuable team resources to focus on strategic, innovation-driven initiatives.

- **Accelerates software delivery:** DevOps practices, such as continuous integration and continuous deployment, establish a rapid feedback loop that allows teams to identify and address issues early in the development cycle. This proactive approach dramatically reduces the cost and complexity of bug fixes, enabling organizations to accelerate software delivery while maintaining high quality.

- **Transforms workforce engagement:** The DevOps culture of shared responsibility and transparency nurtures a more motivated, empowered team environment. Developers and operations professionals feel a deeper sense of ownership and purpose, leading to increased job satisfaction, innovation, and team cohesion.

- **Enhances competitive advantages:** DevOps' accelerated time-to-market capabilities allow organizations to respond more agilely to market changes and customer needs, securing a crucial competitive edge. Improved predictability and reliability in the delivery pipeline also reduce operational risks and enable more accurate project planning.

- **Improves customer experience:** The continuous delivery model ensures customers receive regular updates and new features aligned with their evolving needs, while robust testing and deployment processes maintain high standards of quality and stability, strengthening customer relationships and loyalty.

- **Strengthens security posture:** DevSecOps practices embed security considerations throughout the development lifecycle, creating a more proactive and robust security posture. Automated security testing and continuous monitoring identify vulnerabilities early and ensure ongoing protection without sacrificing development speed. For example, tools like Trivy can be integrated into CI pipelines to scan container images for vulnerabilities, as shown:

```
name: Container Security Scan
on: [push]
jobs:
  scan:
    runs-on: ubuntu-latest
    steps:
      - name: Checkout code
        uses: actions/checkout@v3
      - name: Build image
        run: docker build -t myapp:${{ github.sha }} .
      - name: Scan image for vulnerabilities
        uses: aquasecurity/trivy-action@master
        with:
          image-ref: 'myapp:${{ github.sha }}'
          format: 'table'
          exit-code: '1'
          ignore-unfixed: true
          severity: 'CRITICAL'
```

This scan fails the build if critical vulnerabilities are detected, implementing shift-left security practices.

- **Delivers substantial cost savings:** While initial DevOps implementation may require investment, the long-term cost savings are substantial. Automated processes reduce operational overhead, improve stability, minimize costly downtime, and streamline development, enabling greater output with fewer resources.

- **Fosters a culture of continuous improvement:** DevOps teams regularly analyze their processes, experiment with new approaches, and refine their practices based on data and feedback. This commitment to ongoing optimization ensures organizations continue to evolve and maintain their competitive edge in an ever-changing technological landscape.

Relationship between DevOps, Agile, and Lean methodologies

Let us now talk about how Lean, Agile, and DevOps, three widely adopted methodologies, intersect and build upon each other. Imagine building your dream house. You would not want to wait months to see if the foundation was laid correctly. Instead, you would want to check progress regularly, make adjustments quickly, and ensure every team works together seamlessly, from the plumbers to the electricians. This is exactly what modern software development methodologies help us achieve in the tech world.

Think of Lean, Agile, and DevOps as three best friends who grew up in different neighborhoods but share the same values. Each brings their unique strengths to the table, creating a powerful combination when they work together.

Let us discuss each of them in detail as follows:

- **Lean is the efficiency expert:** Born in the factories of *Toyota*, Lean is like that friend who hates waste and always finds the most innovative way to do things. Imagine preparing a meal. Lean would ensure the following:
  o Buy only the ingredients you need.
  o Arrange your kitchen for maximum efficiency.
  o Cook dishes in the perfect order.
  o Clean as you go.
  o Keep improving your recipe based on feedback.

  Lean's five core principles are all about maximizing value while minimizing waste as follows:
  o Define value (What does your customer want?).
  o Map the value stream (How do we get there with minimal waste?).

- o   Create flow (Keep things moving smoothly).

- o   Establish pull (Only make what is needed).

- o   Seek perfection (Always look for ways to improve).

- **Agile the flexible friend:** If Lean is about efficiency, Agile is about adaptability. Born in 2001, when a group of developers realized traditional methods were too rigid, Agile is like that friend who is great at handling change and loves getting feedback.

  Think of Agile as building a LEGO set without looking at the final picture. Instead of trying to build everything at once, you:

  - o   Build small sections and check if they work.

  - o   Show others and get their input.

  - o   Make adjustments based on feedback.

  - o   Keep improving piece by piece.

  Agile values the following:

  - People over processes.

  - Working software over perfect documentation.

  - Collaboration over rigid contracts.

  - Adapting to change rather than sticking to a plan.

- **DevOps the bridge builder:** DevOps is the newest member of our trio, emerging when organizations realized they needed to bridge the gap between development teams (who build software) and operations teams (who run it). It is like having a translator who helps two groups speak the same language.

  DevOps ensures that:

  - o   Development and operations teams work together seamlessly.

  - o   Changes can be deployed quickly and safely.

  - o   Problems get fixed fast.

  - o   Everything is automated where possible.

  When these three methodologies combine, they create something amazing, as follows:

- o   **Continuous improvement:**

  - ☐   Lean brings the mindset of reducing waste.

  - ☐   Agile adds regular feedback loops.

  - ☐   DevOps automates the process.

o **Customer focus**:

- Lean ensures we are creating value.
- Agile helps us adapt to changing needs.
- DevOps enables quick delivery.

o **Team collaboration**:

- Lean optimizes workflows.
- Agile promotes cross-functional teams.
- DevOps unifies different departments, as shown in the following figure:

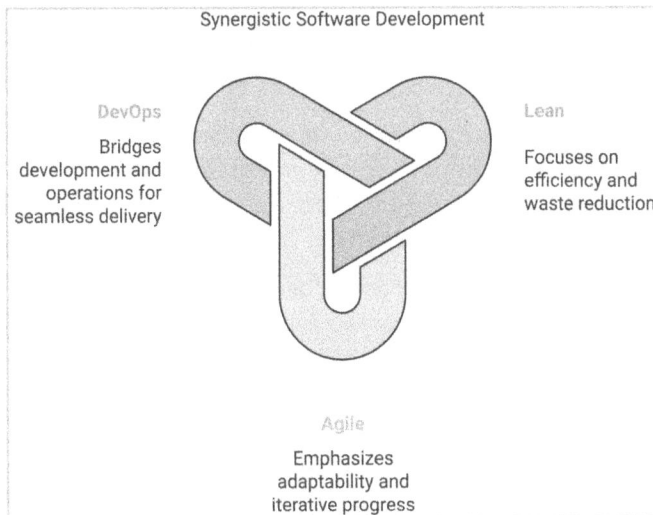

Figure 1.3: *Synergistic software development with DevOps, Lean, and Agile*

When you combine these approaches, you get what we call **Lean DevOps**. It is like having a super-powered development process that:

- Continuously improves (like Lean).
- Adapts quickly (like Agile).
- Delivers reliably (like DevOps).

The beauty of these methodologies is that they all lead to the same goal, delivering value to customers efficiently and effectively. While they emerged from different places and times, they complement each other perfectly in today's fast-paced digital world.

Note: **It is not about rigidly following any one methodology but understanding how they can work together to help your team succeed. After all, the best process is the one that works for your specific needs while keeping everyone, teams and customers alike, happy and productive.**

Overcoming organizational resistance to DevOps

Imagine you are excited about implementing DevOps in your organization, ready to streamline processes and boost efficiency. But instead of enthusiasm, you are met with hesitation, skepticism, and sometimes even outright resistance. This is more common than you might think.

Organizations resist DevOps for the following reasons:

- **Fear of losing control and job security:** Many team members, especially those in operations, worry that automation might make their roles obsolete. For instance, when build and deployment processes become automated, the go-to person for these tasks might feel their position is threatened. As one operations engineer put it, *If everything is automated, what will happen to my job?*

- **Comfort with the status quo:** Let us face it, change can be uncomfortable. Teams that have worked in traditional development and operations silos for years often feel comfortable with their current processes. They may be reluctant to adopt new ways of working, questioning the need for change.

- **Departmental territory concerns:** When DevOps breaks down silos between development and operations, some managers fear losing their turf. The shift to self-managing, cross-functional teams can make traditional department heads nervous about their authority and control.

- **Skills gap anxiety:** Different team members may resist DevOps because they worry about learning new tools and technologies. For example:

    o Developers might hesitate to deal with operational issues.

    o QA teams may feel pressured by faster release cycles.

    o Operations teams might feel overwhelmed by the need to learn new automation tools.

Resistance is overcome by undertaking the following:

- **Start with clear leadership support:** Success starts at the top. Your organization's leadership needs to:

    o Set clear goals for the DevOps transformation.

    o Hold all teams accountable for the success of the initiative.

    o Demonstrate unwavering support for the change.

- **Focus on education and training:** Help your teams build confidence through:

    o Providing comprehensive training on new tools and technologies.

    o Organizing workshops to explain DevOps principles.

- o Creating opportunities for cross-team knowledge sharing.
- o Offering hands-on experience with automation tools.

- **Implement the left-shift approach:** Get operations involved early in the development process by:
  - o Including ops teams in technical architecture meetings.
  - o Involving them in code reviews.
  - o Having them participate in early-stage deployments.
  - o Sharing deployment responsibilities across environments.

- **Build trust through communication:** Open and honest communication is crucial to:
  - o Explain the benefits of DevOps for each team member.
  - o Address concerns promptly and transparently.
  - o Share success stories from other organizations.
  - o Create forums for regular team discussions.

- **Start small and share your wins:** Build confidence through success:
  - o Begin with smaller, manageable projects.
  - o Celebrate early wins, no matter how small.
  - o Document and share improvements in efficiency.
  - o Use metrics to show a positive impact.

- **Create a supportive learning environment:** Mistakes will happen; use them as learning opportunities:
  - o Encourage open discussion about challenges.
  - o Hold regular retrospectives to review processes.
  - o Focus on solutions rather than blame.
  - o Share learnings across teams.

- **Address job security concerns:** Be clear about how roles will evolve:
  - o Explain how automation creates opportunities for more strategic work.
  - o Highlight new skills team members will gain.
  - o Show how DevOps can lead to career growth.
  - o Emphasize the value of cross-functional expertise.

Remember, resistance to DevOps is natural and expected. The key is approaching the transformation with patience, understanding, and a clear plan for supporting your teams through the change. By addressing concerns head-on and providing the necessary support, you can help your organization embrace DevOps and reap its many benefits.

Success in DevOps transformation is not just about tools and processes. It is about people. When you focus on helping your teams understand and embrace the changes, you are much more likely to achieve lasting success in your DevOps journey.

Key DevOps roles and responsibilities

At its heart, DevOps culture emphasizes shared responsibility and mutual understanding. Rather than viewing development and operations as separate entities, organizations embracing DevOps create unified teams where every member share accountability for the entire software lifecycle. This shared ownership model naturally cultivates an environment where cross-functional knowledge-sharing flourishes. Teams make decisions rapidly and solve problems collaboratively while maintaining a steadfast commitment to continuous learning and improvement. By establishing shared goals and metrics, organizations ensure that all team members work cohesively toward common objectives.

The following are some of the essential practices and responsibilities:

- **Automation and infrastructure management:** In a DevOps culture, infrastructure becomes a shared concern rather than an operations-only domain. Teams collectively embrace infrastructure as code practices, ensuring that environment management remains consistent and version-controlled throughout the development lifecycle. Through automated provisioning and scaling of resources, organizations can respond dynamically to changing demands. Container orchestration provides flexible application deployment options, while careful cloud service optimization ensures efficient resource utilization across both development and production environments.

- **Infrastructure as code (IaC):** In modern DevOps environments, infrastructure is defined and managed using code, bringing software engineering practices to infrastructure management. This approach makes infrastructure provisioning consistent, version-controlled, and repeatable.

  For example, using Terraform, teams can define cloud resources in a declarative syntax:

  ```
  provider "aws" {
    region = "us-west-2"
  }

  resource "aws_s3_bucket" "application_data" {
    bucket = "my-app-data-${var.environment}"
  ```

```
    tags = {
      Environment = var.environment
      Project     = "DevOps Demo"
    }
  }
}

resource "aws_s3_bucket_versioning" "versioning" {
  bucket = aws_s3_bucket.application_data.id
  versioning_configuration {
    status = "Enabled"
  }
}
```

This code creates an AWS S3 bucket with versioning enabled. The same code can be used to create identical environments for development, testing, and production, ensuring consistency across the deployment pipeline.

- **Continuous integration and delivery:** The philosophy of continuous improvement manifests through robust integration and delivery practices. Teams implement automated build and test processes that facilitate regular code integration, while streamlined deployment pipelines enable frequent, small releases. Quality gates and security checks are automated throughout the pipeline, ensuring that every change meets established standards before reaching production. This systematic approach to delivery helps organizations maintain high quality while increasing their deployment frequency.

- **Monitoring and feedback:** A successful DevOps culture thrives on comprehensive feedback loops that inform continuous improvement. Real-time application and infrastructure monitoring provide immediate insights into system health, while comprehensive logging and analytics enable deeper analysis of trends and patterns. Teams track performance metrics diligently and integrate user feedback into their development processes. When incidents occur, robust response procedures and thorough post-mortem analyses ensure that teams learn from every experience and strengthen their systems accordingly.

- **Observability and monitoring:** A critical aspect of DevOps is the ability to gain insights into application and infrastructure performance. Modern observability practices combine metrics, logs, and traces to provide a comprehensive view of system behavior.

For example, using Prometheus, teams can query metrics to detect potential issues:

```
# Calculate the rate of HTTP 5xx errors over the past 5 minutes
sum(rate(http_requests_total{status=~"5.."}[5m])) / sum(rate(http_requests_total[5m]))
```

This query calculates the ratio of HTTP 5xx errors to total HTTP requests, providing an error rate percentage that can trigger alerts when it exceeds acceptable thresholds.

- **Security and compliance:** Security in a DevOps culture transcends traditional boundaries to become everyone's responsibility. Teams integrate security testing directly into their development pipelines and automate compliance checking to ensure consistent standards. Regular security audits complement these automated processes, while ongoing security awareness training ensures that all team members understand their role in maintaining system security. This proactive approach to vulnerability management helps organizations stay ahead of potential threats.

- **Team dynamics and collaboration:** The success of DevOps hinges on effective communication and collaboration. Teams establish regular cross-functional synchronization meetings to share updates, discuss challenges, and align priorities. Decision-making processes remain transparent, with clear escalation paths for when issues arise. Knowledge sharing becomes part of the daily routine, supported by collaborative documentation practices that ensure critical information remains accessible to all team members.

  Teams align their tools and practices through shared workflows for version control, deployment procedures, and testing methodologies. This alignment extends to monitoring approaches and incident response protocols, ensuring that everyone follows consistent practices while maintaining the flexibility to adapt to specific needs.

- **Measuring success:** Success in a DevOps culture extends beyond traditional metrics to encompass both technical and business outcomes. Organizations track deployment frequency and lead time for changes to gauge their delivery efficiency. Mean time to recovery and change failure rate provide insights into system stability and reliability. Customer satisfaction metrics help teams understand the real-world impact of their efforts, ensuring that technical improvements translate into tangible business value.

- **Continuous evolution:** The DevOps journey represents an ongoing commitment to improvement rather than a destination. Organizations must regularly assess and adjust their practices, embracing new technologies and methodologies as they emerge. Innovation and experimentation become part of the cultural fabric, with teams encouraged to explore new approaches while maintaining their focus on delivering customer value. Investment in team growth and learning ensures that organizations can sustain their DevOps transformation over the long term.

- **Building for scale:** As organizations grow, their DevOps culture must scale accordingly. This scaling happens through the development of standardized yet flexible processes that teams can adapt to their specific needs. Reusable automation templates reduce duplication of effort, while documented best practices help new teams adopt proven approaches. Mentorship programs and centers of excellence facilitate knowledge transfer and maintain consistency across the organization while allowing for necessary adaptations.

DevOps maturity models and assessment frameworks

A DevOps maturity model serves as a structured framework to evaluate and benchmark an organization's DevOps practices. By assessing a range of elements, such as the level of automation, release frequency, collaboration between teams, and security protocols, a maturity model helps identify where an organization stands in its DevOps journey.

Key benefits of using a DevOps maturity model include:

- **Performance evaluation:** It identifies current strengths and weaknesses across development, operations, and cross-functional teams.

- **Progress benchmarking:** The model helps compare past and current DevOps states to track progress over time.

- **Target setting and building roadmap:** Organizations can determine desired maturity levels, prioritize areas for improvement, and create a strategic roadmap to reach those goals.

- **Enhanced cultural integration:** By examining team collaboration and communication, assessments help foster a cohesive DevOps culture across departments.

Common DevOps maturity models

Several well-established DevOps maturity models provide reliable frameworks for organizations to evaluate their DevOps practices.

The following are the three prominent models:

- **Capability Maturity Model Integration:** Widely used for assessing organizational capabilities, **Capability Maturity Model Integration** (**CMMI**) offers a structured, general framework for evaluating maturity across several business functions. While it is applicable beyond DevOps, it allows organizations to assess operational capabilities and areas for improvement systematically. Due to its broad scope, CMMI can be complex to implement and may lack specificity for DevOps. However, organizations can work with DevOps consultants to apply CMMI principles to DevOps-specific practices effectively.

- **Culture, Automation, Lean, Measurement, Sharing model:** The **Culture, Automation, Lean, Measurement, Sharing** (**CALMS**) model offers a DevOps-focused approach, evaluating cultural and operational dimensions central to DevOps success. Covering cultural shifts, automation, lean practices, metrics, and knowledge sharing, CALMS emphasizes core DevOps values like collaboration and transparency. While its less rigid structure may pose challenges for organizations new to DevOps assessments, CALMS is a holistic and practical option for aligning DevOps practices with an organization's unique culture and goals.

- **IBM DevOps maturity model:** Developed by IBM, this model assesses DevOps capabilities specific to IBM's tools and practices, making it highly detailed and customizable for organizations that use IBM solutions. The IBM model covers DevOps elements such as planning, development, testing, and delivery. Due to its reliance on IBM technologies, it may be less relevant for organizations using other toolsets.

The following are the steps in a DevOps maturity assessment:

Assessing DevOps maturity is an iterative process that provides insight into current practices, risks, and areas for improvement. The assessment typically involves the following steps, as shown in *Figure 1.4*:

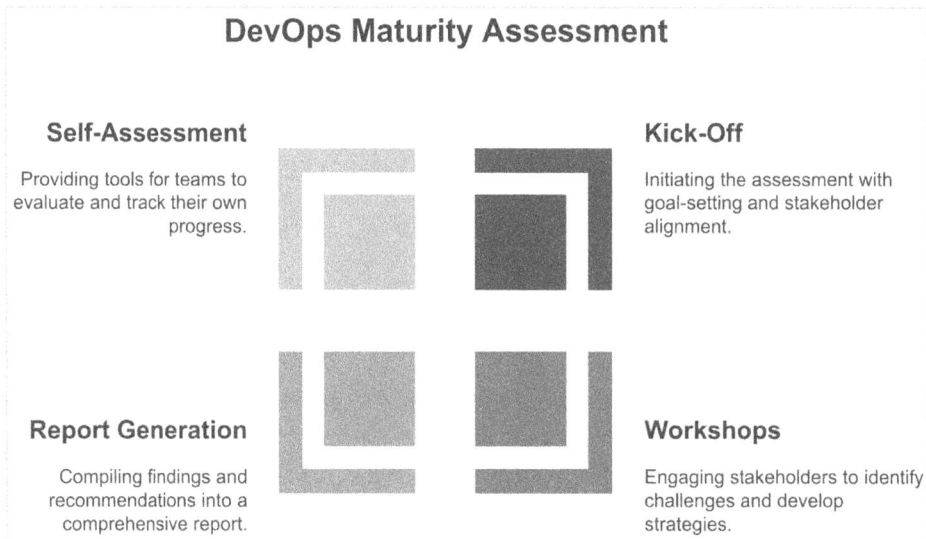

Figure 1.4: DevOps maturity assessment

1. **Kick-off:** The assessment begins with a meeting to define goals and understand the organization's needs, existing pain points, and desired milestones. Stakeholders set high-level objectives and establish timelines and priorities for the assessment.

2. **Workshops:** DevOps consultants work closely with key stakeholders during the workshop phase to identify business drivers, assess existing challenges, and outline a strategic roadmap. **Proof of concepts** (**POCs**) may be implemented to address specific challenges and evaluate potential improvements.

3. **Report generation:** After assessing DevOps practices, the team compiles a report outlining the current maturity level, benchmark comparisons, and recommended improvements. The report typically includes:

    a. A snapshot of the current environment's state.

    b. Key findings and insights across assessment categories.

    c. An improvement roadmap highlighting quick wins and longer-term objectives.

4. **Self-assessment (optional):** Many organizations choose to incorporate self-assessment portals, allowing teams to evaluate their practices through structured surveys and benchmark their DevOps maturity over time. Self-assessment tools can provide high-level insights and guide incremental improvements, allowing teams to gauge progress continuously.

DevOps maturity and DORA metrics

When evaluating DevOps maturity, many organizations now incorporate the **DevOps Research and Assessment** (**DORA**) metrics framework. These research-backed metrics provide quantitative measures of software delivery performance:

- **Deployment frequency:** How often an organization successfully releases to production:

    o **Low performers**: Between once per month and once every six months.

    o **High performers**: Multiple deployments per day.

- **Lead time for changes:** The time it takes from code committed to code successfully running in production:

    o **Low performers**: Between one month and six months.

    o **High performers**: Less than one hour.

- **Mean time to restore (MTTR):** How long it takes to restore service when a service incident occurs:

    o **Low performers**: Between one week and one month.

    o **High performers**: Less than one hour.

- **Change failure rate:** The percentage of changes that result in degraded service and require remediation:

    o **Low performers**: 46-60% of changes fail.

    o **High performers**: 0-15% of changes fail.

These metrics can be measured using specialized DevOps analytics platforms or through custom integration with tools like:

- **Deployment frequency:** CI/CD tools (Jenkins, GitHub Actions, CircleCI)
- **Lead time:** Version control + deployment systems (GitHub + Argo CD)
- **MTTR:** Incident management systems (PagerDuty, Opsgenie)
- **Change failure rate:** Deployment systems + monitoring (GitLab + Prometheus)

By tracking these metrics, organizations can objectively measure their DevOps performance and identify specific areas for improvement.

The following are the key assessment areas in DevOps maturity:

DevOps assessments evaluate various organizational aspects to determine maturity levels. Key areas commonly covered include the following, as shown in *Figure 1.5*:

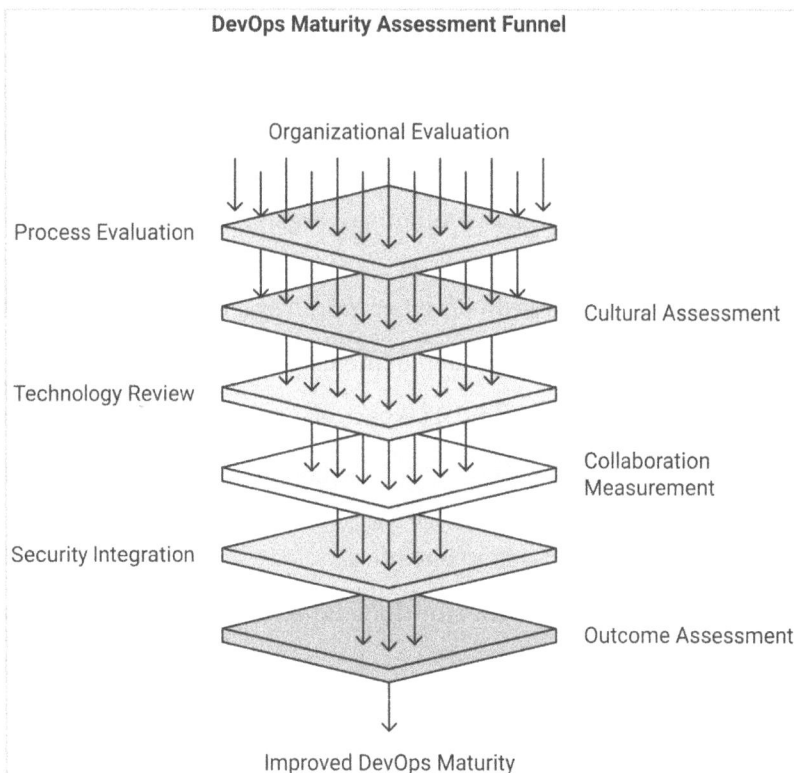

Figure 1.5: DevOps maturity assessment funnel

- **Process:** Evaluate the effectiveness and standardization of processes that support DevOps, such as the use of CI/CD pipelines and workflow automation. Efficient processes help align DevOps practices with corporate policies and business objectives.

- **Culture:** Focuses on cross-team collaboration, transparency, and communication. An integrated DevOps culture enhances the collaboration of development, operations, and testing teams, fostering continuous learning and shared goals.

- **Technology and automation:** Reviews the toolsets and automation practices used in development and deployment processes. The model assesses the extent of automation and whether the tools support continuous integration, delivery, and deployment goals.

- **Collaboration:** Measures the effectiveness of collaboration across different teams. Strong collaboration reduces bottlenecks, encourages cross-training, and aligns teams towards a common purpose, which is essential for DevOps success.

- **Security:** Ensures security protocols are embedded early in the **software development lifecycle (SDLC)**, following DevSecOps principles. A robust security evaluation includes automated compliance checks and security testing at each stage of the DevOps pipeline.

- **Outcomes:** Assesses the impact of DevOps practices on business goals and technical efficiency. This includes identifying workflow recommendations, major risks, backlog improvements, and setting KPIs aligned with Agile best practices.

In conclusion, the DevOps maturity model is essential for helping organizations evaluate, benchmark, and continuously improve their DevOps practices. By choosing the most suitable model and following a structured assessment process, businesses can drive effective DevOps adoption, optimize resource allocation, and accelerate time-to-market. As DevOps maturity evolves, organizations gain greater efficiency, resilience, and agility in delivering high-quality software solutions that align with their strategic goals.

DevSecOps integrating security into DevOps

DevSecOps extends DevOps principles to include security as a shared responsibility throughout the software development lifecycle. Rather than treating security as a final checkpoint before deployment, DevSecOps integrates security practices into every stage of development and operations.

The core principles of DevSecOps include:

- **Shift-left security:** Integrating security testing and verification early in the development process.

- **Security as code:** Managing security policies, configurations, and compliance checks as code.

- **Continuous security validation:** Automating security testing in CI/CD pipelines.

- **Security visibility:** Making security metrics and findings accessible to all teams.

Implementing DevSecOps brings several benefits:

- Early identification and remediation of security issues.

- Reduced cost of fixing security vulnerabilities.

- Improved security posture without slowing development.

- Shared security responsibility across all teams.

DevSecOps tooling examples

Modern DevSecOps implementations leverage various specialized tools:

- **Static Application Security Testing (SAST):** Tools like SonarQube or Checkmarx scan source code for security vulnerabilities.

- **Container scanning:** Tools like Trivy, Clair, or Snyk examine container images for known vulnerabilities.

- **Infrastructure as code scanning:** Tools like Checkov or tfsec analyze IaC templates for security misconfigurations.

- **Secret detection:** Tools like GitGuardian or GitHub Secret Scanning prevent secrets from being committed to repositories.

- **Policy as code:** Tools like **Open Policy Agent** (**OPA**) enforce security policies across the infrastructure.

Here is an example of integrating Trivy container scanning into a CI/CD pipeline using GitHub Actions:

```
name: Security Scan

on: [push, pull_request]

jobs:
  security-scan:
    runs-on: ubuntu-latest
    steps:
      - name: Checkout code
        uses: actions/checkout@v3

      - name: Build image
        run: docker build -t app:${{ github.sha }} .

      - name: Trivy vulnerability scan
        uses: aquasecurity/trivy-action@master
```

```yaml
  with:
    image-ref: 'app:${{ github.sha }}'
    format: 'sarif'
    output: 'trivy-results.sarif'
    severity: 'CRITICAL,HIGH'

- name: Upload Trivy scan results
  uses: github/codeql-action/upload-sarif@v2
  if: always()
  with:
    sarif_file: 'trivy-results.sarif'
```

Another example is managing secrets securely using HashiCorp Vault:

```
# Terraform configuration to set up a Vault secrets engine
resource "vault_mount" "db" {
  path        = "database"
  type        = "database"
  description = "Database secrets engine"
}

resource "vault_database_secret_backend_connection" "postgres" {
  backend       = vault_mount.db.path
  name          = "postgres"
  allowed_roles = ["app"]

  postgresql {
    connection_url = "postgresql://{{username}}:{{password}}@
db.example.com:5432/postgres"
    username       = "vault"
    password       = var.db_admin_password
  }
}

resource "vault_database_secret_backend_role" "app" {
  backend             = vault_mount.db.path
  name                = "app"
  db_name             = vault_database_secret_backend_connection.
ostgres.name
  creation_statements = ["CREATE ROLE \"{{name}}\" WITH LOGIN PASSWORD
‹{{password}}›VALID UNTIL ‹{{expiration}}›;
```

```
GRANT SELECT ON ALL TABLES IN SCHEMA public TO \"{{name}}\";"]
   default_ttl        = 3600
   max_ttl            = 86400
}
```

By implementing these DevSecOps practices and tools, organizations can ensure security is built into their DevOps pipelines rather than added as an afterthought, creating more secure and compliant software delivery processes.

Conclusion

DevOps has clearly emerged as a transformative approach, reshaping software development and IT operations. From its historical origins to its current status as an industry standard, DevOps continues to drive organizations toward faster, more reliable, and customer-focused software delivery. By embracing the principles of collaboration, automation, and continuous improvement, DevOps empowers teams to break down silos, encourage shared ownership, and rapidly adapt to change.

Building on the DevOps foundation, the next chapter will explore containerization technologies like Docker. We will cover the fundamentals of containers, Docker, and Docker Compose and discuss how these tools can help create consistent, reproducible development environments across all stages, from local development to testing and production. This focus on environment parity is a key enabler of the DevOps philosophy.

Join our Discord space

Join our Discord workspace for latest updates, offers, tech happenings around the world, new releases, and sessions with the authors:

https://discord.bpbonline.com

CHAPTER 2

Setting up Development Environments

Introduction

In today's rapidly evolving software development landscape, one of the most critical challenges developers face is not just writing code, it is ensuring that code works consistently across different environments. How many times have you heard (or perhaps said yourself) the infamous phrase, *but it works on my machine*? This chapter tackles this universal challenge head-on.

As we progress through this chapter, we will understand the world of containerization and explore how it has revolutionized the way we create, share, and maintain development environments. Gone are the days of spending hours configuring development machines or debugging environment-specific issues. Instead, we will discover how modern tools and practices enable us to create reproducible, consistent environments that work seamlessly across development, testing, and production stages.

At the heart of our discussion lies Docker, a technology that has fundamentally transformed how we approach containerization. We will explore everything from basic containerization concepts to advanced multi-container orchestration, ensuring you know how to build robust development environments. Whether you are working on a small personal project or a large-scale enterprise application, the principles and practices we will cover will prove invaluable.

As we tackle environment parity, configuration management, and integration with modern CI/CD pipelines, remember that our goal is not just to set up development environments; it is to create a foundation for efficient, reliable, and scalable software development.

The following is a visual roadmap for the upcoming technologies in the chapter:

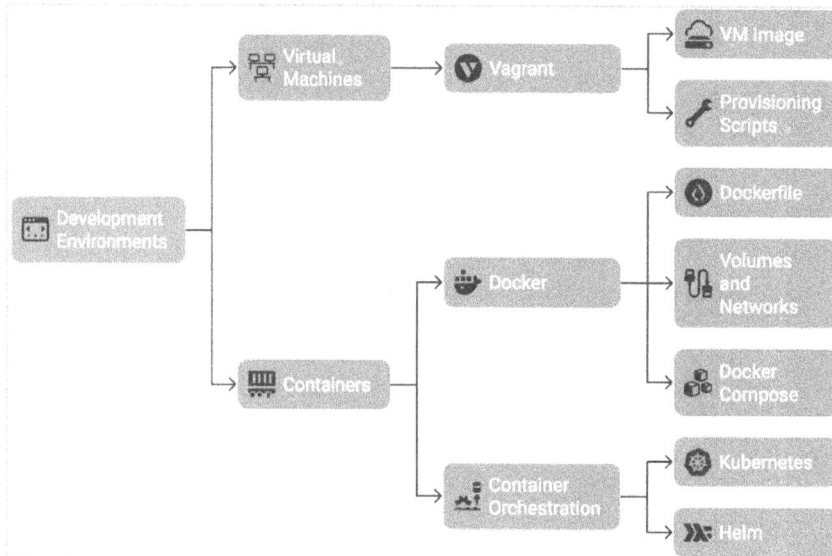

Figure 2.1: Development environments and technologies in this chapter

Structure

We will cover the following topics in this chapter:

- Containerization and its benefits
- Internal working of containers
- Docker and its fundamentals
- Vagrant for creating development environments
- Container orchestration basics
- Environment parity in DevOps
- Managing development environment configurations
- Integration with CI/CD pipelines

Objectives

By the end of this chapter, we will be able to understand the fundamentals of containerization and how it addresses the *it works on my machine* problem that plagues development teams, explain the internal mechanics of containers, including how user space, control groups, and namespaces provide isolation and resource management. We will build, run, and manage Docker containers, from basic images to complex multi-container applications; create reproducible development environments using Docker Compose and Vagrant to ensure consistency across your team; implement environment parity practices to minimize differences between development, testing, and production environments. We will also recognize the basics of container orchestration and how tools like Kubernetes extend container management to production-scale applications; configure and manage development environments using industry best practices and integrate containerized environments with CI/CD pipelines to streamline your development workflow.

These skills are directly applicable to real-world scenarios where you need to onboard new team members quickly, ensure code works reliably across different environments, and establish a foundation for modern DevOps practices. Whether you are working in a startup that needs agile, lightweight development solutions or an enterprise requiring standardized environments across large teams, the container-based approach covered in this chapter offers practical tools to improve your development process and reduce environment-related issues.

Containerization and its benefits

Suppose you are going on a trip. Instead of packing your entire house (like a virtual machine would), you simply grab a suitcase filled with everything you need for your journey. This suitcase represents a Linux container: a smart, self-sufficient package that includes everything an application needs to run smoothly, such as the application code, runtime environment, system libraries, dependencies, and configuration files.

Internal working of containers

Containers revolutionize how we deploy and run applications by offering a lightweight, portable, and consistent environment. However, to truly grasp their mechanics, one must dive beneath the surface to explore the foundational technologies that make them possible. This section will unravel the internals of containers by focusing on the Linux kernel's capabilities, specifically user space, **control groups** (**cgroups**), and namespaces.

User space versus kernel space

In Linux, the operating system is divided into two main spaces: kernel space and user space. The kernel space is where the core of the OS operates, managing hardware and executing essential low-level tasks. Conversely, user space is where applications run, isolated from the kernel to ensure system stability and security.

Containers live in user space. They interact with the kernel through system calls (syscalls[1]), which act as gateways for requesting kernel services, such as accessing files or allocating memory. A container essentially bundles the application and its dependencies into a user space environment, leveraging the host's kernel for execution.

Control groups

Cgroups are a kernel feature that allows the allocation and management of system resources among different groups of processes. They ensure that a containerized application uses a defined set of resources like CPU, memory, and I/O, preventing any single container from monopolizing the host's resources.

Some of the key capabilities of cgroups are as follows:

- **Resource limiting:** Set upper limits for resource usage.
- **Prioritization:** Allocate a larger share of CPU or I/O bandwidth to certain groups.
- **Accounting:** Monitor and report resource usage.
- **Control:** Pause or resume process groups.

Let us take a quick look at the following steps to understand how a cgroup is created in Linux as follows:

1. Create a cgroup directory under the following:

   ```
   # Step 1: Create a cgroup directory
   $ sudo mkdir /sys/fs/cgroup/cpu/mycontainer
   ```

   There are a couple of things to note here:

   a. The **/sys/fs/cgroup/** directory is a special virtual filesystem provided by the Linux kernel, specifically for managing cgroups. It is where you interact with the kernel's cgroup subsystem.

   b. By navigating to **/sys/fs/cgroup/cpu/,** we are working with the CPU subsystem of cgroups. This particular directory allows us to manage CPU usage limits and priorities for processes.

   c. Once the **mycontainer** directory is created, you will notice a bunch of files auto created where you can now configure the resource limits for a specific group of processes.

2. Set CPU quota:

   ```
   # Step 2: Set the CPU quota
   $ echo 100000 > /sys/fs/cgroup/cpu/mycontainer/cpu.cfs_quota_us
   ```

---

1 System calls are the interface between user space applications and the kernel. They allow programs to request services from the operating system's kernel, such as file operations, process creation, or network communication. In containerization, syscalls are the mechanism through which containerized applications interact with the host's kernel, while maintaining isolation at the user space level.

The aforementioned command has two key insights as follows:

a. The **cpu.cfs_quota_us** file defines the quota or the maximum amount of CPU time (in microseconds) that tasks in this cgroup are allowed to use in one scheduling period.

b. Setting **cpu.cfs_quota_us** to 100000 means that the tasks in this cgroup can use 100,000 microseconds (or 100ms) of CPU time every 100ms period. This effectively limits the processes to 100% of a single CPU core.

3. Add a process to the cgroup:

```
# Step 3: Add a process to the cgroup
$ echo $$ > /sys/fs/cgroup/cpu/mycontainer/tasks
```

a. The **$$** is a shell variable representing the **process ID** (**PID**) of the current shell process.

b. The tasks file in the cgroup directory lists all processes that are part of this cgroup. By echoing **$$** into this file, we add the current shell (and any processes it spawns) to the **mycontainer** cgroup.

Once a process is added to the cgroup, its CPU usage is governed by the cgroup's CPU quota.

Any child processes spawned by this process will inherit the same CPU constraints unless explicitly moved to another cgroup. Hence, by creating a directory under **/sys/fs/ cgroup/cpu/**, and then setting a quota, assigning tasks to it, we have effectively created a sandboxed environment where CPU usage is controlled. This ensures that no matter how resource-intensive a process becomes, it will not exceed the CPU quota defined, preventing it from affecting other processes on the system.

Namespaces

Namespaces in Linux provide isolation for various system resources. This isolation ensures that processes within a namespace see their version of the system, separate from the global system resources. Each type of namespace isolates a specific aspect of the system, allowing containers to run as if they were on separate machines, despite sharing the same kernel.

Linux offers a couple of namespaces as follows:

- **PID namespace (pid):** Isolates PIDs so that processes inside a container only see processes within the same namespace.

- **Mount namespace (mnt):** Isolates file system mount points, allowing each container to have its file system hierarchy.

- **Network namespace (net):** Provides isolation for network interfaces, IP addresses, and routing tables.

- **User namespace (user):** Isolates user and group IDs, allowing containers to run with root privileges inside the namespace but as non-root users on the host.

- **Unix time-sharing (UTS) namespace:** Isolates the hostname and **Network Information Service** (**NIS**) domain name, letting containers have their unique identifiers.

- **IPC namespace:** Isolates System V IPC objects and **Portable Operating System Interface** (**POSIX**) message queues.

- **Time namespace:** Isolates the system clocks, allowing containers to have different time or time zone settings.

Let us take an example of the PID namespace and see how we can create it. The following step is going to help us understand the concepts of namespace better:

Create a new PID namespace as follows:

```
$ sudo unshare --pid --fork --mount-proc bash
```

This command has a few components which need an understanding under the hood:

- **unshare:** This command allows creating namespaces, which allows a process to **unshare** certain resources from its parent process and operate within a new namespace.

- **pid:** Specifies that a new PID namespace should be created. This isolates the process IDs.

- **fork:** Ensures that a new process is created within the namespace. Without this, the current shell would still show processes from the host namespace.

- **mount-proc:** Mounts the **/proc** filesystem within the new namespace, allowing the isolated process to see its process tree.

As soon as you run the aforementioned command, a new shell (bash) is started, and you are dropped inside it. This shell is started inside a new PID namespace and the **/proc** filesystem is remounted so when you inspect processes (**ps** or **cat /proc**), it shows only the processes within this new namespace.

```
root [ /home/nissingh ]# ps
PID TTY          TIME CMD
1 pts/2    00:00:00 bash
4 pts/2    00:00:00 ps
```

You can also check another shell on the host and observe with **ps aux | grep bash** that the bash process is running under a different PID on the host, which confirms that the namespace isolates process IDs from global system view.

Hence, now we can understand why namespaces are critical for containers as follows:

- **Process isolation:** Ensures that processes in one container cannot see or interact with processes in another container or the host. This is important for security and preventing accidental interference between containers.

- **Resource independence:** Each container operates as if it is the only process on the system, making it easier to manage applications without worrying about conflicts.

Now that we understand the foundational concepts of containers in Linux, let us delve into Docker, a powerful platform that simplifies the creation, deployment, and management of containers. In this section, we will explore the core components of Docker, including images, containers, and Dockerfiles, which make containerization accessible and efficient for developers and operations teams alike.

Container namespaces, the apartment building analogy

Let us consider an analogy for Linux namespaces.

Imagine a large apartment building (the host operating system) with multiple tenants (containers). Each apartment has:

- **Its own door with a unique lock (PID namespace):** Tenants can only see and interact with people in their own apartment, not other apartments.

- **Its own thermostat and electrical panel (cgroups):** Each tenant has their own resource controls and cannot use more than their allocated electricity or water.

- **A separate mailbox (UTS namespace):** Mail (hostnames, network identifiers) is delivered to the correct apartment without confusion.

- **A private Wi-Fi network (network namespace):** Each apartment has its own network with unique IP addresses that do not conflict with neighbors.

- **Personal storage (mount namespace):** Tenants have their own storage spaces and cannot access other tenants' belongings.

- **Individual intercom system (IPC namespace):** Communications within the apartment stay private.

The building manager (the kernel) ensures all these systems work properly and that tenants remain isolated from each other while efficiently sharing the building's core infrastructure (plumbing, foundation, electrical grid). This is how containers can coexist on the same host while maintaining isolation and resource boundaries.

Docker and its fundamentals

At its core, a container runtime is the software responsible for running containers on a host operating system. Think of it as the engine that powers containerization, it handles the fundamental tasks of starting, stopping, and managing containers. Container runtimes manage the container's lifecycle, establish the isolated environment, and ensure proper resource allocation and security boundaries.

Docker revolutionized the software industry by making containers accessible to developers worldwide. While Docker is often used as a synonym for containerization, it is a complete platform that includes both high-level tools and its container runtime. Docker simplified the complex process of containerization by providing an intuitive way to package, distribute, and run applications in isolated environments.

Several other container runtimes exist in the ecosystem, each with its strengths as follows:

- **containerd:** Originally developed by Docker and later donated to the **Cloud Native Computing Foundation** (**CNCF**), containerd is a lightweight, high-performance runtime that handles container execution and image management. It is now the default runtime for many container platforms.

- **CRI-O:** Developed specifically for Kubernetes, CRI-O is a lightweight alternative that implements the Kubernetes **Container Runtime Interface** (**CRI**). It is optimized for Kubernetes environments and focuses on simplicity and security.

- **rkt:** Created by CoreOS (now part of Red Hat), rkt was designed with security and composability in mind. While no longer actively maintained, it introduced important concepts to the container ecosystem.

Figure 2.2 describes some of the industry-wide used container runtimes, as follows:

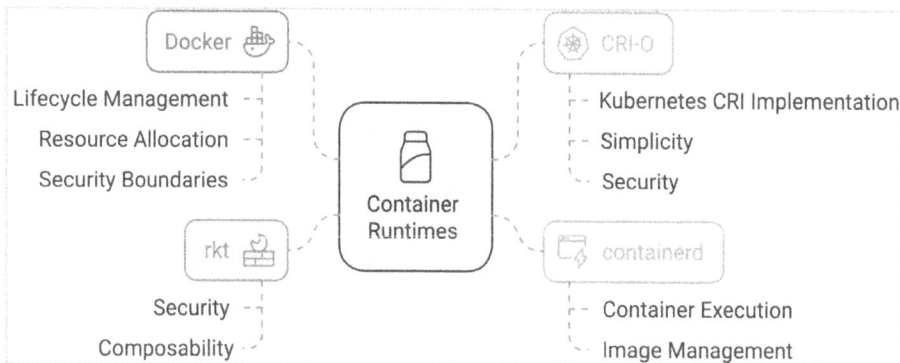

Figure 2.2: *Different types of container runtimes*

Docker's significance lies in its ability to abstract away these low-level runtime complexities, providing developers with a seamless experience through its user-friendly CLI and robust ecosystem of tools. It transforms the intricate process of containerization into accessible commands like docker run and docker build, making container technology approachable for developers of all skill levels.

Docker leverages OS-level virtualization to deliver applications in standardized units called **containers**. Containers package the applications with all necessary dependencies (libraries etc.), ensuring they run consistently across different environments, from development to production. Docker is built around a few foundational concepts as follows:

- **Images:** Immutable, read-only templates containing an application and its dependencies. These serve as the basis for running containers.

- **Containers:** Instances of images that run in isolation from the host and other containers. They create a self-contained environment for applications.

- **Dockerfiles:** Text files with a set of instructions to build an image, automating the process and ensuring consistency.

- **Registry:** A repository (like Docker Hub) where Docker images are stored, shared, and versioned.

Figure 2.3 shows a typical life cycle of how Docker containers are spawned:

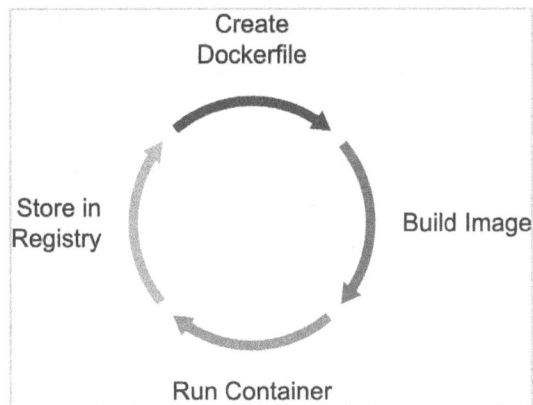

Figure 2.3: Docker workflow cycle

Let us now look at these foundational concepts in a bit more detail.

Docker image

Docker images are like blueprints for containers. They contain the application code, libraries, and configuration files needed to run an application. When you create a Docker container, you are essentially creating an instance from a Docker image. These images are immutable, layered filesystems that follow a union mount design pattern. Each image consists of a series of read-only layers that represent filesystem differences, implemented using **overlay/overlay2** storage drivers in modern Docker installations, as shown:

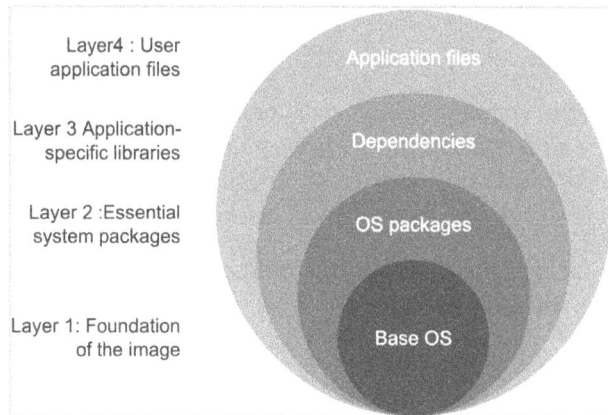

Figure 2.4: *Docker image layer structure*

Each layer in *Figure 2.4* is identified by a cryptographic hash and contains only the filesystem changes from the previous layer. The **Union File System** (**UFS**)[2] combines these layers into a single coherent filesystem view.

Let us now see how we can create a simple Docker image using a Dockerfile. To do this, you need to create a file named exactly as **Dockerfile** in a directory. As a prerequisite, you can head to **https://docs.docker.com/engine/install/** to install the Docker for your variant.

1. Create the Dockerfile in a directory of your choice:

```
# Use an official Python runtime as a base image
FROM python:3.8-slim
# Set the working directory
WORKDIR /app
# Copy the requirements file to install dependencies
COPY requirements.txt
# Install dependencies
RUN pip install --no-cache-dir -r requirements.txt
# Copy the application code to the container
COPY . .
# Expose the port the app runs on
EXPOSE 80
# Define the command to run the application
CMD ["python", "app.py"]
```

2 UFS is a specialized filesystem that layers multiple directories on a single mount point, making them appear as one merged filesystem. In Docker, this allows multiple read-only image layers to be stacked with a writable container layer on top. When a file needs to be modified, it is copied from the read-only layer to the writable layer (copy-on-write), ensuring image layers remain immutable while allowing container modifications.

In the aforementioned Dockerfile, we are primarily doing the following in order:

a. **FROM** sets the base image.

b. **WORKDIR** defines the working directory within the container.

c. **COPY** adds files from the host to the container.

d. **RUN** executes commands, like installing dependencies.

e. **EXPOSE** opens a port on the container.

f. **CMD** defines the command to start the application.

2. Create application files in the same directory:

a. **requirements.txt**: Lists the dependencies of your application (in this case just **flask**):

   ```
   flask
   ```

b. **app.py**: This contains your application code:

   ```
   from flask import Flask
   app = Flask(__name__)


   @app.route('/')
   def hello():
       return «Hello, Docker World!»


   if __name__ == "__main__":
       app.run(host="0.0.0.0", port=80)
   ```

3. Now, you can build the image by running the following command:

   ```
   $ docker build -t my-python-app
   ```

Once you run the aforementioned command you will be able to see your image being built successfully. You can check this by running the following command as well to verify your Docker image status:

```
$docker image ls
REPOSITORY      TAG       IMAGE ID       CREATED          SIZE
my-python-app   latest    a17bbd45cc3e   37 seconds ago   161MB
```

Docker containers

Now that you have a Docker image created in the previous section, you can spin up a Docker container from this image. Since a Docker container is a running instance of a Docker image in its isolated environment, which has its own file system and network stack, you will see how easy it is to port this across different environments.

To create a container from the image built in the previous steps, you need to do the following:

```
$docker run -p 4001:80 my-python-app
 * Serving Flask app ‹app›
 * Debug mode: off
WARNING: This is a development server. Do not use it in a production de-
ployment. Use a production WSGI server instead.
 * Running on all addresses (0.0.0.0)
 * Running on http://127.0.0.1:80
 * Running on http://172.17.0.2:80
Press CTRL+C to quit
172.17.0.1 - - [10/Nov/2024 09:03:30] "GET / HTTP/1.1" 200 -
172.17.0.1 - - [10/Nov/2024 09:03:30] "GET /favicon.ico HTTP/1.1" 404 –
```

You can head over to **http://localhost:4001/** on your browser and should see *Hello, Docker World!*

Let us consider a common pitfall, that is forgetting to map ports.

When you run a container that serves web content or an API, you must explicitly map the container's internal ports to host ports using the **-p** or **--port** flag:

```
# INCORRECT - Service will run but won't be accessible from host
docker run nginx


# CORRECT - Maps host port 8080 to container port 80
docker run -p 8080:80 nginx
```

> **Note:** The port mapping format is `HOST_PORT:CONTAINER_PORT`. Without this mapping, your container's services would not be accessible from your host machine.

Now you know what a Docker image, Docker Container and Dockerfile are, you can also spend time to learn a bit more in-depth about the basics of Docker CLI commands like:

- **docker pull <image_name>:** Pulls an image from a registry, e.g., Docker Hub.

- **docker run <image_name>:** Creates and starts a container from a specified image.

- **docker ps:** Lists all running containers. Use docker **ps** **-a** to see all containers, including stopped ones.

- **docker stop <container_id>:** Stops a running container.

- **docker start <container_id>:** Starts a stopped container.

- **docker build -t <tag>:** Builds an image from a Dockerfile in the current directory.

- **docker logs <container_id>:** Fetches logs from a container, useful for debugging.

- **docker exec -it <container_id> <command>:** Runs a command inside a running container, like opening a shell with bash.

Now that we have mastered the fundamentals of Docker images, containers, and Dockerfiles, let us explore Docker Compose, a powerful tool that helps us manage multi-container applications. While individual containers are great for simple applications, real-world projects often require multiple services working together, such as web servers, databases, caching layers, and message queues. Docker Compose simplifies this complexity by allowing us to define and orchestrate multiple containers using a single **YAML Ain't Markup Language** (**YAML**) file, making it an essential tool in every Docker developer's toolkit.

To summarize:

- **Images** are read-only templates containing application code and dependencies.
- **Containers** are runtime instances of images with their own isolated environment.
- **Dockerfiles** define how to build images through a series of instructions (FROM, RUN, COPY, etc.).
- Every image consists of layers, with each instruction creating a new layer.
- Docker uses a Union File System to combine layers into a single coherent view.

Use Docker build to create images and docker run to start containers.

Understanding Dockerfile

A Dockerfile is a text document containing instructions that Docker uses to automatically build an image. It is essentially a script of commands for creating a Docker container that can run on any platform with Docker installed, as shown:

```
# Base image
FROM ubuntu:20.04

# Set working directory
WORKDIR /app

# Copy files
COPY . /app/

# Install dependencies
RUN apt-get update && apt-get install -y \
    python3 \
    python3-pip \
    && pip3 install -r requirements.txt
```

```
# Expose port
EXPOSE 8080

# Set environment variables
ENV NODE_ENV=production

# Define command to run on container start
CMD ["python3", "app.py"]
```

The aforementioned Dockerfile has the following key elements:

- **FROM:** Specifies the base image to build upon (required as first instruction).
- **WORKDIR:** Sets the working directory for subsequent instructions.
- **COPY/ADD:** Copies files from the host into the container image.
- **RUN:** Executes commands during the build process.
- **EXPOSE:** Documents that the container listens on at runtime.
- **ENV:** Sets environment variables.
- **CMD:** Provides the default command to execute when the container starts.
- **ENTRYPOINT:** Configures the container to run as an executable.

Docker Compose for multi-container applications

As applications grow in a modern software ecosystem, they often need multiple services (e.g., a web server, database, and cache) to work together. Docker Compose simplifies this by allowing you to define and run multi-container applications with a single command. This is accomplished by using a **docker-compose.yml** file to specify the configuration for each service, making it easier to manage and scale multi-container environments.

Let us now take a quick example of how you can use Docker Compose using a **nginx** web server and a **redis** database as follows:

1. Create the directory structure as follows:

   ```
   $ mkdir simple-docker-compose
   $ cd simple-docker-compose
   ```

2. Make sure the directory structure is as follows:

   ```
   simple-docker-compose/
   ├──── docker-compose.yml
   ├──── nginx/
   │     └──── default.conf
   ```

3. Now, you can create a file named **docker-compose.yml** file in the root directory as follows:

```
version: '3.8'

services:
  web:
    image: nginx:latest
    ports:
      - «8080:80"  # Map port 8080 on the host to port 80 in the con
tainer
    volumes:
                    -   ./nginx/default.conf:/etc/nginx/conf.d/default.
conf:ro  # Mount the custom Nginx config
    depends_on:
      - redis

  redis:
    image: redis:latest
    ports:
      - «6379:6379"  # Map Redis default port
```

4. Create **nginx/default.conf** file for a simple NGINX setup:

```
server {
    listen 80;

    location / {
        return 200 ‹Hello, Docker Compose!';
        add_header Content-Type text/plain;
    }

    location /redis {
        default_type text/plain;
        return 200 ‹Connected to Redis!';
    }
}
```

Now, you can run **docker-compose up -d**, which will start the service as follows from inside the **simple-docker-compose** directory. At this point you should be able to see:

```
Network simple-docker-compose_default    Created 0.0s
Container simple-docker-compose-redis-1  Started 0.2s
Container simple-docker-compose-web-1    Started 0.3s
```

You can verify the running container via **docker-compose ps**. You can also head over to your browser and check the following:

- **http://localhost:8080/**: You should see *Hello, Docker Compose!*

- **http://localhost:8080/redis**: You should see *Connected to Redis!*

Docker Compose hence simplifies the orchestration of multi-container setups, enabling you to define, deploy, and manage complex applications with minimal effort. By using a single **docker-compose.yml** file, developers can ensure consistency across environments, whether it is for local development, testing, or staging. From web servers to databases, Compose provides seamless service integration, making it a cornerstone of modern containerized workflows.

Let us consider container rebuilding with Docker Compose.

After changing your application code or Dockerfile, running just **docker-compose up** would not automatically rebuild your containers. Your changes would not be reflected in the running application. Always use:

```
$docker-compose up –build
```

This ensures your containers are rebuilt with the latest code changes. Alternatively, you can run **docker-compose build** first, then **docker-compose up**.

For more persistent and efficient development workflows, consider using volumes to map your local code directory into the container.

However, while Docker excels at running lightweight, isolated services, there are scenarios where replicating a full-fledged development environment, including system configurations and virtual machines, is necessary. This is where Vagrant shines. In the next section, we will explore how Vagrant complements Docker by providing robust tools for creating and managing development environments, giving you the flexibility to tailor your workflows to diverse project requirements.

Microservice blog platform

Let us consider the following real-world scenario.

Scenario: You are building a microservice-based blog platform with three components:

- A frontend service (React) that renders the user interface.

- A backend API service (Node.js) that handles data processing and business logic.

- A database service (MongoDB) that stores the blog posts and user information.

Without Docker Compose, you would need to manage three separate terminals, start each service individually, and manually ensure they are connected properly. Every team member would need to remember several commands to get the environment running.

Solution: By defining all three services in a single **docker-compose.yml** file, you can:

- Launch the entire environment with a single command: **docker-compose up --build**

- Ensure services start in the correct order (database first, then API, then frontend).

- Create a consistent network between services automatically.

- Share environment variables across services.

- Persist database data using volumes.

Here is what the **docker-compose.yml** might look like for this scenario:

```yaml
version: '3.8'
services:
  # MongoDB Database Service
  mongodb:
    image: mongo:latest
    ports:
      - "27017:27017"
    volumes:
      - mongo-data:/data/db
    environment:
      - MONGO_INITDB_ROOT_USERNAME=admin
      - MONGO_INITDB_ROOT_PASSWORD=password

  # Node.js Backend API Service
  backend:
    build: ./backend
    ports:
      - "3000:3000"
    depends_on:
      - mongodb
    environment:
      - MONGODB_URI=mongodb://admin:password@mongodb:27017
      - NODE_ENV=development

  # React Frontend Service
  frontend:
    build: ./frontend
    ports:
      - "8080:80"
```

```
depends_on:
  - backend
environment:
  - REACT_APP_API_URL=http://localhost:3000/api

volumes:
  mongo-data:
```

This real-world example demonstrates how Docker Compose simplifies complex multi-container development environments, improving team productivity and ensuring consistency across development machines.

To summarize:

- Define multiple containers and their configurations in one YAML file.

- Manage networking between containers automatically.

- Support for environment variables, volumes, and dependencies.

- Use **docker-compose up** to start all services and **docker-compose down** to stop them.

- Perfect for local development and testing multi-service applications.

- Enables reproducible environments across the team.

Building a containerized API with data persistence

Apply your Docker and Docker Compose knowledge with this multi-part challenge. The details are as follows:

Challenge 1: Create a Dockerfile for a Node.js API

1. Create a new directory for your project.

2. Create a simple **Express.js** API that:

   a. Has a /route that returns a welcome message.

   b. Has a /status route that returns the current time.

3. Write a Dockerfile that:

   a. Uses Node.js 16 as the base image.

   b. Copies **package.json** and installs dependencies.

   c. Copies the application code.

    d.   Exposes port 3000.

    e.   Sets the startup command.

Challenge 2: Add Redis and Link Services with Docker Compose

1. Create a **docker-compose.yml** file that:

    a.   Defines your API service using the Dockerfile.

    b.   Adds a Redis service with the official Redis image.

    c.   Sets up network connectivity between them.

2. Modify your API to:

    a.   Connect to Redis using the **redis npm** package

    b.   Add a /counter endpoint that increments and returns a visit counter stored in Redis.

Challenge 3: Test your multi-container application

1. Build and run your services using Docker Compose.

2. Use curl, Postman, or your browser to test all endpoints.

3. Verify data persistence by:

    a.   Stopping and restarting the services.

    b.   Checking if the counter maintains its value.

Success criteria:

- Both services start successfully with **docker-compose up**.
- The API can communicate with Redis.
- The counter persists across service restarts.
- All endpoints return appropriate responses.

Vagrant for creating development environments

Vagrant is a tool for building and managing virtualized development environments. It simplifies the setup of consistent environments for developers by using **virtual machines (VMs)** or containers, ensuring that every team member works in an identical setup. With

Vagrant, you can define environments in code, making them portable, reproducible, and easy to share.

Figure 2.5 showcases some of the common benefits of Vagrant:

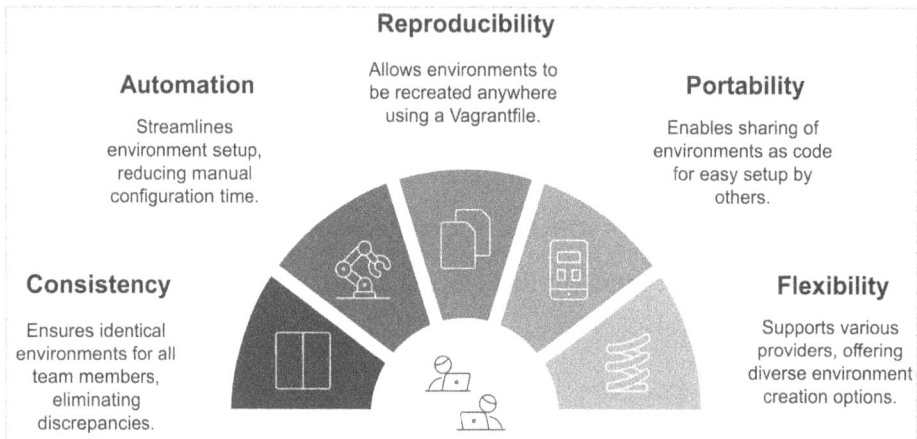

Figure 2.5: *Vagrant benefits*

Let us now take a quick look at how vagrant works.

Vagrant uses a configuration file called a Vagrantfile to define the environment. This file includes the following:

- **Base box:** A preconfigured OS image (e.g., Ubuntu, CentOS).
- **Providers:** The virtualization platform used, like VirtualBox, VMware, or Docker.
- **Provisioners:** Scripts or tools (like Shell, Ansible, Puppet) to automate environment setup.

When you run vagrant up, it performs the following:

- Creates a VM or container from the specified base box.
- Configures the environment based on the Vagrantfile.
- Installs necessary software or dependencies using provisioners.

Setting up a basic development environment

Following are the steps for setting up a basic development environment:

📂 🐾 Download and install Vagrant: (**https://developer.hashicorp.com/vagrant/install?product_intent=vagrant**) and VirtualBox (**https://www.virtualbox.org/wiki/Downloads)** for your operating system.

📄 🐾 Initialize Vagrant in your project directory:

```
$ mkdir python-dev-env
$ cd python-dev-env
$ vagrant init
```

⧉⬿ Update the generated Vagrantfile:

```
Vagrant.configure("2") do |config|
  config.vm.box = «ubuntu/focal64»
  config.vm.provider «virtualbox" do |vb|
    vb.memory = «1024»
    vb.cpus = 2
  end
  config.vm.provision «shell», inline: <<-SHELL
    apt-get update
    apt-get install -y python3 python3-pip
  SHELL
End
```

⧉⬿ Launch the environment

```
$vagrant up
```

The aforementioned commands will do the following:

- Download the Ubuntu base box.
- Create a VM with 1 GB RAM and 2 CPUs.
- Install Python and Pip.

Now you can include SSH (also known as Secure Shell) into the VM by simply doing:

```
$vagrant ssh
```

You can now use this VM for your development work. Similarly, try creating multiple environments (VMs). Hence, by defining environments as code in a Vagrantfile, Vagrant simplifies the process of creating, sharing, and managing development setups. Whether you are working on a single project or a complex multi-machine setup, Vagrant ensures consistency, automation, and efficiency.

To summarize:

- Creates consistent VM-based development environments using a Vagrantfile.
- Works with various providers (VirtualBox, VMware, AWS).
- Supports provisioning tools like Shell, Ansible, and Puppet.
- Use vagrant up to create and start VMs, vagrant ssh to access them.
- Better for cases where you need full OS isolation or specific OS requirements.

Useful when Docker cannot meet your needs (e.g., Windows-specific development).

Container orchestration basics

Container orchestration is the conductor of modern cloud computing. Imagine trying to coordinate hundreds of musicians in an orchestra without a conductor. As applications grow more sophisticated, they are split into numerous specialized containers, each running specific services. However, who manages all these containers across vast networks of computers?

That is where container orchestration shines. It is an automated system that handles the complex choreography of deploying, networking, and scaling containers. Like a skilled conductor, it ensures every container starts at the right time, communicates properly with others, and adapts to changing conditions, all without manual intervention.

Figure 2.6 paints a clear picture of what the overall responsibilities of a container orchestrator are:

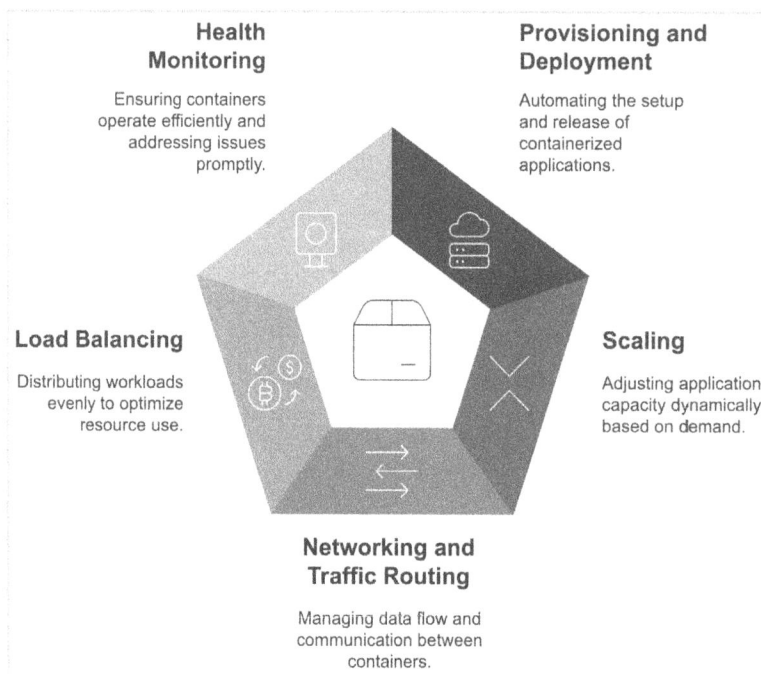

Figure 2.6: *Container orchestrator responsibilities*

Under the hood, container orchestrators are powered by declarative programming, i.e., you describe what you want, and the underlying logic will make it happen. Developers define the desired state of the system (e.g., which containers to run, how to scale them, network requirements) in a configuration file written in YAML or JSON. The orchestration tool then automates the processes to achieve and maintain that state.

The steps in this orchestration process include the following:

1. **Set configurations:**

   a. Developers define container images, networking rules, storage volumes, and resource requirements in a configuration file.

   b. These files are version-controlled for consistency and reusability across development, staging, and production environments.

2. **Deploy containers:**

   a. Containers are deployed to suitable hosts based on predefined constraints (e.g., memory, CPU, proximity to other services).

   For example, Kubernetes uses pods (the smallest deployment unit) to manage groups of containers.

3. **Manage the container lifecycle by fully automating:**

   a. Scaling containers up or down based on traffic.

   b. Migrating containers to other hosts in case of failures.

   c. Load balancing and traffic routing between the services are deployed.

   d. Monitoring health and reachability.

Now, let us quickly take a look at some of the popular container orchestration tools as follows:

- **Kubernetes (K8s):**

  o This is the most widely adopted container orchestration platform, which takes care of automating deployment, scaling, and management of containerized applications.

  o Features include self-healing, load balancing, and portability across cloud providers.

  We will discuss this in detail in *Chapter 10, Kubernetes Essentials*.

- **Docker Swarm:**

  o A lightweight, native clustering and orchestration solution for Docker.

  o Simpler than Kubernetes, ideal for smaller-scale container deployments.

- **Apache Mesos:**

  o A cluster manager for containerized and non-containerized workloads.

  o Often paired with Marathon for managing container orchestration in large, complex environments.

- **Cloud providers' Kubernetes Services:**
  - o **Azure Kubernetes Service (AKS):**
    - ☐ A managed Kubernetes service by Microsoft Azure.
    - ☐ Handles Kubernetes control plane management while users focus on deploying applications.
  - o **Amazon Elastic Kubernetes Service (EKS):**
    - ☐ A managed Kubernetes service from AWS.
    - ☐ Simplifies running Kubernetes in the cloud and integrates deeply with AWS services.
  - o **Google Kubernetes Engine (GKE):**
    - ☐ Google Cloud's managed Kubernetes service.
    - ☐ Offers seamless scaling, monitoring, and integrations with other Google Cloud services.

Now that we have explored the fundamentals of container orchestration, let us turn our attention to another critical aspect of modern software development: environment parity.

The challenges we discussed in container orchestration, maintaining consistency, ensuring scalability, and managing dependencies, lead us naturally to the broader question of how to maintain consistency across different deployment environments. While containers help package our applications consistently, ensuring identical behavior across development, staging, and production environments remains a significant challenge that requires careful consideration.

As we will discover, environment parity builds upon the containerization principles we have just covered, extending them to create a seamless experience across your entire development pipeline. This concept is crucial for maintaining reliability and reducing the, *it works on my machine* syndrome that has plagued development teams for decades.

To summarize:

- Manages the deployment, scaling, and operation of containers across clusters.
- Handles container placement, networking, load balancing, and health monitoring.
- Kubernetes is the most popular orchestration platform for production environments.
- Docker Swarm offers a simpler alternative for smaller deployments.
- Cloud providers offer managed Kubernetes services (AKS, EKS, GKE).
- Uses declarative configurations to define the desired state of the system.

Environment parity in DevOps

Environment parity is a fundamental principle in modern software development that emphasizes keeping all environments, development, staging, and production, as similar as possible. In simple terms, if your application works in one environment, it should work the same way in another.

To understand why this matters, let us explore how environmental parity affects real-world software development and deployment.

Critical gaps

When examining environment parity, we often encounter three fundamental gaps that can cause discrepancies between development and production environments. These gaps have historically created significant challenges for software teams and continue to be relevant today. Understanding these gaps is crucial for addressing the root causes of environment-related issues.

The three gaps are discussed as follows:

- **Time gap:**

  o **Traditional approach**: Weeks or months between code completion and deployment.

  o **Modern approach**: Minutes to hours from commit to production.

  o **Impact**: Shorter time gaps lead to better code quality as developers work knowing their code will be in production quickly.

  The time gap represents perhaps the most significant challenge in maintaining environmental parity. When too much time passes between development and deployment, developers lose context, and the risk of environmental drift increases substantially.

- **Personnel gap:**

  o **Traditional approach**: Different teams handle development and deployment.

  o **Modern approach**: Automated deployments with minimal human intervention.

  o **Key point**: If you cannot deploy with a single button press, you are likely doing it wrong.

  The personnel gap highlights the organizational challenges in maintaining environmental parity. When different teams are responsible for different environments, communication barriers and varying priorities can lead to inconsistencies.

- **Tools gap:**

  o   **Traditional approach**: Different tools and services across environments.

  o   **Example**: Using SQLite in development but PostgreSQL in production.

  o   **Solution**: Use identical backing services across all environments.

  The tools gap represents the technical differences between environments. This gap often emerges from practical compromises made during development, but these shortcuts can lead to significant problems in production.

As teams work to maintain environment parity, they frequently encounter several recurring challenges. Understanding these challenges and their solutions is essential for implementing effective environment parity strategies. The automotive industry provides a compelling example of these challenges and how modern development teams are addressing them.

In automotive software development, teams face a significant challenge: cloud-based development environments often vastly outperform the actual vehicle systems they are designing for. While developers might work in high-performance cloud environments with abundant resources, the final code must run on embedded systems with strict hardware limitations, specific memory constraints, and complex vehicle interfaces. This mismatch between development and production environments can lead to critical issues that only surface when the software is deployed in actual vehicles.

To address this challenge, automotive companies are implementing environment parity through cloud environments that accurately replicate the properties and constraints of physical vehicle components. They use specialized tools to simulate hardware limitations, apply real-time kernel patches, and create development environments that mirror actual vehicle conditions as closely as possible. This approach allows developers to catch potential issues early in the development cycle, reduce dependency on scarce hardware resources, and ensure their software will perform reliably when deployed in real vehicles. The result is more efficient development cycles, reduced testing costs, and, most importantly, more reliable software in the final product.

Best practices for maintaining environmental parity

Based on the lessons learned from various industries and development teams, several best practices have emerged for maintaining effective environment parity. These practices form the foundation of a robust environment parity strategy. They are discussed as follows:

- **Use containerization:** Ensure consistent runtime environments.

- **Automate everything:** Reduce human intervention in deployments.

- **Version control environment configs:** Track all environment settings.

- **Regular testing:** Validate behavior across all environments.

- **Monitor differences:** Actively track and eliminate environment divergence.

Each of these practices contributes to a comprehensive approach to environmental parity, helping teams maintain consistency across their entire deployment pipeline.

Golden rule of environment parity

The most important principle in environment parity is that every commit should be a candidate for deployment. If your environments are not truly identical, you lose the ability to predict how your code will behave in production accurately. This rule should guide all decisions about environment configuration and management.

To summarize:

- Minimize differences between development, testing, and production environments.

- Address the three key gaps: time, personnel, and tools.

- Use containerization to ensure consistent runtime environments.

- Version control environment configurations to track changes.

- Implement regular testing and monitoring to catch differences early.

Follow the golden rule, every commit should be a candidate for deployment.

Managing development environment configurations

After understanding the importance of environment parity, we need to focus on how to manage our development environments effectively. The key challenge lies in maintaining environments that are reliable for experimentation and consistently matched with production.

When development environments drift from production, several critical problems can emerge:

- Changes that work in development may fail in production.

- Inconsistent behavior across different environments.

- Unexpected deployment failures.

- Unintended changes sneaking into deployments.

To avoid these problems, you should follow the following principles for your environment management:

- **Avoid manual changes:**
  - o   All changes should be tracked through user stories.
  - o   Use automated deployment tools consistently.
  - o   Implement changes through the metadata API rather than manual configurations.
  - o   Manual changes in testing or production can lead to environment drift.

- **Balance development environments:**
  - o   Version control enables parallel development work.
  - o   Single shared development environment:
    - ☐   **Pros**: Natural integration of work.
    - ☐   **Cons**: Changes by one developer can affect others.
  - o   Individual environments:
    - ☐   **Pros**: Isolated experimentation.
    - ☐   **Cons**: Requires frequent synchronization.

- **Environment synchronization:**
  - o   Implement daily back-promotions to keep environments in sync.
  - o   Developers must commit work before synchronization.
  - o   Regular sandbox refreshes (typically quarterly to annual).
  - o   Automate synchronization processes where possible.

Integration with CI/CD pipelines

While managing development environments effectively is crucial, integrating them into a robust CI/CD pipeline takes us one step further in maintaining consistency and reliability. The environment management practices we discussed earlier, avoiding manual changes, maintaining synchronization, and implementing proper refresh strategies, form the foundation for successful CI/CD integration. We will spend more time on CI/CD in the upcoming chapters; however, it is essential to understand how our environment management practices enhance our continuous delivery capabilities.

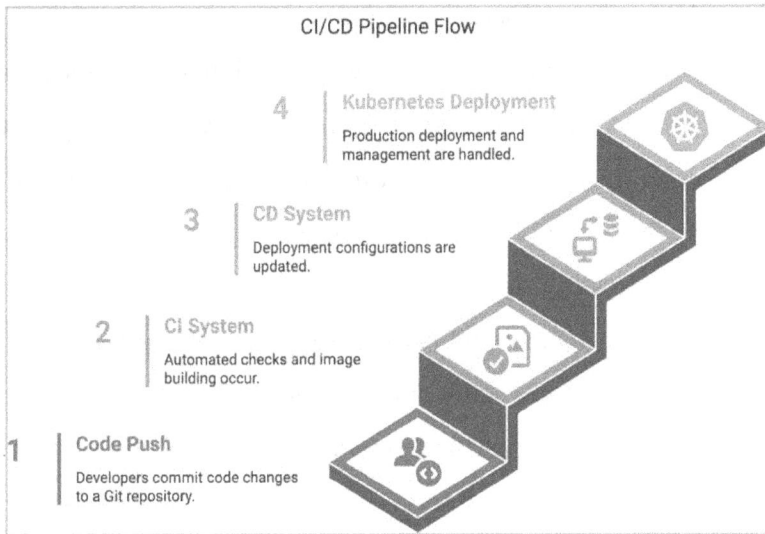

Figure 2.7: CI/CD pipeline for containerized applications from dev to prod

The aforementioned figure illustrates how containerized applications flow through a modern CI/CD pipeline:

1. Developers push code changes to a Git repository.

2. The CI system automatically:

    a. Runs linting and tests to ensure code quality.

    b. Builds a Docker image from the Dockerfile.

    c. Tag the image with a version (typically the **git commit hash**).

    d. Pushes the image to a container registry.

3. The CD system detects the new image and:

    α. Pulls the latest image from the registry.

    β. Updates the deployment configuration.

    χ. Applies the changes to the Kubernetes cluster.

4. Kubernetes handles the production deployment, scaling, and management. This continuous flow ensures that your development environments remain in sync with production, maintaining the environment parity we discussed earlier. The containerized approach guarantees that the exact same code and dependencies that passed testing will be deployed to production.

Let us examine how these practices naturally extend into our CI/CD pipeline architecture across three key areas:

- **Automated environment setup:**
  - o Convert manual environment configurations into declarative pipeline stages.
  - o Implement systematic back-promotion workflows across environments.
  - o Orchestrate environment refresh cycles through automated schedules.
  - o Leverage IaC for consistent environment definitions.

- **Comprehensive testing strategy:**
  - o Maintain strict environment parity throughout testing phases.
  - o Design automated test suites optimized for each environment tier.
  - o Deploy environment-specific validation gates and checks.
  - o Establish dedicated testing pathways for hotfix deployments.

- **Deployment orchestration:**
  - o Replace manual intervention with pipeline-driven deployment flows.
  - o Engineer resilient automated rollback mechanisms.
  - o Enforce deployment consistency through environment templates.
  - o Implement robust change tracking and validation processes.

This integration creates a seamless delivery pipeline while preserving our core principles of environment parity and controlled change management. The result is a reliable, reproducible system that minimizes drift and maintains operational integrity.

Building a Flask and Redis visit counter with Docker Compose

Let us apply what we have learned by building a simple but functional microservice system using Docker and Docker Compose. We will create a Flask application that counts website visits by storing data in Redis.

The following are the project objectives:

- Create a containerized Flask application.
- Connect it to a Redis database for data persistence.
- Use Docker Compose to orchestrate both services.
- Implement basic endpoints to demonstrate the functionality.

Let us discuss the steps as follows:

1. Set up the project structure.

   Create the following directory structure:

```
flask-redis-counter/
├── docker-compose.yml
├── app/
│   ├── Dockerfile
│   ├── requirements.txt
│   └── app.py
└── README.md
```

2. Create the flask application.

   Create app/**requirements.txt**:

```
flask==2.0.1
redis==3.5.3
```

   Create app/**app.py**:

```python
from flask import Flask, jsonify
import redis
import socket
import os

app = Flask(__name__)
cache = redis.Redis(host='redis', port=6379)

def get_hit_count():
    return cache.incr('hits')

@app.route('/')
def home():
    count = get_hit_count()
    return jsonify(
        message="Hello Docker Compose!",
        counter=count,
        container_id=socket.gethostname()
    )

@app.route('/set/<key>/<value>')
def set_key(key, value):
    cache.set(key, value)
```

```python
        return jsonify(
            message=f"Stored {key}",
            key=key,
            value=value
        )


@app.route('/get/<key>')
def get_key(key):
    value = cache.get(key)
    if value:
        value = value.decode('utf-8')
    return jsonify(
        key=key,
        value=value
    )


if __name__ == "__main__":
    app.run(host="0.0.0.0", port=5000, debug=True)
```

3. Create the Dockerfile.

   Create app/Dockerfile:

```dockerfile
FROM python:3.9-slim

WORKDIR /app

COPY requirements.txt .
RUN pip install --no-cache-dir -r requirements.txt

COPY . .

EXPOSE 5000

CMD ["python", "app.py"]
```

4. Create Docker Compose Configuration.

   Create **docker-compose.yml**:

```yaml
version: '3.8'

services:
  web:
```

```
    build: ./app
    ports:
      - "5000:5000"
    volumes:
      - ./app:/app
    environment:
      - FLASK_ENV=development
    depends_on:
      - redis
    restart: always

  redis:
    image: redis:alpine
    ports:
      - "6379:6379"
    volumes:
      - redis-data:/data

volumes:
  redis-data:
```

5. Run the application.

   Run the application with:
   ```
   docker-compose up –build
   ```

6. Test the application.

   Once the services are running, test the endpoints:

   • Visit **http://localhost:5000/** to see the counter increment with each refresh.

   • Set a value with **http://localhost:5000/set/username/developer.**

   • Retrieve the value with **http://localhost:5000/get/username.**

7. Experiment with container resilience.

   Try stopping and restarting the containers:
   ```
   # Stop containers but keep volumes
   docker-compose down

   # Start them again
   docker-compose up
   ```

Note: **The counter value persists because the Redis data is stored in a persistent volume.**

The following are some bonus challenges:

- Add environment variables to configure Redis connection details.

- Implement a /reset endpoint to reset the counter.

- Add basic authentication to the API.

- Create a simple front-end container with NGINX to serve a static website that displays the counter.

This mini project demonstrates several key concepts:

- Containerizing a Python application.

- Using Docker Compose for multi-container orchestration.

- Implementing service-to-service communication.

- Utilizing volumes for data persistence.

- Creating a RESTful API with Flask.

Completing this project will give you hands-on experience with the core concepts covered in this chapter.

Conclusion

By the end of this chapter, we have explored the fundamental building blocks of robust development environments. From containerization basics to advanced environment management techniques, we have established patterns for creating consistent, reproducible workspaces that support modern DevOps practices. The tools and approaches we have discussed: Docker, Vagrant, environment parity, and automated pipelines form the foundation for reliable software delivery.

In the next chapter, we will build upon these environment management principles by exploring version control and Git workflows. While solid development environments provide the workspace for writing code, version control systems like Git provide the framework for managing, tracking, and collaborating on that code. We will see how Git workflows complement our environment management strategies, creating a cohesive approach to software development that emphasizes both stability and agility.

CHAPTER 3
Version Control and Git Workflows

Introduction

Version control is the backbone of modern software development and a critical skill in the DevOps ecosystem. In this chapter, we will explore Git, the industry-standard version control system, and discuss the strategies and techniques that enable seamless collaboration, code management, and continuous integration. We will understand how to effectively create, manage, and synchronize code repositories, understand advanced branching strategies like Gitflow and trunk-based development, and master techniques such as rebasing, cherry-picking, and implementing efficient code review processes. Whether you are working on small team projects or large-scale enterprise systems, this chapter will equip you with the knowledge to implement robust version control workflows that enhance code quality, track changes, facilitate collaboration, and support continuous delivery.

Structure

The chapter covers the following topics:

- Git fundamentals
- Popular Git workflows
- Advanced Git techniques

- Branching strategies

- Pull or merge request best practices

- Code review processes and tools

- Automating code quality with Git Hooks

- Monorepo vs. multi-repo strategies

- Practical infrastructure as code organization

Objectives

By the end of this chapter, you will gain comprehensive knowledge of version control systems with a focus on Git, enabling you to implement robust workflows that enhance code quality and team collaboration. We will understand how to effectively create and manage repositories, understand the mechanics of commits, branches, and merging operations. The chapter will equip you with practical knowledge of popular workflows like Gitflow, GitHub Flow, and trunk-based development, helping you choose the right approach for your projects. We will master advanced techniques such as rebasing, cherry-picking, and working with submodules, while also learning branching strategies that support continuous integration and deployment. Additionally, we will develop skills in creating effective pull requests, implementing code review processes, automating quality checks with Git Hooks, and making informed decisions between monorepo and multi-repo architectures. The chapter includes practical examples and command-line instructions throughout, ensuring you can immediately apply these concepts to transform version control from a mere tracking tool into a strategic asset in your SDLC.

Git fundamentals

Version control is the cornerstone of collaborative software development, and Git has emerged as the definitive tool for managing code across teams and projects. At its core, a Git repository is more than just a storage container, it is a comprehensive historical record of your project's evolution, capturing every change, modification, and creative decision made by developers.

Creating your first repository

To begin your Git journey, you will need to create a repository. Open your terminal and follow these steps:

```
# Create a new directory for your project
$ mkdir my-first-project
$ cd my-first-project

# Initialize a new Git repository
```

```
$ git init

# Verify the repository creation
$ ls -la
```

When you run these commands, Git creates a hidden **.git** directory that will track all changes in your project. This directory contains the entire history and configuration of your repository, serving as the backbone of version control.

Understanding the Git workflow is essential for effective version control. Git maintains your code in distinct states:

[Working Directory] | [Staging Area] | [Local Repository] | [Remote Repository]

When you make changes to files in your working directory, you use **git add** to move them to the staging area. The staging area (or index) holds changes you want to include in your next commit. Using **git commit** transfers these changes to your local repository, creating a permanent snapshot. Finally, **git push** sends these commits to the remote repository for collaboration.

Understanding repositories begins with recognizing their fundamental structure. A repository can exist in multiple forms, local repositories residing on individual developer machines, remote repositories hosted on platforms like GitHub or GitLab, and bare repositories designed specifically for sharing and collaboration

Adding your first files

Let us create and track some files in your repository as follows:

```
# Create a sample Python function
$ cat > calculator.py << EOF
def calculate_total(items):
    """Calculate the sum of all items in the cart"""
    return sum(item['price'] * item['quantity'] for item in items)

if __name__ == "__main__":
    # Test the function
    cart = [
        {'name': 'Keyboard', 'price': 50, 'quantity': 1},
        {'name': 'Mouse', 'price': 25, 'quantity': 2}
    ]
    print(f"Total: ${calculate_total(cart)}")
EOF

# Check the repository status
```

```
$ git status

# Stage the new file
$ git add calculator.py

# Commit the file with a descriptive message
$ git commit -m "Initial commit: Add shopping cart calculator function"
```

Commits are the fundamental units of this tracking system, representing precise snapshots of a project at specific moments in time. Each **commit** is a comprehensive package containing a unique identifier, author information, timestamp, descriptive message, and the exact changes made to the project files.

You can now check the commits as follows:

```
# View commit history
$ git log

# See detailed information about the last commit
$ git show HEAD

# View a compact commit history
$ git log --oneline
```

Similarly, branches in Git extend Git's power by enabling parallel development paths. They allow developers to create isolated environments for experimenting with new features, fixing bugs, or exploring innovative solutions without risking the stability of the main codebase.

Let us take a quick look at how branches in Git work:

```
# List existing branches
$ git branch

# Create a new feature branch
$ git branch feature-login

# Switch to the new branch
$ git checkout feature-login

# Create and switch to a new branch in one command
$ git checkout -b feature-registration

# List all branches
$ git branch
```

Further merging brings these parallel development paths together, integrating changes from different branches into a unified codebase. Merging is a sophisticated process that can occur through different mechanisms, fast-forward merges, and three-way merges.

Fast-forward merge

A fast-forward merge occurs when there are no new changes in the main branch since the feature branch was created. It is like simply moving the pointer forward because there are no conflicting changes.

```
Before merge:          After merge:
main: A -> B           main: A -> B -> C
     |                      ^
feature: B -> C            C (feature branch changes)
```

The following is the example:

```
# Create and switch to main branch
git checkout main

# Create a new feature branch
git checkout -b feature-update

# Make some changes in the feature branch
echo "New feature implementation" > feature.txt
git add feature.txt
git commit -m "Add new feature"

# Switch back to main
git checkout main

# Merge the feature branch
# Since no changes were made in main, this is a fast-forward merge
git merge feature-update

# The merge is straightforward - it simply moves the main branch pointer
```

Three-way merge

A three-way merge happens when both the main branch and the feature branch have unique commits since they diverged. Git must create a new **Merge Commit** that combines the changes. Refer to the following:

```
Before merge:        After merge:
main: A -> B -> D    main: A -> B -> D
                             \          /
feature:    A -> B -> C    \-> C ---' (Merge Commit)
```

The following is an example of three-way merge:

```
# Start from main branch
git checkout main

# Create and switch to a feature branch
git checkout -b feature-login

# Make some changes in feature branch
echo "Login functionality" > login.py
git add login.py
git commit -m "Add login module"

# Switch back to main and make different changes
git checkout main
echo "Main application update" > main.py
git add main.py
git commit -m "Update main application"

# Now merge the feature branch
# This will create a new merge commit
git merge feature-login
```

Interactive learning resources

For hands-on practice with Git concepts, consider using interactive learning tools like Learn Git Branching (**https://learngitbranching.js.org**), which provides visual representations of branches and commits as you enter commands. These tools can significantly accelerate your understanding of Git's branching model and workflow states.

Popular Git workflows

Git workflows are structured approaches to managing code development, branching, and release cycles. Each workflow offers unique strategies for collaboration, code management, and continuous delivery. Understanding these workflows is crucial for teams to establish efficient and predictable software development processes.

Gitflow

Gitflow is a robust, structured workflow designed for projects with complex release cycles and multiple simultaneous versions. It defines a strict branching model that provides clear separation of concerns and supports parallel development.

The following are the key branches in Gitflow:

- **Main branch (master/main):** Represents the official release history.
- **Develop branch:** Serves as an integration branch for features.
- **Feature branches:** For developing new features.
- **Release branches:** Prepare new production releases.
- **Hotfix branches:** Quickly address critical production issues.

Let us look at how Gitflow works:

```
# Initialize Gitflow in an existing repository
$ git flow init

# Start a new feature
$ git flow feature start user-authentication

# Finish a feature (merges back to develop)
$ git flow feature finish user-authentication

# Start a release
$ git flow release start 1.0.0

# Finish a release (merges to main and develop)
$ git flow release finish 1.0.0
```

GitHub Flow

GitHub Flow offers a more lightweight, continuous delivery-focused approach. It simplifies the branching model, making it ideal for teams practicing continuous deployment.

The core principles of GitHub Flow are:

- Main branch always represents production-ready code.
- New features are developed in separate branches.
- Pull requests are used for code review and discussion.
- Continuous integration ensures branch stability.
- Immediate deployment after merge.

GitHub Flow is particularly well-suited for continuous deployment environments where teams release features frequently. It thrives in web applications and services that can be updated without extensive versioning, making it the workflow of choice for many SaaS products and cloud-native applications.

The following is a typical example of GitHub Flow:

```
# Create a new feature branch
$ git checkout -b feature/new-login-system

# Make changes and commit
$ git add .
$ git commit -m "Implement modern login system"

# Push branch to remote repository
$ git push -u origin feature/new-login-system

# Create a pull request on GitHub
# Reviewers check and approve
# Merge directly into main branch
```

Trunk-based development

Trunk-based development (**TBD**) is a streamlined version control strategy designed to enable rapid development and deployment. It revolves around a single main branch (the trunk), with minimal branching overhead. Developers frequently integrate their changes into this branch, ensuring a constantly updated and stable codebase.

The key characteristics of this approach are:

- Single main branch (trunk) where all developers commit.

- Short-lived feature branches (typically lasting hours or days).

- Frequent merges back to the main branch.

- Relies heavily on robust automated testing.

- Supports continuous deployment.

TBD is particularly effective for teams working with microservices and containerized applications deployed via Kubernetes. The short-lived branches and frequent integrations complement container orchestration environments where automated testing and deployment pipelines can quickly validate and deploy incremental changes.

TBD is primarily implemented as follows:

```
# Always start from the main branch
$ git checkout main
$ git pull origin main

# Create a very short-lived feature branch
$ git checkout -b feature/quick-update

# Make minimal, focused changes
$ git add .
$ git commit -m "Implement quick performance optimization"

# Merge back to main quickly
$ git checkout main
$ git merge --no-ff .feature/quick-update

# Push changes
$ git push origin main
```

Each workflow represents a different philosophy of collaboration and code management. The key is finding the approach that maximizes your team's productivity, code quality, and delivery speed.

Advanced Git techniques

Version control is not just about tracking changes; it is about crafting a narrative of code evolution. As developers progress beyond basic Git operations, they discover techniques that transform version control from a simple tracking tool to a sophisticated code management system. Our journey through advanced Git techniques will explore how developers can gain unprecedented control and flexibility in managing complex project histories.

Rebasing

While commits capture snapshots of code, rebasing offers the ability to reshape those snapshots, creating a cleaner, more coherent narrative. Think of rebasing as a storyteller's tool, allowing you to reorganize your project's history into a more logical, linear progression.

The transition from basic branching to rebasing is natural. Where branching creates parallel development paths, rebasing allows you to integrate those paths seamlessly, eliminating unnecessary complexity.

Let us explore the practical implementation of rebasing through the following commands:

```
# Start with a feature branch with multiple commits
$ git checkout feature-auth
$ git log --oneline
abc123 Add password reset functionality
def456 Implement OAuth login
ghi789 Create basic authentication framework

# Perform an interactive rebase to clean up history
$ git rebase -i HEAD~3

# In the editor that opens, you might change:
pick ghi789 Create basic authentication framework
pick def456 Implement OAuth login
pick abc123 Add password reset functionality

# To:
pick ghi789 Create basic authentication framework
squash def456 Implement OAuth login
squash abc123 Add password reset functionality

# This will combine the three commits into one comprehensive commit
# providing a cleaner, more logical history
```

As we move from rebasing to our next technique, we recognize that sometimes we do not want to move entire branches, but only specific commits.

Cherry-picking

Cherry-picking emerges as the natural successor to rebasing, offering even more granular control. If rebasing is about reshaping entire branch histories, cherry-picking is about selecting precise moments of code change and transplanting them with surgical precision.

Building upon the narrative control demonstrated in rebasing, cherry-picking allows developers to select individual commits from one branch and apply them to another, bridging development streams with unprecedented flexibility.

The following command specifies how to use cherry-picking:

```
# Selecting and applying specific commits
$ git cherry-pick abc123

# Integrating select changes across branches
$ git cherry-pick commit1..commit2
```

However, sometimes the complexity of modern software development often requires more than just moving commits. This leads us to our next advanced technique: managing intricate project dependencies.

Submodules

Submodules represent the next evolution in our Git mastery; a technique that transcends simple commit management and enters the realm of comprehensive project architecture. Where cherry-picking manipulates individual commits, submodules allow entire repositories to be nested within one another, creating complex, modular development environments.

The journey from rebasing to cherry-picking to submodules mirrors the increasing sophistication of software development practices, each technique building upon the last to provide more nuanced control, as shown:

```
# Adding a external library as a submodule
$ git submodule add https://github.com/example/library.git libs/library


# Initializing and updating submodule dependencies
$ git submodule init
$ git submodule update -remote
```

Putting it all together

All the advanced strategies that we discussed are not isolated tools but interconnected strategies for managing code:

- **Rebasing:** It provides a clean, linear project history.
- **Cherry-picking:** It allows selective code integration.
- **Submodules:** It enables complex, modular project structures.

A practical workflow can look like:

- Use rebasing to clean the local branch history.
- Cherry-pick specific features across branches.
- Manage shared components using submodules.

As developers master these techniques, they transform from mere code writers to architectural storytellers, capable of crafting intricate, manageable software landscapes.

Branching strategies

In modern DevOps workflows, effective branching strategies play a crucial role in supporting CI/CD. A well-defined branching strategy ensures smooth collaboration, frequent integrations, and reliable deployments while reducing the risk of conflicts and unstable releases. CI/CD demand a branching approach that balances speed, stability, and reliability. The right branching strategy acts as a conveyor belt, moving code from development to production with minimal friction and maximum confidence.

Also, these branching strategies are essential and allow:

- **Parallel development:** Allow multiple developers to work on features, fixes, or experiments without interfering with each other.

- **Code stability:** Isolate unstable code from production-ready code.

- **Frequent integration:** Facilitate regular merges to detect integration issues early.

- **Automated testing and deployment:** Align with CI/CD pipelines to ensure quality and enable quick releases.

Let us now look at popular branching strategies for CI/CD.

Feature branching

The feature branch model serves as the foundational approach for many CI/CD workflows. Each new feature or bug fix gets its own dedicated branch, allowing isolated development and comprehensive testing.

The following code explains how branches are created:

```
# Creating a feature branch
$ git checkout -b feature/user-authentication


# Workflow steps
$ git add .
$ git commit -m "Implement user authentication"


# Continuous Integration trigger
git push origin feature/user-authentication
```

Integration branch approach

An integration branch acts as a staging area for multiple feature branches, providing a consolidated testing environment before production deployment:

```
# A integration branch workflow
$ git checkout develop
$ git merge feature/user-authentication
$ git merge feature/payment-system
```

```
# Run comprehensive tests
# Prepare for release
```

Trunk-based development for high-performance teams

Trunk-based development represents an aggressive CI/CD branching strategy, emphasizing rapid integration and minimal long-lived branches, as shown:

```
# Short-lived feature branch
$ git checkout -b feature/quick-update main
$ git commit -m "Implement performance optimization"


# Rapid merge back to main
$ git checkout main
$ git merge --no-ff feature/quick-update
$ git push origin main
```

Release branch strategy

Release branches provide a structured approach to preparing and stabilizing code for production deployment, as shown:

```
# Create release branch
$ git checkout -b release/v1.2.0 develop


# Perform final testing and stabilization
$ git commit -m "Prepare release 1.2.0"


# Merge to main and develop
$ git checkout main
$ git merge release/v1.2.0
$ git checkout develop
$ git merge release/v1.2.0
```

Branching strategies are the architectural blueprint of modern software development, transforming version control from a simple tracking mechanism into a sophisticated delivery pipeline. The most effective approaches transcend traditional version control, creating intelligent systems that balance speed, quality, and reliability. This foundational understanding of branching strategies enables teams to align development workflows with their CI/CD goals, balancing speed, stability, and collaboration.

Pull or merge request best practices

Pull/merge requests (**PRs/MRs**) are vital for collaborative software development, enabling teams to review, discuss, and approve changes before merging them into the main branch. By adhering to best practices, teams can ensure code quality, reduce defects, and foster better collaboration.

When creating a PR, it is important to keep the changes small and focused. Each PR should ideally address a single feature, bug fix, or improvement. This not only makes the review process quicker but also reduces the likelihood of introducing errors. Additionally, providing a clear title and description is essential. The title should summarize the change concisely, while the description should explain the purpose, any related issues, and how the changes can be tested.

Reviewing a PR is as critical as writing one. Before starting the review, it is essential to understand the context of the changes. Reading the PR description and any linked issues or documentation can provide clarity. During the review, focus on code quality, maintainability, and adherence to standards. Offering constructive feedback is key, suggest improvements clearly and respectfully. Testing the branch locally can also help identify issues that automated tests might miss.

When merging a PR, ensure all automated tests and checks have passed. If the repository uses a continuous integration pipeline, confirm that it has validated the changes. Consider squashing commits if the PR has multiple smaller commits to keep the commit history clean and meaningful. Finally, delete the branch after merging to keep the repository organized.

By following these practices, teams can streamline the code review process and maintain high standards for their codebase.

Code review processes and tools

Code review is a systematic examination of source code by one or more developers who are not the original authors of the code. This collaborative process is a cornerstone of modern software development, serving multiple critical purposes beyond simply identifying bugs. At its core, code review is about collective code ownership, knowledge sharing, and continuous improvement of software quality.

Code reviews provide several key benefits to software development teams:

- **Quality assurance:** By having multiple sets of eyes examine the code, teams can catch potential bugs, design flaws, and performance issues before they make their way into production. This proactive approach significantly reduces the cost and complexity of fixing issues later in the development cycle.

- **Knowledge sharing:** Code reviews serve as an informal training mechanism. Junior developers learn best practices by having their code reviewed by more experienced team members, while senior developers gain insights from fresh perspectives and innovative approaches.

- **Consistency and standards:** Regular code reviews help maintain a consistent coding style, architectural patterns, and adherence to organizational coding standards. This consistency makes the codebase more maintainable and easier to understand.

- **Architectural integrity:** Reviews help ensure that new code aligns with the overall system architecture, preventing technical debt and maintaining the long-term scalability of the software.

Let us now look at the tooling side as well.

Version control platforms and review capabilities

GitHub has revolutionized code reviews by transforming pull requests into collaborative discussion spaces. Its web-based interface allows developers to comment directly on specific lines of code, creating a contextual dialogue around code changes. The platform's integration with various continuous integration tools enables automatic code quality checks, linting, and test run validations, providing immediate feedback during the review process.

GitLab takes collaboration a step further with its comprehensive merge request review system. Beyond simple code comparison, it offers built-in code quality analyzers that can automatically detect potential issues, security vulnerabilities, and coding standard violations. The platform's dashboard provides visual insights into code changes, allowing reviewers to quickly understand the scope and impact of proposed modifications.

Bitbucket, developed by *Atlassian*, offers seamless integration with *Jira* and other project management tools. This integration creates a holistic environment where code reviews are directly linked to specific tasks, issues, and project workflows. Developers can trace the context of code changes, understand their relationship to broader project objectives, and maintain a clear audit trail of development decisions.

Each platform offers distinct advantages for specific development environments:

- GitHub's integration with GitHub Actions enables automated checks that run directly within pull requests, making it ideal for teams already utilizing the GitHub ecosystem for both hosting and CI/CD.

- GitLab's built-in CI/CD pipeline capabilities create a unified experience where code review, testing, and deployment are tightly integrated within a single platform without requiring third-party integrations.

- Bitbucket's deep integration with Jira and Confluence makes it the preferred choice for organizations heavily invested in Atlassian's project management and documentation tools, enabling traceability from requirements to code changes.

- Gerrit's advanced access control model and customizable workflow rules provide enterprises with the governance structure needed for large-scale projects with complex approval hierarchies and compliance requirements.

Specialized code review solutions

Gerrit represents a more specialized approach to code reviews, particularly popular in large-scale and open-source software development. Its web-based interface provides a granular review mechanism where each code change can be scored and commented on by multiple reviewers. Unlike traditional platforms, Gerrit supports a pre-commit review model, allowing teams to approve or reject code before it enters the main codebase.

Phabricator, developed originally by Facebook, offers a comprehensive suite of development collaboration tools. Its standout feature is the ability to conduct deep, multi-stage code reviews that go beyond simple line-by-line comparisons. The platform supports complex workflow integrations, making it particularly useful for organizations with sophisticated development processes and multiple interconnected projects.

Review Board stands out for its cross-platform compatibility, supporting multiple version control systems beyond Git. This flexibility makes it an attractive option for organizations with diverse technological ecosystems. Its intuitive interface allows for detailed code annotations, side-by-side diffs, and comprehensive review tracking, making it easier for teams to maintain high code quality standards across different development environments.

Emerging tools and AI integration

The newest generation of code review tools is increasingly incorporating artificial intelligence and machine learning capabilities. These advanced platforms can now provide intelligent suggestions, predict potential bugs, and offer automated code improvement recommendations. Tools like CodeClimate and DeepSource use sophisticated algorithms to analyze code quality, detect complex anti-patterns, and provide actionable insights that go beyond traditional static code analysis.

Cloud-based code review platforms are also gaining traction, offering scalable solutions that can adapt to growing development teams and increasingly complex software architectures. These platforms provide real-time collaboration features, advanced security scanning, and comprehensive analytics that help organizations understand their code evolution and maintain high-quality standards.

Automating code quality with Git Hooks

Git Hooks are powerful scripts that trigger automatically at specific points in the Git workflow, providing developers with a mechanism to enforce code quality, run automated checks, and maintain consistent development standards. These scripts are stored in the `.git/hooks` directory of every Git repository and can be executed client-side or server-side, offering multiple opportunities for automated validation and enforcement.

Types of Git Hooks

Git provides several hook points throughout the version control lifecycle as follows:

1. **Pre-commit hooks:** Pre-commit hooks run before a commit is finalized, making them ideal for catching issues early in the development process. Typical use cases include:

   a. Running code linters to ensure coding style consistency.

   b. Executing unit tests to verify code functionality.

   c. Checking for forbidden code patterns or security vulnerabilities.

   d. Verifying commit message formatting.

   Example of pre-commit hook (Python with flake8):

   ```sh
   #!/bin/sh
   # Pre-commit hook for comprehensive code quality checks

   echo "Running pre-commit checks..."

   # Run linting
   echo "Checking code style with flake8..."
   flake8 . --count --select=E9,F63,F7,F82 --show-source --statistics
   if [ $? -ne 0 ]; then
       echo "✗ Code does not meet linting standards»
       exit 1
   fi

   # Run code formatter check
   echo "Checking formatting with black..."
   black --check .
   if [ $? -ne 0 ]; then
       echo "✗ Code is not properly formatted»
       exit 1
   fi

   # Run tests
   echo "Running unit tests..."
   pytest -xvs tests/
   if [ $? -ne 0 ]; then
       echo "✗ Tests failed»
       exit 1
   ```

```
fi

echo "✅ All pre-commit checks passed!»
```

2. **Commit-msg hooks:** These hooks validate commit messages, ensuring they meet team-defined standards:

   a. Enforcing commit message length.

   b. Checking for required prefixes (e.g., feature/, bugfix/).

   c. Linking commits to issue tracking systems.

   d. Preventing commits with inappropriate language.

   The following is an example of a commit-msg hook enforcing JIRA ticket ref:

```
#!/bin/sh
# Enforce JIRA ticket ID in commit messages

commit_msg=$(cat "$1")
jira_pattern="[A-Z]+-[0-9]+"

if ! echo "$commit_msg" | grep -E "$jira_pattern" > /dev/null; then
    echo "Error: Commit message must include a
JIRA ticket ID (e.g., PROJ-123)"
    echo "Your commit message: $commit_msg"
    exit 1
fi

echo "✅ Commit message format verified»
```

3. **Pre-push hooks:** Executed before pushing changes to a remote repository, these hooks can:

   a. Run comprehensive test suites.

   b. Check for unpushed local branches.

   c. Verify branch naming conventions.

   d. Perform final code quality checks.

4. **Post-merge hooks:** These run after successfully merging branches, useful for:

   a. Automatically updating dependencies.

   b. Rebuilding local assets.

   c. Notifying team members of significant merges.

   d. Updating local development environment.

The following is an example of a post-merge hook that automatically installs dependencies:

```sh
#!/bin/sh
# Automatically update dependencies after pull or merge

# Check if package.json was changed in the merge
if git diff-tree -r --name-only --no-commit-id ORIG_
HEAD HEAD | grep --quiet "package.json"; then
    echo "📄 package.json changed, updating dependencies...»
    npm install
    echo "✅ Dependencies updated successfully»
fi
```

While Git Hooks provide local automation, they seamlessly integrate with broader continuous integration strategies:

- Serve as a first line of defense for code quality.

- Provide immediate feedback to developers.

- Reduce the load on the CI/CD pipeline by catching issues early.

- Enforce organizational coding standards at the individual developer level.

Hence, Git Hooks represent a powerful automation tool in the modern developer's toolkit. By strategically implementing these scripts, development teams can enforce quality standards, catch potential issues early, and create a more consistent and reliable software development process.

Monorepo vs. multi-repo strategies

Repository management is a critical architectural decision that significantly impacts software development workflows, team collaboration, and project scalability. The choice between monorepo and multi-repo strategies represents a fundamental approach to organizing code, managing dependencies, and structuring large-scale software systems.

Monorepo strategy

A monorepo is a version control approach where all project code, across multiple services, applications, and libraries, exists within a single repository. This strategy consolidates entire software ecosystems into one comprehensive codebase, managed by a single version control system.

Advantages of monorepo

The monorepo approach offers several significant benefits for software development teams. By centralizing code in a single repository, organizations can achieve better cohesion, visibility, and management across their entire codebase.

Let us examine the key advantages of this strategy as follows:

- **Simplified dependency management:** Monorepos provide a centralized approach to managing dependencies, making it easier to:
  - o Ensure consistent versioning across projects.
  - o Implement atomic changes that span multiple components.
  - o Reduce dependency conflicts through direct visibility.
- **Enhanced collaboration:** The unified codebase promotes:
  - o Easier code sharing between teams.
  - o Improved visibility into cross-team dependencies.
  - o Simplified refactoring across multiple projects.
  - o Reduced organizational silos.
- **Consistent tooling and standards:** Monorepos enable:
  - o Uniform code quality checks.
  - o Centralized configuration management.
  - o Easier implementation of organization-wide coding standards.
  - o Simplified continuous integration and deployment.

Challenges of monorepo

Monorepos present several scalability concerns that can impact development workflows. As repositories grow in size, developers experience longer clone and checkout times, which can hinder productivity and create performance challenges, especially when working with very large codebases. The increased complexity of version control operations further compounds these issues. Access control also becomes more intricate in monorepos, with significant challenges in implementing granular permissions and managing potential security risks. Teams must carefully isolate sensitive components to prevent unauthorized access. Additionally, monorepos introduce build and CI/CD complexity, requiring more sophisticated build systems that demand increased computational resources. These architectural challenges translate into longer build and test cycles, which can slow down the overall development process and potentially impact team efficiency.

Multi-repo strategy

In a multi-repo approach, different projects, services, or components are stored in separate, independent repositories. Each repository represents a discrete unit of software, with clear boundaries and independent version control.

Advantages of multi-repo

The multi-repo strategy provides distinct benefits that align particularly well with certain organizational structures and development methodologies. By separating codebases into focused repositories, teams can achieve greater autonomy and specialization.

The following are the primary advantages this approach offers:

- **Architectural isolation:**
  - Clear separation of concerns.
  - Independent scaling of different components.
  - Easier to manage microservices architectures.
  - Simplified ownership and responsibility boundaries.

- **Flexible team organization:**
  - Teams can work independently.
  - Easier to manage access controls.
  - Reduced risk of unintended cross-project changes.
  - Support for diverse technology stacks.

- **Reduced repository complexity:**
  - Smaller, more focused repositories.
  - Faster clone and checkout times.
  - Simplified version control operations.
  - Lower cognitive load for developers.

Challenges of multi-repo

Multi-repo architectures introduce significant challenges in dependency management and collaboration. Organizations face increased overhead when managing inter-project dependencies, making it more challenging to implement system-wide changes and raising the risk of version incompatibilities. Tracking and updating shared libraries become substantially more complex, requiring additional coordination and effort. Collaboration barriers are equally pronounced in multi-repo environments, with reduced visibility across projects creating silos that fragment team understanding and communication. These architectural boundaries make cross-cutting changes more difficult to implement, potentially leading to increased communication overhead and a higher likelihood of duplicated efforts. Teams must invest considerable time and resources in maintaining clear communication channels and establishing robust processes to mitigate these inherent challenges of distributed repository structures.

Factors influencing repository strategy decisions

Repository architecture is not a static choice, but a dynamic decision influenced by multiple organizational and technical factors. Understanding these nuanced considerations helps teams make informed choices about their code management approach:

- **Organization size impact:** Smaller teams typically benefit from the simplicity and unified view provided by monorepos. These compact environments value quick collaboration and reduced overhead. In contrast, larger organizations often require the granular control and independent scaling that multi-repo strategies offer, allowing different teams and departments to manage their codebases with greater autonomy.

- **Project complexity considerations:** The intrinsic complexity of software systems plays a crucial role in repository strategy selection:

  o Monorepos excel in environments where components are deeply interconnected, requiring frequent, coordinated changes across multiple services or libraries.

  o Multi-repo strategies provide clear boundaries and independent deployment paths for loosely coupled services, supporting more distributed system designs.

- **Technological diversity challenges:** The technological landscape of an organization significantly influences repository architecture:

  o Multi-repo approaches accommodate diverse technology stacks, allowing teams to use different programming languages, frameworks, and tools.

  o Monorepos work most effectively in more uniform technological environments where consistent tooling and practices can be easily implemented.

The journey of selecting an optimal repository strategy is far more nuanced than a simple technical decision. It represents a critical intersection of organizational culture, technological capabilities, and future-forward thinking. Organizations must approach this choice as a strategic decision that reflects not just current technological needs, but anticipates future growth, collaboration models, and system complexity. The most effective repository architecture emerges from a deep understanding of an organization's unique DNA, its team dynamics, project interdependencies, technological ecosystem, and long-term innovation goals.

Successful implementation requires more than just selecting a repository approach; it demands a holistic, adaptive mindset. Teams must be prepared to evolve their repository strategy as their software ecosystem grows and transforms. This means creating flexible architectural foundations that can accommodate changing requirements, emerging technologies, and shifting organizational structures. The ideal approach balances technical efficiency with human collaboration, providing developers with tools and structures that enhance productivity while maintaining system clarity and maintainability.

Ultimately, there is no universal perfect repository strategy. Instead, the most effective approach is one that remains inherently adaptable, prioritizes developer experience, and aligns closely with organizational objectives. It should provide the right balance between code sharing and component isolation, between centralized governance and team autonomy. Organizations that view their repository architecture as a living, breathing ecosystem, rather than a static infrastructure, will be best positioned to navigate the complex landscape of modern software development.

By embracing a strategic, thoughtful approach to repository management, teams can create robust, scalable systems that not only meet current technological demands but also provide a solid foundation for future innovation. The key lies in continuous evaluation, open communication, and a willingness to experiment and adjust as technological and organizational needs evolve.

Version controlling configuration and infrastructure code

Effective version control of configuration and infrastructure code is fundamental to modern software development and operations. At its core, this practice requires a comprehensive approach that balances technical precision with collaborative workflow strategies. Organizations should prioritize using declarative configuration formats that clearly define infrastructure states, treating these configurations as immutable artifacts that can be reliably reproduced and tracked.

The foundation of robust infrastructure version control lies in implementing a disciplined approach to repository management. This means storing all configuration code in version control systems like Git, with a strong emphasis on creating meaningful commit messages that provide clear context for changes. Developers and operations teams should establish consistent naming conventions and directory structures that logically represent the infrastructure's architecture, making it intuitive for team members to navigate and understand the configuration ecosystem.

Security cannot be an afterthought in infrastructure version control. Sensitive information must be carefully managed, using sophisticated secret management tools that prevent credentials and API keys from being directly committed to repositories. This approach requires implementing environment-specific secret injection mechanisms and maintaining strict access controls that protect critical infrastructure configurations.

Modularity and reusability are key principles in creating maintainable infrastructure code. By breaking down configurations into smaller, composable modules, teams can create more flexible and adaptable systems. This modular approach allows for easier updates, reduces duplication, and enables more efficient collaboration across different projects and environments.

Continuous integration and validation play a crucial role in maintaining the integrity of infrastructure configurations. Automated pipelines should incorporate comprehensive validation processes, including linting, syntax checking, security scanning, and compliance verification. These automated checks help prevent configuration drift and ensure that infrastructure deployments remain consistent and predictable across different environments.

Documentation emerges as a critical companion to infrastructure code. Beyond the code itself, teams should invest in creating comprehensive README files, inline comments, and metadata that explain configuration setup, assumptions, dependencies, and potential complexities. This documentation serves as a knowledge transfer mechanism, helping both current team members and future contributors understand the infrastructure's design and evolution.

The approach to infrastructure configuration is not static but requires continuous learning and improvement. Teams should regularly review and refactor their configuration code, staying current with emerging tools and best practices. This might involve periodic architecture reviews, attending conferences, and fostering a culture of knowledge sharing that keeps the infrastructure management strategy dynamic and responsive to changing technological landscapes.

Ultimately, effective version control of configuration and infrastructure code is about creating a reliable, secure, and adaptable system that supports rapid deployment while maintaining the highest standards of consistency and reproducibility. It requires a holistic approach that balances technical implementation with collaborative practices, continuous learning, and a commitment to maintaining the highest infrastructure management standards.

Practical infrastructure as code organization

When versioning infrastructure code, the organization of files and directories is crucial. Consider the following examples:

Argo CD Kubernetes manifests are structured as follows:

```
/infrastructure        # Root directory for all infra configurations
|
├── base/              # Base configs shared across all environments
|   ├── kustomization.yaml   # Declares deployment, service, etc.
|   ├── deployment.yaml  #Generic app deployment(no env specifics)
|   └── service.yaml        # Generic service definition
|
└── overlays/              # Environment-specific customizations
    ├── dev/               # Development environment
    |   ├── kustomization.yaml # Patches or extends base
    |   └── config-map.yaml    # Dev-specific ConfigMap values
    |
```

```
└── prod/                      # Production environment
    ├── kustomization.yaml # References base + adds prod-
only resources
        ├── config-map.yaml    # Prod-specific ConfigMap values
        └── hpa.yaml     # Horizontal Pod Autoscaler for production
```

Terraform infrastructure code example:

```
1.
2.  ```hcl
3.  # main.tf - Versioned infrastructure code
4.  provider "aws" {
5.    region = var.aws_region
6.  }
7.
8.  # S3 bucket with versioning enabled
9.  resource "aws_s3_bucket" "artifact_storage" {
10.    bucket = "${var.environment}-artifacts-${var.project_name}"
11.
12.    tags = {
13.      Environment = var.environment
14.      Project     = var.project_name
15.      ManagedBy   = "Terraform"
16.    }
17. }
18.
19. resource "aws_s3_bucket_versioning" "artifact_versioning" {
20.    bucket = aws_s3_bucket.artifact_storage.id
21.
22.    versioning_configuration {
23.      status = "Enabled"
24.    }
25. }
```

Let us consider secret management best practices.

For sensitive information, implement these approaches:

- Use **.gitignore** to exclude files containing secrets.
- Implement secrets scanning with tools like gitleaks or detect-secrets.
- Encrypt sensitive values using tools like **Secrets OPerationS** (**SOPS**) or cloud provider secret management services.
- Use environment variables for local development that are never committed.

Common Git pitfalls and how to avoid them

Even experienced developers encounter challenges with Git. Understanding common pitfalls and their solutions can save substantial time and prevent potential code loss.

Force-pushing dangers

Force-pushing (`git push --force`) overwrites remote history and can cause data loss or disrupt team workflows.

Solution: Use protected branches to prevent force pushes to critical branches like main or develop. When force-pushing is necessary, use the safer **`--force-with-lease`** option:

```
# git push --force-with-lease
```

This command checks if the remote branch has been updated by others before proceeding, preventing accidental overwrites of teammates' work.

Forgetting to pull before committing

Working on outdated code leads to unnecessary merge conflicts.

Solution: Develop a habit of pulling with rebase before starting new work:

```
# git pull --rebase origin main
```

This keeps your local branch up-to-date and creates a cleaner, linear history by placing your local commits on top of the latest remote changes.

Committing sensitive information

Accidentally committing credentials, API keys, or personal data can lead to security breaches.

Solution: Implement a multi-layered approach:

- Configure comprehensive **`.gitignore`** files.
- Set up pre-commit hooks with secrets scanning.
- Use Git-compatible secrets management tools.
- If secrets are accidentally compromised, change them immediately (consider them compromised).

Remember that once information is pushed to a remote repository, it should be considered permanently exposed, even if later removed.

Conclusion

Version control has evolved from a basic tracking tool to a cornerstone of modern DevOps, enabling efficient collaboration, transparency, and reliability. This chapter explored Git workflows, branching strategies, and best practices that elevate version control from a tool to a strategic asset.

Effective version control is more than managing code; it fosters accountability and efficiency. By adopting robust strategies, teams can streamline development, reduce errors, and enhance predictability. Key takeaways include choosing the right workflow, maintaining clean commit histories, enforcing code reviews, and treating infrastructure code with the same rigor as application code.

Since version control is not a one-size-fits-all solution, teams must tailor their approach based on project complexity and organizational needs. Whether using Gitflow for structured releases, GitHub Flow for agility, or trunk-based development for continuous delivery, the goal remains the same: a flexible and efficient code management strategy.

This foundation naturally leads to our next chapter, *Continuous Integration*. While version control organizes collaboration, CI automates the integration and validation of code changes.

In the next chapter, we will explore CI principles, popular tools like Jenkins and GitHub Actions, pipeline automation, testing strategies, artifact management, and best practices for scaling CI in large projects.

Join our Discord space

Join our Discord workspace for latest updates, offers, tech happenings around the world, new releases, and sessions with the authors:

https://discord.bpbonline.com

CHAPTER 4

Continuous Integration Fundamentals

Introduction

Continuous integration (**CI**) is a game-changing method in today's software development landscape, tackling the essential issues of code integration, quality control, and swift delivery. As software complexity grows and development teams become more dispersed, CI stands out as a key practice that helps organizations enhance their software development workflows, minimize integration challenges, and speed up time-to-market. By automatically merging code changes from various contributors, executing immediate automated tests, and offering quick feedback, CI dismantles the traditional barriers between development, testing, and operations teams, promoting a culture of collaboration, openness, and ongoing improvement.

This chapter aims to clarify the principles, tools, and strategies associated with CI, equipping readers with a thorough understanding of implementing, refining, and utilizing CI practices to create more robust, efficient, and high-quality software systems.

Structure

This chapter will cover the following topics:

- Principles and benefits of continuous integration
- Overview of CI tools

- Setting up CI pipelines

- Automated testing in CI

- Code quality check and static code analysis

- Artifact management and versioning

- CI best practices and common pitfalls

- Metrics and KPIs for CI effectiveness

- Scaling CI for large projects and monorepos

- Security considerations in CI pipelines

Objectives

By the end of this chapter, we will discuss the fundamental principles of Continuous Integration and how it transforms software development workflows. We will explore various CI tools, pipeline setup strategies, and automated testing approaches that help teams detect issues early and improve code quality. The chapter will cover critical aspects of artifact management, best practices, and common pitfalls to avoid. Additionally, we will examine how to measure CI effectiveness through metrics, scale CI for larger projects, and implement essential security measures in CI pipelines. This knowledge will equip readers with a comprehensive understanding of how to implement and optimize CI practices to build more reliable, efficient, and high-quality software systems.

Principles and benefits of continuous integration

CI is based on key principles that significantly change the way software development teams work together and provide value. Essentially, CI focuses on establishing a structured method for integrating code, ensuring quality, and obtaining quick feedback.

Some of the core CI principles are as follows:

- **Frequent code commits:** Developers regularly integrate their code changes into a shared repository several times daily. This practice helps avoid large, complicated merges and allows for early detection of conflicts. Each small commit is easier to manage, which minimizes the risk of significant integration issues. For instance, in modern Git workflows, developers push feature updates to branches multiple times per day. A practical example is using GitHub Actions workflows (`.github/workflows/ci.yml`) that trigger on each push to run tests and linters, providing immediate feedback and preventing faulty code from reaching the main branch. This automation reinforces the principle by making it easy to commit frequently while maintaining code quality.

- **Automated build process:** With every code commit, an automatic build process is triggered. This guarantees that the code can be compiled and assembled into a functioning software product right away. Automation eliminates manual build steps, reducing the chance of human error and ensuring a consistent, reproducible build environment. A typical implementation involves using GitLab CI with a **.gitlab-ci.yml** file that includes a **build** stage executing commands like **npm install && npm run build** for a frontend application. If any step in this build process fails, the pipeline halts before proceeding to tests or deployment, ensuring only successfully built code advances through the pipeline.

- **Comprehensive automated testing:** Right after the build, a thorough suite of automated tests is run. These tests check the functionality, performance, and compatibility of the code across various environments. By identifying issues early on, teams can tackle potential problems before they grow.

- **Immediate feedback:** CI systems offer instant feedback to developers regarding the status of their code. If a build fails or tests do not pass, developers receive immediate notifications, enabling them to quickly pinpoint and resolve issues.

- **Single source of truth:** A centralized version control repository acts as the single source of truth for the entire project. This method ensures that all team members are working from the most up to date, validated version of the codebase.

These core principles of CI are not just theoretical ideas; they are effective strategies that offer tangible benefits for development teams. By consistently applying these principles, organizations can experience a range of advantages that tackle significant challenges in software development.

Take the principle of frequent code commits, for example: what may appear to be a straightforward practice of integrating code more regularly actually serves as a robust risk management tactic. Each small, incremental commit simplifies the merging process, reduces integration conflicts, and provides an up-to-date view of the project's status. This method turns the traditional, often stressful integration process into a seamless, predictable workflow.

The benefits of CI emerge organically from its principles as follows:

- **Technical excellence:**

  o **Reduced integration complexity**: Frequent, small commits help avoid large, conflict-prone code changes from piling up.

  o **Rapid bug detection**: Automated testing initiated with each commit identifies defects at their earliest and most manageable stage.

  o **Consistent and reproducible builds**: Automation guarantees that builds remain the same across various environments, preventing *it works on my machine* situations.

o **Enhanced code quality**: The ongoing validation process motivates developers to create more modular and testable code.

- **Organizational transformation:**

    o **Breaking down silos**: CI naturally fosters collaboration by establishing a shared and transparent development process.

    o **Accelerated delivery cycles**: Quick feedback and automated workflows significantly shorten time-to-market.

    o **Increased transparency**: Real-time build and test results offer clear visibility into project progress and potential challenges.

    o **Predictable deployments**: Regular integration and testing lead to more controlled and less risky software releases.

- **Developer productivity and morale:**

    o **Instant feedback loop**: Developers gain immediate insights into how their code performs and its compatibility.

    o **Reduced manual overhead**: Automation handles repetitive and error-prone tasks.

    o **Increased confidence**: Continuous validation reassures developers about code quality and system integrity.

    o **Focus on innovation**: By removing manual integration hurdles, developers can dedicate their efforts to creating value.

The principles of CI extend beyond mere technical practices; they serve as strategic differentiators. By cutting down on waste, reducing rework, and facilitating quicker iterations, CI offers a competitive edge. Organizations that embrace CI can adapt more swiftly to market shifts, produce higher quality software, and foster more engaged and productive development teams.

Overview of CI tools

In the ever-evolving landscape of CI, a variety of powerful tools have surfaced, each designed to meet specific needs and workflows. This section discusses the four prominent CI tools, Jenkins, GitLab CI, GitHub Actions, and CircleCI, emphasizing their main features, advantages, challenges, and the scenarios in which they excel.

Jenkins: Veteran of CI/CD

Jenkins stands as a testament to the evolution of continuous integration, offering a robust, flexible automation platform that has fundamentally transformed software delivery processes. At its core, Jenkins distinguishes itself through an unparalleled ability to adapt to diverse development environments, making it the *Swiss Army knife* of CI/CD tools for organizations of all sizes.

The true technical prowess of Jenkins lies in its POC concept, implemented through the Jenkinsfile. This revolutionary approach allows development teams to define entire build, test, and deployment processes as programmable code, creating reproducible and version-controlled workflows. Unlike traditional static configuration tools, Jenkins leverages a groovy-based **domain specific language (DSL)** that enables developers to create complex, dynamic pipeline configurations with unprecedented flexibility.

What truly sets Jenkins apart is its extensive plugin ecosystem, boasting over 1,500 community-contributed plugins that extend its capabilities across virtually every aspect of software development. From version control system integrations to cloud platform connections, security mechanisms, and testing tools, these plugins transform Jenkins from a simple automation server into a comprehensive integration platform. This extensibility means that organizations can customize their CI/CD processes without modifying the core system, addressing unique technological challenges with remarkable precision.

The distributed build architecture represents another technical marvel of Jenkins. By supporting a master-agent model, Jenkins enables parallel build execution across multiple machines, efficiently distributing computational load and supporting complex, resource-intensive build processes. This architecture allows teams to create sophisticated build environments that can scale horizontally, accommodating everything from small startups to large enterprise deployments.

Security and access control form another critical dimension of Jenkins' technical capabilities. The platform provides robust **role-based access control (RBAC)**, enterprise authentication integrations, comprehensive credential management, and detailed audit logging. These features ensure that continuous integration processes meet the most stringent enterprise security requirements while maintaining the flexibility needed for modern software development.

Perhaps most importantly, Jenkins bridges the gap between legacy systems and cloud-native technologies. Its ability to support both traditional and modern development approaches makes it uniquely positioned in the CI/CD landscape. Recent versions have enhanced Kubernetes and container support, allowing organizations to modernize their build processes without completely abandoning existing infrastructure.

The scripting and extensibility of Jenkins transform it from a mere automation tool into a powerful integration platform. Developers can leverage Groovy scripting to create complex conditional workflows, dynamically configure environments, and implement sophisticated build logic that goes far beyond simple automation. This programmability means that Jenkins can adapt to virtually any build scenario, making it an invaluable tool for teams with unique or complex integration requirements.

However, this power comes with complexity. Jenkins demands a significant investment in configuration and expertise. Its steep learning curve and the need for manual setup can be challenging, particularly for teams new to advanced CI/CD practices. Yet, for organizations willing to invest the time and resources, Jenkins offers unparalleled flexibility and control over their software delivery pipeline.

GitLab CI: Integrated DevOps solution

GitLab CI marks a significant advancement in continuous integration, serving as a complete solution that goes beyond traditional CI/CD frameworks by seamlessly combining source code management, pipeline automation, and DevOps workflows into one unified platform. Unlike separate CI tools, GitLab CI is inherently designed as a full DevOps lifecycle solution, where continuous integration is a core feature rather than an optional extra.

The technical sophistication of GitLab CI is evident in its straightforward configuration and robust declarative approach. Teams can use the `.gitlab-ci.yml` file to outline intricate build, test, and deployment pipelines with a clear, human-friendly YAML syntax. This method makes pipeline configuration accessible, allowing developers to version control their entire CI/CD workflow alongside their application code. The configuration model is both adaptable and standardized, facilitating quick pipeline creation while ensuring a consistent structure across different projects.

Another key aspect of GitLab CI's technical framework is its native support for containers and Kubernetes. The platform accommodates containerization and prioritizes it as a fundamental component. Developers can easily define, build, and deploy containerized applications, benefiting from an integrated container registry and advanced orchestration features. The Auto DevOps functionality enhances this by automatically identifying, building, testing, and deploying applications with minimal setup, significantly lowering the complexity of establishing intricate CI/CD pipelines.

Security and compliance are integral to GitLab CI's architecture. The platform provides extensive security scanning features, including dependency checks, container scanning, and both **Dynamic Application Security Testing** (**DAST**) and **Static Application Security Testing** (**SAST**), along with compliance pipeline capabilities. These built-in security measures ensure that quality and risk management are central to the continuous integration process rather than being treated as secondary concerns.

GitHub Actions: Native GitHub workflow automation

GitHub Actions offers a groundbreaking method for continuous integration and deployment, effortlessly incorporating workflow automation into the software development lifecycle. By integrating CI/CD features within the source code repository, GitHub has changed the way developers think about automation, transforming repositories into robust, self-sufficient delivery platforms.

At the heart of GitHub Actions lies its elegant, declarative workflow configuration using YAML files. This approach allows developers to define complex build, test, and deployment processes directly within their repository, creating a natural, version-controlled approach to workflow management. The ability to define workflows alongside code blurs the lines between source code and delivery mechanisms, promoting a more holistic view of software development.

The marketplace of pre-built actions serves as a powerful ecosystem that dramatically accelerates workflow creation. Developers can leverage thousands of community-contributed actions, spanning from simple build steps to complex deployment scenarios across multiple platforms and technologies. This marketplace transforms GitHub Actions from a simple CI tool into a comprehensive automation platform, enabling teams to quickly assemble sophisticated workflows with minimal custom configuration.

Technically, GitHub Actions shines in its robust support for matrix builds and parallel execution. Developers can effortlessly create complex build matrices that test code across multiple operating systems, programming language versions, and configurations. The platform's ability to dynamically spin up runners and execute jobs in parallel significantly reduces build and test times, providing a performance-oriented approach to continuous integration.

Native integration with GitHub's security and project management tools creates a unique value proposition. Workflow runs are deeply integrated with pull requests, providing instant visibility into build and test status. Security scanning, dependency checks, and compliance verifications become seamless parts of the development process, rather than separate, disconnected activities.

The platform's event-driven architecture represents a significant technical innovation. Workflows can be triggered by a wide range of GitHub events, from code pushes and pull requests to issues, releases, and even external webhook events. This flexibility allows teams to create highly responsive, context-aware automation that goes beyond traditional CI/CD paradigms.

Cost and accessibility are key strengths of GitHub Actions. Free runners for public repositories democratize continuous integration for open-source projects, while flexible pricing models accommodate teams of all sizes. Hosting self-hosted runners provides additional flexibility for organizations with specific infrastructure requirements or compliance constraints.

However, the platform's tight coupling with the GitHub ecosystem is both its greatest strength and potential limitation. Teams deeply invested in GitHub will find an almost frictionless automation experience, but those with complex, multi-repository or multi-platform workflows may encounter challenges. The potential for vendor lock-in remains a consideration for enterprise architects and technology strategists.

GitHub Actions excels in scenarios that align with modern, cloud-native development practices. Its support for containerization, Kubernetes deployments, and cloud platform integrations makes it particularly powerful for teams building modern, distributed applications. The ability to easily define complex deployment strategies, combined with comprehensive secrets management and environment controls, provides a robust platform for continuous delivery.

The learning curve for GitHub Actions is notably gentle compared to more complex CI/CD tools. Its declarative syntax, extensive documentation, and intuitive marketplace make it accessible to developers of all skill levels. This accessibility democratizes advanced workflow automation, enabling smaller teams and individual developers to implement sophisticated CI/CD practices with minimal overhead.

CircleCI: Cloud-native CI/CD platform

CircleCI stands out as a crucial platform in the rapidly changing world of continuous integration and delivery, specifically designed to meet the needs of modern, cloud-native software development. In contrast to traditional CI tools that originated from on-premises systems, CircleCI was built from the ground up as a cloud-native solution, fundamentally changing how teams handle build, test, and deployment automation.

The platform's design philosophy emphasizes speed, scalability, and enhancing developer productivity. By removing the complexities of infrastructure management, CircleCI enables development teams to concentrate on what truly matters, writing code and delivering value. Its cloud-based infrastructure allows for immediate scaling, automatically allocating computational resources to fit the specific requirements of each build and test scenario, thus overcoming the limitations of fixed, manual infrastructure management.

CircleCI's configuration is a prime example of both simplicity and power. The **config.yml** file offers a clear, version-controlled way to define complex CI/CD workflows. This model balances user-friendliness and advanced customization, allowing teams to quickly establish sophisticated pipelines without getting lost in complicated technicalities. Adding orbs and reusable configuration packages further streamlines workflow creation by offering pre-built, community-curated components that can be easily integrated into custom workflows.

Support for various languages and ecosystems is another key aspect of CircleCI's technical design. Unlike many CI platforms with limited language support, CircleCI provides extensive tools for nearly every modern programming language and framework. Whether working with JavaScript, Python, Ruby, Go, or newer technologies, teams can rely on top-notch support, including native dependency management, testing frameworks, and deployment options.

Performance optimization is a core element of CircleCI's architecture. The platform's smart caching, parallel job execution, and advanced resource allocation ensure that build and test processes are completed efficiently. By intelligently distributing computational loads and utilizing cloud infrastructure, CircleCI significantly cuts down overall build times compared to traditional CI methods.

Security and compliance are integral to the design, not just afterthoughts. CircleCI offers a range of security features, including automatic scanning for dependency vulnerabilities, secrets management, detailed access controls, and comprehensive audit logging. These features guarantee that continuous integration processes adhere to the highest enterprise security standards while still allowing for the agility required for fast software delivery.

Understanding the strengths and capabilities of various CI tools is the first step in leveraging them effectively.

Now, let us move on to the practical aspect of CI, specifically setting up CI pipelines. This involves defining triggers, organizing workflows into stages, and executing tasks as jobs. In the next section, we will explore how to structure pipelines for maximum efficiency, regardless of the CI tool you choose.

Setting up CI pipelines

CI pipelines are the backbone of automated software delivery, transforming code changes into deployable artifacts through a structured, repeatable process. Understanding how to effectively configure pipelines is crucial for implementing robust CI strategies. The CI pipeline is essentially an automated sequence of steps that takes code from version control to a production-ready state. It is a series of computational processes that compile, test, analyze, and prepare software for deployment. Unlike manual processes, pipelines ensure consistency, repeatability, and rapid feedback.

Figure 4.1 showcases the various CI sequences as follows:

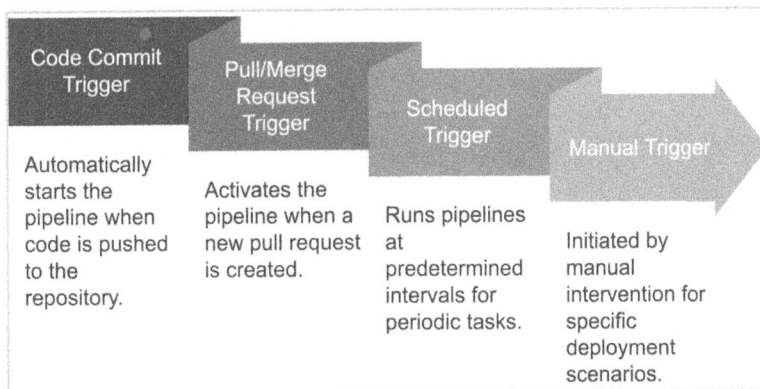

Figure 4.1: CI pipeline sequence

Pipeline stages

Pipeline stages organize the CI/CD process into logical, sequential steps, making workflows more manageable and efficient. Each stage groups related jobs that execute in a defined order to ensure a smooth progression from code integration to deployment. *Figure 4.2* showcases the various CI/CD stages.

The source stage marks the starting point, where the pipeline retrieves the source code from version control, validates the repository state, and performs the initial code checkout. Next, the build stage compiles the source code, resolves dependencies, generates artifacts, and prepares deployable packages.

Once the build is ready, the test stage kicks in, executing various test suites such as unit tests, integration tests, performance tests, and security scans. After testing, the analysis stage ensures the code meets quality and security standards by conducting static code analysis, vulnerability scanning, and compliance verification.

Finally, the deployment stage delivers the build to target environments, which might involve staging deployments, production releases, or cloud infrastructure provisioning. This structured progression ensures every aspect of the software lifecycle is addressed systematically, paving the way for reliable and efficient delivery.

The following figure sums up the overall pipeline stages:

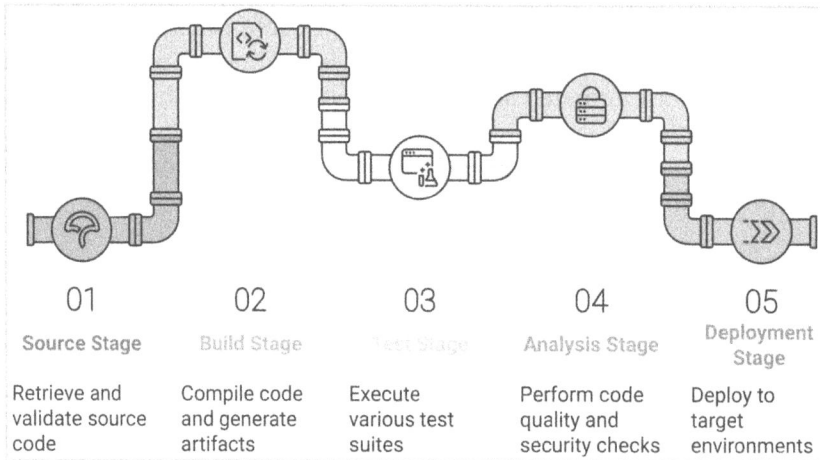

01	02	03	04	05
Source Stage	Build Stage	Test Stage	Analysis Stage	Deployment Stage
Retrieve and validate source code	Compile code and generate artifacts	Execute various test suites	Perform code quality and security checks	Deploy to target environments

Figure 4.2: CI/CD stages

Jobs

In a CI/CD pipeline, jobs represent the smallest executable units, each tasked with a specific function within the pipeline. These functions, which may include compiling code, executing tests, or deploying applications, are isolated and function independently. Jobs can be set up to run one after the other, ensuring that dependencies are honored, or simultaneously, which helps to optimize execution time for tasks that are not related. Each job has a clearly defined success or failure state, which directly influences the progression of the pipeline.

Jobs are defined with precise instructions, typically in the form of scripts, shell commands, or predefined actions. They function within their execution environment, such as a container, virtual machine, or bare-metal system, which is explicitly specified during configuration. This environment ensures that each job has the required tools, libraries, and dependencies to complete its tasks. Jobs often produce outputs, such as build artifacts or logs, which can be consumed by downstream jobs or archived for later analysis. Also, while defining a job, some key considerations must be thought through.

Figure 4.3 showcases these as follows:

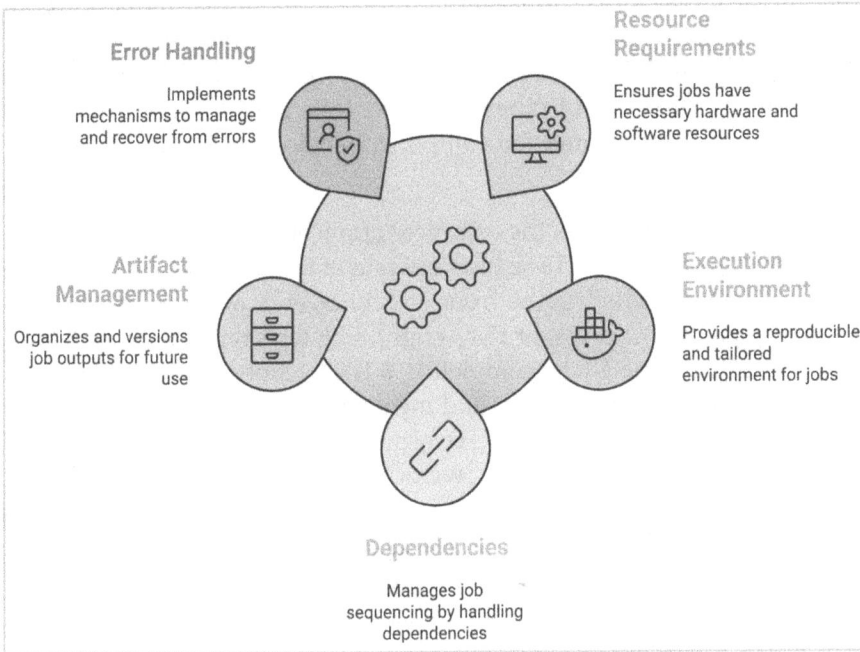

Figure 4.3: *Key considerations for job configuration*

By combining these considerations, jobs are tailored to efficiently and reliably perform their tasks, forming the atomic building blocks of a well-structured CI/CD pipeline. This granular approach ensures flexibility, scalability, and fault isolation, critical for modern DevOps workflows.

Automated testing in CI

Unit testing serves as the first line of defense in automated testing, concentrating on validating individual components or functions in isolation. These tests aim to confirm that specific methods or classes perform as intended, without relying on external systems or dependencies. Unit tests are lightweight and run quickly, making them perfect for providing immediate feedback during the development process. By using mocks or stubs for dependencies, unit tests can replicate the code's functionality being tested without requiring a complete application context. They are especially useful for identifying logical errors, managing edge cases, and verifying essential code paths. In CI pipelines, unit tests are run early, often triggered by each commit or pull request, allowing developers to catch and resolve bugs as soon as they arise.

While unit tests validate isolated pieces of code, integration tests focus on ensuring that different components or services interact correctly. These tests evaluate the communication between modules, such as APIs, databases, and external systems, to ensure seamless functionality across the application. Integration tests often simulate real-world scenarios, such as data exchange between services or interaction with third-party APIs, to identify issues that may arise from misconfigured dependencies or incompatible interfaces. Unlike unit tests, integration tests may require setting up realistic environments with actual databases or mock services. In CI pipelines, these tests are typically run after unit tests to verify the stability of interconnected components before advancing to more extensive system validations.

End-to-end (**E2E**) testing validates the complete application flow by simulating real user interactions from start to finish. These tests operate at the highest level, covering the full stack of the application, including the front end, back end, and any integrated systems. Using tools like Selenium, Cypress, or Playwright, E2E tests replicate user behaviors such as logging in, navigating the UI, or completing a transaction. These tests ensure that the application functions as a cohesive unit and meets business requirements. However, E2E tests are slower and more resource-intensive compared to unit or integration tests, so they are typically reserved for critical workflows or smoke tests. In a CI pipeline, E2E tests are often run in later stages against staging environments to validate the application's readiness for production deployment. For example, in a Python project using GitLab CI, unit tests defined with **pytest** can be run through a simple configuration:

```
test:
  stage: test
  script:
    - pip install -r requirements.txt
    - pytest tests/
```

This ensures comprehensive test coverage is automatically executed on every commit, from unit to integration to end-to-end tests.

The following figure shows test hierarchies:

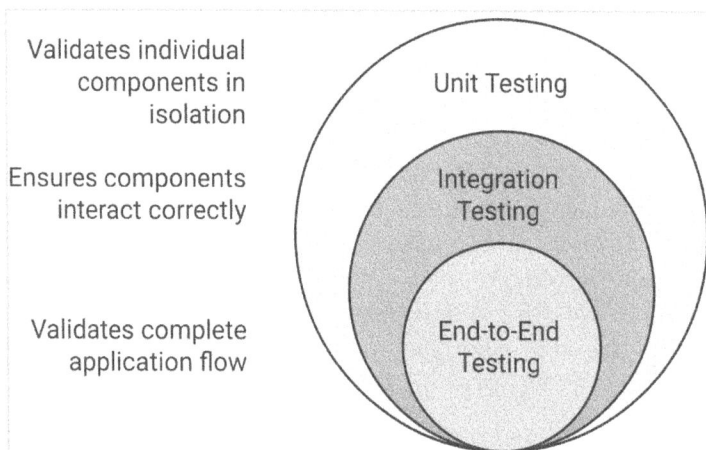

Figure 4.4: Testing hierarchy in CI pipeline

Code quality check and static code analysis

Code quality checks and static code analysis play a crucial role in keeping a strong and secure codebase. They ensure that the code meets established standards and is devoid of common mistakes or vulnerabilities. These methods evaluate the source code without running it, pinpointing potential problems such as code smells, unused variables, inefficient constructs, and security threats. By incorporating these checks into continuous integration pipelines, developers get prompt feedback, allowing them to resolve issues before the code moves on to later phases of the development process.

Static code analysis tools like SonarQube, ESLint, Pylint, and Checkstyle are commonly utilized to uphold best practices and ensure consistency throughout the codebase. These tools can be set up to identify particular issues, such as cyclomatic complexity, deprecated APIs, or hardcoded secrets, and they generate comprehensive reports that pinpoint areas of concern. Additionally, they offer the flexibility to customize rulesets to meet the specific needs of a project or adhere to organizational coding standards.

A practical implementation involves Jenkins integrated with the SonarQube plugin to analyze Java code for vulnerabilities and complexity. The pipeline can be configured to fail if severity levels exceed defined thresholds, ensuring that code quality issues are caught before they reach production. This integration transforms code quality from a manual review process to an automated gate.

In CI pipelines, static code analysis is typically integrated as a pre-build or build stage task. It is often configured to fail the pipeline if critical issues are detected, ensuring that substandard code does not proceed to deployment. This proactive approach reduces technical debt and strengthens security and maintainability. Moreover, static analysis promotes a culture of accountability and continuous improvement within development teams, contributing to higher-quality releases.

Artifact management and versioning

Artifact management and versioning play a crucial role in CI pipelines, making sure that build outputs, like binaries, container images, libraries, or documentation, are stored, tracked, and deployed consistently across different environments. Artifacts are the outcomes of the build process and act as the deployable assets that progress through the CI/CD pipeline. Effectively managing these artifacts guarantees traceability, reproducibility, and consistency, all of which are essential for ensuring reliable software delivery.

Versioning artifacts is critical to uniquely identify builds and facilitate seamless rollbacks or upgrades. A common approach is semantic versioning (e.g., v1.2.0), which uses version numbers to indicate changes, major, minor, or patch. In CI pipelines, automated versioning strategies include embedding build numbers, commit hashes, or timestamps into artifact names, ensuring every build is uniquely identifiable (e.g., `app-1.0.0+build-123` or `app-1.0.0-<commit_sha>`). Tagging artifacts with metadata, such as branch names, environment labels, or release candidates, further aids in tracking and deployment.

Artifact management typically occurs at the build stage, where successful builds are packaged and published to the artifact repository. Subsequent stages, like testing, staging, or production deployment, consume these versioned artifacts, ensuring consistency across the pipeline. For containerized applications, CI systems often use tools like Docker to package applications into images, tag them with unique versions, and push them to registries. For instance, GitHub Actions can automatically tag Docker images with Git commit SHAs and push them to GitHub Container Registry:

```
- name: Build and push Docker image
  run: |
    docker build -t ghcr.io/org/app:${{ github.sha }} .
    docker push ghcr.io/org/app:${{ github.sha }}
```

This ensures every build is uniquely identifiable and traceable back to its source code state.

By decoupling artifacts from the build environment and ensuring version immutability, teams can promote reliable deployments, reduce build duplication, and enable seamless rollbacks when needed.

In large-scale systems, artifact lifecycle management becomes crucial. Policies for artifact retention, cleanup of outdated versions, and promoting artifacts to higher environments (e.g., staging | production) ensure efficient storage utilization and streamlined deployment workflows. Integrating artifact management into CI pipelines establishes a single source of truth for deliverables, enhances traceability, and enables faster, error-free releases.

CI best practices and common pitfalls

While implementing CI can drastically improve productivity and code quality, its effectiveness hinges on following best practices while avoiding common pitfalls. A well-structured CI pipeline combines robust automation, efficient processes, and strong cultural alignment to deliver consistent and scalable results.

Some of the best practices for building a CI pipeline are:

- **Frequent code commits:** Developers should integrate code changes multiple times daily to detect issues early and minimize merge conflicts. Smaller, incremental changes reduce the risk of failures and simplify debugging.

- **Comprehensive automated testing:** Implement a robust test suite that includes unit, integration, and end-to-end tests. Ensure high test coverage across components and make automated testing a mandatory step in the CI pipeline to guarantee code reliability.

- **Optimized build performance:** Focus on keeping build times short, ideally under 10 minutes, by leveraging caching mechanisms, parallelizing tasks, and optimizing test suites. Faster builds provide quicker feedback loops, enhancing developer productivity.

- **Code quality and environment consistency:** Enforce static code analysis, linters, and style guides to maintain clean and consistent code. Adopt IaC to ensure reproducible environments, eliminating discrepancies between development, testing, and production stages.

- **Integrated security practices:** Embed security checks into the CI pipeline by scanning dependencies for vulnerabilities, performing SAST, and implementing access controls. Addressing security early prevents costly fixes in later stages.

- **Monitoring and observability:** Establish detailed logging, performance monitoring, and tracking of key metrics such as build success rates and test coverage. Alerts for failures and degradations help teams respond quickly to issues.

- **Cultural alignment:** Promote a culture of ownership and shared responsibility for building health. Encourage the immediate resolution of build failures, facilitate transparent communication, and foster continuous learning across teams.

Let us now also take a quick look at common pitfalls while building CI pipelines:

- **Neglected testing practices:** Poor test coverage, flaky tests, or overly complex test suites undermine CI reliability. Persistent, unreliable tests can erode team confidence in the CI process and lead to failed deployments.

- **Build and configuration complexity:** Overly intricate build scripts, inconsistent environments, and configuration drift across stages introduce instability. Failure to standardize or simplify pipelines often leads to prolonged debugging and delayed releases.

- **Performance bottlenecks:** Long build execution times, inefficient processes, and poor resource management hinder scalability. As projects grow, failing to optimize pipelines can overwhelm CI systems, slowing feedback loops.

- **Lack of security controls:** Neglecting dependency vulnerability scans, static analysis, or access control mechanisms can expose projects to security risks. Weak authentication and limited visibility into pipeline security further exacerbate these issues.

- **Insufficient monitoring and feedback:** Limited logging, absence of meaningful metrics, and ineffective failure reporting make it challenging to diagnose and fix issues. Without robust observability, teams lack actionable insights into pipeline performance.

- **Process and cultural misalignment:** Treating CI as merely a technical implementation, rather than a shared team responsibility, often leads to disengagement. Lack of collaboration between developers and operations teams prevents continuous improvement and innovation.

By implementing consistent build automation, comprehensive testing, and rigorous quality checks, organizations can significantly minimize integration challenges, catch defects early, and accelerate development cycles. Successful CI requires a balanced approach that combines technical best practices with a collaborative team culture, ultimately transforming software development from a fragmented process into a streamlined, reliable workflow.

Metrics and KPIs for CI effectiveness

Evaluating the effectiveness of CI is essential for teams aiming to improve software quality, boost efficiency, and accelerate delivery. Metrics and **key performance indicators** (**KPIs**) serve as measurable benchmarks that help pinpoint pipeline bottlenecks, track system health, and assess the impact of CI practices. A clear set of metrics allows teams to make informed decisions, streamline processes, and achieve reliable outcomes.

Let us explore the key metrics that organizations should monitor to effectively measure the health and performance of their CI processes, as follows:

- **Build success rate:** This metric measures the percentage of builds that are completed successfully without errors. A high success rate indicates stable pipelines and reliable code quality, while frequent failures highlight underlying issues such as broken tests, configuration errors, or fragile infrastructure.

- **Build time:** Build time refers to the total duration needed to run a CI pipeline, which includes code compilation, testing, and artifact generation. Optimizing build times allows for quicker feedback loops, reducing developer idle time and enhancing productivity.

- **Test coverage:** Test coverage measures the proportion of the codebase that is tested by automated tests. A higher test coverage helps identify potential defects early in the development process. However, it is important to prioritize the quality of coverage over merely achieving a high percentage.

- **Test success rate:** This represents the percentage of tests that have successfully passed within a CI pipeline. A high test pass rate suggests that the code is stable, whereas frequent test failures could indicate regressions or issues with the reliability of the test suites.

- **Mean time to detect (MTTD):** MTTD measures the average time required to spot issues in the CI pipeline following a code change. Quick detection is a key feature of effective CI, helping to stop broken code from moving forward.

- **Mean time to resolve (MTTR):** MTTR calculates the average time taken to fix pipeline failures or code defects once detected. Lower MTTR signifies a team's agility in addressing issues and improving overall stability. Modern CI platforms provide built-in analytics to track these metrics. For example, CircleCI's Insights dashboard shows trends in build durations and failure causes, helping teams identify flaky tests or slow steps. This data-driven approach allows teams to continuously optimize their pipelines based on real performance metrics rather than assumptions.

By systematically monitoring these KPIs, teams can gain a clear understanding of CI performance and its influence on development workflows. Metrics go beyond mere numbers; they provide actionable insights that enable teams to minimize build friction, improve code quality, and streamline delivery processes. Ultimately, assessing and enhancing CI effectiveness leads to consistent, reliable, and high-quality software delivery.

Scaling CI for large projects and monorepos

As projects grow in complexity and size, and especially when utilizing monorepos, scaling CI pipelines becomes critical. Large projects involve multiple teams, diverse workflows, and extensive codebases, while monorepos house the code for multiple projects or services in a single repository. Both scenarios demand a CI system that is performant, efficient, and capable of handling concurrent tasks without bottlenecks.

Some of the strategies for scaling CI for large projects are as follows:

- **Optimized dependency scoping:** Implement change detection logic to determine the specific modules or components impacted by a code change. Only rebuild and test the affected areas instead of triggering the entire pipeline. Tools like Bazel, Lerna, or Nx can assist in defining and managing dependency scopes efficiently within monorepos.

- **Pipeline parallelization:** Use parallel job execution to reduce bottlenecks. CI tools like Jenkins, GitLab CI, CircleCI, and GitHub Actions support distributing tasks across multiple machines or containers. Breaking pipelines into smaller, independent stages also helps balance workload distribution.

- **Dynamic resource allocation:** Adopt containerized CI environments (e.g., Kubernetes clusters) to allocate resources based on job requirements dynamically. Autoscaling ensures resources are available for peak workloads while minimizing costs during idle periods.

- **Incremental builds and caching:** Implement incremental builds to reuse outputs from previous builds and reduce redundant work. Efficient caching strategies for dependencies, artifacts, and test results further improve performance and save computing time.

- **Test sharding:** Divide large test suites into smaller shards that can run concurrently across multiple workers. Tools like Pytest-xdist, JUnit, or Cypress Test Runner support this approach, significantly reducing test execution time. A practical example of scaling is running Cypress tests in parallel on GitHub Actions with the `--record --parallel` flag, which can reduce test execution time dramatically. This approach, combined with intelligent test distribution, allows teams to maintain fast feedback loops even as test suites grow to thousands of tests across complex applications.

- **CI configuration as code:** Manage CI pipelines declaratively with YAML or similar configuration files. This ensures consistency, version control, and easier maintenance as the project grows.

- **Modular pipeline design:** For monorepos, create modular pipelines tailored to individual projects or services. Use CI triggers to run specific pipelines based on changes in particular directories or file types.

Scaling CI for large projects and monorepos requires thoughtful design, resource management, and automation to maintain efficiency and reliability. With the right strategies and tools, teams can ensure fast feedback loops, avoid resource contention, and support seamless collaboration across a growing codebase.

Security considerations in CI pipelines

Securing CI pipelines is essential for maintaining the integrity of software delivery and protecting sensitive data, code, and systems from malicious threats. Since CI pipelines frequently manage source code, credentials, build artifacts, and deployment processes, they become prime targets for attacks. By incorporating strong security measures into CI pipelines, organizations can minimize vulnerabilities and guarantee secure software delivery.

Some of the common risks in CI pipelines are as follows:

- **Exposure of secrets and credentials:** CI pipelines often require access to sensitive information, such as API keys, tokens, or SSH credentials. Improper handling or storage of these secrets can lead to unauthorized access.

- **Compromised dependencies:** Pipelines may inadvertently use compromised third-party libraries, dependencies, or containers, introducing vulnerabilities into the software.

- **Insecure infrastructure:** Misconfigured build agents, exposed CI servers, or insufficient access controls can provide attackers with entry points to the pipeline.

- **Malicious code injection:** Unauthorized or malicious code commits may pass through the pipeline and compromise the software or infrastructure.

- **Supply chain attacks:** CI systems are part of the software supply chain, and weaknesses in pipeline processes or dependencies can lead to supply chain attacks.

Some of the best practices for CI pipelines are as follows:

- Protecting sensitive information such as API keys, tokens, and SSH credentials is crucial. Use secret management tools like HashiCorp Vault, AWS Secrets Manager, or the built-in environment variable managers in CI systems. Avoid hardcoding secrets in your source code or configuration files, and make sure they are encrypted both during transmission and when stored. Regularly rotate your credentials and review access logs to spot any unauthorized usage.

- To secure your CI infrastructure, limit access to CI servers using firewalls, VPNs, or IP whitelisting. Implement **role-based access control (RBAC)** to ensure users only have the permissions they need. Consider using ephemeral build agents that are automatically destroyed after each pipeline run to eliminate lingering vulnerabilities and maintain clean environments for every build.

- Integrate automated security checks into your CI pipelines to catch vulnerabilities early on. Use SAST to analyze your code, **software composition analysis (SCA)** to inspect dependencies, and container scanning to validate image security. **Dynamic Application Security Testing (DAST)** can help identify runtime vulnerabilities. Make sure your pipelines halt further progression if critical vulnerabilities are found. For example, a GitLab CI pipeline can use Trivy to scan Docker images for vulnerabilities:

```
scan:
  stage: security
  image: aquasec/trivy
  script:
    - trivy image myapp:latest
```

This automated security scanning ensures that vulnerable containers never make it to production, shifting security left in the development process.

- To maintain code integrity, require signed commits to verify the authenticity of changes. Enforce peer reviews and automated tests for all pull or merge requests to catch any malicious or accidental issues before they make it into the main codebase. Utilize Git Hooks for pre-commit validations, ensuring that only approved changes move forward in the pipeline.

- Finally, run builds in isolated, sandboxed environments to minimize the impact of any compromised or faulty builds. Prevent CI pipelines from having direct access to production systems by introducing intermediate staging environments.

Security considerations must be a core element of CI pipelines rather than an afterthought. By embracing a shift-left approach, we can weave security into every stage of the development lifecycle. Tools like SonarQube, Trivy, and OWASP ZAP enable automated security checks, while practices such as threat modeling and regular penetration testing provide an important layer of protection.

With these security measures implemented, CI pipelines can become a robust and secure foundation for software delivery, protecting organizations from risks and ensuring compliance with industry standards.

Conclusion

CI marks a significant shift in software development, connecting the process of writing code with dependable delivery. This chapter has highlighted the essential role of CI in contemporary DevOps practices, offering a detailed guide for establishing strong and efficient integration strategies. By grasping the basic concepts and mastering advanced tools such as Jenkins, GitLab CI, and GitHub Actions, developers can view CI as a strategic advantage rather than just a technical necessity.

Exploring the fundamentals of CI shows that effective implementation goes well beyond just automated builds. It requires a comprehensive approach that includes advanced testing methods, thorough code quality assessments, and strategic management of artifacts. By adopting best practices and proactively tackling potential challenges, teams can build resilient pipelines that identify issues early, minimize integration challenges, and speed up software delivery.

The importance of metrics and security highlights the evolution of a CI approach, elevating it from a simple tool to a strategic resource. As software becomes more complex, the ability to scale CI processes is vital, especially for large projects and monorepos. The strategies discussed in this chapter offer a versatile framework for tailoring CI practices to meet various organizational requirements.

In the end, CI is not just a collection of technical practices; it represents a cultural change that fosters transparency, teamwork, and ongoing improvement. By embracing these principles, development teams can build more agile, dependable, and efficient software delivery systems that quickly respond to shifting market needs.

In the next chapter, we will explore IaC, a critical complement to CI practices. We will examine how IaC enables teams to manage and provision infrastructure through code using popular tools like Terraform, AWS CloudFormation, and Ansible. The chapter will cover both declarative and imperative approaches to IaC, detail how to manage cloud resources effectively, and demonstrate best practices for version control, testing, and security in infrastructure code. By integrating IaC with CI/CD pipelines, organizations can achieve complete automation across both application and infrastructure layers, further accelerating the delivery of value to customers.

CHAPTER 5

Introduction to Infrastructure as Code

Introduction

Setting up numerous servers, networks, and storage systems across different cloud environments can be quite complex and time-consuming. Mistakes and inconsistencies can easily occur, leading to a lot of frustrating work. This is why **infrastructure as code (IaC)** has become an essential component of modern DevOps practices.

The traditional approach of using web consoles or executing manual scripts to configure infrastructure is becoming outdated. Today, DevOps teams treat infrastructure as if it were software. They write code to define, deploy, and manage everything from simple storage systems to intricate cloud configurations spanning multiple regions.

In this chapter, we will explore the realm of IaC and examine how it is changing the way teams interact with cloud resources. We will begin by discussing the core concepts of IaC, such as version control, automation, and declarative specifications. You will also discover various IaC methods, including tools like Terraform.

Structure

The chapter covers the following topics:

- Principles and benefits of IaC
- Declarative vs. imperative IaC

- Terraform fundamentals

- Managing cloud resources with IaC

- Version control practices for IaC

- IaC security best practices

- Integrating IaC with CI/CD pipelines

- Managing multi-environment deployments

Objectives

This chapter aims to provide a comprehensive understanding of IaC and its critical role in modern DevOps practices. We will understand how to distinguish between declarative and imperative approaches while mastering core IaC principles, including version control, automation, idempotency, and reusability. The chapter explores key benefits of IaC implementation, such as consistency, speed, and enhanced security, alongside practical skills in Terraform fundamentals (HCL, providers, resources, modules) and AWS CloudFormation (templates, stacks, change sets). We will develop expertise in version control practices, security best practices, including secrets management, and techniques for integrating IaC with CI/CD pipelines.

By the end of the chapter, we will be equipped to manage multi-environment deployments while maintaining consistency across development, staging, and production environments.

Principles and benefits of IaC

IaC revolutionizes how teams design, deploy, and manage IT infrastructure by applying software development principles to infrastructure management. By replacing manual processes with code-based automation, IaC introduces consistency, speed, and scalability to infrastructure operations. This section delves into the core principles and benefits of IaC to provide a foundational understanding.

Let us take a look at the core principles of IaC:

- **Declarative and imperative approaches:**

  o **Declarative**: Focuses on what the desired end state of the infrastructure should look like. IaC determines how to achieve this state. For example, defining an S3 bucket in Terraform by specifying its properties.

  o **Imperative**: Focuses on how to achieve the desired state by specifying step-by-step instructions. For example, writing a script to manually create an S3 bucket using AWS CLI.

- **Idempotency:** Idempotency ensures that running the same code multiple times produces the same result. Regardless of how many times the IaC script is executed, the infrastructure state remains consistent, preventing duplication or unexpected changes.

- **Version control:** IaC relies on version-controlled repositories (e.g., Git) to track changes, collaborate with teams, and maintain a history of infrastructure modifications. This aligns infrastructure management with DevOps best practices.

- **Reusability:** IaC enables reusability through modules, templates, or playbooks. Teams can define standardized configurations for components (e.g., virtual machines, databases) and reuse them across projects, reducing redundancy and errors.

- **Automation:** IaC automates infrastructure provisioning and management, reducing the need for manual intervention. Automation not only improves speed but also minimizes human error.

Let us now talk about the major benefits of using IaC in your organization:

- **Consistency and standardization:** When infrastructure is defined as code, you eliminate the variability that comes with manual provisioning. Every environment, from development to production, is created using the same code, ensuring consistent configurations and reducing environment-specific issues. This standardization dramatically reduces the *it works on my machine* problem and makes troubleshooting more straightforward.

- **Speed and efficiency:** IaC significantly accelerates infrastructure provisioning. What might take hours or days to set up manually can be accomplished in minutes with IaC. This efficiency extends beyond initial provisioning, updates, modifications, and even complete environment rebuilds, becoming quick and reliable operations.

- **Cost reduction:** By automating infrastructure management, organizations can reduce both direct and indirect costs. The direct savings come from requiring fewer person-hours for infrastructure management. Indirect savings arise from reduced errors, faster problem resolution, and the ability to optimize resource usage through code.

- **Enhanced security and compliance:** Infrastructure code can embed security controls and compliance requirements directly into the infrastructure definitions. This approach ensures that security best practices are consistently applied across all deployments. Version control provides audit trails, while automated testing can verify that security policies are being followed.

- **Improved collaboration:** IaC bridges the gap between development and operations teams. By using code to define infrastructure, developers can better understand the infrastructure requirements of their applications, while operations teams can use familiar development practices like code review and testing to manage infrastructure changes.

- **Disaster recovery:** When your infrastructure is defined as code, disaster recovery becomes more reliable and testable. You can regularly validate your recovery procedures by using your IaC configurations to recreate environments in different regions or accounts. This capability provides confidence in your disaster recovery plans and reduces recovery time when incidents occur.

- **Documentation as code:** IaC serves as living documentation of your infrastructure. Instead of maintaining separate documentation that can become outdated, the code itself describes exactly how your infrastructure is configured. This self-documenting nature helps new team members understand the infrastructure and makes knowledge transfer more effective.

Understanding and embracing the principles and benefits of IaC lays the groundwork for managing modern infrastructure effectively. In the next sections, we will explore specific tools and techniques to bring these principles to life.

Declarative vs. imperative IaC

Recognizing the difference between declarative and imperative approaches is essential when dealing with IaC. These two paradigms offer fundamentally different methods for defining and managing infrastructure, each possessing its own advantages and specific scenarios where it excels.

Declarative approach

The declarative approach of doing IaC is mostly about describing the desired end state of your infrastructure. Hence, instead of specifying the steps to create resources, you basically declare what you want the final configuration to look like. Think of it as telling your infrastructure tool, *This is what I want,* or *These are the resources I want to create* rather than *This is how to do it.* Some of the key characteristics of this approach are:

- You define the target state of resources (e.g., *I want 3 web servers with these specifications*).

- The IaC tool handles the implementation details and order of operations.

- The code is idempotent in nature, meaning repeated executions produce the same result.

- The system maintains a state file to track the current infrastructure configuration.

For example, Terraform is one of the most common tools that uses the declarative approach of IaC:

```
1.  resource "aws_instance" "web_server" {
2.    count        = 3
3.    ami          = "ami-0c55b159cbfafe1f0"
```

```
4.    instance_type = "t2.micro"
5.
6.    tags = {
7.      Name = "web-server-${count.index}"
8.    }
9.  }
```

In the aforementioned example, we are provisioning 3 AWS EC2 instances (**count=3**) of type **t2.micro** with the **Amazon Machine Image** (**ami**), along with applying a tag on the machines as web-server-1, web-server-2 and web-server-3.

Imperative approach

The imperative approach explicitly defines the sequence of steps needed to achieve the desired infrastructure state. This method focuses on *how* to perform the changes, specifying each action in detail.

The key characteristics of this approach are:

- You write step-by-step instructions for creating or modifying infrastructure.

- The execution order is explicitly defined.

- Changes are typically executed as a series of commands or scripts.

- More control over the exact implementation process requires careful handling of state and dependencies.

For example, Ansible is a well-known configuration management tool that follows this approach:

```
1.  ---
2.  - name: Configure web servers
3.    hosts: web_servers
4.    become: yes
5.    tasks:
6.      - name: Install nginx
7.        apt:
8.          name: nginx
9.          state: present
10.
11.      - name: Start nginx service
12.        service:
13.          name: nginx
14.          state: started
15.          enabled: yes
```

```
16.
17.        - name: Copy website configuration
18.          template:
19.            src: nginx.conf.j2
20.            dest: /etc/nginx/sites-available/default
21.          notify: Restart nginx
22.
23.        - name: Create document root
24.          file:
25.            path: /var/www/html
26.            state: directory
27.            mode: '0755'
28.
29.        - name: Deploy website content
30.          copy:
31.            src: files/index.html
32.            dest: /var/www/html/index.html
33.
34.      handlers:
35.        - name: Restart nginx
36.          service:
37.            name: nginx
38.            state: restarted
```

The aforementioned Ansible playbook has a step-by-step configuration example of a web server.

Hence, as you can see when comparing declarative and imperative approaches, each offers distinct advantages and challenges for infrastructure management. Declarative tools like Terraform excel in maintainability and predictability as they focus on the desired end state rather than the implementation details. Their built-in state management and idempotent nature make them particularly suitable for large-scale infrastructure deployments and team environments. However, they may require a steeper learning curve to master their specific syntax and behaviors. On the other hand, imperative tools like Ansible offer greater flexibility and familiarity for those with scripting experience. They provide fine-grained control over the execution process and are excellent for configuration management tasks. Though imperative approaches require more careful handling of error conditions and state management, they excel in scenarios that require complex orchestration or specific execution orders. Many organizations adopt a hybrid approach, using declarative tools for core infrastructure provisioning while leveraging imperative tools for configuration management and specialized tasks.

In practice, teams often integrate these approaches with CI/CD pipelines. For example, in Bitbucket Pipelines, developers use feature branches that trigger builds defined in `bitbucket-pipelines.yml`. The pipeline includes steps for linting, testing, and code quality checks before merging to main. This demonstrates how IaC patterns complement broader DevOps workflows beyond just infrastructure provisioning.

Terraform fundamentals

Terraform has revolutionized the way organizations manage their infrastructure and has established itself as a cornerstone of modern DevOps practices. It is an open-source IaC tool created by HashiCorp, which enables software teams to define, provision, and manage infrastructure across multiple cloud providers with consistency and efficiency. At its heart, Terraform uses **HashiCorp Configuration Language (HCL)**, which is a declarative language that strikes a balance between human readability and automation capabilities.

What sets Terraform apart is its practical architecture, which has proven invaluable for both small teams and large enterprises. Terraform has a rich ecosystem of providers and modules, which can be used by teams to orchestrate complex infrastructure deployments while maintaining code reusability and scalability. Whether you are managing cloud resources, on-premises systems, or a hybrid environment, Terraform's unified approach to infrastructure management helps reduce manual work and human error, enforces consistency, as well as accelerates deployment cycles.

In 2023 Terraform landscape evolved significantly when HashiCorp changed Terraform's license from open-source MPL-2.0 to the **Business Source License (BUSL)**. This led to the creation of OpenTofu, a community-driven fork maintained by the Linux Foundation that preserves the open-source nature of the original project. The best part about this is that both Terraform and OpenTofu continue to share the same fundamental concepts and syntax, offering organizations flexibility in choosing the solution that best aligns with their licensing preferences and requirements.

Let us dive into this section, where we will explore the fundamentals of Terraform: HCL, providers, resources, and modules. By the end, you will have a solid understanding of Terraform's core components and how they work together to manage infrastructure efficiently.

HashiCorp Configuration Language

HashiCorp Configuration Language (HCL) is the language used to write Terraform configuration files. It is designed to be both human-readable and machine-parsable, making it easy to define infrastructure as code.

Some of the key characteristics of HCL are:

- **Declarative:** Focuses on defining the desired state of infrastructure.
- **Readable syntax:** Uses a block-based format with clear and intuitive keywords.

- **Extensible:** Allows for variables, outputs, and dynamic expressions to make configurations reusable and scalable.

  The code is as follows:

```
provider "aws" {
  region = "us-east-1"
}

resource "aws_instance" "web" {
  ami           = "ami-0c94855ba95c574c8"
  instance_type = "t2.micro"

  tags = {
    Name = "WebServer"
  }
}
```

In the aforementioned example:

- The provider block specifies the cloud provider (AWS in this case).

- The resource block defines an EC2 instance with properties like the AMI ID and instance type.

Provider

Terraform providers are specialized plugins that serve as the translation layer between Terraform's HCL configuration and the APIs of various infrastructure platforms. Each provider encapsulates the logic needed to authenticate, **create, read, update, and delete (CRUD)** resources within its respective platform, abstracting away the complexity of direct API interactions. Providers implement sophisticated state management mechanisms to track the real-world infrastructure state and detect drift.

They primarily handle:

- **Resource Dependencies:** Determining the correct order of operations.

- **State Refresh:** Syncing Terraform's state with actual infrastructure.

- **Import Support:** Bringing existing resources under Terraform management.

- **Custom Validation:** Enforcing provider-specific rules and constraints.

```
terraform {
  required_providers {
    aws = {
      source  = "hashicorp/aws"
```

```
      version = "~> 4.16.0"
    }
    azurerm = {
      source  = "hashicorp/azurerm"
      version = "~> 3.0.0"
    }
  }
}
```

In the aforementioned example, we are basically doing:

- Declares which providers are required for this configuration.

- Specifies where to source the providers from (hashicorp registry).

- Sets version constraints using semantic versioning (which means to allow patch updates).

Resources

Resources are the most critical building blocks in Terraform. A resource represents a single piece of infrastructure, such as a virtual machine, a storage bucket, or a load balancer.

A resource primarily has the following characteristics:

- **Definition:** A resource block declares what you want to create, modify, or destroy.

- **Arguments:** Specify the properties of the resource (e.g., size, tags, security settings).

- **Naming convention:** Resources are identified by a type (e.g., aws_instance) and a unique name (e.g., web).

```
resource "aws_s3_bucket" "my_bucket" {
  bucket = "my-unique-bucket-name"
  acl    = "private"
}
```

In the aforementioned example:

- The **aws_s3_bucket** resource creates an S3 bucket.

- The **bucket** argument specifies the bucket name.

- The **acl** argument sets the access control to **private**.

Modules

Modules are reusable, self-contained units of Terraform configuration. They allow you to organize and standardize infrastructure code, making it more manageable and scalable.

Some of the key points about modules:

- **Purpose:** Group related resources and logic into a single reusable package.

- **Inputs and outputs:** Accept variables (inputs) and return values (outputs) for flexibility.

- **Structure:** Typically includes a **main.tf** file (core configuration), along with optional variables.tf and outputs.tf files.

- **Registry:** Terraform has an official Module Registry where you can find pre-built modules.

For example, in the following module:

```
module "web_app" {
  source         = "./modules/web_app"
  instance_type = "t2.micro"
  ami            = "ami-0c94855ba95c574c8"
}
```

- The **source** argument specifies the module location (local folder **./modules/web_app**).

- Variables like **instance_type** and **ami** are passed to customize the module's behavior.

The modularity of Terraform complements application build processes. In Jenkins, the build stage may execute a Maven build using **mvn clean install -DskipTests=false** to compile and package a Java application with dependencies. Similarly, Terraform modules enable reusable infrastructure patterns that can be versioned and shared across teams.

Now, if you are wondering how all of this fits together, let us take the following terraform example:

```
# Define the provider
provider "aws" {
  region = "us-east-1"
}


# Create a security group
resource "aws_security_group" "allow_http" {
  name         = "allow_http"
  description = "Allow HTTP traffic"
  ingress {
    from_port   = 80
```

```
    to_port     = 80
    protocol    = "tcp"
    cidr_blocks = ["0.0.0.0/0"]
  }
}

# Create an EC2 instance
resource "aws_instance" "web" {
  ami           = "ami-0c94855ba95c574c8"
  instance_type = "t2.micro"

  vpc_security_group_ids = [aws_security_group.allow_http.id]

  tags = {
    Name = "WebServer"
  }
}
```

As you can recall from this section, in the aforementioned example:

- **Provider block:** Specifies AWS as the provider and sets the region.

- **Security group resource:** Defines a firewall rule to allow HTTP traffic on port 80.

- **EC2 instance resource:** This creates a web server and associates it with the security group.

In this section, we learned that Terraform's HCL, providers, resources, and modules are the foundational elements of infrastructure automation. By understanding these concepts, you can write reusable, scalable, and maintainable infrastructure code to efficiently manage your environments. Whether you are deploying a single server or an entire cloud ecosystem, Terraform provides the tools you need to build a scalable and reproducible infrastructure.

AWS CloudFormation

AWS CloudFormation is a declarative IaC service that utilizes templates formatted in JSON or YAML to programmatically provision and manage AWS resources through what are called **stacks**. It operates by maintaining a **directed acyclic graph (DAG)** of resource dependencies, which aids in determining the optimal order for creating, updating, and deleting resources. Some of the key components of AWS Cloudformation service are:

- **Template anatomy:** This includes essential top-level objects such as AWSTemplateFormatVersion, Description, Resources, and optional sections like Parameters, Mappings, Conditions, and Outputs.

- **Resource definitions:** These are specified using unique logical IDs that correspond to resource types (e.g., **AWS::EC2::Instance**, **AWS::S3::Bucket**) along with their respective property configurations.

- **Change sets:** These provide a preview of proposed infrastructure changes, detailing resource-level modifications before any stack updates are carried out.

- **Drift detection:** This involves a programmatic comparison between the desired state defined in the template and the actual configurations of deployed resources.

- **Nested stacks:** This feature allows for hierarchical template composition, enabling modular infrastructure definitions with parent-child relationships and cross-stack references.

CloudFormation templates are JSON or YAML-formatted text files that describe your AWS infrastructure.

Let us look at an example template:

```
AWSTemplateFormatVersion: '2010-09-09'
Description: 'Basic EC2 instance with a security group'

Parameters:
  InstanceType:
    Description: EC2 instance type
    Type: String
    Default: t2.micro
    AllowedValues:
      - t2.micro
      - t2.small
      - t2.medium

Resources:
  WebServerSecurityGroup:
    Type: AWS::EC2::SecurityGroup
    Properties:
      GroupDescription: Enable HTTP access via port 80
      SecurityGroupIngress:
        - IpProtocol: tcp
          FromPort: 80
```

```
        ToPort: 80
        CidrIp: 0.0.0.0/0

  WebServer:
    Type: AWS::EC2::Instance
    Properties:
      InstanceType: !Ref InstanceType
      ImageId: ami-0c55b159cbfafe1f0
      SecurityGroups:
        - !Ref WebServerSecurityGroup
      Tags:
        - Key: Name
          Value: Web Server

Outputs:
  WebsiteURL:
    Description: Instance public URL
    Value: !Sub http://${WebServer.PublicDnsName}
```

In the aforementioned CloudFormation template, the following are the key components:

- **Parameters:** Input values that can be specified when creating a stack.
- **Resources:** AWS resources to be created.
- **Mappings:** Key-value mappings for resource properties.
- **Conditions:** Conditional resource creation.
- **Outputs:** Values that can be imported into other stacks.
- **References and Functions:** Built-in functions for dynamic values.

Stacks

In AWS CloudFormation, a stack serves as the basic unit for managing a collection of resources. You can view it as a container that organizes and holds all the infrastructure elements specified in a single CloudFormation template. These elements may consist of AWS services such as EC2 instances, S3 buckets, databases, and networking setups.

To create a stack, you typically follow these steps:

1. **Define a template:** Write a CloudFormation template using JSON or YAML to describe your desired resources and configurations.
2. **Launch the stack:** Use the AWS Management Console, CLI, or SDKs to create a stack, specifying the template and any required parameters.

3. **Manage the stack:** Update or delete the stack as needed. CloudFormation ensures all changes are applied in the correct order.

Here is a high-level overview of a CloudFormation stack that deploys a web server:

```
Resources:
  MyEC2Instance:
    Type: AWS::EC2::Instance
    Properties:
      InstanceType: t2.micro
      ImageId: ami-0c94855ba95c574c8
      SecurityGroups:
        - Ref: MySecurityGroup

  MySecurityGroup:
    Type: AWS::EC2::SecurityGroup
    Properties:
      GroupDescription: Allow HTTP traffic
      SecurityGroupIngress:
        - IpProtocol: tcp
          FromPort: 80
          ToPort: 80
          CidrIp: 0.0.0.0/0
```

You can now save this YAML template to a file (e.g., **web-server-stack.yaml**) and then use the AWS CLI command as follows to launch the stack:

```
$ aws cloudformation create-stack --stack-name WebServerStack --template-body file://web-server-stack.yaml
```

You can check the AWS management console to see the progress now. CloudFormation integrates well with container-based testing workflows. For integration testing, Docker Compose is often used to spin up a local database and backend services, while the CI pipeline executes integration tests using Postman Newman CLI to validate API workflows. This demonstrates how IaC tools work alongside container orchestration for comprehensive infrastructure validation. Hence, by using stacks, you can efficiently manage complex cloud environments while ensuring they remain aligned with your defined architecture.

ChangeSet

A ChangeSet in AWS CloudFormation allows you to preview the changes that will be made to your infrastructure before applying them. This feature is particularly useful for minimizing deployment risks by giving you visibility into how an update will affect your resources. With a ChangeSet, you can ensure that updates are intentional and avoid unexpected modifications.

To create and execute a ChangeSet, you can follow these steps:

1. **Create a new template:** Modify your existing CloudFormation template to reflect the desired changes.

2. **Create a ChangeSet:** Use the AWS Management Console, CLI, or SDK to create a ChangeSet for your stack. For example:

   ```
   $ aws cloudformation create-change-set    --stack-
   name MyStack    --template-body updated-template.yaml    --change-set-
   name MyChangeSet
   ```

3. **Review the ChangeSet:** View the ChangeSet details to understand its impact. You can see resource-specific changes categorized as *Add*, *Modify*, or *Remove*.

4. **Execute the ChangeSet:** Once reviewed, execute the ChangeSet to apply the changes:

   ```
   $ aws cloudformation execute-change-set --change-set-name MyChangeSet
   ```

In conclusion, AWS CloudFormation Change Sets is a powerful tool for maintaining control over infrastructure updates. By previewing changes, you can confidently deploy updates with minimal risk, ensuring that your infrastructure evolves as planned while maintaining stability and reliability.

Managing cloud resources with IaC

IaC marks a significant change in how organizations handle and provision their cloud resources. Rather than relying on manual configurations through web consoles or makeshift scripts, IaC allows teams to define their infrastructure using declarative code, integrating software engineering practices into infrastructure management. This method fundamentally alters the way teams engage with and maintain their cloud infrastructure.

At its essence, IaC is based on the principle of declarative definition, where infrastructure is articulated in code that outlines the desired end state instead of detailing the steps to reach it. This means that instead of crafting procedural scripts to build infrastructure, engineers simply specify what they want the final setup to be.

For instance, when setting up a virtual machine, rather than outlining each step of the creation process, you just declare its intended state as follows:

```
resource "aws_instance" "web_server" {
  ami           = "ami-0c55b159cbfafe1f0"
  instance_type = "t2.micro"
  tags = {
    Name = "Web Server"
    Environment = "Production"
  }
}
```

This declarative approach naturally leads to the integration of version control systems like Git, where infrastructure code becomes a living document of your system's evolution. Teams can review changes, understand the reasoning behind specific configurations, and maintain a clear audit trail of all infrastructure modifications. This versioning capability proves invaluable when organizations need to roll back changes or understand how their infrastructure has evolved over time.

Building upon this foundation, the concept of immutable infrastructure emerges as a natural progression. Rather than modifying existing resources in place, teams create new instances with updated configurations and replace the old ones. This approach not only reduces configuration drift but also ensures consistency across environments and simplifies rollback procedures. When changes are needed, entire infrastructure components are replaced rather than modified, maintaining perfect alignment between the declared configuration and the actual state.

The success of this immutable approach heavily depends on proper state management. Organizations must maintain accurate records of their infrastructure state, typically using remote storage solutions like AWS S3 or Azure Storage. By implementing state locking and separating state files for different environments, teams can prevent concurrent modifications while maintaining clear boundaries between development, staging, and production environments.

As infrastructure grows in complexity, effective resource organization becomes crucial. Teams need to structure their infrastructure code with logical grouping of related resources, clear naming conventions, and proper tagging strategies. This organizational clarity flows naturally into environment management, where variables handle environment-specific values while maintaining standardized resource configurations across different deployment stages.

The structured nature of IaC also facilitates better cost management and optimization. Organizations can implement systematic resource tagging for cost allocation, automate scaling based on demand patterns, and establish regular cleanup procedures for unused resources. This proactive approach to cost management ensures that infrastructure remains economically optimal without sacrificing performance or reliability.

Security and compliance considerations weave seamlessly into this structured approach. By encoding security policies directly into infrastructure definitions, organizations can ensure the consistent application of encryption, IAM roles, and network security controls across all environments. Regular security audits and compliance monitoring become more straightforward when security policies are explicitly defined in code.

The culmination of these interconnected practices yields significant benefits for organizations. Teams achieve greater consistency and reliability through eliminated configuration drift and reduced human error. The standardized nature of IaC facilitates rapid environment provisioning and easy replication across regions, while self-documenting code improves team collaboration and knowledge sharing. Furthermore, the systematic approach to resource management leads to optimized utilization and more efficient cost control.

This comprehensive approach to infrastructure management has become essential for modern cloud operations. By embracing IaC, organizations position themselves to handle increasingly complex infrastructure requirements while maintaining security, efficiency, and reliability. As cloud technologies continue to evolve, the structured and systematic nature of IaC provides a solid foundation for future growth and innovation.

Version control practices for IaC

By leveraging a **version control system** (**VCS**) like Git, IaC enables teams to treat infrastructure definitions as software, making it possible to track changes, collaborate effectively, and maintain consistency across environments. A well-implemented version control strategy ensures that infrastructure is not only reliable but also auditable, repeatable, and scalable.

Infrastructure evolves rapidly in modern development workflows. Changes could involve updates to cloud resources, scaling configurations, network rules, or security policies. Without version control, the following issues are evident:

- **Loss of traceability:** There is no record of who made changes, when, or why.

- **Environment drift occurs:** Inconsistent configurations emerge across environments.

- **Rollbacks are difficult:** Reverting to a stable state becomes error-prone and time-consuming.

Hence, we also need to ensure that a clear and logical repository structure is maintained while implementing or managing IaC effectively.

There are several ways to achieve this, as follows:

- **Repository organization:**

    o **Monorepo**: A single repository contains all IaC configurations for various environments, services, and modules.

        ▪ The advantages of this approach are easier to track dependencies, centralized visibility, simpler CI/CD pipelines.

        ▪ **Challenges**: Requires careful planning to avoid conflicts in large teams.

    o **Multi-repo**: Separate repositories for distinct environments, services, or teams.

        ▪ **Advantages**: Clear ownership boundaries, easier to scale across teams.

        ▪ **Challenges**: Cross-repository dependencies can complicate workflows.

- **Environment-specific management:** Managing multiple environments effectively requires a strategic approach to configuration organization and deployment workflows. Two primary methodologies have emerged as industry standards: directory-based separation and branch-based separation, each offering distinct advantages for environment management.

  Directory-based separation creates a clear hierarchical structure where each environment maintains its own dedicated directory. This approach enables teams to organize configurations with explicit boundaries while keeping common elements centralized.

  A typical directory structure might look like this:

```
infrastructure/
├── environments/
│   ├── dev/
│   │   ├── main.tf
│   │   └── variables.tf
│   ├── staging/
│   │   ├── main.tf
│   │   └── variables.tf
│   └── prod/
│       ├── main.tf
│       └── variables.tf
├── modules/
│   ├── networking/
│   ├── compute/
│   └── storage/
└── shared/
    └── provider.tf
```

Version control practices extend beyond infrastructure code. GitHub Actions, for instance, runs ESLint for JavaScript codebase quality checks and uploads results to the GitHub Code Scanning dashboard. This same versioning discipline applied to infrastructure ensures consistent quality across all aspects of the technology stack.

This structure allows teams to maintain environment-specific configurations while sharing common modules and provider configurations. Each environment can define its own variable values, resource sizing, and security configurations while inheriting standardized architectural patterns from shared modules.

Branch-based separation, on the other hand, leverages version control workflows to manage environment configurations. This approach treats infrastructure changes like software releases, where changes flow from development through staging and finally to production through a series of controlled promotions. Teams create environment-specific branches (dev, staging, prod) and use pull requests to promote changes between environments.

This workflow enables:

- Thorough review of infrastructure changes before promotion.
- Automatic testing and validation at each stage.
- Clear audit trail of configuration changes.
- Ability to roll back changes if issues arise.
- Integration with existing CI/CD pipelines.

Both approaches can be combined to create a robust environment management strategy. For instance, using directory-based separation for environment-specific configurations while leveraging branch-based workflows for change promotion ensures both organizational clarity and controlled deployment processes. This combination provides teams with the flexibility to manage environment-specific requirements while maintaining consistent deployment practices across their infrastructure lifecycle.

Version control practices in IaC are not just a technical requirement; they are essential to effective infrastructure management today. By organizing repositories—whether using a monorepo or multi-repo strategy and managing environments through directory-based or branch-based separation, organizations can create a solid foundation for evolving their infrastructure.

These practices ensure that changes to infrastructure are traceable, reversible, and consistently implemented across different environments. By applying the same level of scrutiny to infrastructure definitions as they do to application code, teams can maintain clarity in their deployment processes while remaining adaptable to new requirements. This structured approach to version control helps minimize environment drift, reduce operational risks, and enables teams to scale their infrastructure confidently.

As organizations increasingly adopt cloud-native architectures and face complex deployment challenges, the importance of these version control practices grows. They establish a framework for effective collaboration, uphold security standards, and guarantee that infrastructure changes can be reliably deployed across all environments. In the end, effective version control in IaC turns infrastructure management from a source of uncertainty into a smooth, predictable process that fosters both stability and innovation.

IaC security best practices

Security in IaC requires a shift-left approach, integrating security controls directly into infrastructure definitions rather than applying them as an afterthought. This proactive stance ensures that security becomes an inherent part of infrastructure deployment rather than a reactive measure.

Secrets management stands at the forefront of IaC security. Rather than embedding sensitive information like API keys, passwords, or certificates directly in code, organizations should leverage dedicated secrets management solutions such as HashiCorp Vault or AWS Secrets Manager.

Infrastructure code should reference these external secrets:

```
data "aws_secretsmanager_secret_version" "db_password" {
  secret_id = "database/password"
}


resource "aws_db_instance" "main" {
  password = data.aws_secretsmanager_secret_version.db_password.secret_
string
  # other configurations...
}
```

Network security requires careful consideration of access patterns and isolation. Implement the principle of least privilege by default, using security groups and network ACLs to control traffic flow.

Resources should be placed in private subnets unless public access is explicitly required:

```
resource "aws_subnet" "private" {
  vpc_id     = aws_vpc.main.id
  cidr_block = "10.0.1.0/24"

  map_public_ip_on_launch = false
}
```

Identity and access management (**IAM**) policies should follow the principle of least privilege, granting only the permissions necessary for resources to function.

Role-based access control (**RBAC**) should be implemented consistently across all environments as follows:

```
resource "aws_iam_role" "app_role" {
  assume_role_policy = jsonencode({
    Version = "2012-10-17"
    Statement = [
      {
        Action = "sts:AssumeRole"
        Effect = "Allow"
        Principal = {
          Service = "ec2.amazonaws.com"
        }
```

```
      }
    ]
  })
}
```

Automated security scanning should be integrated into the deployment pipeline. Tools like **checkov**, **tfsec**, or **Snyk** can identify security misconfigurations, compliance violations, and potential vulnerabilities before infrastructure changes reach production.

Integrate these scans into your CI/CD pipeline:

```
security_scan:
  script:
    - checkov -d .
    - tfsec .
  rules:
    - if: $CI_PIPELINE_SOURCE == "merge_request_event"
```

Resource encryption should be enabled by default for data at rest and in transit. This includes storage volumes, databases, and communication channels:

```
resource "aws_s3_bucket" "data" {
  bucket = "example-bucket"

  server_side_encryption_configuration {
    rule {
      apply_server_side_encryption_by_default {
        sse_algorithm = "AES256"
      }
    }
  }
}
```

Security practices also encompass artifact management in CI/CD workflows. In GitLab, artifacts like **.jar** or **.zip** files are stored using the **artifacts:** keyword and retained for deployment stages. This ensures that all deployable components, including infrastructure definitions, maintain proper security throughout the pipeline.

Regular security audits and compliance checks ensure ongoing adherence to security standards. Implement monitoring and logging to track infrastructure changes and detect potential security incidents.

Use tags to identify security-critical resources and maintain clear ownership:

```
resource "aws_instance" "web" {
  # ... other configurations
```

```
  tags = {
    Environment     = "Production"
    SecurityLevel   = "High"
    DataClass       = "Confidential"
    Owner           = "Platform-Team"
  }
}
```

By incorporating these security practices into IaC workflows, organizations can ensure that their infrastructure remains secure and compliant throughout its lifecycle. This approach not only protects resources and data but also establishes a foundation for scaling secure infrastructure deployments across the organization.

Integrating IaC with CI/CD pipelines

Infrastructure as Code becomes truly powerful when integrated into **continuous integration and continuous deployment (CI/CD)** pipelines, enabling automated testing, validation, and deployment of infrastructure changes. This integration transforms manual infrastructure modifications into automated, repeatable processes that maintain consistency and reliability across environments.

A well-architected IaC pipeline typically flows through several stages:

```
# Example GitLab CI/CD Pipeline for Terraform
stages:
  - validate
  - plan
  - apply
  - test


terraform_validate:
  stage: validate
  script:
    - terraform init
    - terraform validate
    - tflint
    - checkov -d .


terraform_plan:
  stage: plan
  script:
    - terraform init
    - terraform plan -out=tfplan
```

```
artifacts:
  paths:
    - tfplan

terraform_apply:
  stage: apply
  script:
    - terraform apply -auto-approve tfplan
  when: manual
  only:
    - main
```

Beyond automation, successful CI/CD integration requires visibility. Jenkins can be integrated with Prometheus and Grafana to visualize pipeline metrics such as success rate, average build time, and test flakiness. This observability extends to infrastructure deployments, helping teams understand the impact of IaC changes on overall system reliability.

The pipeline begins with the validation stage, where infrastructure code undergoes static analysis, syntax checking, and security scanning. This ensures that basic errors and security misconfigurations are caught early, before any changes reach the target environment. Tools like tflint for Terraform linting and checkov for security scanning become integral parts of this stage.

The planning stage generates a detailed execution plan showing exactly what changes will be made to the infrastructure. This plan is reviewed by team members through pull requests, enabling thorough scrutiny of proposed changes. Critical changes can be flagged for additional review, while routine updates might proceed automatically based on predefined criteria.

The application stage executes the approved changes, transforming the infrastructure to match the desired state. This stage often includes safeguards like manual approvals for production deployments or automatic approvals for lower environments. Post-deployment testing verifies that the infrastructure changes meet functional and security requirements.

By integrating IaC with CI/CD pipelines, organizations establish a standardized process for infrastructure changes that combines automation with appropriate controls. This integration ensures that infrastructure evolves in a controlled, predictable manner while maintaining security and compliance requirements.

Managing multi-environment deployments

Managing infrastructure across multiple environments requires a balanced approach that maintains consistency while accommodating environment-specific needs. Organizations typically establish a hierarchy of environments, development, staging, and production, each serving distinct purposes in the infrastructure lifecycle. By leveraging environment-specific variable files and modular configuration structures, teams can maintain common architectural patterns while allowing for necessary variations in scaling, security, and resource allocation. For instance, development environments might favor flexibility and cost-effectiveness with smaller instance sizes and relaxed security controls, while production environments demand high availability, strict security measures, and robust monitoring. State management becomes crucial in this context, with each environment maintaining its own state file to prevent cross-environment conflicts. A well-structured promotion process ensures that infrastructure changes flow systematically from development through staging to production, with appropriate testing and validation at each stage. This approach enables organizations to maintain a reliable, secure, and cost-effective infrastructure across all environments while ensuring that each environment serves its intended purpose in the development and deployment pipeline.

For organizations with complex infrastructure requirements, advanced build systems provide additional capabilities. Bazel build system in Google-style monorepos supports fine-grained caching and parallel builds for massive codebases. This same level of sophistication can be applied to infrastructure management, where large-scale deployments benefit from intelligent caching and parallel execution of infrastructure changes.

Conclusion

IaC has transformed infrastructure management from manual, error-prone processes to programmable, version-controlled deployments. Throughout this chapter, we have seen how IaC incorporates software engineering principles into infrastructure operations, enabling teams to create reproducible, scalable, and secure deployments. Tools like Terraform and AWS CloudFormation provide powerful declarative approaches, which when combined with robust version control practices and security measures, establish a foundation for modern infrastructure management. The integration of IaC with CI/CD pipelines automates infrastructure changes while maintaining reliability and security, allowing organizations to scale efficiently while preserving consistency across all environments. As cloud technologies advance, IaC principles become increasingly vital for organizations striving to maintain competitive advantage in a rapidly evolving technology landscape.

In the next chapter, we will build upon our infrastructure foundation by exploring continuous delivery and deployment practices. We will distinguish between continuous delivery and continuous deployment while examining robust deployment pipelines and strategies, including Blue/Green, Canary, and Rolling Updates. The chapter will cover feature flags, trunk-based development, database schema automation, and environment promotion. We will also address critical operational concerns like rollback strategies, monitoring, security considerations, and compliance requirements to help you implement reliable, secure deployment processes that accelerate your software delivery lifecycle.

CHAPTER 6

Continuous Delivery and Deployment

Introduction

In this chapter, we will explore the essentials of continuous delivery and continuous deployment, focusing on how these practices automate and streamline the software release process. We will delve into the key differences between the two, build robust deployment pipelines, and examine advanced deployment strategies such as Blue/Green, Canary, and Rolling Updates. We will learn about feature flags, trunk-based development for safe, incremental releases, and strategies for automating database schema changes. The chapter also covers environment promotion, artifact management, and effective rollback techniques. Additionally, we will highlight the importance of monitoring, observability, and security in deployment pipelines while addressing compliance and auditing requirements. Finally, we will explore metrics and KPIs to measure the effectiveness of your CD processes.

Structure

This chapter covers the following topics:

- Continuous delivery vs. continuous deployment
- Building deployment pipelines
- Deployment strategies

- Feature flags and trunk-based development
- Automating database schema changes
- Environment promotion and artifact management
- Rollback strategies
- Observability in CD
- Security considerations in deployments
- CD metrics and KPIs
- Compliance and auditing in CD pipelines

Objectives

By the end of this chapter, readers will be able to differentiate between continuous delivery and continuous deployment, construct robust deployment pipelines with automated testing and quality gates, and implement various deployment strategies, including Blue/Green, Canary, and Rolling Updates. Learners will master feature flags and trunk-based development for incremental releases, develop techniques for automating database schema changes, and establish effective environment promotion and artifact management workflows. They will create comprehensive rollback strategies, integrate observability practices to monitor deployments, apply security best practices throughout the pipeline, define relevant metrics to measure CD effectiveness and implement compliance mechanisms for regulatory requirements. These skills will enable practitioners to design delivery processes that balance rapid innovation with operational stability, resulting in frequent, reliable software releases while maintaining system integrity and performance. By mastering these concepts, teams can achieve a resilient, scalable, and efficient software delivery process that meets technical and business objectives.

Continuous delivery vs. continuous deployment

In contemporary software development, **continuous delivery** (**CD**) and continuous deployment are frequently confused, yet they signify different practices with unique objectives. Grasping these distinctions is essential for selecting the appropriate strategy that aligns with your organization's requirements and limitations. Both concepts are built on the principles of **continuous integration** (**CI**), enhancing automation throughout the software release process.

Let us look further into these two critical practices that have revolutionized modern software delivery.

Continuous delivery

Continuous delivery is an approach where your software is always in a deployable state, but the actual deployment to production is triggered manually. Think of it as having your finger on the launch button; everything is ready to go, but you decide when to press it. It focuses on automating the delivery of software to ensure it is always in a deployable state. The primary goal is to make deployment a routine and predictable process.

In a continuous delivery pipeline:

- Each change is subjected to rigorous automated testing, including unit, integration, and end-to-end tests.

- While the software is ready for deployment at any time, an explicit manual approval step is typically required before deploying to production.

- Artifacts (builds, container images, etc.) are generated once and promoted across environments (e.g., dev, staging, production), as shown in the following figure:

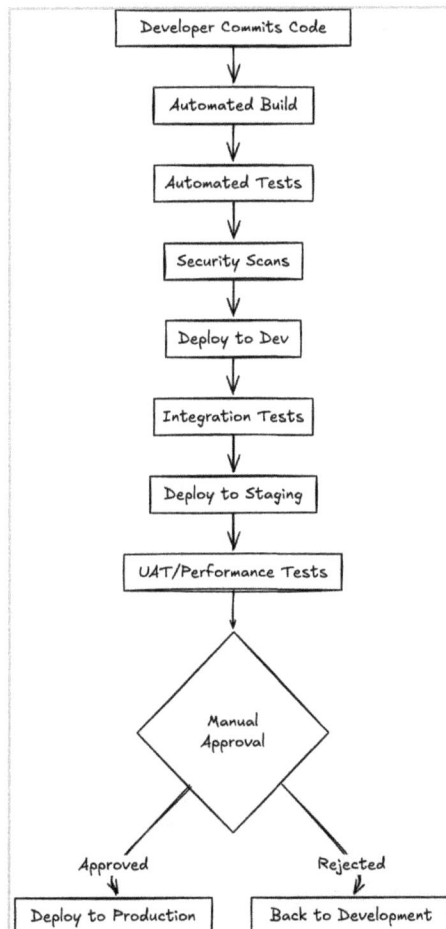

Figure 6.1: Continues delivery process

Figure 6.1 shows the continuous delivery process, where we can see a structured approach where code moves through various stages of validation before reaching production. Some of the key characteristics of continuous delivery are:

- **Frequent releases:** Teams aim to release frequently, even daily or weekly. This is achieved through the automated pipeline shown in *Figure 6.1*, which streamlines everything up to the manual approval stage.

- **High confidence:** Automated tests provide confidence that changes will not break existing functionality. Notice how the pipeline includes multiple testing stages (automated tests, integration tests, UAT/performance tests).

- **Environment consistency:** The same deployment artifacts are used across all environments to prevent discrepancies. The flow shows consistent progression through dev, staging, and production environments.

Now let us look at how continuous development is different from continuous deployment in the next section.

Continuous deployment

Continuous deployment takes automation one step further by eliminating the manual approval step entirely. Every change that passes the automated tests is automatically deployed to production. This approach minimizes time-to-market and ensures users receive updates as soon as they are ready, as shown in the following figure:

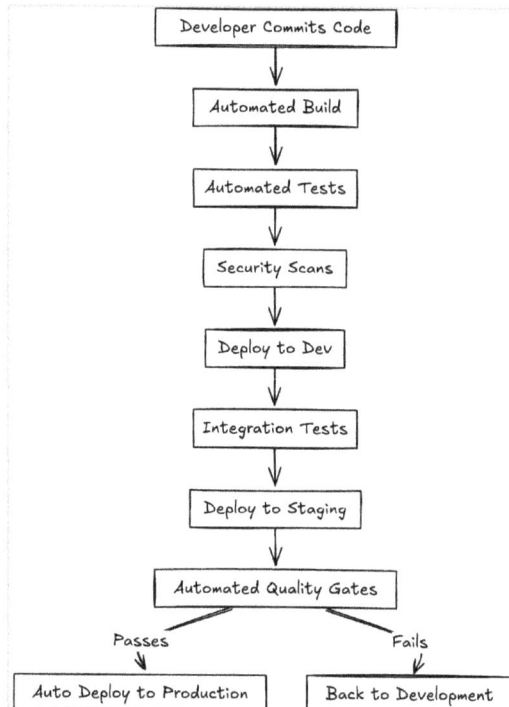

Figure 6.2: Continuous deployment

Figure 6.2 shows that, similarly, we see a fully automated process with no manual intervention points. The key characteristics of continuous deployment are:

- **No manual intervention:** Changes are deployed without human involvement. Notice how the pipeline flows directly from automated quality gates to production deployment.

- **Smaller, incremental releases:** Changes are deployed in small batches, reducing the risk of large-scale failures. This is facilitated by the continuous nature of the pipeline.

- **Immediate feedback:** Users and monitoring systems provide rapid feedback, enabling quick iterations. The automated quality gates ensure immediate validation of deployments.

Both continuous delivery and continuous deployment are innovative practices that enhance the software delivery process. continuous delivery guarantees that software is always ready for deployment with human intervention, while continuous deployment takes automation a step further by delivering changes immediately. By grasping their distinctions, advantages, and applicable scenarios, you can determine which method aligns best with your organization's objectives and limitations. Ultimately, the aim remains consistent: to provide users with high-quality software in an efficient and dependable manner.

Building deployment pipelines

A deployment pipeline is the backbone of any CD and continuous deployment process. It represents the sequence of stages that code changes go through, from development to production. A well-designed pipeline ensures that every change is tested, validated, and deployed consistently and reliably.

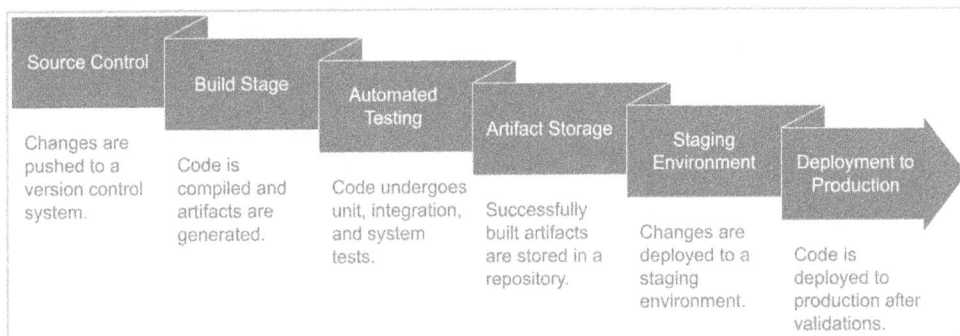

Figure 6.3: Deployment pipeline stages

Figure 6.3 showcases the deployment pipeline, which consists of several sequential stages that code changes must pass through before reaching production. Starting with source control, where developers push their changes to a version control system (like Git). This feeds into the build stage, where the code is compiled, and artifacts are generated—these could be executables, containers, or other deployable assets. The code then moves to automated testing, where it undergoes various tests (unit, integration, system) to verify functionality. Successfully tested code moves to artifact storage, where built artifacts are stored in a repository (like Artifactory or Nexus) for safekeeping and versioning. From there, changes are deployed to a staging environment for final validation in a production-like setting. Finally, after all validations are passed, the code reaches the deployment to production stage, where it is released to end users.

Each stage acts as a quality gate, ensuring only well-tested, verified code reaches production. If any stage fails, the pipeline stops, and developers are notified to fix issues before the code can progress further. This systematic approach helps maintain high-quality standards and reduces the risk of deploying faulty code to production.

Best practices for building deployment pipeline

Creating an effective deployment pipeline is essential for today's software delivery. These pipelines act as the automated route for code to transition from development to production, guaranteeing quality and reliability throughout the process. Although the exact implementation can differ depending on your organization's requirements, several best practices have become recognized as industry standards. These practices not only boost the reliability of your deployments but also improve team productivity and the overall quality of the software.

Here are the key best practices that organizations should keep in mind when constructing their deployment pipelines, along with practical examples for implementation:

- **Automation first:**
  - o   Implement automated dependency updates using tools like Dependabot.
  - o   Set up automated security scanning with tools like SonarQube and OWASP.
  - o   Use automated environment provisioning with IaC.

  As shown here, we can implement an automated GitHub Actions workflow that handles dependency updates and security scanning:

  ```
  # Example GitHub Actions workflow
  name: CI/CD Pipeline
  on: [push]
  jobs:
    build-test-deploy:
      runs-on: ubuntu-latest
      steps:
        - uses: actions/checkout@v2
        - name: Auto-dependency update
  ```

```
        uses: dependabot/dependabot-core@v3
    - name: Security scan
        uses: sonarsource/sonarqube-scan-action@master
```

- **Fail fast:**

  o Run critical tests early in the pipeline.

  o Implement pre-commit hooks for basic validations.

  o Use build timeouts to prevent hanging pipelines.

  Here is an example of a pre-commit hook implementation that ensures basic validations:

```bash
# Pre-commit hook example
#!/bin/bash
# Run linting
npm run lint || exit 1
# Run unit tests
npm run test:unit || exit 1
# Run security checks
npm audit || exit 1
```

- **Pipeline as code:**

  o Store pipeline configurations in version control.

  o Use templates for common pipeline patterns.

  o Implement reusable pipeline components.

  The following is an example of a Jenkins Shared Library implementation showing reusable pipeline components:

```groovy
// Jenkins Shared Library example
def call(Map config) {
    pipeline {
        agent any
        stages {
            stage('Build') {
                steps {
                    script {
                        dockerBuild(
                            registry: config.registry,
                            image: config.image
                        )
                    }
```

```
            }
          }
        }
      }
    }
```

- **Parallelization:**

    o   Run independent tests concurrently.

    o   Implement matrix builds for multi-platform testing.

    o   Use distributed build systems.

    The following example demonstrates parallel test execution in GitLab CI:

```
# GitLab CI parallel execution
test:
  parallel: 3
  script:
    - npm run test:split
  artifacts:
    reports:
      junit: junit.xml
```

- **Monitoring and logging:**

    o   Track pipeline performance metrics.

    o   Implement comprehensive error logging.

    o   Set up alerts for pipeline failures.

    The following is an example of implementing pipeline monitoring using Prometheus metrics:

```
# Pipeline monitoring implementation
from prometheus_client import Counter, Histogram

# Define metrics
pipeline_runs = Counter('pipeline_runs_
total', 'Total number of pipeline runs')
stage_duration = Histogram('stage_duration_
seconds', 'Duration of pipeline stages')

def monitor_pipeline_execution():
    pipeline_runs.inc()
    with stage_duration.time():
        execute_pipeline_stage()
```

Deployment strategies

Selecting the appropriate deployment strategy is essential for achieving seamless and dependable updates in production environments. In this section, we will examine three popular strategies: Blue/Green deployments, Canary deployments, and Rolling Updates. Each method presents distinct advantages and disadvantages, making them ideal for various situations.

Blue/Green deployment

Blue/Green deployment involves maintaining two identical environments: one (Blue) running the current version and the other (Green) hosting the new version. Traffic is switched from the Blue environment to the Green environment once the new version is validated.

Here is how it works:

1. Deploy the new version to the Green environment.

2. Perform tests and validations in the Green environment.

3. Redirect traffic from Blue to Green once satisfied.

4. Retain the Blue environment as a fallback option.

The pros are:

- **Instant rollback:** Switching traffic back to the Blue environment is fast and straightforward.

- **Minimal downtime:** The transition is seamless for users.

- **Safe testing:** The Green environment provides an isolated space for validation.

The cons are:

- **Infrastructure costs:** Requires duplicating environments, increasing resource usage.

- **Setup complexity:** Managing two environments can be operationally challenging.

Modern deployment strategies are increasingly implemented using IaC tools. For example, with Kubernetes and Istio, Blue/Green deployment can be achieved through declarative configurations:

```yaml
# Create two deployments: myapp-blue and myapp-green
apiVersion: networking.istio.io/v1beta1
kind: VirtualService
spec:
```

```
hosts:
- myapp.example.com
http:
- route:
  - destination:
      host: myapp-green
```

For Rolling Updates using Helm:

```
helm upgrade myapp ./myapp-chart --set image.tag=v2 --reuse-values
# Use --atomic and --wait for safe deployments
```

Canary deployment

Canary deployment gradually rolls out changes to a subset of users before a full release. This approach allows teams to monitor the impact of changes on a smaller scale.

Here is how it works:

1. Deploy the new version to a small percentage of users.

2. Monitor the system for errors, performance, and user feedback.

3. Gradually increase the user base if no issues are detected.

The pros are:

- **Risk mitigation:** Limits exposure to issues by starting with a small user base.

- **User feedback:** Provides early insights into user experience and system behavior.

- **Scalability:** Adjustments can be made incrementally.

The cons are:

- **Monitoring complexity:** Requires robust monitoring and observability tools.

- **Longer deployment times:** Full rollout takes longer compared to other methods.

Rolling Updates

Rolling Updates incrementally deploy new versions of software by replacing the existing instances in a controlled manner. Unlike Blue/Green or Canary deployments, this strategy does not require duplicate environments or traffic splitting but focuses on gradually updating the system to minimize risk.

Here is how it works:

1. A small percentage (e.g., one or two instances) of the current version is replaced with the new version.

2. These updated instances are monitored to ensure stability and correctness.

3. The process is repeated for the remaining instances until all are running the new version.

The pros are:

- **No additional environments:** Eliminates the need for duplicate infrastructure, reducing costs.

- **Minimal downtime:** Ensures service continuity as changes occur incrementally.

- **Quick recovery:** If an issue is detected, the rollout can be paused or reverted for only the affected instances.

The cons are:

- **Complexity in validation:** Testing and monitoring must occur at every step to avoid widespread issues.

- **Slower deployment:** Replacing instances incrementally takes more time than other strategies.

- **Stateful systems challenges:** Rolling Updates may cause compatibility issues in systems with tightly coupled components or shared state.

Feature flags and trunk-based development

Modern software teams strive to deliver features rapidly without compromising quality or stability. Two critical techniques that enable this agility are feature flags and trunk-based development. Both approaches focus on improving collaboration, reducing risk, and enabling faster releases.

Feature flags

Feature flags, also known as **feature toggles**, allow developers to control the visibility of features in the application without deploying new code. They decouple deployment from feature release, enabling partial or selective activation of features.

Here is how feature flags work:

1. Developers wrap feature-related code with a conditional flag (e.g., if statements or configuration settings).

2. Flags can be controlled dynamically via configuration files, API calls, or dashboards.

3. Features can be activated for specific user groups, regions, or timeframes.

The pros are:

- **Incremental rollouts:** Enables gradual exposure of new features, minimizing risk.

- **Quick rollbacks:** Deactivating a problematic feature is as simple as toggling the flag.

- **Testing in production:** Safely validate features in a real-world environment without affecting all users.

The cons are:

- **Technical debt:** Flags need careful management to avoid the accumulation of stale toggles.

- **Complexity:** Overuse can make the codebase harder to understand and maintain.

- **Performance overhead:** Flag checks can introduce slight runtime overhead.

Let us look at the use case.

Feature flags are ideal for beta testing, A/B experiments, and controlled feature rollouts, enabling teams to gather feedback and iterate quickly.

Code-level implementation

Here is how feature flags can be implemented at the code level:

```java
// Java Spring Boot example
@Value("${feature.enable-new-checkout:false}")
private boolean isNewCheckoutEnabled;

if (isNewCheckoutEnabled) {
    showNewCheckoutFlow();

}
```

Using LaunchDarkly SDK for dynamic control:

```java
LDClient ldClient = new LDClient("sdk-key");
boolean showFeature = ldClient.boolVariation("new-ui", user, false);
```

Integration with CI/CD pipelines:

```yaml
# GitHub Actions example
- name: Enable new feature
  run: launchdarkly-cli flag set new-ui true
```

This allows teams to toggle features without redeployment, enabling safer releases and easier rollbacks.

Trunk-based development

Trunk-based development is a source control strategy where all developers commit to a single main branch (trunk). Instead of long-lived feature branches, developers integrate small, frequent changes, ensuring the trunk is always in a deployable state.

Here how trunk-based development works:

1. Developers work on small changes that are completed within a day or two.

2. Changes are committed to the trunk after passing automated tests.

3. Feature flags are often used to isolate incomplete work.

The pros are:

- **Fast integration:** Frequent commits reduce merge conflicts and integration challenges.

- **Continuous deployment ready:** Ensures the trunk is always production ready.

- **Simplified workflow:** Eliminates the complexity of managing multiple branches.

The cons are:

- **Requires discipline:** Developers must maintain high-quality commits and test coverage.

- **Incomplete features:** Feature flags are essential to prevent partially implemented changes from being visible.

- **Limited flexibility:** It may not suit teams working on long-term or experimental features.

Use case: Trunk-based development is widely used in teams practicing continuous integration and continuous deployment, especially in fast-paced environments like startups or SaaS companies.

Hence, feature flags and trunk-based development create a strong partnership that enhances agility, safety, and speed in software delivery. Trunk-Based development encourages a smooth workflow with regular integrations, while feature flags help reduce the risks tied to deploying incomplete or experimental features. Together, they allow teams to deliver value to users confidently without compromising stability or causing delays.

By adopting these practices, organizations can foster a culture of continuous improvement and experimentation. Developers can implement changes more quickly, test in production safely, and easily adjust or revert based on immediate feedback. In the end, this collaboration speeds up innovation and enables teams to concentrate on providing high-quality software that effectively and reliably meets user needs.

Automating database schema changes

Automating database schema changes is a critical aspect of ensuring that applications and their underlying data structures evolve seamlessly. In the realm of **continuous delivery (CD)**, this practice ensures that database changes are synchronized with application updates, minimizing risks of failures or downtime.

This section delves into the importance of automating schema changes, best practices, and tools that facilitate the process.

Need for database automation

Databases are often the backbone of applications, and schema changes are inevitable as features evolve. Traditionally, manual database updates have been prone to errors and have been slow, and difficult to coordinate across environments. Automation addresses these challenges by:

- **Ensuring consistency:** Schema changes are applied consistently across all environments (development, staging, production).

- **Reducing risk:** Automated scripts reduce human errors that can corrupt data or break applications.

- **Speeding up deployments:** Changes are applied as part of the deployment pipeline, eliminating delays caused by manual processes.

- **Enabling rollbacks:** Automation supports controlled rollbacks if issues arise during schema changes.

The best practices for automating schema changes are as follows:

- **Version control for schema:**

    o   Always maintain database schema changes in version control alongside application code. This ensures traceability and collaborative visibility.

    o   Use migration files or scripts to define schema changes (e.g., adding tables, altering columns). Ensure these scripts are clear, descriptive, and auditable for review processes.

- **Idempotent scripts:** Write idempotent scripts, which can be executed multiple times without negative effects. This is particularly useful for retries or when deploying changes to multiple environments.

    o   **Example**: When creating a table, include checks such as IF NOT EXISTS to avoid redundant errors if the table already exists.

- **Backward compatibility:** Design schema changes to be backward-compatible, allowing the application to continue functioning even during updates. This avoids downtime or user disruptions.

    o   **Example 1**: Instead of removing a column immediately, add the new column in one release and phase out the old column in a later release.

    o   **Example 2**: When renaming fields, use aliasing or transitional mappings.

- **Automated testing for schema:** Validate schema changes with robust automated tests before production deployment. These tests can include:

    o   Checking for syntax errors in migration scripts.

    o   Running migrations in a staging environment to simulate production behavior.

o Verifying data integrity and ensuring application compatibility through integration and SQL-based test cases.

- **Gradual rollouts:**

    o Implement strategies like Blue/Green or Canary deployments for schema updates. This approach involves deploying changes incrementally to a subset of database nodes before applying them globally.

    o Combine gradual rollouts with real-time monitoring tools to detect issues early, such as performance degradation or unexpected application errors.

Several tools simplify automating database schema changes, integrating seamlessly with CI/CD pipelines:

- **Flyway:** A lightweight tool for version-controlled migrations with support for multiple databases. Flyway applies migration scripts in a sequential order to ensure consistency across environments.

- **Liquibase:** A robust open-source tool that allows you to track, version, and deploy database changes. It offers features like database diff generation and rollback scripts.

- **Alembic:** A Python-based tool designed for SQLAlchemy applications, making it ideal for Python-centric environments.

- **Rails ActiveRecord migrations:** Built into Ruby on Rails, enabling seamless database changes within the Rails ecosystem.

- **Entity framework migrations:** Used in .NET environments to manage schema updates with a focus on **object-relational mapping** (**ORM**).

These tools provide features like versioning, rollbacks, and compatibility checks, making them indispensable for modern software teams. By adhering to best practices and leveraging the right tools, teams can ensure consistency, reduce risks, and maintain high application uptime. When implemented correctly, automated schema management enables developers to focus on innovation while ensuring the stability and scalability of their systems.

Here is how to integrate database migrations into your CI/CD pipeline:

```
# GitHub Actions with Flyway
jobs:
  flyway-migrate:
    runs-on: ubuntu-latest
    steps:
      - uses: actions/checkout@v2
      - name: Flyway Migration
```

```
run: |
  docker run --rm -v $(pwd)/sql:/flyway/sql flyway/flyway \
    -url=jdbc:mysql://db:3306/app \
    -user=root \
    -password=secret migrate
```

For rollback capability:

```
# Maintain versioned migration files
V1__init.sql  # Forward migration
U1__init.sql  # Undo migration


# Enable rollback support
flyway.undoEnabled=true
```

This automation ensures database changes are version-controlled and tested before production deployment.

Environment promotion and artifact management

Effective environment promotion and artifact management are integral to maintaining a reliable and repeatable CD process. These practices ensure that artifacts, such as build outputs, configuration files, and dependencies, are managed systematically and deployed consistently across environments, from development to production.

Environment promotion

Environment promotion involves moving software artifacts through predefined stages, development, staging, testing, and production based on validation criteria. Key considerations include:

- **Stage gates:** Define clear criteria for promoting artifacts between environments, such as passing tests or meeting performance benchmarks.

- **Immutable artifacts:** Once an artifact is built, ensure it remains unchanged throughout its lifecycle to guarantee consistency between environments.

- **Automated promotion:** Use CI/CD pipelines to automate the promotion process, minimizing manual intervention and reducing the risk of errors.

The benefits are:

- Ensures consistent deployments across environments.

- Streamlines the release process with predictable results.

- Reduces the chances of *it works on my machine* issues.

Artifact management

Artifact management focuses on storing, versioning, and distributing software artifacts efficiently. A robust artifact management strategy includes:

- **Centralized storage:** Use artifact repositories like JFrog Artifactory, Nexus Repository, or AWS CodeArtifact to store artifacts securely and provide easy access.

- **Version control:** Assign unique version identifiers to artifacts to track changes and ensure reproducibility.

- **Retention policies:** Define policies to retain or clean up artifacts based on their age or usage to optimize storage.

The benefits are:

- Simplifies dependency management.

- Improves the traceability and auditability of releases.

- Enhances collaboration among teams by providing a single source of truth for artifacts.

Both environment promotion and artifact management are the backbone of reliable software delivery. By adopting structured workflows, leveraging specialized tools, and adhering to best practices, teams can ensure seamless transitions between environments and maintain a high level of confidence in their releases. These strategies not only enhance efficiency but also play a crucial role in maintaining the stability and integrity of production systems.

Rollback strategies

Rollback strategies are essential for ensuring that if a deployment fails, you can quickly and safely revert to a stable state. In modern CD pipelines, the ability to rollback is a critical component of minimizing downtime and maintaining application reliability.

Let us explore several rollback strategies and how they can be effectively implemented in a CD environment:

- **Rollback to previous artifact version:** One of the most straightforward rollback strategies is reverting to a previous, stable version of the application. This is particularly useful when the newly deployed version introduces critical bugs or performance issues.

    o **How it works:**

        - Every deployment creates an artifact (e.g., a Docker image, a JAR file, or a binary).

        - In case of failure, the system can automatically or manually deploy the previous version of the artifact to the same environment.

o **Example**: If you are using a containerized deployment, you might maintain a version history of Docker images. When a deployment fails, you can roll back by redeploying the previous image.

o **The pros are**:

■ Simple to implement, especially with artifact management tools (e.g., Nexus, Artifactory).

■ Provides a reliable and quick recovery method.

o **Con**: May not be suitable if the failure is related to database migrations or state changes, as rolling back the code without addressing data changes can cause inconsistencies.

- **Database rollbacks:** When deployments include database schema changes (e.g., migrations), rolling back the code alone might not be enough. A rollback, in this case, must also account for reverting database changes, such as undoing schema migrations or restoring data.

o **How it works**:

■ **Database versioning**: Tools like Flyway or Liquibase allow you to version database changes. If a deployment fails, you can rollback the database schema to its previous state using the same tool.

■ **Data backups**: Periodically back up critical data before running migrations. In case of failure, restore the database from the backup.

o **Example**: If you are deploying an application with a database schema change, and the deployment causes issues, you can use Flyway to undo the migration or restore from a backup.

o **The pros are**:

■ Ensures the integrity of the application's data layer.

■ Allows for both code and data state rollback.

o **The cons are**:

■ Database rollbacks can be complex and risky, especially with large or highly interconnected databases.

■ Restoration from backups may lead to data loss if not carefully managed.

- **Canary deployments and Blue/Green deployments:** These deployment strategies are designed for safe, gradual rollouts. If the new version of the application causes issues, the system can easily roll back by reverting traffic to the stable version.

o **How it works**:

- **Canary**: Traffic is routed in phases to the new version, with automated checks to detect problems (e.g., error rates, latency).

- **Blue/Green**: After testing the Green environment, the traffic is switched from Blue to Green. If there is an issue, traffic can be switched back to Blue instantly.

o **Example**: In a Canary deployment, you could route 10% of the traffic to the new version. If no issues are detected after a set period, you increase the traffic percentage until 100% of users are on the new version.

o **The pros are**:

- Reduces risk by minimizing the exposure of the new version.

- Quick and easy to switch back to the stable environment.

o **The cons are**:

- Requires infrastructure to support multiple environments.

- May involve more complexity in managing traffic routing and monitoring.

- **Feature flags (Feature Toggles):** Feature flags allow you to control which features are enabled in the deployed application without needing to redeploy the entire application. This gives you fine-grained control over which parts of the application are exposed to users.

o **How it works**:

- Feature flags can be implemented to hide or expose new features in the application.

- If a feature causes issues, you can disable the flag to turn off the feature without needing to roll back the entire deployment.

o **Example**: If a new feature introduced in the deployment causes errors, you could use a feature flag to disable that feature while keeping the rest of the application functional.

o **The pros are**:

- Provides flexibility without requiring full application rollbacks.

- Can be used for partial rollbacks, targeting specific users or features.

o **The cons are**:

- Managing and maintaining feature flags can become complex over time.

- Risks introducing feature flag debt, where flags linger long after the feature is no longer needed.

- **Automated health checks and rollback triggers:** Automated health checks are an essential part of many rollback strategies. By continuously monitoring the system's health after a deployment, you can automate the rollback process if certain conditions are met (e.g., high error rates, slow response times).

  o **How it works:**

    ▪ Health checks can monitor system performance, error rates, and other key metrics.

    ▪ If a failure threshold is exceeded (e.g., 5% error rate), the deployment pipeline automatically triggers a rollback.

  o **Example:** After deploying a new version of the application, health checks might automatically monitor for 5xx errors or slow response times. If these metrics exceed a threshold, the system can automatically roll back to the previous version.

    ```
    # Helm rollback in pipeline
    helm upgrade myapp ./chart --install || helm rollback myapp


    # Kubernetes deployment rollback
    kubectl rollout undo deployment/myapp


    # Database rollback with Liquibase
    liquibase rollbackCount 1 \
        --url="jdbc:mysql://..." \
        --username=user \
        --password=pass
    ```

    These commands can be integrated into CI/CD pipelines to automatically revert failed deployments, ensuring minimal downtime.

  o **The pros are:**

    ▪ Reduces the need for manual intervention, leading to faster recovery.

    ▪ Provides continuous monitoring and quick reaction to deployment failures.

  o **The cons are:**

    ▪ Requires robust health checks and monitoring in place.

    ▪ It might not detect all types of failures (e.g., UI issues that do not trigger backend errors).

Whether you are reverting to a previous version of your application, undoing database changes, or using feature flags , having well-defined rollback strategies will help ensure that your deployments are resilient and can be quickly reversed in the event of failure. By incorporating these strategies into your CD pipeline, you can minimize downtime, reduce the impact of deployment failures, and maintain a seamless user experience.

Observability in CD

Observability in CD extends beyond conventional monitoring by emphasizing the understanding of a system's internal states through its external outputs. It empowers teams to proactively identify, analyze, and resolve issues within complex and dynamic deployment environments. Observability is especially crucial in CD pipelines, where rapid and frequent deployments can lead to unforeseen behaviors.

At its essence, observability in CD relies on three primary signals: metrics, logs, and traces. Metrics deliver quantitative insights into system performance, including latency, error rates, and throughput. Logs provide comprehensive records of events and interactions within the system, assisting teams in pinpointing specific failure points or anomalies. Traces enhance this understanding by illustrating the flow of requests across distributed systems, granting end-to-end visibility into system behavior.

The ever-changing nature of CD pipelines necessitates that observability systems are crafted for real-time insights. When a new deployment occurs, observability tools can quickly detect shifts in application behavior or performance. For example, if a recent release results in higher error rates or latency, observability systems can identify the impacted services and aid in diagnosing root causes. This capability is particularly vital in intricate systems, where failures are seldom isolated and often affect multiple components.

Contemporary observability tools, such as OpenTelemetry, Datadog, and Honeycomb, are increasingly being integrated into CD pipelines to deliver actionable insights. These tools facilitate automated alerting, anomaly detection, and correlation analysis, enabling teams to address issues promptly. Additionally, by capturing historical trends and deployment data, observability systems support continuous improvement, assisting teams in refining deployment practices and enhancing system resilience.

In summary, observability is a cornerstone of effective continuous delivery, providing the visibility needed to ensure that deployments are safe, reliable, and efficient. By embedding observability practices into CD pipelines, teams can minimize downtime, enhance user experience, and build confidence in their ability to deploy changes at speed.

Here is how to implement observability in practice:

```yaml
# Prometheus setup (values.yaml for Helm)
prometheus:
  prometheusSpec:
    externalLabels:
      cluster: prod
    serviceMonitorSelector:
```

```
    matchLabels:
        team: devops
```

Creating Grafana dashboards with Jsonnet:

```
panels:
  - title: Deployment Success Rate
    targets:
      - expr: sum(increase(deployment_success_total[5m])) by (app)
```

Distributed tracing with Spring Boot:

```
spring:
  sleuth:
    sampler:
      probability: 1.0
  zipkin:
    base-url: http://jaeger-collector:9411
```

Security considerations in deployments

Security is crucial in CD environments where changes occur regularly and may introduce vulnerabilities. To achieve secure deployments, it is important to adopt a proactive and systematic approach to identify, mitigate, and monitor potential risks throughout the pipeline. This section highlights key security considerations for deployments and effective strategies to address them:

- **Secure the deployment pipeline:** The deployment pipeline is the backbone of CD and must be protected against unauthorized access and potential attacks. Use **role-based access control (RBAC)** to restrict who can modify or trigger deployments. Secrets such as API keys, database credentials, and private certificates should be encrypted and managed with tools like HashiCorp Vault or AWS Secrets Manager. To maintain transparency and accountability, audit pipeline actions by logging all activities, including deployment triggers and configuration changes. Regular reviews of these logs can help identify and mitigate security risks.

- **Validate artifacts:** Artifacts deployed to production should always be verified to ensure their integrity and authenticity. Signing artifacts using cryptographic methods, such as Docker Content Trust or Sigstore, prevents tampering. Additionally, supply chain security practices, like verifying third-party dependencies with tools such as SLSA, help protect against vulnerabilities introduced through external libraries. Before deployment, always validate checksums of artifacts to detect corruption or unauthorized changes.

- **Secure deployment configurations:** Configurations often contain sensitive information, making them a prime target for attackers. Deployments should follow best practices, such as isolating environments (development, staging, production) to minimize the blast radius of a potential breach. Embrace immutable infrastructure tools like Terraform or Kubernetes to enforce secure and consistent configurations across environments. Avoid hardcoding secrets into configuration files; instead, leverage secrets management tools to inject sensitive data securely during runtime.

- **Continuous security testing:** Security testing should be an integral part of the deployment process to identify vulnerabilities before they reach production. **Static Application Security Testing (SAST)** tools like SonarQube analyze source code for security issues early in the development cycle. **Dynamic Application Security Testing (DAST)** simulates attacks on the running application to identify vulnerabilities like SQL injection or cross-site scripting. For containerized applications, use tools like Trivy or Aqua to scan container images for vulnerabilities before deploying them.

- **Secure rollback and recovery:** Rollbacks are a critical part of deployment strategies but must also be handled securely. Ensure that rolling back does not reintroduce outdated vulnerabilities or misconfigurations. Regular backups of critical data and configurations should be maintained, with tested recovery procedures to ensure seamless restoration in case of failure or compromise. After a rollback, conduct scans to confirm the environment's integrity and ensure that no residual vulnerabilities remain.

- **Monitor and respond to threats:** Post-deployment security requires continuous monitoring and rapid response capabilities. Real-time monitoring tools like Prometheus, Splunk, or Datadog help track system behavior and detect anomalies. Implement **intrusion detection and prevention systems (IDS/IPS)** to identify and block suspicious activities. Additionally, having a clear incident response plan with defined roles and procedures ensures that your team can quickly address and mitigate security threats as they arise.

- **Ensure compliance:** For organizations in regulated industries, deployments must comply with legal and industry standards such as GDPR, HIPAA, or ISO 27001. Compliance requires maintaining detailed audit trails of deployment activities and ensuring secure data-handling practices, such as encryption for data in transit and at rest. Tools like **Open Policy Agent (OPA)** or Kyverno can enforce compliance policies in deployment pipelines, ensuring adherence to security and privacy standards.

Security considerations are crucial for protecting deployments in a continuous delivery environment. By focusing on the pipeline, validating artifacts, securing configurations, and incorporating continuous security testing, teams can establish a strong defense against vulnerabilities. Additionally, monitoring and compliance play a key role in enhancing security by ensuring that issues are identified and resolved quickly while meeting legal and industry standards. By proactively integrating these practices into the deployment process, organizations can deliver software securely, quickly, and with confidence.

CD metrics and KPIs

Measuring the success of CD is essential to ensure the process is delivering value effectively. Metrics and **key performance indicators** (**KPIs**) provide data-driven insights into the health, efficiency, and reliability of the CD pipeline.

These measurements help identify bottlenecks, optimize workflows, and maintain a high level of quality in deployments:

- **Deployment frequency:** This metric measures how often changes are successfully deployed to production. High deployment frequency indicates that the pipeline is efficient, and teams can deliver value rapidly. It reflects the maturity of automation and confidence in the process.

- **Lead time for changes:** Lead time tracks the duration between committing code and deploying it to production. Shorter lead times indicate streamlined processes, enabling faster delivery of features and bug fixes while maintaining responsiveness to customer needs.

- **Change failure rate (CFR):** CFR measures the percentage of deployments that lead to failures requiring remediation, such as rollbacks or patches. A low CFR signals robust testing and validation processes, while a high CFR highlights areas for improvement in pre-deployment checks.

- **MTTR:** MTTR calculates the average time taken to restore services after a deployment-related failure. Lower MTTR demonstrates a team's ability to detect and address issues quickly, minimizing user impact and downtime.

- **Pipeline efficiency:** Pipeline efficiency measures the ratio of time spent in productive activities (e.g., building, testing, deploying) versus idle or waiting time. High efficiency ensures faster and more predictable releases, reducing wasted time and resources.

- **Deployment success rate:** This KPI reflects the percentage of deployments completed without errors. A high success rate indicates a stable and reliable pipeline, reducing risks associated with production releases.

- **Business impact metrics:** Metrics like user engagement, revenue growth, or reduced churn help connect CD performance to business outcomes. These measurements provide a broader perspective, ensuring the pipeline supports overall organizational goals.

Tracking CD metrics and KPIs enables teams to assess performance, detect inefficiencies, and continuously improve their processes. By focusing on deployment frequency, lead time, and recovery metrics alongside business outcomes, organizations can ensure their CD pipelines are aligned with both technical excellence and strategic objectives.

Compliance and auditing in CD pipelines

Compliance and auditing are essential components of CD, especially for organizations operating in regulated industries. They ensure adherence to legal, security, and industry standards, such as GDPR, HIPAA, PCI DSS, and ISO 27001, while maintaining transparency and accountability throughout the deployment process. Incorporating compliance into CD pipelines minimizes risks, avoids penalties, and fosters customer trust.

Organizations can achieve this through several key approaches, as follows:

- **Automating policy enforcement:** Automated tools like OPA and Kyverno can be integrated into CD pipelines to enforce compliance policies. These tools validate configurations, access controls, and deployment practices to ensure they align with organizational standards before changes are approved for release.

- **Maintaining audit trails:** Comprehensive audit trails record every action in the pipeline, such as who triggered a deployment, what changes were made, and when. Tools like Jenkins, GitLab, and Kubernetes provide detailed logs that support internal reviews and external audits. Regular log reviews help identify suspicious activity and improve accountability.

- **Securing sensitive data:** Data encryption (both in transit and at rest) and proper secrets management are vital to ensure compliance with data protection regulations. Tools like HashiCorp Vault or AWS Secrets Manager secure sensitive credentials and access tokens, reducing the risk of exposure.

- **Segregation of duties (SoD):** Enforcing separation between roles, such as developers, testers, and operators, prevents conflicts of interest and unauthorized changes. RBAC mechanisms in CI/CD tools ensure that only authorized personnel can approve or deploy changes to production environments.

- **Periodic compliance reviews:** Regular compliance audits assess the effectiveness of security and governance practices in the pipeline. These reviews ensure ongoing adherence to regulations and help prepare for external audits by providing documented evidence of compliance efforts.

- **Retaining artifacts and logs:** Regulations often require retaining build artifacts, logs, and deployment records for a specified period. Artifact repositories like Nexus or JFrog Artifactory, combined with centralized log management tools, ensure this data is securely stored and easily retrievable when needed.

- **Integrating compliance testing:** Compliance testing ensures that deployments meet regulatory and organizational requirements. Automated checks for security vulnerabilities, license compliance, and data privacy regulations can be built into the pipeline using tools like SonarQube or Checkmarx.

By automating policy enforcement, securing sensitive data, and maintaining detailed records, organizations can seamlessly integrate compliance into their workflows. These practices not only reduce the risk of non-compliance but also build a strong foundation of trust and accountability for all stakeholders.

Conclusion

This chapter explored the distinction between continuous delivery and continuous deployment, highlighting their shared goal of streamlining software releases while differing in automation levels. We examined how to build robust deployment pipelines with integrated testing and artifact management, and compared deployment strategies like Blue/Green, Canary, and Rolling Updates for mitigating risks. Feature flags and trunk-based development demonstrated how to enable faster iterations while maintaining stability.

We addressed critical aspects, including automating database schema changes, environment promotion workflows, and implementing effective rollback strategies. The chapter emphasized observability practices for real-time system insights, security considerations to protect pipelines, and metrics like deployment frequency and MTTR to measure effectiveness. Finally, we explored compliance and auditing requirements for regulated environments.

By mastering these practices, organizations can deliver software with confidence, speed, and reliability, achieving the balance between rapid innovation and operational stability needed for modern software delivery.

In the next chapter, we will understand configuration management, a critical complement to the deployment practices covered here. We will examine tools like Ansible, Puppet, and Chef that ensure consistency across environments. We will cover configuration management principles, creating idempotent infrastructure definitions, managing secrets securely, and version controlling configuration data. We will learn strategies for testing configuration code, detecting configuration drift, and integrating these practices with CI/CD pipelines. Additionally, we will address compliance and security considerations specific to configuration management. This knowledge will further strengthen your ability to maintain reliable, secure, and consistent environments throughout your delivery pipeline.

CHAPTER 7

Configuration Management

Introduction

Configuration management (CM) is a practice in modern DevOps that enables teams to maintain consistency and reliability across environments, from development to production. Automating the management of configurations eliminates manual errors, accelerates deployments, and ensures that systems behave predictably as they scale. At its core, CM relies on principles like idempotency and convergence to ensure that desired states are applied consistently, regardless of the initial conditions.

This chapter explores the fundamentals of CM and its implementation using tools like Ansible, Puppet, and Chef. You will learn how to manage configurations at scale, securely handle secrets, version control configuration data, and test configuration code for reliability. We will also address detecting and remediating configuration drift and integrating these practices into CI/CD pipelines. Through a hands-on exercise, you will create an Ansible playbook to configure a multi-node application, gaining practical insights into automating system and application setup. This knowledge will equip you to build reliable, scalable, and secure systems in your DevOps journey.

Structure

The chapter covers the following topics:

- Principles of configuration management

- Ansible
- Puppet
- Chef
- Idempotency and convergence
- Managing secrets
- Version controlling configuration data
- Testing configuration management code
- Detecting and remediating configuration drift
- Integrating with CI/CD pipelines
- Compliance and security

Objectives

By the end of this chapter, we will gain comprehensive knowledge of CM principles and their critical role in modern DevOps practices. We will become proficient in implementing and comparing major CM tools, including Ansible, Puppet, and Chef while mastering core concepts like idempotency and convergence to ensure consistent system states across environments.

The chapter will equip us with practical skills for securely managing sensitive information, applying version control to configuration data, and designing effective testing frameworks for configuration code. We will learn strategies to detect and remediate configuration drift, integrate CM into CI/CD pipelines, and enforce compliance and security standards through automation. Through hands-on exercises, we will develop the ability to create and deploy Ansible playbooks for multi-node applications, gaining valuable experience in automating system and application configuration that will serve as a foundation for building reliable, scalable, and secure systems throughout your DevOps journey.

Principles of configuration management

This section will help you understand the fundamental principle of CM and explain why CM is important in modern DevOps practices. We will also identify key challenges that CM addresses. However, before this, let us first understand what CM is in the next subsection.

Introduction to configuration management

Imagine you are managing a chain of restaurants. Each location must have identical kitchen setups, cooking procedures, and quality standards. CM in IT works similarly, ensuring all servers and systems follow the same recipe for setup and maintenance.

In technical terms, CM is the process of systematically handling changes to ensure consistency and reliability in systems, applications, and environments. It automates the management of infrastructure and application configurations to reduce errors, enhance scalability, and improve operational efficiency.

In simpler terms:

- It is about making sure all systems are configured correctly and identically.

- If something changes, those changes are tracked and managed efficiently.

The need for CM arrives primarily from the following need of the modern dynamic environment:

- **Scaling:** Adding new servers or containers to handle increased load.

- **Frequent deployments:** CI/CD pipelines deploying code multiple times a day.

- **Complexity:** Managing multiple environments (development, staging, production) across diverse platforms.

In the absence of proper configuration management, organizations face significant operational challenges. Manual processes introduce a high risk of errors and inconsistencies across systems, while the phenomenon of configuration drift makes troubleshooting increasingly complex and time-consuming. Furthermore, any attempts to scale up systems require substantial manual effort, creating bottlenecks and inefficiencies in the deployment process. These issues collectively highlight the critical importance of implementing robust configuration management practices.

Key principles of configuration management

The following are some of the key principles of configuration management:

- **Consistency and standardization:** Consistency and standardization form the bedrock of effective configuration management. At its core, this principle ensures that all systems and environments maintain identical configurations, establishing a single source of truth across the infrastructure. For instance, when deploying applications, using a unified script or playbook for both staging and production environments guarantees that all environments remain perfectly aligned, eliminating the *it works on my machine* syndrome that often plagues development teams.

- **Automation:** Automation stands as a transformative principle in configuration management, fundamentally changing how organizations handle infrastructure. By leveraging tools like Ansible, Puppet, and Chef, teams can automate repetitive tasks such as software installation and network configuration. This automation not only accelerates deployment processes but also significantly reduces human error, leading to more reliable and consistent system configurations. The impact is particularly noticeable in large-scale deployments, where manual configuration would be both time-consuming and error prone.

- **Idempotency:** Idempotency represents a crucial concept in configuration management where repeated application of the same configuration should yield identical results. This principle ensures that configuration tasks are safe to repeat without causing unintended side effects. For example, when a configuration script runs to install a specific software package, it should intelligently check if the package is already present and only proceed with installation if necessary. This approach provides stability and predictability in configuration management processes.

- **Version control:** Version control brings software development best practices to configuration management by treating configuration files as code. This approach involves storing all configuration files in version control systems like Git, creating a comprehensive history of changes. This historical record proves invaluable when troubleshooting issues, as teams can easily track changes and roll back to previous stable configurations if problems arise. The ability to maintain this detailed change history while collaborating across teams makes version control an indispensable part of configuration management.

- **Reusability:** The principle of reusability emphasizes creating modular, flexible configuration components that can be applied across multiple projects or environments. By developing reusable modules or roles, organizations can significantly reduce duplication of effort and maintain consistency across their infrastructure. For instance, a well-designed configuration module for setting up a web server can be reused across different applications and projects, saving time while ensuring standardization.

- **Detecting and preventing configuration drift:** Configuration drift management focuses on maintaining system stability by preventing unplanned deviations from the desired state. This principle acknowledges that systems naturally tend to diverge from their intended configuration over time due to manual changes, updates, or environmental factors. Modern configuration management tools address this challenge by continuously monitoring systems and automatically correcting any detected deviations, ensuring long-term stability and reliability.

- **Security and compliance:** Security and compliance integration in configuration management ensures that all systems consistently meet organizational and regulatory security standards. This principle goes beyond simple security configurations to encompass continuous monitoring and enforcement of security policies. It involves automatically implementing security measures such as port management, package updates, and access controls across all systems, making security an integral part of the configuration management process rather than an afterthought.

Hence, CM is essential for maintaining consistency, reducing errors, and enabling scalability in dynamic IT environments. By following the principles of consistency, automation, idempotency, version control, reusability, drift detection, and security, organizations can effectively manage complex infrastructures.

Ansible

Configuration management is an essential aspect of modern IT operations, ensuring consistency and automation across environments. Ansible stands out as a leading tool in this domain due to its simplicity, agentless architecture, and versatility. Designed for automation, Ansible helps manage infrastructure, deploy applications, and orchestrate complex workflows with minimal effort. Unlike traditional methods requiring manual intervention or complex configurations, Ansible uses straightforward YAML-based playbooks, making it accessible and powerful for administrators and developers alike.

At its core, Ansible operates by connecting to target systems (referred to as hosts) over SSH and executing instructions to bring those systems into a desired state. Whether installing software, managing users, or deploying applications, Ansible's modular architecture makes it a go-to choice for organizations of all sizes. This section dives into the three fundamental components of Ansible: playbooks, roles, and modules, offering practical insights and examples to demonstrate their utility.

Let us now talk about the core concepts of Ansible.

Playbooks

Playbooks are the cornerstone of Ansible automation. They define a series of tasks to be executed on specified hosts. Written in YAML, playbooks provide a human-readable yet machine-executable way to describe configurations and workflows.

The following is an Ansible playbook example of installing and configuring NGINX:

```yaml
# File: nginx_setup.yml
- name: Install and configure Nginx
  hosts: web_servers
  become: yes  # Run tasks with elevated privileges
  tasks:
    - name: Install Nginx
      apt:
        name: nginx
        state: present
      notify: Restart Nginx

    - name: Ensure Nginx is running
      service:
        name: nginx
        state: started
        enabled: true
```

```
handlers:
  - name: Restart Nginx
    service:
      name: nginx
      state: restarted
```

This example showcases how a single playbook can automate the installation and configuration of NGINX across multiple servers. Running this playbook ensures that NGINX is consistently installed and operational. The playbook has three important sub-components as well:

- **Tasks:** Defined under the tasks section, each task specifies an action, such as installing software or starting a service.

- **Handlers:** Used for actions triggered by changes, such as restarting a service after a configuration change.

- **Inventory integration:** The host field maps to groups or individual systems in the inventory file.

Roles

Roles enable the modularization and reuse of Ansible configurations. They provide a structured approach to organizing tasks, variables, templates, and other components required for specific functionality. The following is a directory structure of an Ansible role:

```
my_role/
├── tasks/
│   └── main.yml          # Defines the tasks
├── templates/
│   └── nginx.conf.j2     # Jinja2 template for Nginx configuration
├── vars/
│   └── main.yml          # Default variables
├── handlers/
│   └── main.yml          # Handlers for notifications
├── defaults/
│   └── main.yml          # Default variables
├── meta/
│   └── main.yml          # Metadata about the role
```

For example, let us look at a basic NGINX web server role:

```
# tasks/main.yml
- name: Install nginx
```

```
    apt:
      name: nginx
      state: present
    become: true

  - name: Configure nginx
    template:
      src: nginx.conf.j2
      dest: /etc/nginx/nginx.conf
    notify: restart nginx

  # templates/nginx.conf.j2
  server {
      listen {{ nginx_port }};
      server_name {{ server_name }};
      root {{ web_root }};

      location / {
          index index.html;
      }
  }

  # defaults/main.yml
  nginx_port: 80
  server_name: example.com
  web_root: /var/www/html

  # handlers/main.yml
  - name: restart nginx
    service:
      name: nginx
      state: restarted
```

You can use this role as follows:

```
  - hosts: webservers
    roles:
      - nginx_role
```

The advantages of an Ansible role are:

- **Reusability:** Roles can be reused across different projects and environments.

- **Organization:** Helps manage complex configurations by breaking them into smaller, manageable components.

- **Scalability:** Simplifies scaling configurations to multiple hosts or environments.

Modules

Modules are Ansible's workhorses. These small programs execute specific tasks, such as managing packages, users, files, or services. Modules are designed to be idempotent, ensuring the desired state without making unnecessary changes. Some of the commonly used modules are:

- **apt or yum:** Manage package installations.

- **service:** Start, stop, or restart services.

- **file:** Manage files and directories.

- **user:** This command adds or removes users.

- **template:** Deploy dynamically rendered configuration files.

Let us take an example of a **file** module:

```
- name: Manage directories
  hosts: all
  tasks:
    - name: Create a directory
      file:
        path: /var/www/html
        state: directory
        mode: '0755'

    - name: Remove a file
      file:
        path: /var/www/html/old_file.txt
        state: absent
```

Similarly, let us take an example of a template module where the template module generates configuration files dynamically using Jinja2 templates:

- **Create a template file (templates/nginx.conf.j2):**
```
server {
    listen {{ nginx_port }};
```

```
    server_name {{ nginx_server_name }};
    root {{ nginx_root }};
}
```

- **Use the template in a playbook:**

```
- name: Deploy Nginx configuration
  hosts: web_servers
  tasks:
    - name: Upload Nginx config
      template:
        src: templates/nginx.conf.j2
        dest: /etc/nginx/nginx.conf
      notify: Restart Nginx

  handlers:
    - name: Restart Nginx
      service:
        name: nginx
        state: restarted
```

- **Define variable:**

```
nginx_port: 80
nginx_server_name: example.com
nginx_root: /var/www/html
```

In conclusion, Ansible's playbooks, roles, and modules empower organizations to automate infrastructure management effectively. Playbooks provide a clear way to define tasks, roles bring reusability and organization, and modules perform granular actions with precision.

Puppet

Puppet is a robust configuration management tool designed to automate the provisioning, configuration, and management of infrastructure. By using Puppet, organizations can ensure that systems remain consistent, scalable, and compliant across diverse environments. Puppet employs a declarative approach, where administrators define the desired system state, and Puppet ensures that state is achieved and maintained.

This section explores three critical components of Puppet, manifests, modules, and Hiera, that form the foundation for its functionality. Practical examples are included to illustrate how these components work together to manage infrastructure efficiently.

Manifests

Manifests are the primary building blocks in Puppet. They are written in Puppet's **domain-specific language** (**DSL**) and define the desired state of resources, such as packages, services, files, and users. The following is an example of installing and managing NGINX using Puppet manifests:

```
# Basic manifest example (webserver.pp)
package { 'nginx':
  ensure => 'installed',
}

service { 'nginx':
  ensure  => 'running',
  enable  => true,
  require => Package['nginx'],
}

file { '/etc/nginx/nginx.conf':
  ensure  => 'present',
  source  => 'puppet:///modules/nginx/nginx.conf',
  notify  => Service['nginx'],
  require => Package['nginx'],
}
```

The key features to note in the manifests are:

- **Declarative syntax:** Specify the desired state without procedural instructions.

- **Resource types:** Manage system components like packages, services, and files.

- **Dependency management:** Use attributes like subscribe and require defining dependencies between resources.

Modules

Modules are self-contained collections of manifests and related files that encapsulate specific functionality. They help organize Puppet code and enable reuse across multiple environments. The structure of a **puppet** module is:

```
apache/
├── manifests/
│   └── init.pp        # Main manifest defining the module
├── files/
```

```
|   └─ custom.html    # Static files to be managed
├─ templates/
|   └─ vhost.conf.erb  # ERB templates for dynamic files
├─ examples/
|   └─ init.pp        # Example usage of the module
├─ metadata.json      # Metadata describing the module
```

You can create a module as follows:

1. Define the module structure using the **puppet module generate** command:

   ```
   puppet module generate my_apache
   ```

2. Write the main manifest (**manifests/init.pp**):

   ```
   class apache {
     include apache::install
     include apache::config
     include apache::service
   }

   class apache::install {
     package { 'apache2':
       ensure => installed,
     }
   }

   class apache::config {
     file { '/etc/apache2/sites-enabled/000-default.conf':
       ensure  => file,
       content => template('apache/vhost.conf.erb'),
     }
   }

   class apache::service {
     service { 'apache2':
       ensure => running,
       enable => true,
     }
   }
   ```

The advantages of modules are:

- **Reusability:** Modules can be shared within teams or uploaded to the Puppet Forge for broader use.

- **Modularity:** This simplifies managing configurations by breaking them into logical components.

- **Scalability:** It is easily extendable to manage complex systems.

Hiera

Hiera is Puppet's key-value lookup tool, designed to separate configuration data from code. By storing environment-specific or node-specific data in Hiera, administrators can write generic manifests that adapt dynamically based on the data. The configuration structure of Hiera is as follows:

```
# hiera.yaml
---
version: 5
hierarchy:
  - name: "Per-node data»
    path: "nodes/%{trusted.certname}.yaml"
  - name: "Common data"
    path: "common.yaml"
```

The following is a Hiera data (**common.yaml**):

```
apache::docroot: /var/www/html
apache::port: 8080
apache::servername: example.com
```

Now you can use this in Hiera as follows:

```
class apache ($docroot, $port, $servername) {
  file { $docroot:
    ensure => directory,
  }

  file { "$docroot/index.html":
    ensure  => file,
    content => '<h1>Welcome to Apache Server!</h1>',
  }

  file { '/etc/apache2/sites-enabled/000-default.conf':
```

```
  ensure  => file,
  content => template('apache/vhost.conf.erb'),
}

service { 'apache2':
  ensure => running,
  enable => true,
 }
}
```

The major benefits of Hiera are:

- **Data abstraction:** Decouple data from code for greater flexibility.
- **Scalability:** Manage configurations for thousands of nodes efficiently.
- **Granularity:** Specify data at global, environment, or node levels.

Puppet's manifests, modules, and Hiera form a powerful trio for managing infrastructure. Manifests provide the foundation for defining system states, modules enable modularity and reuse, and Hiera ensures data abstraction and flexibility.

Chef

Chef is a powerful configuration management tool that automates the provisioning, deployment, and management of infrastructure. With its Ruby-based **domain-specific language** (**DSL**), Chef enables administrators and developers to define the desired state of systems using a code-driven approach. By employing concepts like cookbooks, recipes, and resources, Chef allows users to write reusable and modular configuration code, making it scalable and maintainable across diverse environments.

This section explores the core components of Chef, cookbooks, recipes, and resources and demonstrates their use with practical examples.

Cookbooks

A cookbook is a fundamental unit of configuration and policy distribution in Chef. It contains all the components required to configure a system, including recipes, attributes, files, templates, libraries, and more.

The following is the structure of a cookbook:

```
my_cookbook/
├── recipes/
│   └── default.rb        # Main recipe for the cookbook
├── attributes/
```

```
│   └── default.rb          # Default attribute definitions
├── files/
│   └── default/            # Static files to be deployed
├── templates/
│   └── default/            # ERB templates for dynamic configuration
├── libraries/              # Custom Ruby libraries
├── metadata.rb             # Metadata about the cookbook
├── README.md               # Documentation for the cookbook
```

You can create a cookbook as follows:

1. Use the **chef generate** command to create a new **cookbook**:

   ```
   chef generate cookbook my_cookbook
   ```

2. Add configuration code in the **recipes/default.rb** file.

Recipes

Recipes are the core of a Chef cookbook. They define the specific configurations to apply to nodes by using resources as follows:

```
# File: recipes/default.rb
package 'apache2' do
  action :install
end

service 'apache2' do
  action [:enable, :start]
end

file '/var/www/html/index.html' do
  content '<h1>Welcome to Apache Server!</h1>'
  owner 'www-data'
  group 'www-data'
  mode '0644'
end
```

The key features of recipes are:

- **Declarative style:** Specify the desired state of resources.

- **Resource-driven:** Use Chef resources to manage packages, services, files, and more.

- **Modularity:** Divide complex configurations into smaller, reusable recipes.

Resources

Resources are the building blocks of Chef recipes. Each resource represents a specific piece of system configuration, such as a package, file, or service. Some of the commonly used resources are as follows:

- **package:** Manages software packages.

- **service:** Controls system services.

- **file:** Manages files and directories.

- **template:** Deploys configuration files using ERB templates.

- **user:** Creates or manages user accounts.

For example, let us undertake the following steps, using the template resource:

1. Create a **template** file (**templates/default/vhost.conf.erb**):

```
<VirtualHost *:80>
    ServerName <%= node['apache']['server_name'] %>
    DocumentRoot <%= node['apache']['docroot'] %>
</VirtualHost>
```

2. Using the **template** in the recipe:

```
template '/etc/apache2/sites-available/000-default.conf' do
  source 'vhost.conf.erb'
  variables(
    server_name: 'example.com',
    docroot: '/var/www/html'
  )
  notifies :restart, 'service[apache2]'
end
```

3. Define node attributes in **attributes/default.rb**:

```
default['apache']['server_name'] = 'example.com'
default['apache']['docroot'] = '/var/www/html'
```

Chef's cookbooks, recipes, and resources provide a powerful and flexible framework for automating infrastructure management. Cookbooks encapsulate configurations into reusable packages, recipes define specific actions, and resources manage individual components. By mastering these concepts, users can create scalable and maintainable configurations tailored to their infrastructure needs.

Idempotency and convergence

Idempotency and convergence are foundational concepts in configuration management, ensuring that systems reliably achieve and maintain their desired state.

Idempotency means that applying the same configuration repeatedly has no additional effect if the system is already in the desired state. For instance, an Ansible task like:

```
- name: Ensure Apache is installed
  apt:
    name: apache2
    state: present
```

This ensures that Apache is installed. If Apache is already present, Ansible skips the task, avoiding unnecessary reinstallation. This prevents redundant operations, reduces errors, and ensures predictable outcomes. Similarly, in Puppet, a manifest like:

```
package { 'apache2':
  ensure => present,
}
```

This ensures that the Apache package is installed. Puppet checks the system's state and only acts if the package is missing. Repeated runs of such configurations always produce the same system state without introducing side effects.

Convergence, on the other hand, refers to the process of gradually bringing a system to its target state, automatically correcting deviations. Configuration management tools like Chef, Puppet, and Ansible achieve this by applying only the necessary changes during each execution cycle. For example, a Chef resource like:

```
file '/etc/motd' do
  content 'Welcome to the server!'
  owner 'root'
  group 'root'
  mode '0644'
end
```

This ensures that the **/etc/motd** file exists with the specified content, ownership, and permissions. If the file already matches the desired state, Chef does nothing. If it does not, the Chef updates or creates the file. This approach guarantees that systems converge toward the desired state over time, ensuring consistency.

In Puppet, convergence is evident in the way resources are applied. For example:

```
file { '/etc/motd':
  ensure  => file,
  content => 'Welcome to Puppet-managed server!',
```

```
  owner   => 'root',
  group   => 'root',
  mode    => '0644',
}
```

If the file exists and matches the desired configuration, Puppet takes no action. If there are discrepancies, Puppet makes the necessary changes to bring the file to the defined state.

In conclusion, both idempotency and convergence are essential for effective configuration management, enabling consistent, efficient, and reliable automation. By leveraging these principles, you can ensure that systems remain stable and predictable, even in complex environments.

Managing secrets

Managing secrets effectively is critical in configuration management to protect sensitive information such as passwords, API keys, and certificates. Configuration management tools offer various methods to handle secrets securely. For instance, Ansible uses Vault, which encrypts sensitive data files with a password. An encrypted file can be included in playbooks, and Ansible decrypts it during runtime:

```
vars_files:
  - secrets.yml
```

Here, **secrets.yml** contains sensitive information encrypted with Ansible Vault. Similarly, Puppet leverages Hiera to manage secrets hierarchically. Encrypted values can be stored in configuration files and accessed using secure lookups:

```
$password = lookup('database::password')
```

Chef integrates with external secret management tools like HashiCorp Vault or AWS Secrets Manager, retrieving secrets dynamically during runtime.

For example, using the **vault** cookbook:

```
password = vault('secret/data/database', 'password')
```

Beyond these basic implementations, organizations should implement a comprehensive secret management strategy that includes:

- **Centralized secret storage:** Using dedicated secret management tools like HashiCorp Vault, AWS Secrets Manager, or Azure Key Vault to store and manage secrets separately from configuration code.

- **Dynamic secret generation:** Implementing on-demand, short-lived credentials that automatically expire after use, reducing the risk window if credentials are compromised.

- **Secret rotation policies:** Automatically rotating secrets on a regular schedule to limit the damage potential of leaked credentials.

- **Least privilege access:** Ensuring that systems and users only have access to the specific secrets they need to perform their functions.

- **Audit logging:** Maintaining detailed logs of all secret access attempts, both successful and failed, to detect potential security breaches.

- **Environment-specific secrets:** Managing different sets of secrets for development, testing, and production environments to maintain separation of concerns.

- **Integration with identity management:** Tying secret access to existing identity and access management systems to ensure proper authentication and authorization.

- **Encryption at rest and in transit:** Ensuring that secrets are always encrypted, both when stored and when transmitted between systems.

- **Disaster recovery plans:** Implementing backup and recovery procedures for secret management systems to prevent operational disruptions.

Best practices include restricting access to secrets through **role-based access control** (**RBAC**), auditing secret access, and rotating secrets regularly. Always avoid hardcoding secrets directly in configuration files to minimize security risks. Leveraging tools specifically designed for secret management ensures that sensitive data remains protected and traceable.

Version controlling configuration data

Version controlling configuration data is essential to ensure traceability, collaboration, and accountability in managing system configurations. By storing configurations in **version control systems** (**VCS**) like Git, teams can track changes, roll back to previous versions, and collaborate effectively.

For instance, storing Ansible playbooks, Puppet manifests, or Chef cookbooks in a Git repository allows for:

- **Change history:** Every change to the configuration code is recorded, enabling teams to understand what changed, who made the change, and why.

- **Collaboration:** Teams can work concurrently on different branches, merging changes through pull requests or merge requests for review and discussion.

- **Rollback:** If a new configuration introduces issues, reverting to a stable version is straightforward.

A comprehensive approach to version controlling configuration data includes:

- **Repository structure:** Organizing configuration code in a logical structure that separates environments, roles, and components. For example:

```
├─ environments/
│   ├─ development/
│   ├─ staging/
│   └─ production/
├─ roles/
│   ├─ web_server/
│   ├─ database/
│   └─ load_balancer/
└─ modules/
    ├─ security/
    ├─ monitoring/
    └─ networking/
```

- **Branching strategy:** Implementing a branching model such as Gitflow or GitHub Flow that aligns with the organization's deployment strategy. This typically includes:

  o A main/master branch representing the current production state.

  o Feature branches for new configurations or changes.

  o Release branches for staging and testing configurations before production deployment.

  o Hotfix branches for urgent production fixes.

- **Pull request workflow:** Enforcing code reviews through pull requests before merging changes to main branches. This provides:

  o Peer validation of changes.

  o Knowledge sharing across the team.

  o Early detection of potential issues or conflicts.

- **Tagging and releases:** Creating tags for stable releases and important milestones to mark specific points in the repository's history:

```
$git tag -a v1.2.3 -m "Release 1.2.3 - Security hardening"
```

- **Integration with CI/CD:** Automatically validating configuration changes when committed to the repository:

  o Syntax checking and linting.

  o Unit and integration testing.

  o Security scanning.

- **Documentation:** Maintaining README files, change logs, and architectural documentation alongside the configuration code to provide context and guidance.

- **Artifact management:** Using artifact repositories to store compiled or packaged configurations for deployment, especially for large-scale environments.

- **Git Hooks:** Implementing pre-commit and pre-push hooks to enforce standards and prevent accidental commits of sensitive information.

Best practices include enforcing code reviews, using meaningful commit messages, and tagging stable releases for production. Coupling version control with CI/CD pipelines ensures configurations are tested and deployed consistently across environments, enhancing reliability and efficiency. By adopting these practices, organizations can maintain a complete audit trail of infrastructure changes, facilitate knowledge sharing across teams, and recover quickly from configuration issues when they arise.

Testing configuration management code

Testing configuration management code ensures that configurations work as intended and do not introduce unexpected issues. A robust testing strategy includes:

- **Unit testing:** Tools like Test Kitchen for Chef or **rspec-puppet** for Puppet validate individual modules or resources. For example:

```
describe 'my_module::my_class' do
  it { is_expected.to contain_file('/etc/config').with_
content('configuration data') }
end
```

- **Integration testing:** Validate configurations in an environment resembling production. For example, Ansible integrates with Molecule to test playbooks:

```
# Initialize a Molecule scenario
$ molecule init scenario --driver-name docker


# Test the playbook
$ molecule test
```

- **Linting and syntax checks:** Tools like **ansible-lint**, **puppet-lint**, or **cookstyle** for Chef ensure that code adheres to best practices and is free from syntax errors.

- **Automated testing in CI/CD:** Integrate tests into CI pipelines to validate changes before deployment. For example, a GitHub Actions pipeline for Ansible might include steps to lint and test playbooks:

```
jobs:
  test:
    runs-on: ubuntu-latest
```

```
steps:
  - name: Checkout code
    uses: actions/checkout@v3
  - name: Install Ansible
    run: sudo apt install ansible -y
  - name: Run Lint
    run: ansible-lint playbooks/
  - name: Test with Molecule
    run: molecule test
```

Testing ensures reliability, prevents regressions, and builds confidence in deploying changes. Regularly updating and improving tests as configurations evolve is crucial for maintaining high-quality infrastructure.

Detecting and remediating configuration drift

Configuration drift occurs when the actual state of a system diverges from its desired state defined in configuration management tools. Drift can happen due to manual changes, untracked updates, or unexpected modifications, leading to inconsistencies, security vulnerabilities, and system instability.

Tools like PuppetDB, Ansible Tower, and Chef Automate offer features to monitor and report on system state discrepancies. For example, Puppet periodically applies manifests and logs deviations:

```
puppet agent -test
```

This command compares the current system state with the defined manifests and outputs any differences. Chef's chef-client performs similar checks, ensuring nodes comply with their recipes. Ansible's check mode simulates playbook execution without making changes:

```
ansible-playbook site.yml -check
```

This dry run highlights what would change, enabling early detection of drift.

Once detected, remediating drift involves reapplying configurations. Puppet and Chef do this automatically during their execution cycles, while Ansible requires running the playbooks.

Tools like AWS Config or HashiCorp Sentinel can enforce compliance policies, triggering alerts or automated remediation actions for deviations.

The best practices for drift management are as follows:

- **Automated monitoring:** Schedule regular runs of configuration management tools to detect and resolve drift proactively.

- **Immutable infrastructure:** Adopt practices like rebuilding systems from code rather than manual fixes.

- **Audit and alerting:** Set up logs and notifications for unauthorized changes.

- **Version control:** Store all configurations in Git to ensure consistency and accountability.

Using robust detection and remediation strategies ensures systems stay aligned with their intended configurations, reducing downtime and maintaining security.

Integrating with CI/CD pipelines

Configuration management tools like Ansible, Puppet, and Chef are essential for maintaining consistency and repeatability in modern CI/CD workflows. By integrating these tools into CI/CD pipelines, teams can automate the testing, validation, and application of configurations during the software delivery process, ensuring a seamless and reliable deployment.

In practice, configuration management code is typically stored in version control systems like Git. CI pipelines are triggered to run automated checks such as linting, syntax validation, and unit tests when changes are committed. For example, Ansible configurations can be validated using ansible-lint, while Puppet manifests can be checked with puppet-lint. These steps help identify issues early, reducing the risk of configuration-related failures.

Once the configuration code passes validation, it is deployed to staging environments as part of the CD process. This deployment is often automated using orchestration tools such as Jenkins, GitLab CI/CD, or GitHub Actions, which execute the configurations on target systems. Tools like Ansible can apply playbooks to set up environments, while Puppet and Chef enforce the desired state of infrastructure and applications.

Integrating configuration management into CI/CD also allows for enhanced security and compliance. Sensitive data, such as API keys or credentials, can be managed through secure secret management solutions like HashiCorp Vault, AWS Secrets Manager, or Puppet Hiera. These tools ensure that secrets are dynamically retrieved and securely applied during pipeline execution.

Feedback mechanisms are another critical aspect of this integration. Monitoring tools like Prometheus or Chef Automate provide insights into the system state post-deployment, enabling teams to identify and address any deviations promptly. This feedback loop ensures that configurations remain aligned with the desired state throughout the deployment lifecycle.

By embedding configuration management into CI/CD pipelines, organizations achieve a high degree of automation, consistency, and reliability in their deployment processes. This integration minimizes manual intervention, reduces errors, and accelerates delivery cycles, empowering teams to focus on innovation rather than routine operational tasks.

Compliance and security

Compliance and security are critical aspects of configuration management, ensuring that systems adhere to organizational policies, industry regulations, and security best practices. A robust configuration management strategy helps automate these processes, reducing human error and maintaining consistency across environments.

To enforce compliance, configuration management tools like Puppet, Ansible, and Chef can define and enforce system policies. For example, using Puppet, you can ensure that a specific security baseline is met, such as enabling a firewall:

```
service { 'ufw':
  ensure => running,
  enable => true,
}
```

Security is further strengthened by integrating compliance scans into your workflows. Tools like Chef InSpec or OpenSCAP can validate that systems meet defined compliance standards. For instance, InSpec can check for password policy compliance:

```
describe file('/etc/login.defs') do
  its('content') { should match /PASS_MAX_DAYS\s+90/ }
end
```

Secret management tools like HashiCorp Vault, AWS Secrets Manager, or Ansible Vault are integrated into configuration workflows to secure sensitive data. These tools securely store and provide credentials, keys, and other sensitive information during runtime. This ensures that secrets are not hardcoded into configuration files, mitigating the risk of accidental exposure.

Automating compliance checks and ensuring the secure handling of sensitive data is integral to maintaining a secure and compliant environment. These practices meet regulatory requirements and strengthen the overall security posture of systems.

Conclusion

Configuration management has become an indispensable practice in modern infrastructure operations. In this chapter, we explored how tools like Ansible, Puppet, and Chef provide robust frameworks for managing infrastructure at scale. These tools, combined with principles like idempotency and convergence, enable organizations to maintain consistent, reliable, and secure system configurations across their infrastructure.

The integration of configuration management with version control systems and CI/CD pipelines has transformed infrastructure management from manual processes into automated, repeatable operations. By treating infrastructure as code, organizations can apply software development best practices to their infrastructure management, enhancing collaboration, change tracking, and quality control.

As infrastructure continues to grow in complexity, effective configuration management becomes increasingly critical. Whether managing a handful of servers or thousands of containers, the ability to automate, version, test, and secure configurations remains fundamental to successful infrastructure operations.

In the next chapter, we will explore observability through the **Tracing, Events, Metrics, Profiling, Logs, and Exceptions** (**TEMPLE**) framework. We will examine how these components work together to provide comprehensive visibility into modern distributed systems. We will understand how to implement tracing to follow requests across services, collect and analyze metrics for performance monitoring, utilize logs and exceptions for troubleshooting, and leverage profiling and events for deeper system insights. This foundation in observability will complement your configuration management skills to create robust, resilient systems.

Join our Discord space

Join our Discord workspace for latest updates, offers, tech happenings around the world, new releases, and sessions with the authors:

https://discord.bpbonline.com

CHAPTER 8
Observability with TEMPLE

Introduction

In modern distributed systems, understanding what is happening inside your applications and infrastructure has become increasingly complex. Traditional monitoring approaches often fall short of providing the deep insights needed to troubleshoot issues in distributed, microservices-based architectures. This is where observability comes in.

Observability goes beyond traditional monitoring by providing deep insights into system behavior through multiple complementary approaches. While monitoring tells you when something is wrong, observability helps you understand why it is wrong. The TEMPLE framework represents the six key pillars of modern observability:

- **Tracing:** Following requests as they flow through distributed systems.
- **Events:** Capturing and analyzing discrete occurrences in your system.
- **Metrics:** Measuring and tracking quantitative data over time.
- **Profiling:** Analyzing performance characteristics at the code level.
- **Logging:** Recording detailed system and application activities.
- **Exceptions:** Tracking and managing application errors and failures.

Together, these pillars provide a comprehensive framework for understanding system behavior, troubleshooting issues, and maintaining healthy applications. This chapter explores each pillar in detail, examining the tools, practices, and methodologies that make effective observability possible.

As we investigate each aspect of the TEMPLE framework, we will see how these components work together to provide a complete picture of system health and performance. We will also explore how observability practices integrate with modern development approaches and how machine learning is increasingly being used to derive deeper insights from observability data.

Structure

This chapter covers the following topics:

- Introduction to TEMPLE
- Tracing
- Events
- Metrics
- Profiling
- Logs
- Exceptions
- SLIs, SLOs, and SLAs
- Incident response and alerting
- Observability-driven development

Objectives

By the end of this chapter, readers will understand the comprehensive TEMPLE framework for observability in modern distributed systems, gaining practical knowledge of how to implement and integrate its six key pillars, tracing, events, metrics, profiling, logs, and exceptions. Readers will learn to select appropriate tools like Jaeger, Prometheus, and OpenTelemetry to build robust observability solutions, establish meaningful **service level indicators (SLIs)**, **service level objectives (SLOs)**, and **service level agreements (SLAs)**, and design effective incident response and alerting strategies.

The chapter will enable readers to apply observability-driven development practices that treat telemetry as a first-class requirement, incorporate machine learning techniques for anomaly detection and root cause analysis, and understand how observability contributes to system reliability and performance optimization. Readers will develop skills to correlate signals across different observability pillars, implement centralized logging and distributed tracing, conduct performance profiling with minimal overhead, and leverage event-driven context to enhance debugging capabilities. These competencies will empower readers to maintain visibility and control over increasingly complex distributed architectures while continuously improving system reliability.

Introduction to TEMPLE

Observability is the ability to understand the internal state of a system by analyzing its external outputs. Since modern software systems are distributed, dynamic, and highly complex, observability is a cornerstone for maintaining reliability, diagnosing issues, and ensuring a seamless user experience.

While monitoring tells us what is happening, observability helps us understand why it is happening. This distinction is crucial because monitoring focuses on predefined metrics and alerts, while observability empowers teams to explore unanticipated questions and uncover hidden system behaviors.

Observability today plays a key part in modern systems because these systems today are built on microservices, serverless architectures, and containerized environments. These introduce flexibility but also increase the complexity of troubleshooting and performance tuning. A well-designed observability strategy helps teams:

- **Identify problems quickly:** Reduce **mean time to detect (MTTD)** and **mean time to resolve (MTTR)**.

- **Understand root causes:** Go beyond symptoms to uncover the true source of issues.

- **Improve system reliability:** Proactively address issues before they escalate.

- **Enhance user experience:** Ensure smooth, consistent performance for end-users.

Observability focuses on gathering, analyzing, and acting on data such as traces, metrics, logs, and events. This is where the TEMPLE framework comes into play.

TEMPLE is a structured approach to observability that organizes the essential data signals into six interconnected pillars:

- **Tracing:** Tracks the lifecycle of individual requests or transactions across system components, providing insights into latencies, dependencies, and bottlenecks. Tools like Jaeger and Zipkin are commonly used for this purpose.

- **Events:** Represents state changes within a system, such as user actions, service deployments, or error conditions. Events are vital for understanding sequences and context.

- **Metrics:** Numerical measurements that capture system performance and behavior over time, such as CPU usage, memory utilization, and request rates. These are collected and visualized using tools like Prometheus and Grafana.

- **Profiling:** Focuses on analyzing resource consumption at a fine-grained level, identifying inefficient code paths or resource-heavy processes.

- **Logs:** Provide detailed, time-stamped records of events within a system. Logs are essential for debugging and audit trails, and centralized logging solutions like the ELK Stack make it easier to aggregate and search them.

- **Exceptions:** Captures and categorizes runtime errors that disrupt application functionality. Exception tracking tools like Sentry are valuable for pinpointing issues in code.

The interconnectedness of these stacks is where the real value of TEMPLE comes out. For example:

- A high latency metric (Metrics) could trigger a trace (Tracing) that shows a specific service call taking too long.

- Logs provide additional context about the failing service, and an exception tracker identifies the root cause, a misconfigured database query.

- Meanwhile, events log the deployment of a recent update, highlighting when the problem began.

By combining these signals, engineers gain a holistic view of their systems, making troubleshooting and optimization far more efficient.

Now that we have laid the foundation with the TEMPLE framework, let us look into its first pillar, Tracing. We will explore how distributed tracing helps untangle the complexities of modern, interconnected systems.

Tracing

Tracing is the process of following the journey of a request or transaction as it flows through a system. In distributed systems, where a single request might traverse multiple microservices, databases, and external APIs, tracing provides visibility into how components interact and how much time each step takes.

At its core, tracing involves tracking the lifecycle of a request across system components. Each trace consists of:

- **Spans:** The fundamental units of a trace, representing individual operations or service calls. Each span includes details like:

  o   Start and end times

  o   Operation name (e.g., database query)

  o   Metadata (e.g., status codes, user IDs)

- **Parent-child relationships:** Traces link spans hierarchically, showing how operations relate. For example, a span for an API request might include child spans for database queries and external API calls.

Tracing helps answer questions such as:

- Which services were involved in processing a request?

- Where are the bottlenecks or high latencies?

- Did the request succeed, fail, or encounter retries?

By breaking down complex workflows into individual spans (smaller operations) within a trace (the full journey), tracing offers invaluable insights into system behavior.

Distributed tracing

Distributed tracing extends traditional tracing to systems composed of multiple services, capturing:

- **End-to-end visibility:** Tracks a request from its source to its destination across services.

- **Context propagation:** Maintains a unique identifier for a request across services, enabling correlation.

- **Latency analysis:** Identifies slow components within the request's lifecycle.

Each trace consists of:

- **Spans:** Represent individual operations or processes (e.g., a database query or an HTTP call).

- **Parent-child relationships:** Show how spans relate, creating a hierarchical view of a request's path

The core components of distributed tracing primarily include:

- **Trace context propagation:** To track a request as it flows through various services, distributed tracing tools rely on context propagation. The context includes identifiers that link all spans belonging to the same trace:

  o **Trace ID**: A unique identifier for the entire request lifecycle.

  o **Span ID**: A unique identifier for each operation (span) within the trace.

  o **Parent span ID**: Used to establish the parent-child relationship between spans.

  The context is typically passed between services using:

  o HTTP Headers (e.g., X-B3-TraceId, X-B3-SpanId in the B3 Propagation Format).

  o gRPC Metadata or custom middleware for RPC-based systems.

Standards like W3C Trace Context provide interoperability between tracing systems.

- **Instrumentation:** Instrumentation is the process of embedding tracing logic into applications. This is achieved by:
  - o Using client libraries (e.g., OpenTelemetry SDKs) to generate spans for specific operations.
  - o Wrapping critical code paths, such as database queries, HTTP requests, or message processing, to create meaningful spans.
  - o Automatically instrumenting frameworks (e.g., Spring, Django) to reduce manual effort.

- **Sampling:** To avoid overwhelming the system with telemetry data, traces are sampled. There are two common approaches:
  - o **Head-based sampling**: Decides whether to collect a trace at the start of its lifecycle.
  - o **Tail-based sampling**: Analyzes complete traces before deciding which ones to retain, often based on latency, error rates, or other conditions.

Tools like Jaeger and Zipkin support configurable sampling strategies to balance performance and data fidelity.

Jaeger and Zipkin are some of the common tools used for distributed tracing. Let us break down the core mechanics of how tools like Jaeger and Zipkin work, along with the key technologies that power distributed tracing.

Both Jaeger and Zipkin are distributed tracing systems designed to track the flow of requests across microservices. While their architectures differ in complexity, they share similar core components and workflows, summarized here:

- **Instrumentation:**
  - o Applications are instrumented using tracing libraries (e.g., OpenTelemetry) to generate spans for operations.
  - o Each span includes metadata like trace IDs, span IDs, operation names, and timestamps.

- **Context propagation:**
  - o Trace context is passed between services using protocols like HTTP headers (e.g., B3 format) or gRPC metadata.
  - o This ensures all spans related to a single request are linked together in a hierarchical trace.

- **Data collection:**
  - o Agents (Jaeger) or direct client libraries (Zipkin) send spans to a central system.
  - o Data transport relies on efficient protocols such as HTTP, Thrift, or Protobuf.

- **Data processing:**
  - o Collectors validate, deduplicate, and enrich spans before storage.
  - o Sampling strategies (e.g., head-based or tail-based) manage the volume of trace data.

- **Storage:**
  - o Traces are stored in backends like Elasticsearch, Cassandra, or MySQL, depending on scalability needs.
  - o Both tools support in-memory storage for development use cases.

- **Visualization:**
  - o Web-based UIs allow users to query and analyze traces.
  - o Features include timeline views of traces, latency analysis, and service dependency graphs.

Both Jaeger and Zipkin provide essential tracing capabilities to visualize request flows, identify bottlenecks, and diagnose issues in distributed systems. Jaeger is suited for large, high-scale environments, while Zipkin is ideal for smaller setups or quick prototyping. Together, they form a critical part of modern observability stacks, enabling teams to optimize system performance and reliability.

Events

Events often occupy a gray area in the world of observability. Despite being a distinct pillar, the term *events* is frequently misunderstood due to its generality. At a high level, almost all telemetry data could be classified as events—after all, logs, traces, and even metrics record occurrences in time. However, in the context of observability, events specifically refer to change events: external actions or occurrences that directly impact the observed system.

Change events represent significant activities or shifts that alter the behavior of a system. These events are particularly valuable because they provide context for investigating anomalies, diagnosing failures, and understanding system behavior.

Examples of change events:

- **Deployments:** Application code releases or infrastructure updates.
- **Configuration changes:** These are adjustments to application settings or environment variables.
- **Scaling events:** Auto-scaling triggers that modify resource allocation.
- **Disaster recovery (DR) events:** Traffic rerouting or failover scenarios.
- **User traffic patterns:** Surges during holidays, public events, or marketing campaigns.
- **Experiment rollouts:** A/B tests or feature toggles.

For instance, during Uber's early days, Halloween represented a spike in user traffic, requiring constant system monitoring by SREs. Over time, as the business scaled globally, the impact of this holiday became less pronounced. Yet, it remains a classic example of how external factors like holidays, concerts, or sporting events can influence system behavior.

Distinction between events and logs

On the surface, events might resemble logs; they are structured records of what happened and when. However, the requirements and design trade-offs for handling events differ significantly from those for logs, as shown:

- **Data reliability:**

  o **Logs**: Some data loss may be tolerable. For instance, a bug causing repeated error messages does not require storing every identical log.

  o **Events**: Reliability is critical. Missing a deployment event could hinder debugging and delay incident resolution.

- **Precision and querying:**

  o **Logs**: Typically queried for patterns, aggregates, or statistical insights. Exact matches are rarely necessary.

  o **Events**: Queries often target specific instances, such as identifying the exact deployment that introduced a bug.

- **Volume and scales:**

  o **Logs**: Generated in high volumes, requiring pipelines to down-sample or throttle the data.

  o **Events**: Occur less frequently, allowing for more rigorous capture and storage requirements.

Role of events in observability

Events serve as critical context for understanding other telemetry data like metrics, traces, and logs. For example:

- A spike in error logs might correlate with a recent deployment event.

- Metrics indicating increased latency could align with an auto-scaling event.

- Traces showing prolonged request times might coincide with configuration changes.

By surfacing events alongside other observability data, operators can identify root causes more efficiently and establish better correlations between changes and outcomes.

Some technical challenges with events are as follows:

- **Granularity and precision:** Events must capture detailed metadata to enable precise filtering and querying. For instance, a deployment event might need fields like service name, version, environment, and timestamp.

- **Consistency across systems:** In distributed systems, ensuring consistent event formats and timestamps across services is critical for meaningful analysis. Synchronizing clocks using NTP or PTP protocols is a common solution.

- **Low-latency pipelines:** To maintain system responsiveness, event pipelines must process and store data in near real-time. Techniques include batching and compression to optimize throughput.

- **Integration with other observability pillars:** Events must integrate seamlessly with metrics, traces, and logs for correlation. For example, OpenTelemetry allows tagging spans and metrics with event metadata for unified analysis.

In the next section, we will look into metrics, exploring how numerical data provides valuable insights into system health, performance, and usage patterns.

Metrics

Metrics are fundamental to observability, providing a structured, numerical representation of a system's behavior over time. Unlike logs, which capture detailed, contextual information about specific events, or traces, which show the flow of requests through a system, metrics aggregate quantitative data, offering a high-level view of system health and performance. The key characteristics of metrics are:

- **Aggregated data:** Metrics focus on trends rather than granular details. For example, instead of logging every request, a metric might report the number of requests per second.

- **Time-stamped values:** Each metric is associated with a timestamp, forming a time-series dataset that can be analyzed for patterns.

- **Dimensionality:** Metrics are often tagged with labels (e.g., region, service, instance) to allow filtering and grouping during analysis.

The following list lets you know what to monitor with metrics:

- **Infrastructure health:**

  o **CPU utilization**: Tracks system load, identifies bottlenecks, and helps with capacity planning.

  o **Memory usage**: Monitors memory leaks or inefficient resource use.

  o **Disk I/O and network throughput**: Detects hardware limitations or configuration issues.

- **Application performance:**

  o **Request rate (RPS)**: Measures incoming traffic. Spikes or dips can indicate scaling issues or downtime.

  o **Error rate**: Tracks failures in the system (e.g., HTTP 500 responses).

  o **Latency**: Measures the time it takes for a request to be processed. High latency may indicate performance bottlenecks or resource contention.

- **Business-level metrics:** Metrics such as revenue per transaction, active user counts, or orders processed provide direct insights into the system's impact on business goals.

Metrics also stand out due to their focus on quantitative aggregation and efficiency. Unlike logs, which capture rich, unstructured, or structured details of individual events, metrics summarize behavior. For example, a log may record every HTTP request, while a metric simply counts the number of requests within a defined interval. This aggregation allows metrics to be lightweight, making them ideal for high-level monitoring and alerting.

In contrast to traces, which visualize the path of individual requests across services, metrics provide a macro-level view of system behavior. They can identify issues (e.g., a spike in error rate), while traces help trace those issues to their root cause.

Metrics are usually stored in **time-series databases** (**TSDBs**), optimized for fast write speeds and efficient querying. Tools like Prometheus store metrics in compressed, chunked formats and index them by label to facilitate high-performance queries. For instance:

```
rate(http_requests_total{status="500"}[5m])
```

This query calculates the rate of HTTP 500 errors over the past five minutes, providing insights into system reliability.

Metrics are not standalone solutions but integral components of the observability ecosystem. They highlight what is happening, while logs and traces delve into why it is happening. Together, they empower teams to maintain system reliability, optimize performance, and align technical performance with business objectives.

Profiling

Profiling is the process of examining the runtime characteristics of a system or application to understand its behavior, identify bottlenecks, and optimize performance. While metrics provide a high-level view of a system's health and traces illustrate the flow of requests, profiling focuses on the internal workings of a system, such as CPU usage, memory allocation, thread activity, and execution time of code paths.

Profiling captures granular, low-level details about how a system or application consumes resources. This data is typically collected at runtime and provides insights such as:

- **CPU profiling:** How much processing time-specific functions or threads consume.

- **Memory profiling:** Patterns of memory allocation, usage, and leaks.

- **I/O profiling:** Time spent on disk or network operations.

- **Concurrency profiling:** Thread activity and synchronization issues.

Unlike logs and metrics, profiling often focuses on a narrow time window or specific workload, making it ideal for debugging and performance tuning. Profiling is also an essential tool because it helps in:

- **Identifying bottlenecks:** Pinpoints resource-intensive code paths or system components.

- **Optimizing performance:** Improves response times and reduces resource consumption.

- **Preventing outages:** Detects inefficiencies that could lead to failures under heavy load.

- **Guiding resource allocation:** Helps in capacity planning by identifying which resources are under or over-utilized.

Working of profiling

Profiling tools hook into an application or system at runtime, collecting data on resource usage and execution flow. This involves:

- **Sampling vs. instrumentation:**

  o **Sampling profilers**: Periodically collect stack traces, offering a lightweight way to analyze performance with minimal overhead. Tools like py-spy (Python) and Go pprof use this approach.

  o **Instrumentation profilers**: Inject code to collect detailed metrics for every function call. While more precise, this method introduces higher overhead.

- **Data collection:** Profiling data is collected as a set of metrics (e.g., CPU cycles, memory allocations) or flame graphs, which visually represent the time spent in each code path.

- **Analysis and visualization:** Profiling tools generate reports or interactive visualizations to help developers understand hotspots and inefficiencies.

Some of the common tools for profiling are:

- **System-level profiling:**

  o **perf (Linux)**: Captures detailed performance data for processes and the kernel.

- o **eBPF**: A powerful framework for collecting profiling data directly from the kernel with minimal performance overhead.

- **Application-level profiling:**

    - o **Go pprof**: Built-in Go profiling library for CPU, memory, and block profiling.

    - o **VisualVM**: For Java applications, it provides thread dumps and heap analysis.

    - o **dotnet-trace**: Captures profiling data for .NET applications.

- **Distributed profiling:** In distributed systems, tools like Parca or Pixie collect and visualize profiles across multiple services, enabling end-to-end performance analysis.

Let us take an example in GoLang where we can try using the pprof tool to enable a profiler endpoint (`localhost:6060`) for a Go application, as shown in the following snippet. Developers can use this to collect and analyze CPU or memory profiles in real-time.

```go
import (
    "net/http"
    _ "net/http/pprof"
)

func main() {
    go func() {
        http.ListenAndServe("localhost:6060", nil)
    }()
    // Your application code here
}
```

However, profiling does not come for free, and there are some challenges in profiling as well:

- **Overhead:** Instrumentation-based profiling can impact application performance, making it less suitable for production. Sampling-based profilers mitigate this at the cost of reduced precision.

- **Data volume:** Profiling generates large amounts of data, requiring efficient storage and visualization solutions.

- **Interpreting results:** Profiles can be complex, and drawing actionable conclusions requires domain knowledge and experience.

Profiling complements metrics, logs, and traces by providing a detailed view of how resources are utilized within a system. By leveraging profiling, teams can fine-tune their applications, reduce costs, and ensure optimal performance under varying workloads.

Logs

Logs are detailed, time-stamped records of events and activities generated by applications, systems, or infrastructure. Unlike metrics, which provide aggregated numerical data, logs capture context-rich, unstructured information that is invaluable for debugging, auditing, and understanding system behavior. Logs are textual representations of discrete events. They typically include details such as:

- **Timestamp:** When the event occurred.

- **Log level:** Severity of the event (e.g., DEBUG, INFO, WARN, ERROR).

- **Message:** Human-readable description of the event.

- **Metadata:** Contextual information (e.g., service name, request ID, user ID).

The following is an example of a JSON log:

```
{
  "timestamp": "2025-01-05T14:23:45Z",
  "level": "ERROR",
  "service": "payment-service",
  "message": "Payment processing failed",
  "transactionId": "12345",
  "userId": "67890"
}
```

As you can see, logs provide the granularity needed to investigate the specific sequence of events leading to an issue, making them essential for debugging and root cause analysis. So logs are quite important in the observability story.

OpenTelemetry enhancing logging

OpenTelemetry (**OTel**) is an open-source framework that standardizes the collection, processing, and export of observability data, including logs. By providing consistent APIs and SDKs, OTel simplifies the process of integrating logging into your observability strategy. Some of the key features of OTel Logging are:

- **Unified context across signals:** OTel associates logs with traces and metrics using shared context propagation. For example, logs include trace IDs and span IDs, enabling developers to correlate logs with distributed traces.

- **Vendor-neutrality:** OTel supports exporting logs to multiple backends, such as Elasticsearch, Splunk, or Google Cloud Logging, giving you flexibility in choosing a log storage solution.

- **Structured logging support:** OTel encourages the use of structured logging, ensuring logs are machine-readable and easy to query.

- **Instrumentation libraries:** Pre-built OTel libraries automatically collect logs from popular frameworks and systems, reducing the burden on developers.

The following is an example of OTel logging:

```
from opentelemetry import trace
from opentelemetry.sdk.logs import LoggingHandler
import logging

# Set up OTel tracer and handler
tracer = trace.get_tracer("example-tracer")
otel_handler = LoggingHandler()

# Configure Python logging
logger = logging.getLogger(__name__)
logger.setLevel(logging.INFO)
logger.addHandler(otel_handler)

# Generate a log with trace context
with tracer.start_as_current_span("example-span"):
    logger.info("Processing user request")
```

In this example, the log message **Processing user request** will include a trace context, enabling developers to correlate it with distributed traces.

Centralized logging

Centralized logging aggregates logs from multiple systems into a single location for storage, querying, and visualization. While OpenTelemetry enables log collection and enrichment, tools like **Elasticsearch, Logstash, and Kibana (ELK)**, or cloud-native services like AWS CloudWatch or Google Cloud Logging handle log storage and analysis.

You can use OTel and send your logs to Elasticsearch as well, for example:

- **Instrument your application:** Use OTel SDKs to generate structured, enriched logs.

- **Set up OTel Collector:** Configure the OTel Collector to export logs to Elasticsearch:

```
exporters:
  otlp:
    endpoint: "http://localhost:4317"
  elasticsearch:
    endpoints: ["http://localhost:9200"]
```

```
service:
  pipelines:
    logs:
      receivers: [otlp]
      exporters: [elasticsearch]
```

- **Query logs in Elasticsearch:** Use Kibana to visualize and search logs, now enriched with trace and span IDs for correlation.

By using OTel alongside centralized logging tools, you gain both depth and breadth in observability. Logs, enriched with trace context and structured for analysis, become a cornerstone of monitoring, debugging, and optimizing modern distributed systems.

Exceptions

Exceptions are runtime anomalies or errors that occur during the execution of an application. Unlike metrics or logs, which provide generalized insights into system performance and behavior, exceptions specifically highlight unexpected issues in the code or system. They are essential in observability as they help pinpoint failures and provide detailed context for troubleshooting. An exception is a signal that something went wrong during execution. It could result from:

- Invalid user inputs (e.g., attempting to divide by zero).

- External service failures (e.g., a database timeout or a failed API call).

- Code bugs (e.g., accessing a null pointer or an uninitialized variable).

Exceptions typically include:

- **Error message:** A description of the error.

- **Stack trace:** A detailed list of function calls leading to the error.

- **Timestamp and metadata:** Information about when and where the error occurred.

Although logs may capture exceptions as part of their messages, exceptions serve a more specific purpose in observability:

- **Structured context:** Exceptions inherently include structured details like the stack trace, making it easier to identify the root cause of issues.

- **Criticality:** While logs can be used for all types of events, exceptions often indicate serious or blocking errors that require immediate attention.

- **Volume:** Exceptions are typically fewer but more significant compared to logs, which are generated at a much higher volume.

In distributed systems, capturing and correlating exceptions across services is critical for understanding system-wide failures. Observability platforms and tools play a key role in this:

- **Aggregating exceptions:** Observability systems like Sentry or Datadog automatically collect exceptions from multiple services, group similar ones, and display trends.

- **Correlating with traces:** Using tools like OpenTelemetry, exceptions can be captured and linked to traces. For instance, an exception occurring during a database query in a specific span of a trace will include details about the span (e.g., trace_id and span_id).

- **Visualizing exception data:** Tools such as Sentry, Rollbar, and New Relic provide detailed dashboards showing:

  o The frequency of specific exceptions.

  o Affected services or users.

  o The code paths where the exceptions originated.

- **Alerting on exceptions:** Exception-monitoring tools can be configured to send alerts when new or critical exceptions occur.

OpenTelemetry provides a standardized way to capture exceptions as part of spans in a trace. The following is an example in Python:

```python
from opentelemetry import trace
from opentelemetry.trace.status import Status, StatusCode
from opentelemetry.sdk.trace import TracerProvider
from opentelemetry.sdk.trace.
export import ConsoleSpanExporter, SimpleSpanProcessor

# Configure Tracer
trace.set_tracer_provider(TracerProvider())
tracer = trace.get_tracer(__name__)
trace.get_tracer_provider().add_span_
processor(SimpleSpanProcessor(ConsoleSpanExporter()))

try:
    # Generate a span
    with tracer.start_as_current_span("example-operation") as span:
        # Simulate an error
        result = 10 / 0
except Exception as e:
    # Record the exception in the span
    span.record_exception(e)
    span.set_status(Status(StatusCode.ERROR, str(e)))
```

In the above code, when the exception is raised (**10/0**), it is captured and recorded in the trace span. The span is marked with a failure status (**StatusCode.ERROR**). This trace, including the exception details, can be exported to observability tools like Jaeger or Zipkin for further analysis.

Some of the best practices for exception handling are:

- **Never swallow exceptions:** Avoid silently catching exceptions without logging or re-throwing them. It makes debugging much harder.

- **Use structured metadata:** Include context (e.g., user ID, request ID) with exceptions to aid in debugging.

- **Track trends:** Monitor the frequency of exceptions over time to detect emerging issues.

- **Integrate with alerting:** Configure alerts for critical exceptions to ensure immediate response.

By treating exceptions as a first-class signal in observability, organizations can gain deeper insights into system failures and respond more effectively to production issues.

SLIs, SLOs, and SLAs

In modern software systems, SLIs, SLOs, and SLAs are crucial concepts for defining, monitoring, and maintaining the reliability of services. Observability plays a central role in enabling organizations to measure and act on these service-level metrics.

SLIs

SLIs are the quantitative metrics that reflect the performance or quality of a service. They provide measurable values to track specific aspects of system behavior. Examples include:

- **Latency:** Response times for API requests (e.g., 95th percentile under 200 ms).

- **Availability:** Percentage of successful requests (e.g., 99.9%).

- **Error rate:** The proportion of failed requests over a period (e.g., 0.1%).

- **Throughput:** Number of transactions per second.

Observability systems collect telemetry data (metrics, traces, logs, etc.) to calculate SLIs. For example, a distributed tracing tool can measure API latency, while metrics systems like Prometheus can track error rates or availability.

SLOs

SLOs are the targets or thresholds set for SLIs. They define what good enough looks like for a system or service. For instance:

- API response time must remain under 200 ms for 95% of requests.

- 99.5% of requests must be successful within a 30-day period.

SLOs provide context to observability data. They help prioritize issues based on whether or not the service is meeting its objectives. Observability dashboards can visualize SLO performance over time, enabling proactive monitoring.

SLAs

SLAs are formal agreements, often contractual, between a service provider and its customers. They specify the minimum performance standards (often derived from SLOs) and the consequences of failing to meet them, such as penalties or refunds.

Observability ensures that SLA compliance can be measured and validated with reliable, real-time data.

Observability provides the foundation for measuring SLIs, tracking SLO compliance, and ensuring SLA adherence. By collecting telemetry signals like metrics, traces, and logs, observability enables precise measurements of key SLIs such as latency, availability, and error rates. For example, metrics systems can provide granular visibility into system health, while distributed tracing tools measure request-response times to assess latency. Observability also supports real-time monitoring of SLOs, allowing teams to visualize compliance and receive alerts when thresholds are breached. This integration ensures that issues can be identified and addressed proactively before SLA violations occur. Furthermore, observability empowers incident management by providing detailed telemetry data to diagnose and resolve the root causes of reliability issues. It bridges the gap between operational metrics and customer satisfaction, fostering a culture of proactive reliability management. By linking SLIs, SLOs, and SLAs to telemetry data, observability transforms service reliability into a measurable, actionable process.

Incident response and alerting

Incident response and alerting are critical components of maintaining system reliability and ensuring that teams can quickly detect, respond to, and mitigate issues in production environments. In the highly distributed, fast-paced world of modern software, the ability to react swiftly to incidents can make the difference between a minor hiccup and a catastrophic outage. Observability is the foundation that powers effective incident response and alert mechanisms, enabling organizations to stay proactive and minimize downtime.

Incident response refers to the structured process of detecting, investigating, and resolving issues in a system. The goal is to restore normal operations as quickly as possible while minimizing the impact on users and the business.

A well-designed incident response process involves:

- **Detection:** Identifying potential issues through monitoring and telemetry signals.

- **Triage:** Prioritizing incidents based on their severity and impact.

- **Investigation:** Diagnosing the root cause using observability tools like logs, traces, and metrics.

- **Mitigation:** Taking corrective actions to minimize or eliminate the issue.

- **Postmortem:** Analyzing the incident to learn from it and prevent future occurrences.

Observability ensures that every step of this process is data driven. For instance, metrics provide insights into system health, logs reveal granular details about errors, and traces offer visibility into how requests propagate through the system.

Role of alerting

Alerting is the mechanism that notifies teams when an incident occurs. Effective alerting relies on well-defined triggers based on telemetry data and SLOs. Alerts should be actionable, specific, and free from unnecessary noise to avoid alert fatigue. Key principles of alerting include:

- **Granularity:** Alerts should correspond to meaningful events or threshold breaches, such as latency exceeding an SLO or error rates spiking.

- **Prioritization:** Not all alerts are equal. Critical alerts (e.g., service outages) should demand immediate attention, while lower-priority ones (e.g., slow performance) can be addressed later.

- **Context:** Alerts should provide enough information to help responders quickly understand the issue, including metadata like timestamps, affected components, and potential causes.

Observability tools like Prometheus, Grafana, and OpenTelemetry often integrate with alerting platforms such as PagerDuty, Opsgenie, or Slack to route alerts to the right team at the right time.

Observability significantly enhances incident response and alerting by enabling proactive detection, streamlined diagnosis, and faster resolution of system issues. It provides a unified view of telemetry data, metrics, traces, and logs, which helps identify anomalies and correlate signals for RCA. For instance, rising API latencies captured as metrics can trigger alerts, while traces and logs provide a rich context for immediate investigation. Observability tools also enable enriched alerts with metadata like timestamps, affected components, and failure details, ensuring responders have actionable information.

Moreover, integration with platforms like OpenTelemetry allows seamless alignment between observability and alerting systems. For example, latency SLIs defined in

Prometheus using OpenTelemetry-collected metrics can trigger alerts when thresholds are breached. These alerts, routed through tools like PagerDuty or Slack, include links to related traces and logs, helping teams rapidly pinpoint and resolve the issue. Observability also facilitates automated remediation for certain incidents, like scaling services during traffic spikes, and supports continuous learning through historical telemetry data for post-incident analysis. By integrating observability into incident response, organizations transition from reactive firefighting to a proactive, efficient approach to system reliability.

Observability-driven development

Observability-driven development (ODD) represents a paradigm shift in software engineering where observability requirements are treated as first-class citizens during the development lifecycle alongside functional requirements. In this approach, developers instrument their code with telemetry data points before implementing business logic, ensuring that every significant code path, state transition, and system interaction is inherently observable. This involves strategic placement of trace points, metric collectors, and structured logging statements that capture not just the occurrence of events but also their context, causality, and impact on system behavior.

The technical implementation of ODD typically begins at the architectural level, where services are designed with built-in telemetry endpoints and standardized instrumentation libraries. For instance, developers might leverage OpenTelemetry's auto-instrumentation agents alongside custom span attributes to capture business-specific context. Critical sections of code are augmented with detailed tracing that includes custom attributes, baggage propagation across service boundaries, and explicit parent-child span relationships that reflect the system's execution model. This granular instrumentation enables teams to understand complex distributed transactions and diagnose issues without requiring additional code deployment.

Performance optimization in ODD is achieved through continuous metric collection and analysis. Engineers instrument their code to emit high-cardinality metrics that track not just traditional **Rate, Errors, Duration** (RED) metrics but also business-specific indicators like queue depths, cache hit ratios, and custom histograms of operation latencies. These metrics are typically implemented using statsd-style collectors or direct integration with time-series databases like Prometheus, allowing for real-time aggregation and analysis. The instrumentation includes detailed labels and tags that enable precise filtering and correlation of metrics across different system dimensions.

Error handling and debugging in ODD follow a structured approach where exceptions and error conditions are enriched with contextual information before being propagated. This involves implementing custom error types that carry additional metadata, correlation IDs, and state information that can be used to reconstruct the error context. Developers create explicit error boundaries in their applications, each accompanied by detailed logging that captures the stack trace, relevant variable states, and system conditions at the time of failure. This information is then correlated with distributed traces and metrics to provide a comprehensive view of system behavior during failure scenarios.

Data consistency and state management in ODD require sophisticated instrumentation of database operations and cache interactions. Engineers implement detailed tracking of database query patterns, cache invalidation events, and state transitions, often using aspect-oriented programming techniques or middleware interceptors. This includes recording query execution plans, cache hit/miss ratios, and data access patterns, which are then used to optimize performance and identify potential bottlenecks. The instrumentation extends to tracking distributed transactions and capturing the causal relationships between different data operations across service boundaries.

Integration testing in ODD leverages the observability infrastructure to validate system behavior. Test suites are designed to verify not just functional correctness but also the presence and accuracy of telemetry data. This includes assertions on trace propagation, metric emission, and log correlation. Engineers implement test fixtures that simulate various system conditions and verify that the observability data correctly reflects these scenarios. This approach ensures that observability remains a reliable tool for understanding system behavior even as the codebase evolves.

Resource utilization and capacity planning in ODD are supported by the comprehensive instrumentation of system resources. This includes tracking memory allocation patterns, garbage collection metrics, thread pool utilization, and IO operations. Engineers implement custom collectors that monitor these resources at a granular level, often using JMX beans in Java applications or similar mechanisms in other languages. The collected data is used to generate resource utilization profiles that inform scaling decisions and capacity planning.

Machine learning in observability

Traditional rule-based monitoring and alerting systems have evolved into sophisticated machine learning-powered observability platforms that can detect complex patterns and anomalies across distributed systems. At its core, ML in observability leverages historical telemetry data, including metrics, traces, and logs, to establish baseline behaviors and identify deviations that might indicate potential issues. These systems employ various ML techniques ranging from time-series analysis and clustering to deep learning models that can process high-dimensional observability data in real-time.

Anomaly detection forms the cornerstone of ML-powered observability, where algorithms continuously analyze metrics to identify unusual patterns that deviate from learned normal behavior. For instance, advanced techniques like **long short-term memory (LSTM)** networks and Prophet models can capture seasonal patterns in service latencies, while isolation forests and one-class SVMs excel at detecting point anomalies in resource utilization metrics. These models account for complex seasonality, trend patterns, and the inherent noise in production systems, reducing false positives that often plague traditional threshold-based alerting systems.

RCA benefits significantly from ML-driven approaches that can automatically correlate anomalies across different services and identify potential causal relationships. **Graph neural networks (GNNs)** process service dependency graphs to trace the propagation of failures, while attention mechanisms help highlight the most relevant metrics and logs during incident investigation. These systems learn from historical incident data to recognize patterns in system behavior that preceded past failures, enabling proactive identification of potential issues before they impact end users.

Log analysis has been transformed by **natural language processing (NLP)** techniques that can automatically cluster similar log messages, extract meaningful patterns, and identify anomalous log sequences. Advanced models like BERT and GPT variants are fine-tuned on domain-specific log data to understand the semantic meaning of log messages, while techniques like LogParse and DeepLog learn the structural patterns in log sequences. This enables the automatic detection of novel error messages and the identification of subtle system misbehaviors that might be missed by traditional regex-based approaches.

Performance prediction and capacity planning leverage ML models trained on historical resource utilization patterns to forecast future system behavior. These models, often based on techniques like XGBoost or Neural Prophet, can predict resource requirements across different time horizons, enabling proactive scaling decisions. The models incorporate multiple factors, including historical usage patterns, deployment events, and external factors like time of day or special events, providing accurate predictions that account for both regular patterns and exceptional circumstances.

Automated remediation systems powered by **reinforcement learning (RL)** represent the cutting edge of ML in observability. These systems learn optimal response strategies for different types of system issues by training on historical incident data and simulated environments. For example, RL agents can learn to automatically adjust resource allocation, reroute traffic, or restart services based on observed system states while considering complex trade-offs between service availability, cost, and performance objectives.

Feature extraction and dimensionality reduction techniques play a crucial role in processing the high-dimensional data generated by modern observability systems. Techniques like autoencoders and **principal component analysis (PCA)** help identify the most relevant signals from thousands of metrics, while more advanced approaches like variational autoencoders can learn compact representations that capture complex system behaviors. These reduced representations not only improve model performance but also help engineers understand the key factors driving system behavior.

The integration of ML with observability pipelines presents unique challenges in production environments. Engineers must design systems that can handle streaming data processing, model retraining, and concept drift detection while maintaining low latency. This often involves techniques like online learning and sliding window approaches to continuously update model parameters as system behavior evolves. Additionally, the systems must be designed with interpretability in mind, providing clear explanations for why certain patterns were flagged as anomalous or why specific remediation actions were recommended.

Conclusion

The TEMPLE framework introduced in this chapter establishes a comprehensive approach to observability in modern distributed systems, integrating tracing, events, metrics, profiling, logs, and exceptions into a cohesive observability strategy. This integration, coupled with advanced tooling like Jaeger, Prometheus, and the ELK Stack, enables organizations to maintain visibility and control over increasingly complex architectures.

The rise of observability-driven development and the establishment of clear SLIs, SLOs, and SLAs demonstrate a maturation in how organizations approach system reliability. By treating observability as a fundamental requirement rather than an afterthought, teams can build more resilient and maintainable systems. This evolution is further enhanced by machine learning capabilities that enable predictive analytics, automated anomaly detection, and intelligent root cause analysis.

As we look to the future, the convergence of OpenTelemetry standardization, eBPF-based observability, and AI-driven analytics promises even more sophisticated observability solutions. The TEMPLE framework provides a foundation for incorporating these advances while maintaining a clear focus on the essential aspects of system observability. Organizations that successfully implement these practices and tools will be well-equipped to handle the challenges of modern distributed systems while continuously improving their reliability and performance.

In the next chapter, we will cover the essential concepts and best practices to maximize Docker usage.

Join our Discord space

Join our Discord workspace for latest updates, offers, tech happenings around the world, new releases, and sessions with the authors:

https://discord.bpbonline.com

CHAPTER 9

Containerization and Docker Best Practices

Introduction

Containerization has changed remarkably the way applications are developed, deployed, and maintained in current software ecosystems. The whale at the heart of this change is Docker, a powerful platform enabling developers to build applications into lightweight, portable containers along with all dependencies. Containers have built up to be the very foundation of modern DevOps workflows. They allow teams to build, ship, and run applications across diverse environments, from local development machines to large-scale production clusters, seamlessly.

This chapter explores the most essential concepts and best practices to maximize Docker usage. The basic study is really about the architecture and components of Docker, focusing on how the Docker Engine, images, containers, and registries interact with the entire development and deployment experience. With that, we can go through practical ways of writing efficient and maintainable Dockerfiles, including advanced techniques such as multi-stage builds to optimize image size and build performance.

Security is a vital part when we talk about containerized environments. We will cover ways to scan container images for vulnerabilities, configure secure container runtimes, and properly manage sensitive data. Networking is yet another major concern and dealing with that will be covered in this chapter, showing the Docker networking models, how to configure container-to-container communication and outbound connectivity.

To manage stateful applications, we will cover persistent data storage using Docker volumes, ensuring that data survives container restarts and upgrades. For multi-container applications, we will explore Docker Compose, a powerful tool for defining and running complex application stacks with minimal effort. Additionally, we will examine container registries and strategies for managing and versioning container images effectively.

Debugging and troubleshooting containers can be challenging, but with the right tools and techniques, it becomes manageable. This chapter will provide practical guidance on identifying and resolving common issues in containerized environments. Finally, we will emphasize Docker security best practices, highlighting steps to minimize risks and ensure a robust container ecosystem.

As containerization is integral to DevOps, we will also discuss how Docker integrates seamlessly with CI/CD pipelines, enabling automated builds, testing, and deployments. By the end of this chapter, you will have a comprehensive understanding of Docker and the confidence to apply its best practices to streamline your workflows, enhance security, and improve application performance. Let us embark on this journey into the world of containerization and Docker excellence!

Structure

The chapter covers the following topics:

- Docker architecture and components
- Writing efficient Dockerfiles and multi-stage builds
- Security scanning for container images
- Docker networking models
- Managing persistent data with volumes
- Docker Compose for multi-container applications
- Container registries and image management
- Debugging and troubleshooting containers
- Docker security best practices
- Integration with CI/CD pipelines

Objectives

This chapter aims to provide you with a comprehensive understanding of Docker's architecture and components, enabling you to build efficient containerized applications. You will learn to write optimized Dockerfiles and implement multi-stage builds for creating lightweight, production-ready images. The chapter will equip you with the knowledge to implement security scanning for container images, helping you identify and mitigate vulnerabilities before deployment. We will gain proficiency in configuring Docker networking models to facilitate communication between containers and external systems according to your application requirements.

The chapter will also teach you how to effectively manage persistent data using Docker volumes, ensuring data durability across container lifecycles. We will develop skills in orchestrating multi-container applications with Docker Compose, simplifying complex application deployments. Additionally, we will learn strategies for efficient container registry usage and image management to streamline your workflow. The chapter provides practical approaches to debugging and troubleshooting containerized environments, helping you identify and resolve common issues efficiently.

By the end of this chapter, we will be able to implement Docker security best practices to minimize risks and ensure robust container security. Finally, we will understand how to integrate Docker into CI/CD pipelines, enabling automated build, test, and deployment workflows that enhance productivity and reliability in your software delivery process.

Docker architecture and components

Understanding Docker's architecture and components is fundamental to mastering containerization. Docker provides a robust and efficient platform for creating, deploying, and managing containers. It achieves this by following a client-server model where various components work together seamlessly to deliver a streamlined containerization experience. *Figure 9.1* showcases some of the core components of the docker ecosystem:

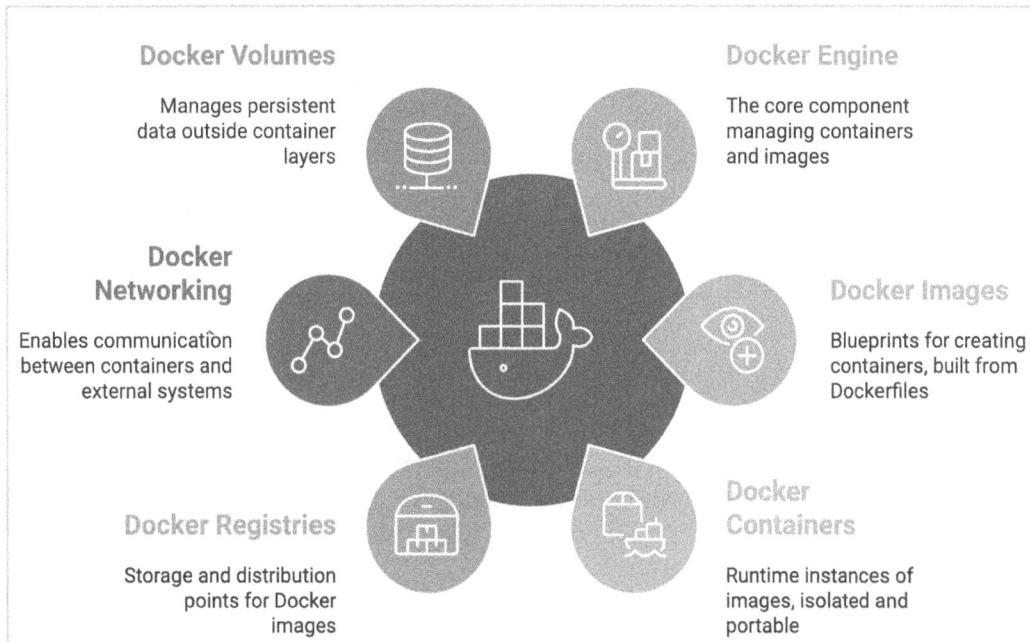

Docker Volumes
Manages persistent data outside container layers

Docker Engine
The core component managing containers and images

Docker Networking
Enables communication between containers and external systems

Docker Images
Blueprints for creating containers, built from Dockerfiles

Docker Registries
Storage and distribution points for Docker images

Docker Containers
Runtime instances of images, isolated and portable

Figure 9.1: *Core components of Docker*

Docker Engine

The Docker Engine is the core of the Docker platform and consists of three main parts:

- **Docker Daemon (dockerd):** The Docker daemon is the heart of Docker's architecture. It runs as a background process on the host machine and is responsible for managing all Docker objects, including images, containers, volumes, and networks. The daemon listens for Docker API requests and orchestrates container operations such as starting, stopping, and monitoring containers.

- **Docker CLI (docker):** The Docker **command line interface** (**CLI**) is the primary way users interact with Docker. It allows users to issue commands to the Docker daemon to manage images, containers, networks, and more. For example, commands like `docker run` or `docker build` are sent to the daemon via the CLI.

- **REST API:** The REST API provides programmatic access to Docker functionality. This API is used by the Docker CLI and can also be used directly by external tools to integrate Docker into custom workflows or automation scripts.

Docker images

A Docker image is a lightweight, standalone, and immutable blueprint for creating containers. Images are built using a **Dockerfile**, which contains instructions for assembling the image layer by layer. Each layer in an image represents a filesystem change, making image builds efficient through caching mechanisms. Docker images are stored in registries and pulled by the Docker daemon to instantiate containers.

The key technical aspects are as follows:

- **Union File System (UnionFS):** Docker uses UnionFS to combine multiple layers into a single, unified file system. This ensures the reusability of layers across different images, optimizing storage and speeding up builds.

- **Content addressable storage:** Each layer is identified by a unique SHA-256 digest, ensuring that identical layers are reused across images.

Docker containers

A Docker container is a runtime instance of a Docker image. It is isolated, portable, and lightweight, containing everything needed to run an application, including the code, runtime, libraries, and configuration files. Containers run on the same kernel as the host machine but are isolated through technologies like namespaces and cgroups.

The key technical features are as follows:

- **Namespaces:** Namespaces provide process isolation, ensuring that containers have their own view of the filesystem, process tree, and network interfaces.

- **Control groups (cgroups):** Limit and allocate resources (CPU, memory, IO) to ensure containers do not consume excessive host resources.

- **UnionFS:** Ensures that containers can share image layers, reducing redundancy and speeding up container startup.

Docker registries

Docker registries store and distribute Docker images. The most common registry is Docker Hub, but organizations often set up private registries for security and control. Registries support versioning, allowing developers to manage multiple versions of an image using tags.

The key technical details are as follows:

- **Layer distribution:** When pulling an image, the Docker daemon downloads only the layers not already present locally, optimizing bandwidth and time.

- **Authentication and access control:** Docker registries implement authentication mechanisms and RBAC to restrict image access

Docker networking

Networking is an essential part of Docker, enabling containers to communicate with each other and with external systems. Docker provides multiple networking drivers, as follows:

- **Bridge:** The default driver for standalone containers, providing isolated container-to-container communication on a single host.

- **Host:** Containers share the host's networking stack for performance-critical applications.

- **Overlay:** Enables multi-host networking by creating a distributed network across multiple Docker daemons.

- **None:** No networking is configured; it is useful for highly isolated containers.

- **Custom plugins:** Docker supports third-party plugins for advanced networking needs.

Docker volumes

Volumes are Docker's solution for managing persistent data that needs to survive container restarts. Unlike the container's writable layer, volumes are managed outside the UnionFS, making them more efficient and persistent.

The technical features are as follows:

- **Mounting mechanism:** Volumes can be mounted directly into the container's filesystem, ensuring efficient access.

- **Data sharing:** Volumes can be shared between multiple containers, facilitating data exchange.

How Docker components work together:

- A developer writes a Dockerfile to define the application's environment.

- The `docker build` command uses the Docker CLI to instruct the Docker daemon to build an image from the Dockerfile.

- The resulting image is stored locally or pushed to a registry for distribution.

- When the `docker run` command is issued, the Docker daemon pulls the image (if it is not already available locally) and creates a container using the image.

- The container is connected to a network, and volumes are mounted as needed to provide the required resources for the application.

- The Docker daemon monitors the container's lifecycle, handles logging, and ensures resource constraints are maintained.

By abstracting complexities and offering seamless integration across its components, Docker simplifies application deployment and management, making it indispensable in modern software development and DevOps workflows.

Writing efficient Dockerfiles and multi-stage builds

Efficient Dockerfiles are the cornerstone of building optimized, secure, and lightweight container images. They ensure faster builds, reduced image sizes, and improved maintainability, making your containerized applications more portable and production ready.

Let us now look at the best practices for writing efficient Dockerfiles as follows:

- **Use a minimal base image:** Start with lightweight base images like **alpine** or **debian-slim** to minimize image size.

  ```
  FROM alpine:latest
  ```

- **Leverage caching:** Docker caches layers during the build process. To maximize caching, order your instructions so that layers that change less frequently come first.

  ```
  # Install dependencies first (infrequent change)
  RUN apt-get update && apt-get install -y build-essential

  # Add application code last (frequent change)
  COPY app/ /app
  ```

- **Minimize layers:** Combine multiple RUN instructions into a single one to reduce the number of layers.

```
RUN apt-get update && apt-get install -y \
    curl \
    git \
    && rm -rf /var/lib/apt/lists/*
```

- **Avoid adding secrets:** Never hard-code sensitive information (e.g., API keys) in the Dockerfile. Use environment variables or secret management tools instead.

- **Use .dockerignore:** Exclude unnecessary files (e.g., **node_modules**, **.git**) from the build context by specifying them in a **.dockerignore** file to improve build performance.

```
node_modules/
.git/
```

- **Specify explicit versions:** Pin specific versions of dependencies to ensure reproducibility and stability.

```
RUN apt-get install -y nodejs=14.17.0
```

Multi-stage builds

Multi-stage builds allow you to create smaller, production-ready images by separating the build and runtime environments into multiple stages. This eliminates unnecessary build-time dependencies from the final image. For example:

```
# Stage 1: Build
FROM node:16 as build

# Set working directory
WORKDIR /app

# Copy dependencies
COPY package.json package-lock.json ./

# Install dependencies
RUN npm install

# Copy source code
COPY . .

# Build the application
```

```
RUN npm run build

# Stage 2: Production
FROM nginx:alpine

# Copy built assets from the build stage
COPY --from=build /app/build /usr/share/nginx/html

# Expose port 80
EXPOSE 80

# Start Nginx server
CMD ["nginx", "-g", "daemon off;"]
```

In the aforementioned Dockerfile, there are two key stages:

- **Build stage:**
  - o Uses the Node.js image to install dependencies, copy the source code, and build the application.
  - o All intermediate files (e.g., **node_modules**) stay in the build stage.
- **Production stage:**
  - o Uses the lightweight **nginx:alpine** image to serve the built assets.
  - o Only the necessary files (**/app/build**) are copied to the production image, reducing size and attack surface.

The primary benefits of multi-stage builds are:

- **Smaller final image size:** No build-time dependencies are included in the production image.
- **Improved security:** Only essential files are present in the runtime environment.
- **Cleaner builds:** Separates concerns between build and runtime stages, making the Dockerfile easier to maintain.

By following these practices and leveraging multi-stage builds, you can create Docker images that are lean, efficient, and production ready.

Security scanning for container images

Container security is critical in production environments, and securing your container images is one of the first lines of defense. Container images often include system libraries, application dependencies, and configurations that can introduce vulnerabilities. Security scanning helps identify and mitigate these risks before deploying containers in production. Security scanning for container images involves analyzing the image's layers, filesystem, and configurations to detect known vulnerabilities, misconfigurations, and outdated software. Scanning tools typically reference vulnerability databases, such as the **National Vulnerability Database (NVD)**, to flag **Common Vulnerabilities and Exposures (CVEs)**.

Some of the key steps in image security scanning are:

- **Integrate scanning into CI/CD pipelines:** Automate security checks at every stage of your CI/CD pipeline to catch vulnerabilities early in development.

- **Scan both base and application layers:** Base images often carry vulnerabilities, so ensure they are scanned along with your custom application layers.

- **Update images regularly:** Vulnerabilities are continuously discovered, so keep base images and dependencies up to date.

- **Use trusted base images:** Prefer official or verified base images from trusted sources to reduce the risk of pre-existing vulnerabilities.

- **Minimize image layers:** Avoid adding unnecessary layers and dependencies to reduce the attack surface.

Security scans also complement observability by ensuring that the underlying container images are free of vulnerabilities that could compromise system reliability and performance. Scanning results can be integrated into monitoring tools, generating alerts for newly detected vulnerabilities, and enabling teams to respond quickly.

By adopting robust scanning practices and tools, you can significantly reduce the risk of deploying vulnerable container images, ensuring a secure and resilient environment.

Docker networking models

Docker networking provides the foundation for communication between containers, services, and external systems. It ensures that containers can securely and efficiently interact within the same host, across a cluster, or with external networks. Docker supports several networking models, each optimized for different use cases:

- **Bridge network:** This is the default network for standalone containers on a single host. Containers on the same bridge network can communicate with each other directly using private IP addresses, while external access requires explicit port mapping.

  For example, `docker network` create `my_bridge` creates a custom bridge network, and `docker run --net=my_bridge` attaches a container to it.

- **Host network:** By using the host's network stack, this model eliminates the isolation layer between the container and the host. Containers share the host's network interface and IP address, reducing latency and network overhead. For example, `docker run --net=host` runs a container using the host's network, which is ideal for low-latency applications.

- **Overlay network:** This model is designed for multi-host communication, often used in Docker Swarm or Kubernetes. It creates a distributed virtual network, allowing containers running on different hosts to communicate seamlessly. Docker uses a key-value store (e.g., etcd or Consul) to manage this network. For example, `docker network create -d overlay my_overlay` creates an overlay network for distributed services

- **Macvlan network:** Containers are assigned unique MAC addresses, making them appear as physical devices on the network. This model is ideal for integrating with existing network infrastructure, especially when direct, static IP address assignment is required, such as for legacy systems or network-restricted environments. For example, `docker network create -d macvlan --subnet=192.168.1.0/24 macvlan_net` creates a `macvlan` network for assigning specific IPs to containers.

- **None network:** This model disables all networking, providing a completely isolated environment. Containers cannot communicate with other containers or external systems. It is useful for security-focused use cases or when networking is unnecessary. For example, `docker run --net=none` disables networking for a container, providing complete isolation.

Managing persistent data with volumes

In containerized applications, managing persistent data is critical for ensuring data durability and consistency, even when containers are recreated or updated. Docker provides volumes as a robust mechanism to persist data outside the container's ephemeral filesystem. Unlike bind mounts or temporary storage, volumes are managed by Docker, offering better portability, isolation, and ease of use.

Volumes are storage objects that Docker manages outside the container's filesystem. They reside in a directory on the host (usually **/var/lib/docker/volumes/**), separate from the container lifecycle, ensuring data persists independently of container restarts or deletions.

Working of Docker volumes

Docker volumes can be used in three primary ways:

- **Anonymous volumes:** These are created automatically when no specific volume is specified.

  ```
  $ docker run -v /data busybox
  ```

  Here, Docker creates a **volume** and mounts it to **/data** in the container.

- **Named volumes:** Explicitly created and named for reusability.

```
docker volume create my_volume
docker run -v my_volume:/data busybox
```

- **Volume sharing:** A single volume can be mounted across multiple containers for shared access.

```
docker run -d --name container1 -v shared_volume:/data busybox
docker run -d --name container2 -v shared_volume:/data busybox
```

Persistent data is essential for various scenarios in containerized applications. For example, databases like MySQL or PostgreSQL store critical files that must survive container restarts to prevent data loss. Configuration files, such as application settings or SSL certificates, can be persisted to ensure consistency across container deployments. Additionally, application logs are often stored in volumes, enabling developers to analyze and debug system behavior over time.

To effectively manage volumes, it is important to follow best practices. Organizing volumes with meaningful names helps identify their purpose and maintain clarity. Regular backups of volume data safeguard against unexpected failures; for instance, using the **docker cp** or **tar** utilities allows you to save and restore critical data. Cleaning up unused or orphaned volumes with **docker volume prune** prevents unnecessary storage consumption. Monitoring volume usage helps optimize resource allocation and detect potential issues before they escalate. For large-scale applications, leveraging external storage drivers like NFS, AWS EFS, or Azure Files ensures scalable and distributed storage, enhancing the reliability and accessibility of persistent data. These strategies enable efficient data management while ensuring the resilience and scalability of containerized systems.

Docker Compose for multi-container applications

Docker Compose is a powerful tool for defining and managing multi-container applications. By using a simple YAML configuration file, developers can describe the services, networks, and volumes that their application needs and then orchestrate everything with a single command. Docker Compose simplifies application lifecycle management, making it easier to build, deploy, and scale containerized applications.

Some of the key benefits of Docker Compose are as follows:

- **Declarative configuration:** Define all components of the application in a single **docker-compose.yml** file.

- **Multi-container orchestration:** Easily manage complex applications with multiple interdependent services.

- **Portability:** Share the configuration file across teams and environments for consistent deployments.

- **Simplified commands:** Use simple commands like **docker-compose up** and **docker-compose down** to manage the entire stack.

Let us explore a basic use case where we deploy a web application with a backend (Python Flask) and a database (MySQL) using Docker Compose as follows:

```yaml
version: '3.9'
services:
  web:
    image: python:3.9
    container_name: flask_app
    working_dir: /app
    volumes:
      - ./app:/app
    ports:
      - "5000:5000"
    command: >
      sh -c «pip install flask mysql-connector-python &&
            python app.py»
    depends_on:
      - db
  db:
    image: mysql:8
    container_name: mysql_db
    environment:
      MYSQL_ROOT_PASSWORD: rootpassword
      MYSQL_DATABASE: flaskdb
      MYSQL_USER: flaskuser
      MYSQL_PASSWORD: flaskpassword
    ports:
      - "3306:3306"
    volumes:
      - db_data:/var/lib/mysql
volumes:
  db_data:
```

In the aforementioned Docker Compose, we have the following:

- **Services:**
  - o The web service runs a Python Flask application, mounts the local **./app** directory for code changes, and maps port 5000 on the host to the container.

o The **db** service runs a MySQL database with environment variables defining credentials and configuration.

- **Volumes:** A named volume **db_data** is defined for persisting MySQL data, ensuring durability across container restarts.

- **Dependencies:**

o The **depends_on** key ensures that the **db** service starts before the web service.

- **Commands:** The web service installs dependencies and starts the Flask application using app.py.

You can run the following command to start the entire stack:

```
$ docker-compose up
```

This will:

o Build and start the web and db containers.

o Automatically link the containers via an internal Docker network.

Similarly, you can stop and remove the whole stack by:

```
$ docker-compose down --volumes
```

This example illustrates how Docker Compose simplifies the management of multi-container applications. It abstracts the complexity of individual container configurations, enabling developers to focus on building and deploying their applications efficiently. By using a single configuration file, teams can ensure consistency across development, testing, and production environments.

Container registries and image management

Container registries are centralized repositories for storing, sharing, and managing Docker images. They play a significant role in the distribution and versioning of containerized applications across different environments. Public container registries, such as Docker Hub, enable developers to easily access and pull pre-built images for common use cases. On the other hand, private container registries allow organizations to store proprietary images securely, allowing them to decide who can use and deploy them. Some popular private registries include Amazon **Elastic Container Registry (ECR)**, **Google Container Registry (GCR)**, and **Azure Container Registry (ACR)**. The management of images in registries includes tagging, versioning, and ensuring the right version is used across environments. Image tags often adhere to semantic versioning or other naming conventions to distinguish between stable releases, development versions, or experimental builds. Also, registry management should clean out the old images no longer in use to prevent unused storage and deploy only valid, secure, and tested images.

Container registries must be integrated into CI/CD workflows to achieve effective image management. This integration allows for the automation of the image build, test, and push process, ensuring that the latest image versions are always available for deployment. Docker images can be built on a developer's local machine, pushed to a registry, and later pulled by production environments, ensuring consistency across various deployment stages. In addition, registries often support automated vulnerability scanning to identify and address security issues in container images before they are deployed. This helps maintain security and compliance since security flaws in containerized applications can be catastrophic. Tools like Clair, Trivy, and Docker's own security scanning features give insights into image vulnerabilities. With these security tools integrated into the CI/CD pipeline, teams prevent vulnerabilities from reaching production. Efficient image management practices, including careful versioning, regular scanning, and automated workflows, are essential for maintaining security, reducing friction in deployment, and ensuring that containerized applications perform as expected across all stages of the lifecycle.

Debugging and troubleshooting containers

Containers are often hard to debug and troubleshoot because they are transient and isolated, but the right tools and approaches can effectively overcome these challenges. The most common technique for diagnosing container issues is inspecting logs. Docker provides the **docker logs** command that lets you view the output of a container's standard output and standard error. This can often help you uncover the cause behind application crashes or processes that crashed or behaved unreliably in other ways. If the container's not starting properly or not working right enough that logs simply do not speak to the failure, you should need to take more direct hands-on approaches towards the container with docker exec, such as manually browsing files, making diagnostic runs, or even troubleshooting the container's environment at your discretion. For example, you could run **docker exec -it <container_id>** bash to get an interactive shell inside the container, where you can explore the file system, check environment variables, and run commands to diagnose what is wrong.

Besides just providing basic logging and shell access, Docker also gives you several additional tools that help to make debugging easier. The **docker inspect** command will give an idea of configuration details about the container in terms of the network settings or the runtime parameters that could be critical if you wish to understand what is configured, how it might have been wrongly configured, and so on, because networking can cause containers sometimes to fail in silent mode and other times when it is behaving mysteriously. Docker also integrates with monitoring tools like Prometheus, Grafana, and ELK Stack, which can provide more advanced observability into container performance and health metrics over time. These tools allow you to monitor resource utilization (CPU, memory, disk), detect anomalies, and visualize logs and metrics in real-time. When debugging, it is also crucial to eliminate the possibility that the problem is related to the host machine, networking, or external dependencies, which often affect container behavior. In bigger environments, with tools such as Kubernetes, there are more layers of monitoring and debugging capabilities, including things like health checks, readiness probes, and more detailed error messages at the time of a pod deployment failure. Debugging containers requires a systematic approach, combining real-time inspection, thorough logging, and external tools to identify and resolve issues.

Docker security best practices

Docker security is one of the critical concerns when using containers in production. Containers, by design, isolate applications from the host system, but this isolation is compromised if not properly managed. To ensure that containerized applications are secure, it is essential to adopt best practices at every stage of the container lifecycle, starting from building images to deploying containers in production. One of the fundamental principles of Docker security is minimizing the attack surface. This can be achieved by using the principle of least privilege, such as running containers with non-root users whenever possible. Avoiding running containers as root limits the potential impact of a security breach, preventing attackers from gaining full control over the host system. Another best practice is to use minimal base images, such as Alpine Linux, that contain only the necessary components for the application's operation. This minimizes the amount of possible vulnerabilities and keeps the container image smaller as well as easier to secure.

In addition to ensuring the container image is secured, it should also be free from known vulnerabilities. Security scanning tools, such as Trivy, Clair, and Docker's built-in security features, can automatically scan images for vulnerabilities before they are deployed to production. Integrating these tools into your CI/CD pipeline allows you to identify and address security flaws early in the development process, reducing the risk of deploying vulnerable images. Another critical area of Docker security is securing the communication between containers. Options include using encrypted communication channels between containers, as well as Docker's built-in security features such as user namespaces, which isolate containers from each other and from the host system. Additionally, with Docker Compose or orchestrators like Kubernetes, one needs to configure network policies and firewalls so that only those containers are allowed to communicate with each other, thereby reducing the attack surface even further.

To further reinforce Docker security, it is advisable to follow the principle of immutability; the container image being built and then deployed should never be changed afterward. Any necessary changes should rather be done at the image level to redeploy in place, while the running containers should not change. This tends to minimize instances of accidental as well as malicious tampering with the environment. Docker also has security features like Content Trust, which ensures that only signed images are pulled from registries, and Docker Secrets for securely managing sensitive information like passwords or API keys. Finally, always keep Docker and its dependencies up to date, as security patches and updates are frequently released to address newly discovered vulnerabilities. Regularly applying these updates is a crucial part of maintaining a secure Docker environment. By following the Docker security best practices outlined here, you will be able to minimize the likelihood of security breaches and ensure that your containerized applications are more secure and reliable.

Integration with CI/CD pipelines

When using Docker, it must be integrated into CI/CD pipelines to automate the processes involved in building, testing, and deploying application containerization. The streamlined integration of Docker into such workflows adds speed, consistency, and reliability across the software delivery lifecycle. There is a core need behind Docker's integration in CI/CD pipeline automation: This refers to the automation of the creation and testing of images. Once developers push code changes to a version control system like Git, the CI/CD pipeline initiates the building of a new Docker image. Tools such as Jenkins, GitLab CI, GitHub Actions, and CircleCI can automate this by defining pipeline steps that include building Docker images with `docker build` commands and pushing them to a container registry using `docker push`. This ensures that each code change brings a new, versioned Docker image to deploy. Building images automatically at each commit prevents the tedious manual effort of building images, hence reducing human errors and ensuring that the development and production environments remain consistent.

Another important aspect is testing when using Docker with CI/CD pipelines. The containerized environment allows for automated tests, including unit, integration, and end-to-end tests, to be executed in the validation of code changes in a consistent and isolated environment. For instance, tests may be run inside Docker containers as part of the CI process so that developers know whether their application will work as expected before it gets deployed. Tools like Docker Compose are often used within the CI/CD pipeline to simulate multi-container applications. For instance, a developer can use the tool to test scenarios involving interactions between several services or containers. Security is another important aspect of using Docker in CI/CD. This way, tools such as Trivy, Clair, or Docker's security scanning features could be integrated into the pipeline, automatically scanning Docker images for known vulnerabilities before pushing them to the registry or deploying. This approach catches security flaws early in the development cycle, making it impossible for insecure images to be allowed into production.

Once the Docker image satisfies all tests and security scans, the pipeline can deploy it to staging or production environments, making the final product ready for use. In modern DevOps practices, integrating with container orchestration tools such as Kubernetes, Docker Swarm, or Amazon ECS is pretty common in CI/CD pipelines. These tools automate the deployment and scaling of containers, leaving a containerized application dispersed across the infrastructure efficiently and resiliently. This is because fully automating the build and testing, as well as the deployment of Docker images, streamlines the delivery of software, minimizes errors, and reduces delays. This ensures that Docker is integrated into CI/CD pipelines, fostering an efficient and reliable workflow, allowing teams to deliver applications to production securely and quickly with a high quality but with consistency in every environment.

Conclusion

Containerization has fundamentally reshaped how modern applications are developed, deployed, and scaled, offering significant flexibility, consistency, and speed advantages. Throughout this chapter, we have explored the best practices and tools that make Docker an essential part of the DevOps workflow. From understanding Docker's architecture and components to writing efficient Dockerfiles, managing multi-container applications with Docker Compose, and handling persistent data with volumes, we have covered the critical elements that ensure containers are built and maintained effectively.

We also discussed the importance of security, highlighting practices such as image vulnerability scanning, running containers with non-root users, and using secure container registries. Integrating Docker with CI/CD pipelines further enhances the development cycle by automating containerized applications' building, testing, and deployment, ensuring fast, reliable, and secure releases. By following Docker security best practices and adopting a proactive approach to debugging and troubleshooting, you can build resilient and secure containerized environments. As you continue to apply these best practices, Docker will enable you to streamline development, reduce operational complexity, and accelerate the delivery of high-quality applications. Mastery of Docker and containerization tools will empower you to manage applications at scale, integrate with robust DevOps workflows, and adapt to the ever-evolving needs of modern software delivery.

In the next chapter, we will build upon the containerization concepts covered here and explore how Kubernetes extends these capabilities for large-scale deployments. We will learn about Kubernetes architecture, its key components like pods, deployments, and services, and how to manage containerized applications at scale effectively. The chapter will cover advanced topics such as stateful applications, configmaps and secrets, horizontal pod autoscaling, and implementing robust networking and storage solutions. Additionally, you will discover how to leverage Kubernetes' rich ecosystem of tools for monitoring, logging, and security, enabling you to build and maintain resilient, production-grade container orchestration environments that can handle the demands of modern distributed applications.

Join our Discord space

Join our Discord workspace for latest updates, offers, tech happenings around the world, new releases, and sessions with the authors:

https://discord.bpbonline.com

Kubernetes Essentials

Introduction

This chapter explores **Kubernetes (K8s)**, the leading platform for automating the deployment, scaling, and management of containerized applications. We will cover Kubernetes architecture, including clusters, nodes, control planes, and core objects like Pods, ReplicaSets, and Deployments.

We will examine Kubernetes networking, services, persistent storage, and configuration management with ConfigMaps and Secrets. The chapter also addresses security through RBAC, explains scaling via autoscaling and Rolling Updates, and introduces Helm for package management.

Additionally, we will cover monitoring, logging, security best practices, and GitOps for Kubernetes application management. By the end of this chapter, we will understand how to manage and scale containerized applications using Kubernetes effectively.

Structure

The chapter covers the following topics:

- Kubernetes architecture and components
- Pods, ReplicaSets, and Deployments

- Kubernetes networking and services

- Persistent storage

- ConfigMaps and Secrets

- Kubernetes RBAC

- Autoscaling and Rolling Updates

- Kubernetes Operators

- Helm charts for application deployment

- Kubernetes monitoring and logging

- Kubernetes security

- GitOps with Kubernetes

Objectives

By the end of this chapter, we will gain a comprehensive understanding of Kubernetes architecture and its core components, enabling you to configure and manage Pods, ReplicaSets, and Deployments effectively. We will understand how to implement Kubernetes networking, create appropriate service types, and set up persistent storage solutions for stateful applications.

The chapter will equip you with the knowledge to manage application configurations using ConfigMaps and Secrets and apply RBAC for proper security governance. We will learn how to configure autoscaling and implement Rolling Updates for zero-downtime deployments, as well as utilize Kubernetes Operators for managing complex applications. Additionally, you will learn to deploy applications using Helm charts, implement monitoring and logging solutions, apply security best practices to protect Kubernetes workloads, and implement GitOps workflows for Kubernetes application management.

Kubernetes architecture and components

Kubernetes architecture is designed to automate the deployment, scaling, and management of containerized applications. It is built around a client-server model, where the master node (or control plane) manages the overall cluster, and worker nodes (or minions) run the applications and workloads.

Let us break down the main components of Kubernetes architecture:

- **Master node (control plane):** The master node is the brain of the Kubernetes cluster. It manages the cluster's state, ensuring that the desired state of applications (as described in configuration files) is maintained. The control plane consists of the following key components:

o **API server**: The API server is the entry point for all Kubernetes REST commands, allowing users and components to interact with the cluster. It processes incoming requests, validates them, and serves the data. It also ensures the API is available and responds to queries for cluster resources.

o **Controller manager**: The controller manager is responsible for maintaining the desired state of the cluster. It ensures that nodes, replicas, and other resources match the desired configuration. Common controllers include the ReplicationController, which ensures that the specified number of replicas of a Pod are running, and the NodeController, which manages node health.

o **Scheduler**: The scheduler is responsible for assigning Pods to worker nodes based on resource availability. It takes into account the current state of the cluster (like node CPU, memory, and disk usage) and ensures that the Pods are placed optimally to meet the desired state of the application.

o **etcd**: etcd is a distributed key-value store that holds the configuration data and the state of the entire cluster. It is the source of truth for Kubernetes, storing details about nodes, Pods, and configurations. etcd ensures that the desired state is always available and can be recovered if needed.

- **Worker nodes:** The worker nodes are responsible for running containerized applications and services. These nodes contain the necessary components to run and manage the containers.

  Key components of the worker node include:

o **Kubelet**: The kubelet is an agent that runs on each worker node. It ensures that containers are running in Pods and continuously monitors the state of containers. If a container fails, the kubelet restarts it to match the desired state. The kubelet communicates with the API server to report the status of containers and nodes.

o **Kube proxy**: The kube proxy runs on each worker node and manages networking for Pods. It maintains network rules that allow communication between different services in the cluster. The kube proxy forwards traffic to the appropriate Pod or service by updating iptables or IPVS rules based on the current state of services in the cluster.

o **Container runtime**: The container runtime is the software responsible for running containers. Kubernetes supports different runtimes like Docker, containerd, or CRI-O. The runtime pulls container images and runs containers within Pods.

- **Kubernetes objects:** Kubernetes organizes and manages containers using a variety of objects. Some of the most important objects are:

o **Pods**: A Pod is the smallest and simplest Kubernetes object. It represents one or more containers that are tightly coupled and share the same network namespace, storage, and lifecycle. Pods are the units that Kubernetes schedules and manages.

o **ReplicaSets**: A ReplicaSet ensures that a specified number of replicas of a Pod are running at all times. If a Pod fails or is terminated, the ReplicaSet automatically creates new Pods to match the desired count.

o **Deployments**: A Deployment provides declarative updates to applications, ensuring that the desired number of replicas are running. It manages Rolling Updates, rollbacks, and versioning of applications, making it easier to maintain a desired application state.

o **Namespaces**: Namespaces provide a mechanism to partition the cluster into multiple virtual clusters, allowing for better resource management, security, and access control. Namespaces help organize and isolate workloads within a single Kubernetes cluster.

o **Services**: A service is an abstraction that exposes a set of Pods as a network service. It allows Pods to communicate with each other without worrying about their IP addresses, providing load balancing and DNS resolution.

• **Cluster management and communication:** Kubernetes clusters rely heavily on intercommunication between components, both within the control plane and between the control plane and worker nodes. Here is how it works:

o The **API server** communicates with all components, including the controller manager, scheduler, and kubelet, using the Kubernetes API.

o The **controller manager** communicates with etcd to store cluster state and with the API Server to manage resources.

o The **scheduler** uses the API Server to track available nodes and schedules Pods based on resource availability.

o The **kubelet** on each node regularly communicates with the API Server, reporting the status of Pods and containers. The Kube Proxy handles networking and load balancing, routing traffic to the correct Pods.

• **High availability and fault tolerance:** Kubernetes is designed to provide high availability and fault tolerance:

o **etcd** stores critical cluster data, and multiple replicas of etcd can be deployed across different nodes to ensure data availability and redundancy.

o The **control plane components** (**API server, scheduler, controller manager**) can be replicated across multiple nodes to ensure high availability.

o **Pods** and **ReplicaSets** ensure that applications remain available even in the case of failures. If a Pod fails or is terminated, a new Pod will be scheduled automatically.

Pods, ReplicaSets, and Deployments

In Kubernetes, Pods, ReplicaSets, and Deployments are the building blocks that ensure your applications run reliably and efficiently.

Each of these serves a specific purpose:

- **Pods:** The smallest and simplest Kubernetes object that encapsulates one or more containers.

- **ReplicaSets:** Ensure that a specified number of Pod replicas are running at all times.

- **Deployments:** Provide a declarative way to manage application updates, scaling, and rollbacks.

Let us break them down step by step.

Pods

A Pod is the basic deployable unit in Kubernetes. It represents a single instance of an application and can run one or more containers that share the same network namespace and storage volumes. Pods are ephemeral; if a Pod crashes, Kubernetes does not restart it directly. Instead, higher-level controllers like ReplicaSets handle this responsibility.

The main features of Pods are:

- **Container grouping:** Allows tightly coupled containers (e.g., a web server and a logging agent) to share resources.

- **Networking:** All containers in a Pod share the same IP address and can communicate using localhost.

- **Storage:** Containers in a Pod can share mounted volumes.

You can create a Pod as shown in the following example:

```
apiVersion: v1
kind: Pod
metadata:
  name: example-pod
  labels:
    app: demo
spec:
  containers:
    - name: nginx-container
      image: nginx:1.21
      ports:
        - containerPort: 80
```

Save this file as **pod-example.yaml**.

Now you can run it as follows:

1. Create a **pod**:

```
kubectl apply -f pod-example.yaml
```

2. View **pods**:

```
kubectl get pods
```

3. Delete a **pod**:

```
kubectl delete pod example-pod
```

A key aspect to note is that Pods are not self-healing. If a Pod fails, it will not restart unless managed by a ReplicaSet or Deployment.

Let us discuss ReplicaSets in the next sub section.

ReplicaSet

A ReplicaSet ensures a specified number of identical Pods are running at all times. If a Pod fails or is deleted, the ReplicaSet creates a new one to maintain the desired state.

The following are some of the key features of ReplicaSets:

- **Self-healing:** Automatically replaces failed Pods.

- **Scaling:** Easily increase or decrease the number of Pod replicas.

Let us take the following example and create a **replicaset-example.yaml** file as follows:

```
apiVersion: apps/v1
kind: ReplicaSet
metadata:
  name: example-replicaset
  labels:
    app: demo
spec:
  replicas: 3
  selector:
    matchLabels:
      app: demo
  template:
    metadata:
      labels:
        app: demo
```

```
   spec:
     containers:
       - name: nginx-container
         image: nginx:1.21
         ports:
           - containerPort: 80
```

Now, you can create a replica by running the following command:

```
$ kubectl apply -f replicaset-example.yaml
```

You can scale a **replicaset** also by running the following:

```
$ kubectl scale replicaset example-replicaset --replicas=5
```

Finally, you can delete the **replicaset** by running:

```
$ kubectl delete replicaset example-replicaset
```

While ReplicaSets are powerful, they are rarely used directly. Instead, Deployments provide additional functionality and manage ReplicaSets for you.

Deployments

A Deployment is a higher-level abstraction that manages ReplicaSets and provides declarative updates for Pods. Deployments simplify tasks like Rolling Updates, rollbacks, and scaling.

Some of the key features of deployments are:

- **Declarative updates:** Specify the desired state, and Kubernetes handles the rest.
- **Rolling updates:** Update Pods incrementally without downtime.
- **Rollback:** Revert to a previous Deployment version if something goes wrong.

Let us take the following example and create a **deployment-example.yaml** file:

```
apiVersion: apps/v1
kind: Deployment
metadata:
  name: example-deployment
  labels:
    app: demo
spec:
  replicas: 3
  selector:
    matchLabels:
      app: demo
```

```
template:
  metadata:
    labels:
      app: demo
  spec:
    containers:
      - name: nginx-container
        image: nginx:1.21
        ports:
          - containerPort: 80
```

You can run the following commands to manage your deployments:

- Create a **deployment**:

  ```
  $ kubectl apply -f deployment-example.yaml
  ```

- Update a **deployment**:

  ```
  $ kubectl set image deployment/example-deployment nginx-
  container=nginx:1.22
  ```

- Rollback a **deployment**:

  ```
  $ kubectl rollout undo deployment/example-deployment
  ```

Deployments ensure zero-downtime updates and maintain application availability, making them the preferred way to manage Pods and ReplicaSets.

You can clearly see how Pods, ReplicaSets, and Deployments all work together in unison in Kubernetes. In summary:

- Pods are the smallest deployable units in Kubernetes, encapsulating one or more containers.

- ReplicaSets ensure a desired number of Pod replicas are running at all times.

- Deployments provide a declarative approach to managing application updates, scaling, and rollbacks.

These components form the foundation for running and managing containerized applications in Kubernetes. Understanding how to use them effectively ensures reliable, scalable, and maintainable deployments.

Kubernetes networking and services

Kubernetes networking ensures that all components within the cluster can communicate efficiently. It provides a consistent way for Pods to communicate with each other and with external clients while abstracting the complexities of network configuration.

Kubernetes implements a flat networking model that adheres to the following principles:

- **Each Pod has a unique IP address:** This allows Pods to communicate directly with one another without requiring **Network Address Translation** (**NAT**).

- **Flat network structure:** Pods can reach other Pods across nodes as though they were on the same network.

- **Localhost communication:** Containers in the same Pod share the same network namespace and communicate via localhost.

- **Pod-to-external communication:** Pods can access the internet and external networks if the cluster is configured appropriately.

Networking components

Kubernetes networking components ensure seamless communication within the cluster and external access to applications. They abstract complexities like IP allocation, routing, and load balancing. Understanding these components is crucial for managing traffic flow and troubleshooting issues.

The core components are:

- **Container Network Interface (CNI):** A standard interface used by Kubernetes to manage network configurations. Popular CNI plugins include Calico, Flannel, and WeaveNet, each offering unique features like network policies and advanced routing.

- **kube-proxy:** A cluster component responsible for maintaining network rules and forwarding traffic to the appropriate Pods via Services. It ensures seamless communication between Pods and external clients.

- **DNS (CoreDNS):** Kubernetes uses CoreDNS for internal service discovery. Each Service in the cluster gets a DNS name, making it easy for applications to locate and communicate with one another.

Kubernetes services

Services provide a consistent way to expose applications running in Pods. Since Pods are ephemeral, their IPs can change over time. Services address this issue by offering stable endpoints that dynamically route traffic to the appropriate Pods.

The following are the types of services:

- **ClusterIP (Default):** Exposes the **Service** within the cluster. It assigns a virtual IP address that other Pods can use to access the **Service** as follows:

```
apiVersion: v1
kind: Service
metadata:
```

```
    name: clusterip-service
spec:
  selector:
    app: demo
  ports:
    - protocol: TCP
      port: 80
      targetPort: 80
  type: ClusterIP
```

- **NodePort:** Exposes the **Service** on a static port of each node, allowing external access to the cluster.

```
apiVersion: v1
kind: Service
metadata:
  name: nodeport-service
spec:
  selector:
    app: demo
  ports:
    - protocol: TCP
      port: 80
      targetPort: 80
      nodePort: 30007
  type: NodePort
```

- **LoadBalancer:** Integrates with cloud provider APIs to provision an external load balancer for distributing traffic to the **Service**.

```
apiVersion: v1
kind: Service
metadata:
  name: loadbalancer-service
spec:
  selector:
    app: demo
  ports:
    - protocol: TCP
      port: 80
      targetPort: 80
  type: LoadBalancer
```

- **ExternalName:** Maps a **Service** to an external DNS name, enabling access to external systems by aliasing them in the cluster.

```
apiVersion: v1
kind: Service
metadata:
  name: externalname-service
spec:
  type: ExternalName
  externalName: external.example.com
```

Ingress

Ingress is an API object that manages external access to Services, typically HTTP and HTTPS traffic. It acts as a reverse proxy, routing requests to the appropriate Service based on rules. The main features of this component are:

- Supports host and path-based routing.
- Handles SSL/TLS termination.
- Balances load across multiple Services.

The following is an example of an **Ingress spec**:

```
apiVersion: networking.k8s.io/v1
kind: Ingress
metadata:
  name: example-ingress
spec:
  rules:
    - host: demo.example.com
      http:
        paths:
          - path: /
            pathType: Prefix
            backend:
              service:
                name: clusterip-service
                port:
                  number: 80
```

In summary, Kubernetes networking and Services are integral to application communication and connectivity. With components such as CNI, kube-proxy, and CoreDNS, Kubernetes offers a robust and scalable networking solution. Services and Ingress objects further simplify exposing applications, ensuring reliable and secure access both within and outside the cluster.

Persistent storage

Persistent storage in Kubernetes allows stateful applications to store and retrieve data even when Pods are rescheduled or restarted. Unlike ephemeral storage tied to a Pod's lifecycle, persistent storage ensures data durability across Pod lifetimes.

Kubernetes abstracts storage management using **Persistent Volumes (PVs)** and **Persistent Volume Claims (PVCs)**. This approach decouples storage provisioning from application deployment, allowing for greater flexibility and scalability.

Let us now look at each of the storage management components:

- **PV:** A PV is a storage resource provisioned by an administrator or dynamically by the cluster. It represents actual storage, such as a disk in the cloud, a local disk, or a network file system.

- **PVC:** A PVC is a request for storage by a Pod. It specifies the desired capacity, access modes, and other requirements. Kubernetes binds the PVC to an appropriate PV based on the request.

- **Storage classes:** Storage classes define the characteristics of dynamically provisioned storage, such as performance tiers or replication policies. They allow administrators to abstract and manage storage backends efficiently.

Persistent storage is crucial for stateful applications, as it ensures data persistence and durability. Kubernetes abstracts storage management with PVs, PVCs, and storage classes, offering a flexible and scalable solution for diverse storage needs.

ConfigMaps and Secrets

In Kubernetes, ConfigMaps and Secrets are essential tools for managing application configuration and sensitive data separately from the application code. This separation enables greater flexibility, security, and reusability in deploying and managing containerized applications.

Basically, ConfigMap is a key-value store used to manage non-sensitive configuration data. ConfigMaps allow you to pass environment variables, configuration files, or command line arguments to your applications without hardcoding them into the container image.

For example, you can create a **ConfigMap** as follows:

```
apiVersion: v1
kind: ConfigMap
metadata:
```

```
  name: example-config
data:
  app.properties: |
    feature.enabled=true
    app.timeout=30
  log.level: "debug"
```

You can use this configuration as follows by attaching it as an **env** variable or a volume in a Pod:

```
apiVersion: v1
kind: Pod
metadata:
  name: configmap-example
spec:
  containers:
    - name: app-container
      image: nginx
      env:
        - name: LOG_LEVEL
          valueFrom:
            configMapKeyRef:
              name: example-config
              key: log.level
      volumeMounts:
        - mountPath: "/etc/config"
          name: config-volume
  volumes:
    - name: config-volume
      configMap:
        name: example-config
```

Finally, you can apply this as:

```
$ kubectl apply -f configmap.yaml
$ kubectl apply -f pod-using-configmap.yaml
$ kubectl get configmap example-config -o yaml
```

Similarly, you can create a **Secret** from either a manifest file as follows:

```
apiVersion: v1
kind: Secret
metadata:
```

```
  name: example-secret
type: Opaque
data:
  username: dXNlcg== # base64-encoded 'user'
  password: cGFzc3dvcmQ= # base64-encoded 'password'
```

You can make use of them in your Pod **spec** as follows:

```
apiVersion: v1
kind: Pod
metadata:
  name: secret-example
spec:
  containers:
    - name: app-container
      image: nginx
      env:
        - name: DB_USERNAME
          valueFrom:
            secretKeyRef:
              name: example-secret
              key: username
        - name: DB_PASSWORD
          valueFrom:
            secretKeyRef:
              name: example-secret
              key: password
```

Both ConfigMaps and Secrets are foundational tools for managing application configuration and sensitive data in Kubernetes. By separating configuration from application code, these tools enhance security, portability, and operational efficiency, making them indispensable in modern Kubernetes workflows.

Kubernetes RBAC

RBAC in Kubernetes is a mechanism for managing access to cluster resources based on user roles. It enforces the principle of least privilege, ensuring that users, applications, or processes only have the permissions necessary to perform their tasks. RBAC enhances security by preventing unauthorized access to critical resources and providing fine-grained control over actions like creating, modifying, or viewing specific objects within the cluster. This makes it especially useful in multi-tenant environments and for meeting organizational compliance requirements.

RBAC consists of four key components such as Roles, ClusterRoles, RoleBindings, and ClusterRoleBindings.

A Role defines a set of permissions within a specific namespace, while a ClusterRole applies permissions across the entire cluster. These roles are assigned to users, groups, or service accounts via RoleBindings or ClusterRoleBindings, which link the defined permissions to the appropriate subjects.

For example, imagine a user named **john-doe** who needs permission to view Pods in the development namespace. You can create a role called pod-reader that allows actions like get, list, and watch on Pods.

Then, you bind this role to **john-doe** using a **RoleBinding** as follows:

```
apiVersion: rbac.authorization.k8s.io/v1
kind: Role
metadata:
  namespace: development
  name: pod-reader
rules:
  - apiGroups: [""]
    resources: ["pods"]
    verbs: ["get", "list", "watch"]
---
apiVersion: rbac.authorization.k8s.io/v1
kind: RoleBinding
metadata:
  name: read-pods-binding
  namespace: development
subjects:
  - kind: User
    name: john-doe
    apiGroup: rbac.authorization.k8s.io
roleRef:
  kind: Role
  name: pod-reader
  apiGroup: rbac.authorization.k8s.io
```

Applying these configurations ensures **john-doe** can only view Pods in the development namespace and nothing more. By defining clear roles and bindings, Kubernetes RBAC provides a robust framework for securing resources and enforcing access control.

Autoscaling and Rolling Updates

Kubernetes offers powerful mechanisms to ensure application performance and reliability through autoscaling and Rolling Updates. These features enable dynamic resource management and seamless deployment updates, thereby minimizing downtime and requiring minimal manual intervention.

Autoscaling in Kubernetes adjusts the number of Pods in a Deployment or ReplicaSet based on resource usage or custom metrics. This ensures applications can handle varying workloads efficiently without over-provisioning resources.

Kubernetes provides two primary types of autoscaling:

- **Horizontal Pod Autoscaler (HPA):** Scales the number of Pods up or down based on CPU, memory, or custom metrics. For instance, if CPU usage exceeds 80%, the HPA adds more Pods to handle the load.

- **Cluster autoscaler:** Adjusts the number of nodes in the cluster by adding or removing nodes based on resource requests from Pods.

The following is an example of an HPA that scales a **Deployment** named **example-deployment** based on CPU usage:

```yaml
apiVersion: autoscaling/v2
kind: HorizontalPodAutoscaler
metadata:
  name: example-hpa
spec:
  scaleTargetRef:
    apiVersion: apps/v1
    kind: Deployment
    name: example-deployment
  minReplicas: 2
  maxReplicas: 10
  metrics:
    - type: Resource
      resource:
        name: cpu
        target:
          type: Utilization
          averageUtilization: 80
```

When CPU usage exceeds 80%, Kubernetes automatically increases the number of Pods in an example deployment. Conversely, it reduces Pods when usage drops, ensuring cost efficiency and optimal performance.

Rolling updates, on the other hand, allow Kubernetes to update applications incrementally, replacing Pods one by one while ensuring minimal downtime. This approach maintains application availability by gradually deploying new versions while keeping the older version active. Rolling updates are managed via Deployments, which ensure zero-downtime transitions.

For example, if a new application version is released, Kubernetes terminates an old Pod and starts a new one, repeating this process until all Pods are updated. This prevents service interruptions and allows users to verify the latest version as it rolls out.

To update a Deployment's image, you can use the following command:

```
$ kubectl set image deployment/example-deployment nginx-
container=nginx:1.22
```

Kubernetes automatically performs the rolling update, ensuring only a fraction of Pods are updated at any time, as defined by the Deployment's maxUnavailable and maxSurge parameters.

Kubernetes Operators

Kubernetes Operators are specialized controllers that extend Kubernetes' capabilities to manage complex, stateful applications. They utilize **Custom Resource Definitions (CRDs)** to define new types of resources and implement domain-specific logic to automate application management tasks. With Operators, you can automate lifecycle activities like deploying, scaling, upgrading, backing up, and recovering applications, eliminating the need for manual intervention. This is particularly useful for applications that require advanced configurations or custom workflows, such as databases or distributed systems.

Operators continuously monitor the cluster state and reconcile it to match the desired configuration defined in the custom resources. For example, a MySQL operator can manage the deployment of a MySQL cluster, ensuring the correct number of replicas, handling failover, and performing automated backups. By embedding operational knowledge into Kubernetes, operators enable consistent and reliable management of applications while simplifying operational overhead.

The following is an example of deploying a Redis cluster using a Redis Operator. The custom resource defines the desired state of the cluster:

```
apiVersion: redis.example.com/v1
kind: RedisCluster
metadata:
  name: example-redis-cluster
spec:
  replicas: 3
  version: "6.2"
  storage:
    size: 10Gi
```

When applied, the Redis Operator reads this configuration and creates the necessary Pods, configures master-slave replication, and monitors the cluster for health. If a Pod fails, the Operator automatically replaces it to maintain availability.

By automating repetitive and complex tasks, Kubernetes Operators empower teams to manage applications at scale with greater efficiency and reliability.

Helm charts for application deployment

Helm is a Kubernetes package manager that simplifies the deployment and management of applications in a Kubernetes cluster. A Helm chart is a pre-configured Kubernetes application definition containing all the resources necessary to deploy and manage an application. Charts enable developers and operators to package, share, and reuse configurations, making application deployment faster and more consistent. They support templating, allowing dynamic configuration for different environments (e.g., staging, production) without modifying the core deployment files.

Using Helm charts, you can deploy complex applications with a single command, managing dependencies, upgrades, and rollbacks effortlessly. For example, instead of writing multiple YAML files to deploy a web application, database, and monitoring tools, a single Helm chart can encapsulate all the configurations and deploy them as a cohesive unit. Helm also provides versioning, which ensures the reproducibility and traceability of deployments.

To deploy a NGINX application with Helm, first search for the official Helm chart:

```
$ helm search repo nginx
```

Then, we can install the chart as:

```
$ helm install my-nginx bitnami/nginx
```

This command deploys the NGINX application with default configurations, and you can customize it by overriding values:

```
$ helm install my-nginx bitnami/nginx --set service.type=LoadBalancer
```

Helm charts streamline Kubernetes application deployment, reducing the complexity of managing multiple resources while ensuring flexibility and ease of maintenance.

Kubernetes monitoring and logging

Monitoring and logging are crucial for understanding the health, performance, and behavior of applications running in Kubernetes. Kubernetes provides a rich ecosystem of tools and integrations to help operators collect, visualize, and analyze metrics and logs from the cluster. Monitoring tools, such as Prometheus, focus on metrics like CPU usage, memory consumption, and request rates, enabling proactive detection of issues. Logging solutions, such as Elasticsearch or Fluentd, capture application logs and system events, providing detailed insights into system behavior and debugging capabilities.

An integrated monitoring and logging setup allows teams to correlate metrics with logs, enabling efficient troubleshooting and performance optimization. For example, monitoring can alert operators about high latency in a service, while logs can provide specific details about errors or exceptions causing the issue.

Kubernetes security

Kubernetes security ensures that your cluster and workloads are protected against threats, both internal and external. A secure Kubernetes environment involves safeguarding the infrastructure, cluster components, workloads, and communication between them. It also includes enforcing strict access controls and protecting sensitive data like secrets.

Key security measures include implementing RBAC to restrict user and application permissions, using network policies to isolate Pods and control traffic flow, and enabling **mutual TLS (mTLS)** for secure communication between components. Encrypting Secrets and sensitive data at rest, as well as ensuring secure image practices like vulnerability scanning, are crucial to mitigating risks.

For example, consider using a **NetworkPolicy** to restrict traffic between Pods:

```yaml
apiVersion: networking.k8s.io/v1
kind: NetworkPolicy
metadata:
  name: restrict-frontend
  namespace: default
spec:
  podSelector:
    matchLabels:
      app: frontend
  policyTypes:
    - Ingress
  ingress:
    - from:
        - podSelector:
            matchLabels:
              app: backend
```

This policy ensures that only Pods labeled **app: backend** can communicate with the **app: frontend** Pods. This isolates your frontend services from unwanted or malicious traffic, reducing the attack surface.

By leveraging Kubernetes' built-in security features alongside external tools for runtime protection, vulnerability scanning, and compliance auditing, you can build a robust defense against potential threats and ensure the reliability of your workloads.

GitOps with Kubernetes

GitOps with Kubernetes is an approach that uses Git repositories as the single source of truth for both application code and infrastructure configurations. In this setup, Kubernetes clusters are managed by declarative configuration files (like YAML) stored in Git, allowing changes to be made by simply committing to the repository. Tools like Argo CD and Flux continuously monitor the Git repository for updates, automatically applying those changes to the Kubernetes cluster, ensuring that the cluster's state matches the desired configuration. This process brings several benefits, such as enhanced consistency, as the cluster always reflects the state defined in Git, and improved auditability since all changes are versioned and tracked. By automating the deployment and configuration process, GitOps accelerates release cycles, reduces manual intervention, and allows for easier rollbacks by reverting Git commits. Security is enhanced by ensuring that sensitive data, like passwords, is managed separately using tools such as Vault or SealedSecrets. Ultimately, GitOps with Kubernetes simplifies continuous delivery workflows, making infrastructure management more efficient and less prone to errors.

Conclusion

Kubernetes has firmly established itself as the industry standard for container orchestration, providing powerful tools and capabilities to manage containerized applications at scale. By understanding its architecture, core components, and advanced features such as auto-scaling, Rolling Updates, and Helm for package management, you are equipped with the knowledge to effectively deploy, manage, and scale applications in a Kubernetes environment. Concepts like Pods, ReplicaSets, and Deployments are central to application management, while networking, persistent storage, and configuration management with ConfigMaps and Secrets ensure a robust and secure infrastructure. With the added flexibility of Kubernetes RBAC, operators, and GitOps integration, Kubernetes offers a comprehensive approach to continuous delivery and operational efficiency. Moreover, effective monitoring, logging, and security practices are critical for maintaining a reliable and secure system. As you continue to explore Kubernetes, mastering these concepts will enable you to harness its full potential in automating and optimizing your containerized workflows.

In the next chapter, we will discuss the principles of DevSecOps and the practical strategies to implement them in our workflows.

CHAPTER 11
DevSecOps

Introduction

In today's fast-paced software development world, speed and agility often take center stage. As the saying goes, *with great power comes great responsibility*. The accelerated pace of DevOps cannot come at the expense of security. Enter DevSecOps, a transformative approach that seamlessly integrates security into every phase of the DevOps pipeline.

This chapter will explore how security becomes an integral, non-negotiable part of development and operations. DevSecOps is not just a set of tools or processes; it is a cultural shift that fosters collaboration between developers, operations teams, and security experts. It aims to embed security practices into workflows without hindering productivity, ultimately achieving the holy grail of fast, reliable, and secure software delivery.

Through this chapter, you will learn not only the principles of DevSecOps but also practical strategies to implement them in your workflows. We will focus on automating security checks, managing vulnerabilities, protecting sensitive information, and building a mindset where security is everyone's responsibility. By the end, you will see how DevSecOps can help you deliver robust and secure systems while maintaining agility.

Structure

This chapter covers the following topics:

- Principles of DevSecOps

- Shifting security left

- Static Application Security Testing

- Dynamic Application Security Testing

- Software composition analysis

- Secrets management with tools like HashiCorp Vault

- Container and infrastructure security in DevSecOps

- Identity and access management

- Compliance automation in DevSecOps

- Threat modeling in DevOps workflows

- Security chaos engineering

Objectives

This chapter aims to transform readers' understanding of security within the software development lifecycle by comprehensively exploring DevSecOps principles and practices. Readers will journey through the critical transformation of security from an isolated function to an integrated, proactive approach embedded throughout the development process. The objective is to equip technical professionals with the knowledge and skills to implement robust security measures seamlessly within DevOps workflows, focusing on practical strategies that balance speed, innovation, and comprehensive protection.

Specifically, the chapter will guide readers in mastering key security methodologies, including Static and Dynamic Application Security Testing, software composition analysis, and advanced techniques for secrets management and infrastructure protection. Participants will learn to shift security left, implementing early detection and mitigation strategies that prevent vulnerabilities from entering production environments. The chapter will demystify complex concepts like threat modeling, identity and access management, and security chaos engineering, providing actionable insights for creating a security-first culture that empowers development teams to build resilient, secure systems without compromising operational efficiency.

In conclusion, readers will not only understand the theoretical foundations of DevSecOps but will also gain practical skills to implement comprehensive security practices that protect organizations from evolving digital threats while maintaining the agility and speed essential in modern software development.

Principles of DevSecOps

At its core, DevSecOps integrates security practices seamlessly into the DevOps lifecycle. Unlike traditional approaches where security is considered an afterthought, DevSecOps makes security a shared responsibility among development, operations, and security teams. This collaborative and proactive approach ensures that security does not become a bottleneck but rather an enabler of innovation and trust.

Let us break down the key principles with examples to demonstrate how they apply in real-world scenarios:

- **Security as code:** Security is treated like any other part of the development process, written as code, version-controlled, and automated. For instance, tools like HashiCorp Sentinel or **Open Policy Agent** (**OPA**) allow teams to define security policies as code, ensuring that only compliant configurations are deployed. A developer can write a rule that prevents an AWS S3 bucket from being created without encryption enabled, and this rule is automatically enforced during deployments.

- **Shifting security left:** Instead of waiting until the end of the development cycle, DevSecOps shifts security practices earlier into the process. By using tools like **Static Application Security Testing** (**SAST**) during code commits, developers can identify vulnerabilities such as SQL injection or **cross-site scripting** (**XSS**) right in their IDE. For example, a developer working on a Python application might use Bandit to scan for security issues in their code before it is even pushed to the repository.

- **Automation of security processes:** Automation is the backbone of DevSecOps. It ensures consistency and reduces manual effort. Tools like Dependabot or Snyk can automatically scan your codebase for known vulnerabilities in dependencies and propose fixes. Imagine a scenario where a critical vulnerability is discovered in a library your application relies on, tools like these will alert the team and even provide a patched version, all without human intervention.

- **Collaboration and shared responsibility:** Security is no longer the sole responsibility of a separate team. DevSecOps fosters collaboration across developers, operations, and security engineers. For instance, consider a team using GitHub Actions for CI/CD. Developers, operations engineers, and security specialists work together to include automated security tests, such as secret scanning and container vulnerability checks, into the pipeline, ensuring security is part of everyone's workflow.

- **Continuous security:** Security does not stop at deployment; it is an ongoing process. Tools like Aqua Security or Falco monitor running containers for unusual behavior, such as unauthorized file changes or unexpected network connections. A practical example is a Kubernetes-based microservices application where these tools continuously scan containers for vulnerabilities and enforce runtime security policies.

- **Threat-driven approach:** DevSecOps emphasizes understanding and addressing specific threats. Threat modeling workshops allow teams to identify potential risks early. For example, when designing a financial application, a team might identify risks related to API abuse or sensitive data exposure. Based on this, they implement rate-limiting and encrypt sensitive data in transit using TLS.

- **Metrics and feedback loops:** Measuring security effectiveness is critical for improvement. Metrics such as MTTD and MTTR vulnerabilities are commonly used. For instance, a team tracking these metrics might notice a high MTTR for critical vulnerabilities and prioritize efforts to reduce it by streamlining their patching process.

- **Fostering a security-first culture:** A cultural shift is essential for the success of DevSecOps. Training sessions, secure coding workshops, and gamified exercises like capture-the-flag challenges help build awareness. For example, a company might host regular security hackathons where developers compete to find and fix vulnerabilities in a controlled environment, fostering learning and collaboration.

By embracing these principles, teams can ensure that security becomes an enabler of speed and quality rather than an obstacle. Real-world examples like automated dependency scanning, policy enforcement, and proactive threat modeling highlight how DevSecOps can make systems both secure and efficient.

Shifting security left

Shifting security left is one of the core principles of DevSecOps, emphasizing the need to integrate security measures as early as possible in the **software development lifecycle (SDLC)**. Traditionally, security checks were performed at the end of the development process, often during testing or pre-release phases. This approach, while common, frequently led to delays, increased costs, and vulnerabilities going unnoticed until late in the process. By shifting security left, teams proactively address security issues during the early stages of development, reducing risk and enhancing efficiency.

Meaning of shifting security left

To shift left means to move security considerations to the earliest phases of the development pipeline, starting at design and continuing through coding, building, and testing. The goal is to detect and mitigate vulnerabilities as soon as possible, ideally before they enter production. For instance, if a developer writes code that exposes sensitive data via an unsecured API, early detection can prevent this vulnerability from being propagated further. You can achieve this by doing the following:

- **Integrate security into design and planning:** Security should be a part of initial design discussions and requirements gathering. For example, during the design phase of a web application, teams should identify potential threats, such as SQL injection or XSS attacks, and plan mitigations like input validation and secure database queries.

- **Adopt secure coding practices:** Developers must be trained in secure coding techniques to avoid common vulnerabilities. Implementing guidelines like the OWASP Top 10 ensures teams are aware of risks and how to prevent them. For instance, validating all user inputs can prevent injection attacks.

- **Use SAST:** Tools like SonarQube, Checkmarx, and Fortify analyze source code for vulnerabilities before the code is compiled. For example, a Java developer using SonarQube might receive real-time feedback in their IDE about insecure code patterns, allowing them to fix issues before they commit the code.

- **Automated code scanning in CI pipelines:** Security tools should be integrated into **continuous integration (CI)** pipelines to automate vulnerability checks. For example, GitHub Actions can be configured to run dependency scanners like Snyk or Dependabot whenever code is pushed, ensuring that libraries with known vulnerabilities are flagged and updated.

- **Perform threat modeling early:** Threat modeling involves identifying potential attack vectors and weaknesses during the design phase. For instance, a team building a microservices-based architecture might identify risks related to inter-service communication and implement TLS encryption to mitigate eavesdropping.

- **Peer code reviews with a security focus:** Code reviews should include checks for security vulnerabilities. For example, during a review, a team member might spot a hardcoded password in the source code and suggest using a secrets management tool like HashiCorp Vault.

- **Test for security at every stage:** Automated security tests, including unit and integration tests, should validate the robustness of the system. For instance, a test case for a login API might simulate a brute force attack to ensure account lockout mechanisms are working.

- **Use development tools with built-in security features:** Many modern IDEs and platforms include plugins or extensions that detect vulnerabilities in real-time. For example, IntelliJ IDEA offers plugins for static code analysis, highlighting potential security issues as developers write code.

To understand this a bite better, consider a fintech company developing a mobile banking app. During the design phase, the team performs a threat model and identifies risks like MITM attacks on API communications. They implement TLS encryption as part of the API design. Later, during development, they use SAST tools integrated into their CI pipeline to detect insecure coding practices like using outdated cryptographic algorithms. This early focus on security ensures the app is robust against known threats before it even reaches production.

Shifting security left transforms security from a final checkpoint into a continuous, proactive process. By embedding security at every stage, teams can build faster, safer, and more reliable systems, ultimately fostering a culture of accountability and trust across the organization.

Static Application Security Testing

Static Application Security Testing (**SAST**) is a method of analyzing application source code, bytecode, or binaries to identify security vulnerabilities early in the software development lifecycle. Unlike dynamic testing methods that examine running applications, SAST focuses on identifying flaws in the application's internal logic, design, and structure without executing the code. It is often referred to as white-box testing because it requires visibility into the codebase.

SAST is a cornerstone of the shift-left security approach, as it enables developers to detect and address vulnerabilities while they are still coding, reducing the cost and time required to fix them later.

SAST tools scan codebases and use rules or patterns to identify vulnerabilities. These tools flag issues like SQL injection, XSS, insecure API usage, hardcoded credentials, and more. The process typically involves:

- **Code parsing:** The SAST tool reads the code, breaking it into components such as variables, functions, and modules.

- **Rule matching:** The tool applies a set of pre-defined security rules to identify patterns that could lead to vulnerabilities.

- **Reporting:** It generates a detailed report highlighting the vulnerabilities, their severity, and remediation steps.

For example, if a developer uses unsensitized user input to construct a database query, an SAST tool would flag it as a potential SQL injection vulnerability and suggest using prepared statements.

SAST is most effective when integrated early and often in the development process. Here are some key points in the lifecycle where SAST can be applied:

- **During development:** Developers can use SAST tools integrated into their IDEs to detect vulnerabilities as they write code.

- **In CI/CD pipelines:** Automating SAST scans as part of the CI/CD workflow ensures that code is scanned every time changes are pushed.

- **Code reviews:** SAST tools complement peer code reviews by providing an additional layer of security checks.

Some common SAST tools are:

- **SonarQube:** An open-source tool with support for multiple languages and integration capabilities with IDEs and CI/CD pipelines.

- **Checkmarx:** A widely used enterprise tool that provides deep code analysis and integration with CI/CD systems.

- **Fortify Static Code Analyzer:** This offers robust analysis for a wide range of programming languages and compliance standards.

- **Bandit:** A Python-specific SAST tool that identifies common security issues in Python code.

SAST is a powerful tool for building secure applications, but its effectiveness depends on how well it is integrated into the development process. By combining SAST with other security measures and fostering a culture of secure coding, organizations can significantly reduce the risk of vulnerabilities in their applications.

Dynamic Application Security Testing

Dynamic Application Security Testing (DAST) is a method of security testing that examines applications while they are running to identify vulnerabilities. Unlike SAST, which analyzes source code, DAST focuses on the application's runtime behavior, testing its external interfaces and interactions. Often referred to as black box testing, DAST simulates attacks from the perspective of a malicious user, making it an essential part of the security testing toolkit.

A real-world example for DAST can be to imagine a team building a healthcare web application with sensitive patient data. Before going live, they use OWASP ZAP to scan the application. The tool identifies an XSS vulnerability in the feedback form that allows attackers to inject malicious scripts. The team fixes the vulnerability by sanitizing user input and retesting with the DAST tool to ensure the issue is resolved. This proactive approach prevents potential exploitation and protects user data.

DAST tools interact with a running application to identify vulnerabilities by sending various inputs, inspecting responses, and looking for security weaknesses. Here is how it typically works:

- **Application setup:** The application is deployed in a testing or staging environment.

- **Test execution:** The DAST tool performs scans, attempting to exploit vulnerabilities such as SQL injection, XSS, broken authentication, and misconfigurations.

- **Analysis and reporting:** It generates a report detailing discovered vulnerabilities, their severity, and remediation recommendations.

For example, a DAST tool might inject malicious SQL queries into input fields to test for SQL injection vulnerabilities. If the application fails to sanitize the input, the tool flags it as a security risk.

When to use DAST

DAST is most effective for testing the security of deployed applications and systems:

- **Post-deployment testing:** To ensure applications meet security standards before production release.

- **Continuous testing:** In staging environments as part of CI/CD pipelines to identify vulnerabilities introduced by recent changes.

- **Third-party components:** To test security when the source code is unavailable, such as for vendor applications or APIs.

DAST is an essential component of a robust security strategy, complementing SAST and other security measures. By continuously testing applications in real-world scenarios, teams can detect and fix vulnerabilities before attackers exploit them, ensuring safer and more reliable systems.

Software composition analysis

Software composition analysis (**SCA**) is a security practice focused on managing risks associated with third-party and open-source software components used in modern applications. These components accelerate development but can introduce vulnerabilities if not properly managed. SCA tools help organizations identify, monitor, and mitigate risks in their software supply chain by analyzing dependencies and their associated vulnerabilities.

SCA operates by scanning an application's codebase, build files, and dependency trees to identify all open-source and third-party components. Once identified, the components are compared against vulnerability databases like the **National Vulnerability Database** (**NVD**) or vendor-specific advisories to detect known issues. For example, if your project relies on an outdated version of a popular library like Log4j, an SCA tool will flag it due to the critical vulnerabilities associated with earlier versions.

In a DevSecOps workflow, integrating SCA into the CI/CD pipeline ensures that vulnerabilities in dependencies are detected early. Developers can be alerted when they attempt to add insecure libraries or outdated versions to their projects, enabling immediate remediation. By combining this with a robust dependency management strategy, teams can proactively address risks before they reach production.

Using SCA is not just about finding vulnerabilities; it also helps maintain compliance with licensing requirements. Many open-source projects have licenses that impose restrictions on how the software can be used. SCA tools provide insights into the types of licenses associated with dependencies, helping teams avoid potential legal risks. For instance, if a project inadvertently includes a component with a restrictive GPL license, the SCA tool will highlight the issue.

In practice, tools like Sonatype Nexus IQ, Snyk, and WhiteSource are widely used for SCA. These tools integrate seamlessly with development environments and CI/CD pipelines, automating the process of scanning and reporting. For example, Snyk can provide real-time feedback in the developer's IDE, suggesting safer alternatives for vulnerable dependencies. This immediate visibility allows developers to make informed decisions about their software stack.

The importance of SCA becomes evident in incidents like the Log4Shell vulnerability in 2021, where a critical flaw in Log4j, an open-source logging library, exposed thousands of applications to remote code execution attacks. Organizations that had robust SCA practices in place were able to quickly identify and patch affected systems, minimizing their exposure.

To maximize the benefits of SCA, teams should adopt the following practices:

- Automate SCA scans in the CI/CD pipeline to ensure all builds are secure.

- Regularly monitor for updates to third-party components and prioritize upgrading high-risk dependencies.

- Educate developers about secure dependency management to foster a culture of proactive security.

- Continuously assess and update policies around acceptable licenses and component usage to align with business needs.

SCA is more than just a tool; it is a critical part of modern application security. By integrating SCA into DevSecOps workflows and pairing it with practices like Static and Dynamic Application Security Testing, teams can address vulnerabilities at every layer of their applications. This holistic approach ensures that open-source and third-party components contribute to innovation without compromising security or compliance.

Secrets management with tools like HashiCorp Vault

In modern DevOps environments, managing secrets such as API keys, database credentials, encryption keys, and certificates is critical to maintaining security. Secrets management ensures that these sensitive pieces of information are securely stored, accessed, and rotated to minimize the risk of exposure. Tools like HashiCorp Vault provide robust solutions for secrets management, making it easier to enforce security best practices across development and operational workflows.

In traditional workflows, secrets were often hardcoded into application code, configuration files, or environment variables. This practice not only made secrets difficult to update but also exposed them to potential breaches if the code or files were inadvertently shared or leaked. With secret management tools like Vault, secrets are centralized in a secure storage mechanism, encrypted at rest and in transit, and accessed programmatically through controlled policies.

HashiCorp Vault is a widely used tool for secrets management. It allows teams to dynamically generate secrets, manage access policies, and automate secret rotation. For example, instead of storing a static database password in application code, Vault can generate temporary credentials with a specified **time-to-live** (TTL), limiting their validity and reducing the impact of compromised secrets.

Using Vault involves the following core principles:

- **Centralized storage:** Vault provides a secure, central repository for managing secrets. It encrypts secrets with advanced algorithms and stores them in a backend of your choice, such as Consul, etcd, or a traditional database.

- **Dynamic secrets:** Unlike static secrets, Vault can generate secrets on the fly. For instance, when an application needs database access, Vault can create a unique, time-bound username and password. This ensures that secrets are never reused and can be automatically revoked when no longer needed.

- **Access policies:** Vault uses fine-grained access controls through its policy framework. Developers or applications can only access the secrets they are authorized to use. For example, a policy might allow a frontend application to retrieve API keys but not database credentials.

- **Audit logging:** All interactions with Vault are logged, providing a comprehensive audit trail for security compliance and incident investigation.

A typical implementation workflow with Vault might look like this:

- **Initialization and unsealing:** The Vault is initialized by a trusted operator, and its master key is split into multiple unseal keys. These keys must be used collaboratively to unseal the Vault and make it operational.

- **Secret storage:** Secrets such as AWS credentials, database passwords, or SSH keys are stored in the Vault. They are encrypted using Vault's encryption engine before being persisted to storage.

- **Access via authentication methods:** Applications or users authenticate to Vault using methods like Kubernetes service accounts, AWS IAM roles, or AppRole. Upon authentication, Vault issues a token with specific permissions based on defined policies.

- **Programmatic retrieval:** Applications interact with Vault's API or CLI to fetch secrets securely. For instance, a CI/CD pipeline can retrieve a GitHub token from Vault during a deployment stage.

- **Dynamic secret generation and rotation:** Vault dynamically generates and rotates secrets as needed. For example, database credentials might be refreshed every hour, ensuring that stale secrets cannot be exploited.

To better understand this, consider a microservices-based application running in Kubernetes. Each service requires access to an external payment gateway's API. Instead of embedding the API keys in configuration files, the keys are stored in Vault. When a service starts, it authenticates with Vault using its Kubernetes service account token. Vault then provides the API key dynamically, scoped to the service's identity and with a TTL of one hour. If the key is compromised, it becomes useless after expiration.

Container and infrastructure security in DevSecOps

In a DevSecOps environment, security is not an afterthought; it is an integral part of every stage of development, deployment, and operations. As organizations increasingly adopt containers and IaC for their applications, ensuring the security of both containers and the underlying infrastructure becomes essential. Containers, while providing significant advantages in scalability, portability, and efficiency, also introduce new challenges that require careful attention to security. Similarly, IaC allows teams to automate infrastructure provisioning but also brings the risk of misconfigurations and vulnerabilities if not properly secured.

Security for containers and infrastructure must be tackled holistically with a unified strategy that spans both environments, ensuring that threats are addressed at every layer, from the code in containers to the infrastructure that runs them.

In DevSecOps, container and infrastructure security go hand in hand. Containers themselves are lightweight and isolated, but vulnerabilities within the container image or improper runtime configurations can open the door to attacks. Similarly, infrastructure security ensures that the environment hosting containers is protected with proper access control, network isolation, and secure configurations. When combined, these two layers form a secure foundation for your applications and services. Several critical aspects must be carefully addressed for container and infrastructure security in DevSecOps to create a comprehensive security strategy. These key areas of focus include:

- **Image and dependency security:** Container images are the building blocks of your application in a containerized environment. It is essential to ensure that the images you are using are free of vulnerabilities. Container images often contain a variety of dependencies, including open-source libraries and third-party components, which can introduce risks. Just as in infrastructure security, managing these dependencies is crucial. Tools like Trivy, Anchore, and Clair can scan for known vulnerabilities within container images before they are deployed.

  On the infrastructure side, vulnerabilities in the environment hosting containers must be identified and managed. IaC tools like Terraform or CloudFormation define and provision infrastructure in a repeatable, automated way. While this increases operational efficiency, it also raises the risk of misconfigurations. Ensuring that your IaC templates follow best practices is as important as securing your container images. Tools like Checkov and tflint scan IaC for security flaws, such as overly permissive access rights or unsecured resources.

- **Runtime security:** Once containers are deployed, ensuring their security during runtime is critical. Containers are often vulnerable to attacks that can exploit misconfigured or weak security policies, such as privilege escalation or container breakout. Implementing runtime security tools like Falco can detect suspicious activity, such as unauthorized access to resources, abnormal system calls, or attempts to break container isolation.

At the infrastructure level, securing the underlying hosts or cloud platforms that run containers is equally important. Limiting access to only the necessary ports and services, using firewalls and network segmentation, and applying security patches regularly can minimize the attack surface. Tools like Kubernetes NetworkPolicies and AWS Security Groups can help enforce strict communication boundaries between components, ensuring that containers only communicate with the services they are authorized to.

- **Secrets management:** Both containers and infrastructure often require access to sensitive data, such as API keys, database credentials, and encryption keys. Hardcoding secrets directly into container images or configuration files is a dangerous practice, as it exposes sensitive information to anyone who has access to the image or the code repository.

  Tools like HashiCorp Vault provide a secure way to store and manage secrets. Vault integrates with both container environments (such as Kubernetes) and infrastructure, enabling the automated, secure retrieval of secrets. For example, Vault can dynamically generate database credentials for a container at runtime, ensuring that secrets are not hardcoded and are only accessible to the services that need them.

- **Access control and identity management:** Managing who has access to containers and infrastructure is a key part of both container and infrastructure security. Implementing strong IAM policies ensures that only authorized users and services can interact with critical systems.

  In a containerized environment, Kubernetes provides native access control mechanisms through RBAC, which allows you to define roles and permissions for users and services. Similarly, cloud platforms like AWS, Azure, and GCP provide IAM tools that control who can provision or modify infrastructure. Ensuring that both infrastructure and containers are protected by appropriate access controls helps prevent unauthorized changes and potential breaches.

- **Continuous monitoring and auditing:** Security does not stop once the system is deployed. Continuous monitoring and auditing are essential to detect and respond to security incidents. Both containers and infrastructure should be continuously monitored for abnormal behavior, performance issues, or security breaches. Tools like Prometheus and Grafana can provide real-time insights into container health, while Datadog and ELK Stack can aggregate logs and metrics for both containers and infrastructure, providing a centralized view of system activity.

To understand this better, assume that there is a company running a microservices architecture on Kubernetes that integrates container and infrastructure security into its DevSecOps pipeline. They use Trivy to scan all container images for known vulnerabilities before they are deployed to the cluster. Simultaneously, Checkov scans their Terraform IaC files to ensure that resources are securely configured, with no excessive permissions or open access points.

When deploying the application, sensitive information, such as database credentials, is not stored in the container images. Instead, HashiCorp Vault dynamically generates secure credentials for each microservice at runtime. Access to both the container environment and the underlying cloud infrastructure is tightly controlled through Kubernetes RBAC and AWS IAM policies, ensuring only authorized users and services can make changes.

By combining these tools and practices, they create a secure, automated environment where both containers and infrastructure are protected at every layer, from development through to production.

Identity and access management

Identity and access management (IAM) is a critical aspect of securing both containerized applications and infrastructure in a DevSecOps pipeline. IAM ensures that the right users and systems have the appropriate level of access to resources, minimizing the risk of unauthorized actions, data breaches, or accidental misconfigurations. Effective IAM practices are foundational to ensuring that security is integrated into every layer of the DevOps process.

In a DevSecOps context, IAM is not just about controlling access but also about enforcing the principles of least privilege, ensuring that only authorized entities can interact with sensitive systems and data. This extends beyond users and includes roles, machines, and services. By automating and managing access controls effectively, IAM becomes a key tool in securing both infrastructure and applications throughout the development lifecycle.

The core principles of IAM in DevSecOps are:

- **Least privilege access:** The principle of least privilege is essential in DevSecOps. This means granting only the minimal permissions necessary for a user or service to perform its required tasks. By adhering to this principle, organizations reduce the risk of privilege escalation and limit the potential impact of a security breach. For example, a developer may need access to code repositories but should not have the ability to deploy to production environments. Similarly, a container may need to access a specific database but should not have unrestricted access to all services.

- **RBAC:** RBAC is a widely adopted approach for managing access to resources. It involves assigning roles to users and systems and then associating specific permissions with those roles. In Kubernetes, for example, RBAC enables you to define who can create, modify, or delete resources like Pods, Services, or Deployments. The key benefit of RBAC is that it simplifies managing large numbers of users and services by grouping them into roles, reducing administrative overhead.

- **Separation of duties:** Separation of duties ensures that critical actions require multiple parties or systems to execute, preventing conflicts of interest or fraudulent activity. For example, in a deployment pipeline, separating the roles of a developer who writes the code from the administrator who deploys the code to production helps maintain accountability and reduces the risk of unauthorized changes.

- **Automation of access policies:** In a dynamic DevSecOps environment, manually managing IAM policies can become cumbersome and error prone. Automating IAM policies ensures that access controls are consistently applied across all systems and services. Tools like AWS IAM, Azure Active Directory, and Google Cloud IAM allow you to define policies that automatically apply to users, services, and infrastructure components.

- **Continuous auditing and monitoring:** IAM is not a set-and-forget solution; continuous monitoring and auditing of IAM policies and permissions are crucial. Regular audits help identify excessive permissions, orphaned accounts, or misconfigured access controls. Tools like AWS CloudTrail or Kubernetes Audit Logs allow teams to track access and changes, enabling quick detection of anomalous activities.

We can expand this with an example by using a global e-commerce company that uses IAM principles across its DevSecOps pipeline to ensure secure access to both its infrastructure and containerized applications. Developers have access to the code repositories and CI/CD pipeline but are restricted from deploying directly to production environments.

Using Kubernetes RBAC, they assign different roles to their development, operations, and security teams. For instance, developers can only view logs and configure test environments, while only operations teams have permission to deploy to production.

On the infrastructure side, they use AWS IAM to enforce access policies for cloud resources. Developers are granted temporary credentials through AWS STS, which expire after a defined period, ensuring that access is always time-bound. They also employ MFA for all users with access to sensitive infrastructure, adding an additional layer of protection.

With continuous monitoring using AWS CloudTrail and Kubernetes Audit Logs, the company can track any changes in permissions or access, ensuring that no unauthorized actions go unnoticed.

Compliance automation in DevSecOps

In the rapidly evolving world of DevSecOps, maintaining compliance across development, deployment, and operational processes can be a challenging task. Compliance requirements, whether industry-specific (like HIPAA, PCI-DSS, GDPR) or organizational standards, demand that security, privacy, and regulatory protocols are followed rigorously. Traditional approaches to compliance often involve manual checks and reviews, which can slow down the DevOps pipeline and increase the risk of errors or omissions. Compliance automation is a game-changer for integrating these requirements seamlessly into the DevSecOps workflow.

By automating compliance processes, organizations can continuously enforce policies and ensure that compliance standards are met without hindering the speed and flexibility that DevOps brings. Compliance automation integrates with existing CI/CD pipelines, IaC tools, and containerized environments to provide a real-time, proactive approach to compliance.

Compliance automation is crucial in modern DevSecOps practices for several reasons:

- **Speed and agility:** DevSecOps is about faster delivery without compromising on security and compliance. Manual compliance checks can delay deployments and create bottlenecks, undermining the very speed that DevOps aims for. Automated compliance checks ensure that security and regulatory requirements are consistently met without slowing down the pipeline.

- **Continuous monitoring:** Regulations and security standards are not static; they evolve over time. With manual compliance processes, it is difficult to keep up with changing regulations. Automating compliance ensures that your systems are continuously monitored and deviations from compliance policies are detected in real time.

- **Reduced human error:** Manual compliance checks are prone to mistakes and oversights. Automated tools eliminate human error, ensuring more consistent and reliable compliance management.

- **Scalability:** As organizations scale, maintaining compliance across multiple teams, environments, and infrastructures becomes increasingly complex. Automation provides a scalable way to manage compliance requirements across vast, distributed systems.

- **Auditability and reporting:** Automated compliance systems often include built-in reporting capabilities, making it easier to provide detailed audit logs. These logs serve as proof that compliance standards have been met and can be used for internal audits or external regulatory reviews.

To understand the need for compliance a bit better, imagine a financial services company that must comply with PCI-DSS regulations. They use a DevSecOps pipeline with compliance automation integrated into their CI/CD process. The company uses Terraform to manage its cloud infrastructure, and they have written compliance checks into its code using Checkov to ensure that only secure configurations are applied, such as encrypted storage and restricted access to sensitive systems.

Additionally, every time a container image is built, tools like Anchore automatically scan for known vulnerabilities, and any image that contains vulnerabilities that violate PCI-DSS rules is flagged and blocked from deployment. The pipeline also includes OPA policies that ensure sensitive customer data is never hardcoded into the application code and is always encrypted.

To monitor their compliance post-deployment, the company uses Prisma Cloud to scan their running infrastructure for any misconfigurations or violations of security best practices. In case of a non-compliant event, such as an insecure API or exposed database, alerts are sent out, and automated workflows are triggered to remediate the issue.

Finally, the company generates regular compliance reports using Chef InSpec, which tracks the state of their infrastructure and application environments. These reports are automatically compiled and ready to be submitted to regulators or internal auditors.

The benefits of compliance automation are as follows:

- **Time saving:** Automating compliance tasks reduces the manual effort involved in ensuring compliance, freeing up resources to focus on other critical areas of DevSecOps.

- **Consistency:** Automated tools apply compliance policies uniformly, ensuring that all environments, whether dev, test, or production, are consistently compliant.

- **Proactive security:** By continuously monitoring and auditing compliance standards, automated tools allow teams to detect and address potential issues before they become risks.

- **Scalability:** As infrastructure grows, maintaining manual compliance becomes increasingly difficult. Automation scales with the infrastructure, ensuring compliance is maintained across complex, distributed systems.

Compliance automation is a key enabler for achieving continuous, seamless compliance in a DevSecOps environment. By automating infrastructure, policy checks, vulnerability scans, and continuous monitoring, organizations can maintain compliance without sacrificing the speed and flexibility that DevSecOps promises. Automated compliance is essential not only for meeting regulatory requirements but also for protecting data, mitigating risks, and ensuring that security is built into every stage of the software development lifecycle. With the right tools and practices, compliance becomes an ongoing process rather than a hurdle to be overcome.

Threat modeling in DevOps workflows

Threat modeling is an essential practice for identifying potential security risks and vulnerabilities in applications and infrastructure before they are exploited. By proactively addressing threats in the early stages of the DevOps workflow, organizations can reduce the likelihood of security breaches, mitigate risks, and ensure that security is seamlessly integrated into development processes. In the fast-paced world of DevOps, where code is continuously deployed and infrastructure is constantly changing, threat modeling is a proactive measure that helps teams anticipate and address security challenges.

In the context of DevSecOps, threat modeling is integrated into the CI/CD pipeline and applied across both the development and operational environments. It involves mapping out potential attack vectors, understanding the possible impact of a threat, and developing mitigation strategies—all while aligning with Agile development practices.

Threat modeling is crucial in DevOps primarily because of the following reasons:

- **Proactive security planning:** DevOps is built around continuous integration, continuous delivery, and automation, which speed up software development and deployment. However, this speed often leaves little room for manual security checks. Threat modeling allows teams to identify and mitigate security risks during the planning phase before they are integrated into the system. By considering threats from the outset, teams can design secure applications and infrastructure, minimizing vulnerabilities that could be exploited later.

- **Shifting security left:** Traditionally, security has been an afterthought, often addressed late in the development process or after deployment. In DevOps, security is shifted left, meaning it is integrated early in the development lifecycle. Threat modeling plays a crucial role in this shift, as it helps developers and security teams think about potential vulnerabilities in code, containers, infrastructure, and APIs right from the start.

- **Identifying attack vectors:** Threat modeling helps identify all potential ways an attacker could compromise the system. Whether it is through exposed endpoints, misconfigured access controls, or vulnerabilities in third-party libraries, threat modeling provides teams with a comprehensive view of possible attack vectors. By understanding these vectors, teams can build defenses against them before they become real threats.

- **Building a security-first culture:** Integrating threat modeling into DevOps workflows reinforces the importance of security throughout the entire organization. It encourages collaboration between development, security, and operations teams and promotes a security-first mindset. As security risks are increasingly recognized as a shared responsibility, threat modeling provides a common framework for all teams to discuss, assess, and prioritize security risks.

Some key steps in threat modeling for DevOps include:

1. **Define security objectives and scope:** The first step in threat modeling is defining the security objectives of the project. What are you trying to protect, and what are the potential consequences of a breach? It is crucial to establish what data, resources, or systems are most valuable and need the most protection. This includes understanding regulatory requirements, customer privacy, and financial considerations. The scope should also define which parts of the system (application code, APIs, databases, infrastructure) will be included in the threat modeling process. For example, for a healthcare application, the primary concern might be patient data, which is subject to HIPAA regulations. In this case, protecting patient

privacy and ensuring that data is encrypted both at rest and in transit would be key objectives.

2. **Identify and map assets:** Identifying and mapping the assets—both technical (servers, databases, code, etc.) and non-technical (user trust, brand reputation)—helps prioritize the areas that need the most attention. Understanding the architecture and workflows of the application allows you to pinpoint where vulnerabilities are most likely to occur. This step involves creating **data flow diagrams (DFDs)** to illustrate how information moves through the system. For example, in a microservices architecture, assets might include sensitive customer data stored in a database, authentication tokens, and API endpoints that interface with other services. Mapping these assets will help highlight where encryption, access controls, and security checks are needed.

3. **Identify potential threats:** Once the assets are defined, the next step is to identify potential threats. A useful framework for this is the STRIDE methodology, which helps classify threats based on common categories:

   a. **Spoofing**: Impersonating another user or system.

   b. **Tampering**: Altering data or code maliciously.

   c. **Repudiation**: Denying actions or events (lack of logging).

   d. **Information disclosure**: Unauthorized access to sensitive information.

   e. **Denial of service (DoS)**: Disrupting or denying access to services.

   f. **Elevation of privilege**: Gaining unauthorized access or privileges.

   Teams should also consider threats based on their specific environment—cloud infrastructure, containers, and third-party dependencies all introduce unique risks.

4. **Analyze the threats and vulnerabilities:** After identifying potential threats, the next step is to analyze their likelihood and impact. This involves considering factors such as:

   a. How likely is this threat to occur?

   b. What would the impact be if it occurred?

   c. What existing defenses or mitigation strategies are in place?

   d. This step helps teams prioritize threats and focus on the most significant risks first.

   For example, consider a misconfigured API endpoint that exposes sensitive customer data; it might be a high-likelihood threat with a significant impact. On the other hand, a theoretical DoS attack on a less critical system might be less likely and have a lower impact.

5. **Mitigate and build defenses:** Based on the analysis, the next step is to develop strategies to mitigate the identified threats. This includes implementing preventive measures, such as:

   a. Input validation to prevent injection attacks.

   b. Encryption to protect sensitive data at rest and in transit.

   c. Rate limiting and firewall rules to mitigate DoS attacks.

   d. Access controls ensure that only authorized users or systems can access critical resources.

   The mitigation strategies should be integrated directly into the DevOps pipeline to ensure that they are continuously enforced. Automation tools like OWASP ZAP for security scanning or SonarQube for static analysis can be used to check code for vulnerabilities in real-time.

6. **Monitor and iterate:** Threat modeling is not a one-time exercise; it is an ongoing process. As systems evolve, new threats emerge, and previously identified risks may change. Continuous monitoring of the application, infrastructure, and security defenses is essential to staying ahead of potential threats. Teams should incorporate automated security testing into their CI/CD pipeline to identify new vulnerabilities or weaknesses as the system is developed and deployed.

Threat modeling is a vital component of DevSecOps, enabling teams to proactively identify and mitigate security risks throughout the development lifecycle. By shifting security left and integrating threat modeling into the DevOps workflow, organizations can reduce the likelihood of breaches, ensure compliance, and maintain the integrity of their applications and infrastructure. With the right tools, practices, and collaboration, threat modeling becomes an ongoing, automated process that ensures security is an intrinsic part of the software development lifecycle.

Security chaos engineering

As the DevOps landscape continues to evolve, the complexity of modern systems, especially those built using microservices, cloud-native applications, and containers, presents new challenges in maintaining a secure environment. In this context, **security chaos engineering** (SCE) has emerged as a critical discipline for proactively identifying and mitigating vulnerabilities rather than reacting to breaches after they occur. By embracing the concept of chaos engineering, where controlled disruptions are introduced into systems to test their robustness, teams can simulate security incidents in a safe, testable environment and ensure that security is resilient, even in the face of unexpected challenges.

While traditional chaos engineering typically focuses on system reliability and resilience, SCE extends this practice by intentionally testing a system's security posture under adversarial conditions. The goal is to continuously assess and strengthen security measures by introducing security-related failures into the system before real attackers can exploit them.

Why SCE matters is explained as follows:

- **Proactive security testing:** Security testing in most organizations tends to occur in the later stages of development or in response to known vulnerabilities. Security chaos engineering shifts this mindset by proactively testing systems in real-time. It forces teams to confront security failures head-on, ensuring that systems are secure even when unexpected threats occur. With security chaos engineering, you are not just waiting for an attacker to find vulnerabilities; you are actively looking for them.

- **Ensuring real-world resilience:** In today's world of distributed systems and cloud-native architectures, attacks can come from anywhere. Simply relying on vulnerability scans or penetration tests is not enough because they typically focus on known threats. Security chaos engineering, on the other hand, tests the unknown. It introduces a controlled environment where simulated attacks, compromised components, and other adversarial events are used to verify if the security infrastructure can withstand them.

- **Building a security-first culture:** Security chaos engineering aligns well with the principles of DevSecOps, where security is everyone's responsibility. It requires collaboration between security, development, and operations teams to ensure that security concerns are addressed at every level. This shared responsibility model encourages a deeper understanding of security risks and the creation of secure systems rather than simply patching vulnerabilities after the fact.

Some practical examples of security chaos engineering are:

- **Simulating an insider threat:** To understand how well your system would react to an insider threat, you could simulate the scenario where an employee gains elevated privileges or intentionally misuses their access. This could be done by testing the ability of your access control and logging systems to detect unusual behavior or unauthorized access to sensitive data.

- **API vulnerabilities:** A common attack vector in modern applications is through APIs. Security chaos engineering might simulate an attacker exploiting a vulnerability in an exposed API endpoint by injecting malicious payloads or attempting unauthorized access. Testing this proactively ensures that your API rate limits, input validation, and authentication are working effectively.

- **Container security testing:** Containers are highly dynamic and often involve rapid deployments. By introducing chaos into your container environment, such as simulating the breach of a container's security perimeter or manipulating network policies, you can test how well your container security platform responds. You could also test your incident response protocols to ensure quick detection and mitigation.

- **Simulating data exfiltration:** A major security concern is the potential for data exfiltration. Chaos engineering can simulate scenarios where a security breach leads to unauthorized access to customer data. You could observe if your encryption, data masking, and monitoring systems can detect and stop the exfiltration process before it causes damage.

Some of the popular tools for security chaos engineering are:

- **Gremlin:** A popular chaos engineering platform that enables teams to simulate various failures, including security breaches, in a controlled manner. It can simulate scenarios such as service crashes, network disruptions, and container security tests.

- **Chaos Monkey:** A tool from Netflix's chaos engineering suite that randomly terminates instances to ensure that the system can recover gracefully. While primarily used for system reliability, it can also be adapted to test security controls.

- **Simian Army:** Also from Netflix, the Simian Army suite provides tools for testing various fault scenarios. Some parts of the suite are designed specifically to test security, such as Security Monkey, which identifies security policy violations in your infrastructure.

- **Toxiproxy:** A tool for simulating network disruptions and failures in APIs, allowing teams to test how their security mechanisms handle network failures, service interruptions, and security risks under uncertain conditions.

Security chaos engineering is a powerful tool in the DevSecOps toolkit that allows organizations to continuously assess their security posture in the face of unpredictable, adversarial events. By proactively testing systems under realistic attack scenarios, teams can identify weaknesses before they are exploited by malicious actors. This approach fosters a security-first mindset, drives collaboration, and ensures that security is deeply embedded into the development lifecycle.

Ultimately, the goal of security chaos engineering is not just to prevent breaches but to create a resilient system capable of withstanding the challenges and threats of the ever-evolving digital landscape. By embracing uncertainty and chaos, organizations can build more secure, robust, and adaptive systems.

Conclusion

DevSecOps represents a fundamental shift in approaching security within the software development lifecycle. By integrating security practices at every stage of development and operations, organizations create a proactive, security-first culture that safeguards the entire pipeline. From secure containerization to automated compliance and threat modeling, DevSecOps transforms security from a potential bottleneck to an enabler of innovation and trust.

As systems become increasingly complex, the principles outlined in this chapter become crucial for minimizing risks and maintaining robust security. Security is no longer an afterthought, but a continuous responsibility shared across all teams, enabling businesses to innovate with confidence and resilience.

In the next chapter, we will explore continuous testing, a critical companion to DevSecOps. We will discuss automated testing strategies that ensure software quality, covering methodologies like **Test-Driven Development** (**TDD**) and **Behavior-Driven Development** (**BDD**). Building on the security foundations we have established, continuous testing will provide the mechanisms to validate and verify the reliability of our increasingly sophisticated software systems.

Join our Discord space

Join our Discord workspace for latest updates, offers, tech happenings around the world, new releases, and sessions with the authors:

https://discord.bpbonline.com

CHAPTER 12

Continuous Testing and Quality Assurance

Introduction

In today's fast-paced software development landscape, ensuring quality is no longer an afterthought; it is a continuous process embedded in every stage of the development lifecycle. Continuous testing is the backbone of this approach, enabling teams to validate their code early, often, and efficiently. By automating testing and integrating it into the CI/CD pipelines, teams can identify and address issues as soon as they arise, reducing the risk of defects making their way into production.

Imagine that you are working on a team building a critical application, and every new feature or fix you add could potentially break something that was already working. Without a robust testing strategy, the risk of delivering a buggy product skyrocket. This is where continuous testing comes in; it is like having a safety net that ensures every change to your codebase is tested rigorously, giving you confidence in your software's quality.

This chapter will cover the principles and practices of continuous testing, starting with foundational methodologies like **Test-Driven Development (TDD)** and **Behavior-Driven Development (BDD)**. We will explore how to design effective test strategies, from unit tests that validate individual pieces of code to integration and end-to-end tests that ensure the entire system works harmoniously. Along the way, we will introduce you to powerful tools like Selenium, Cypress, and performance testing frameworks and show you how to manage test data and maintain your test suites in CI/CD pipelines.

Continuous testing is not just about writing tests; it is about fostering a culture of quality. By the end of this chapter, we will not only understand the technical aspects of testing but also appreciate how it fits into the bigger picture of delivering reliable, high-quality software. Let us get started.

Structure

The chapter covers the following topics:

- Continuous testing principles
- Test-Driven Development
- Behavior-Driven Development
- Unit, integration, and end-to-end testing strategies
- Performance and load testing tools
- API and contract testing
- UI testing with Selenium or Cypress
- Test data management
- Maintaining test suites in CI/CD pipelines
- Code coverage analysis and reporting

Objectives

This chapter aims to equip readers with the knowledge and skills necessary to implement effective continuous testing practices throughout the software development lifecycle. After completing this chapter, we will understand the core principles of continuous testing and be able to integrate them with modern development methodologies. We will learn how to implement TDD using the Red-Green-Refactor cycle and apply BDD techniques to foster collaboration between technical and non-technical stakeholders. The chapter will enable us to design comprehensive testing strategies spanning unit, integration, and end-to-end testing while helping us select appropriate performance and load testing tools to validate application scalability. We will gain proficiency in developing API and contract testing approaches for microservice architectures and creating automated UI tests using tools like Selenium and Cypress.

Additionally, we will master best practices for test data management, including anonymization and synthetic data generation techniques. The chapter will guide you in configuring and maintaining efficient test suites within CI/CD pipelines and analyzing code coverage reports to identify areas requiring additional testing. By mastering these concepts, you will be equipped to build robust testing frameworks that ensure software reliability, maintain code quality, and support rapid, confident delivery of features to production environments.

Continuous testing principles

Continuous testing (**CT**) is a core practice in modern software development, ensuring that quality checks happen at every stage of the development lifecycle. Unlike traditional testing, which often occurs late in the process, CT integrates testing activities into the entire development workflow, enabling rapid feedback and reducing the time between detecting and resolving defects.

Here are the key principles of CT:

- **Early and frequent testing:** Testing should begin as soon as development starts and should occur continuously. By identifying and fixing issues early, teams avoid the cost and complexity of addressing defects later in the lifecycle. This is often summarized as shift-left testing, where testing moves closer to the design and development phases.

- **Automated testing at scale:** Manual testing cannot keep up with the speed of modern development cycles. Automated tests, covering unit, integration, end-to-end, performance, and security aspects, form the backbone of CT. Automation ensures consistency, reduces human error, and allows tests to be run frequently and efficiently.

- **Integration with CI/CD pipelines:** Continuous Testing thrives in environments where tests are seamlessly integrated into **continuous integration** (**CI**) and **continuous deployment/delivery** (**CD**) pipelines. Every code change triggers a series of automated tests, providing instant feedback on whether the change is safe to merge or deploy.

- **Comprehensive coverage:** CT aims for broad test coverage across various dimensions, including:

  o **Functional coverage**: Ensuring that each feature behaves as expected.

  o **Non-functional coverage**: Testing performance, scalability, and security aspects.

  o **Code coverage**: Measuring how much of the codebase is tested, ensuring that critical paths are not overlooked.

- **Feedback loops:** Fast feedback is critical in CT. Developers should receive test results promptly after each change. Whether it is a failed test or a performance bottleneck, this rapid feedback allows issues to be resolved quickly, preventing them from snowballing into larger problems.

- **Risk-based testing:** Not all tests are equally important. CT prioritizes high-risk areas of the application, ensuring that critical functionalities are tested more thoroughly. This approach optimizes testing efforts and aligns them with business priorities.

- **Testing in production:** While traditionally avoided, testing in production has become an accepted practice in CT to validate real-world scenarios. Techniques like canary releases, A/B testing, and chaos engineering allow teams to test in live environments with minimal risk.

- **Continuous improvement:** CT is an evolving process. Teams regularly analyze test results, coverage metrics, and failure patterns to refine their testing strategies, remove redundant tests, and address gaps. The goal is to make the testing process more efficient and effective over time.

To understand this better, consider a team working on an e-commerce platform. Each time a developer pushes code for a new feature (e.g., adding a product filter), the CI pipeline triggers:

- Unit tests validate the functionality of the filter logic.

- Integration tests ensure the filter works well with the search and cart systems.

- End-to-end tests simulate a user applying the filter and verifying the results.

- Performance tests check if the new feature impacts search response times.

To illustrate these principles in action, consider a popular electronic commerce platform implementing a new promotional feature. When a developer adds functionality for a *Buy Two Items, Get One Free* promotion, several automated tests would immediately execute upon code check-in. Without CT, this new discount logic might silently interfere with the standard checkout process, potentially causing revenue loss or customer frustration. With properly implemented CT, automated tests would verify that the promotional pricing works correctly while simultaneously confirming that standard purchasing flows remain unaffected.

Similarly, for a food delivery service application expanding its restaurant network, CT would automatically verify multiple aspects of the system whenever a new establishment is added to the platform. Tests would confirm that the restaurant's menu displays correctly with accurate descriptions, pricing information loads properly, and that the entire order process, from adding items to cart through payment processing functions flawlessly. This comprehensive verification happens continuously rather than as a manual effort before launch, significantly reducing the risk of customers encountering errors when interacting with newly added restaurants.

These examples demonstrate how CT shifts quality assurance from being a distinct phase to becoming an integral, ongoing aspect of development that provides immediate feedback throughout the software development lifecycle.

The test results provide immediate feedback, allowing the developer to fix any issues before merging the code. This continuous process ensures that only high-quality code reaches production.

CT fosters a culture of quality and trust within the development team. By embedding testing into every step of the process, teams can innovate faster, deliver more reliable software, and meet users' ever-growing expectations. It is not just about finding bugs but about preventing them and ensuring confidence in every release.

Test-Driven Development

Test-Driven Development (**TDD**) is a transformative approach to software development that places testing at the heart of the coding process. By writing tests before implementation, TDD ensures that the software is built to meet predefined requirements from the start. This approach minimizes bugs, promotes clean design, and encourages a disciplined development mindset.

Let us explore the nuances of TDD through its workflow, practices, and impact on modern development.

TDD operates on a structured and iterative cycle, often referred to as Red-Green-Refactor:

- **Red, write a failing test case:** The developer writes a test for the desired functionality, which will initially fail because the functionality has not been implemented yet. This step defines the scope and requirements of the code to be written. For example, we begin by writing a test that defines our expectations. For a password validation function, our test might look like this:

```python
def test_password_validation():
    # Test for minimum length requirement
    assert validate_password("short") == False

    # Test for valid password
    assert validate_password("GoodPass123") == True

    # Test for empty password
    assert validate_password("") == False
```

  Running this test results in failure, exactly what we want at this stage. This failure guides our implementation and ensures we are building exactly what we need.

- **Green, write the minimum code required to pass the test:** The goal is to write just enough code to make the test pass without worrying about optimization or elegance. Let us write a simple code to pass our test:

```python
def validate_password(password):
    MINIMUM_LENGTH = 8
    return len(password) >= MINIMUM_LENGTH
```

- **Refactor, improve the code without changing its functionality:** After the test passes, the developer refactors the code to improve readability, performance, or structure, ensuring the tests still pass.

The main benefits of this approach are:

- **Change with confidence:** Comprehensive tests serve as a safety net when modifying code during critical deployments or urgent fixes, preventing unintended side effects.

- **Superior design emergence:** Writing tests before implementation naturally leads to more modular, loosely coupled code. Teams have consistently found that TDD helps identify design flaws before they become deeply embedded in the system.

- **Living documentation:** Tests become an invaluable resource for team knowledge transfer. New team members can understand system behavior by reading through test cases.

- **Reduced debugging time:** By catching issues early in the development cycle, TDD significantly cuts down the time spent on debugging and fixing production issues.

To appreciate the practical application of TDD, consider how it might be applied in two common scenarios:

In the development of a financial services application, a team might be tasked with creating a loan eligibility calculation feature. Following TDD principles, before writing any implementation code, a developer would first create a test that defines the expected behavior: For applicants with annual income exceeding 50,000 currency units and age between 21 and 55 years, the system should return an eligibility status of *Qualified for Personal Loan*. Initially, this test would fail because the function does not exist yet. The developer would then implement the minimum code required to make this test pass, focusing specifically on the defined business rules. After ensuring the test passes, the code would be refactored for optimization and readability while maintaining the passing test status.

Similarly, when implementing social media functionality like a content appreciation feature, the developer would begin by writing a test specifying that *when a user clicks the appreciation button on a post, the appreciation count should increase by exactly one, and the button state should change to indicate the user has appreciated the content.* This test-first approach ensures that the implementation will satisfy the exact requirements, preventing scope creep and unnecessary complications. The resulting code tends to be more modular, focused, and maintainable because it was written specifically to address the test requirements.

These examples demonstrate how TDD guides developers to write precisely the code needed to fulfill the requirements, no more, no less resulting in cleaner, more maintainable codebases that align closely with business needs.

However, there are some challenges as well in TDD:

- **Initial learning curve:** Adopting TDD often requires developers and teams to unlearn traditional coding approaches and embrace a new mindset. Writing tests before code can feel counterintuitive, especially for those accustomed to coding first and testing later. This paradigm shift necessitates training and practice, which may lead to initial resistance or slower productivity. For teams new to TDD, overcoming the learning curve can be challenging without adequate support, mentorship, and patience.

- **Increased development time:** One of the most cited criticisms of TDD is that it initially takes more time compared to traditional approaches. Writing tests first, especially for edge cases and integration scenarios, can be time-consuming. However, this upfront investment is often misunderstood, as it reduces debugging and maintenance time later. Nonetheless, teams with tight deadlines or insufficient resources may find the upfront time commitment a significant hurdle.

- **Test maintenance overhead:** As projects grow, maintaining a comprehensive suite of tests can become a burdensome task. Changing requirements, refactoring, or updating libraries often necessitate updates to existing tests, which can slow down development. This problem is exacerbated in projects where test coverage is poorly planned or where test logic becomes tightly coupled to implementation details, leading to brittle tests that frequently break.

- **Overhead for simple applications:** TDD can feel like overkill for small, straightforward projects or prototypes where rapid iteration is a priority. In these cases, the additional effort of writing tests first might outweigh the benefits, especially if the project has a short lifecycle or is unlikely to see significant scaling. Balancing the practicality of TDD with the nature of the application can be a challenge for teams working on a diverse portfolio of projects.

- **Difficulty in testing non-deterministic behavior:** TDD is inherently easier to apply for deterministic code, where inputs reliably produce the same outputs. However, when dealing with non-deterministic behavior, such as asynchronous operations, multi-threaded programs, or systems that rely on external APIs, writing effective tests can become complex. Developers must often rely on mocks, stubs, or other testing aids, adding layers of complexity to the process.

To gain the most out of TDD, it is important to follow some best practices, such as:

- **Start with the smallest test:** Begin with the simplest failing test possible. Teams often fall into the trap of writing complex tests initially, making the process unnecessarily difficult.

- **Maintain test focus:** Each test should verify one specific behavior. If a test name requires multiple clauses to describe what it is testing, it is probably trying to do too much.

- **Embrace the refactor phase:** Many teams rush through or skip refactoring, but this phase is crucial for maintaining code quality and preventing technical debt.

By addressing these challenges and following best practices, teams can maximize the benefits of TDD while mitigating potential drawbacks. Proper implementation ensures that TDD remains an effective tool for improving code quality, fostering collaboration, and enhancing long-term project success.

Behavior-Driven Development

Behavior-Driven Development (**BDD**) is a software development methodology that extends the principles of TDD by emphasizing collaboration and a shared understanding of software behavior among stakeholders. Introduced by *Dan North* in the mid-2000s, BDD focuses on describing application functionality in terms of user behavior and business outcomes, using a language accessible to both technical and non-technical participants.

BDD helps bridge the gap between developers, testers, product managers, and business stakeholders by using plain language descriptions of features and their expected behavior. These descriptions often take the form of scenarios written in a structured format, enabling all parties to contribute to and validate the understanding of the system being developed.

The core principles of BDD are:

- **Collaboration:** BDD encourages close collaboration among all stakeholders to define features, ensuring a shared understanding of requirements and eliminating ambiguities.

- **Ubiquitous language:** A key aspect of BDD is the use of a common, domain-specific language that everyone on the team understands, fostering clear communication.

- **Focus on behavior:** The methodology focuses on the behavior of the system from the user's perspective, emphasizing what the system should do rather than *how* it should be implemented.

- **Test automation:** BDD often integrates with testing tools to automate the execution of behavioral scenarios, enabling continuous feedback and validation throughout development.

Typically, BDD follows the following steps:

1. **Discovery:** Teams collaborate to explore and define the desired behavior of the application. This involves discussing user stories, scenarios, and edge cases.

2. **Formulation:** Behavior is expressed in structured scenarios using a human-readable format, commonly written in Gherkin syntax. Each scenario consists of steps written as:

   a. **Given**: Defines the initial context or setup.

   b. **When**: Specifies the action or event.

   c. **Then**: Describes the expected outcome.

3. **Automation:** Scenarios are automated using BDD tools that map the plain-text steps to the underlying test code. Tools like Cucumber, SpecFlow, and Behave are commonly used for this purpose.

4. **Execution and refinement:** Automated tests are executed, and feedback is incorporated into the development process. Scenarios may be refined as requirements evolve.

Hence, the benefits of TDD are:

- **Improved communication:** By involving all stakeholders in the process, BDD fosters better communication and ensures that software meets business expectations.

- **Enhanced alignment:** BDD ensures that development efforts align with user needs and business goals, reducing the risk of building unnecessary or misaligned features.

- **Early detection of issues:** The collaborative nature of BDD helps identify gaps and ambiguities in requirements early, saving time and effort later.

- **Increased test coverage:** The structured approach of BDD encourages thorough testing of various scenarios, improving the reliability of the software.

- **Living documentation:** BDD scenarios double as documentation, describing the system's behavior in a way that remains relevant as the system evolves.

BDD has become a staple of Agile and DevOps practices. By fostering collaboration, improving understanding, and aligning development with business goals, BDD empowers teams to deliver high-quality software that meets user needs. As organizations increasingly focus on delivering value quickly, BDD serves as a vital methodology for achieving both technical excellence and stakeholder satisfaction.

BDD becomes particularly powerful when applied to real-world applications. Consider a travel reservation platform developing a hotel search feature. Using Gherkin syntax, business analysts, developers, and quality assurance specialists would collaboratively define a scenario:

- Given a customer is searching for accommodation in *Goa*.

- When they select stay dates from June 15 to June 20 for 2 adults.

- Then they should see a list of available properties with.

- And each property should display nightly rates.

- And each property should show availability status for selected dates.

- And sorting options should be available for price and customer ratings.

This structured approach ensures all stakeholders share a common understanding of the expected behavior. Business stakeholders can verify that the specified behavior aligns with business objectives, developers gain clear acceptance criteria before implementation begins, and testers receive precise verification points for validation.

For a healthcare application implementing appointment scheduling, a BDD scenario might specify:

- Given a patient has selected a physician and appointment time.

- When they confirm the appointment booking.

- Then they should receive an immediate on-screen confirmation.

- And an SMS confirmation should be delivered to their registered mobile number within 2 minutes.

- And the appointment should appear in their patient portal calendar.

The significant advantage of this approach is how it transforms requirements from potentially ambiguous documentation into concrete, executable specifications that serve multiple purposes: as requirements, as development guidance, and as automated tests. This bridges the communication gap between technical and non-technical stakeholders, fostering collaboration and ensuring that everyone works toward the same well-defined goals.

Unit, integration, and end-to-end testing strategies

Software testing ensures the reliability, performance, and functionality of applications by identifying bugs or issues before deployment. Different testing strategies target various layers of the software stack, with unit, integration, and end-to-end testing forming the foundation of a robust testing approach. Each type plays a critical role in validating the software at specific levels of complexity and interaction.

Before looking into specific testing strategies, we need to understand the testing pyramid, a concept that guides us in balancing different types of tests. At the base, we have numerous unit tests, followed by a smaller number of integration tests, and finally, a few end-to-end tests at the top.

Foundation of unit testing

Unit testing forms the bedrock of our testing strategy. These tests focus on individual components, functions, or classes in isolation. Think of unit tests as quality checks for the smallest building blocks of our application.

Here is how we can implement effective unit tests:

```
class PaymentCalculator:
    def calculate_total(self, amount, tax_rate):
        return amount + (amount * tax_rate)
```

```
def test_payment_calculation():
    calculator = PaymentCalculator()
    # Test standard calculation
    assert calculator.calculate_total(100, 0.2) == 120
    # Test zero tax scenario
    assert calculator.calculate_total(100, 0) == 100
```

The key aspects of unit testing are:

- Tests should be isolated and independent.

- Each test should focus on a single piece of functionality.

- Use descriptive names that explain the test scenario.

- Include both positive and negative test cases.

Integration testing

Moving up the pyramid, integration testing verifies that different components work together harmoniously. These tests ensure that our units collaborate effectively in real-world scenarios. Consider this example of testing user registration:

```
def test_user_registration():
    user_service = UserService(DatabaseConnection())
    notification_service = NotificationService()

    # Test the registration flow
    new_user = user_service.register("john.doe@example.com", "password123")
    assert new_user.is_active == True
    assert notification_service.verify_welcome_email(new_user.email)
```

To get the best out of the integration tests, you should ideally:

- Test realistic scenarios involving multiple components.

- Use test databases that mirror production setups.

- Focus on component boundaries and interactions.

- Include error handling and edge cases.

End-to-end testing

End-to-end (E2E) tests validate entire user workflows at the pyramid's peak. These tests ensure that all system components work together to deliver the expected user experience. Here is an example of an E2E test for an e-commerce checkout:

```
def test_complete_checkout_flow():
    # Initialize test environment
    webdriver = WebDriver()
    test_user = create_test_user()

    # Execute checkout flow
    webdriver.login(test_user)
    webdriver.add_product_to_cart("Test Product")
    webdriver.proceed_to_checkout()
    webdriver.fill_shipping_details()
    webdriver.complete_payment()

    # Verify order completion
    assert webdriver.get_order_confirmation_status() == "SUCCESS"
```

To implement these testing strategies effectively, consider the following structure:

- **Development phase:**
  - o Start with unit tests for new features.
  - o Add integration tests as components come together.
  - o Finish with E2E tests for critical user paths.

- **Testing distribution:**
  - o 70% Unit tests for thorough coverage of business logic.
  - o 20% Integration tests for component interactions.
  - o 10% E2E tests for critical user journeys.

- **Automation and CI/CD:**
  - o Automate all test levels in your pipeline.
  - o Run unit and integration tests on every commit.
  - o Schedule E2E tests for major releases.

By implementing these testing strategies effectively, we create a robust quality assurance process that catches issues early and ensures our software's reliability. The key is finding the right balance between these different testing levels while keeping maintenance overhead manageable.

These testing strategies become clearer when examined through the lens of real-world applications.

For unit testing in transportation service applications, developers might isolate the fare calculation component to verify its correctness under various conditions:

- Testing that the formula (*Distance × Base Rate + Time Factor + Applicable Taxes*) calculates correctly for standard journeys.

- Verifying behavior with boundary conditions such as minimum fare for very short distances.

- Confirming that special rate adjustments apply correctly during peak demand periods.

- Ensuring the calculation handles edge cases like zero distance requests appropriately.

Each test isolates this specific component, using mock objects to simulate interactions with location services, traffic estimation, and payment processing systems.

Integration testing for financial services applications demonstrates how components work together. When testing money transfer functionality, integration tests would verify that:

- The account management service correctly debits the sender's account balance.

- The transaction processing service properly records the transfer details with accurate timestamps.

- The receiving account service correctly credits the recipient's balance.

- The notification service delivers appropriate alerts to both parties.

- The security service properly logs the transaction for audit purposes.

These tests focus on the interactions between multiple components rather than their individual behaviors.

End-to-end testing captures complete user workflows, simulating actual customer experiences. For an electronic commerce platform, an E2E test might verify the entire purchase process:

1. User authentication and login.
2. Product search with specific criteria.
3. Filtering results by brand, price range, and user ratings.
4. Adding selected items to the shopping cart.
5. Applying promotional discounts or coupon codes.
6. Completing the checkout process with address selection.
7. Processing payment through multiple payment gateway options.
8. Receiving order confirmation and delivery estimates.

This comprehensive approach ensures that all system components work together correctly to deliver the expected user experience, validating the application from the user's perspective rather than focusing on internal technical implementations.

By implementing these different testing levels in appropriate proportions, development teams create a robust quality assurance framework that balances thoroughness with efficiency.

Performance and load testing tools

Performance and load testing are essential components of ensuring that an application or system can handle the expected user load without compromising its stability or responsiveness. These tests simulate different levels of traffic and monitor how well the application performs under stress. Performance testing focuses on validating system speed, responsiveness, and resource usage, while load testing assesses the system's ability to handle expected or peak user activity. Various tools are available that can assist in automating these tests, providing valuable insights into how a system behaves under different conditions.

Performance testing is critical because it identifies bottlenecks in an application, allowing developers to pinpoint areas where optimizations are necessary. Load testing helps to evaluate the system's capacity, ensuring that it can handle the anticipated number of users without degradation in performance. Without these tests, systems may experience slowdowns, crashes, or other failures when subjected to high usage levels. It is crucial to run these tests in various environments (development, staging, production) to verify the system's behavior at every stage of the lifecycle.

When conducting performance and load testing, there are several key metrics to monitor to evaluate the health and performance of your system under load.

These include:

- **Response time:** The amount of time it takes for the system to respond to a request. High response times may indicate bottlenecks or inefficient code.

- **Throughput:** The number of requests that the system can handle per unit of time, typically measured in **requests per second** (**RPS**). This metric helps to assess the scalability of the application.

- **Error rate:** The percentage of requests that result in errors. A high error rate during load testing may suggest that the system is unable to handle the load effectively.

- **Concurrent users:** The number of users interacting with the system at the same time. Monitoring this helps determine if the system can scale to meet demand during peak usage.

- **Resource utilization:** CPU, memory, and network usage during the test. These metrics help identify system constraints and potential areas for optimization.

Some of the best practices for performance and load testing are:

- **Test in realistic environments:** Always run tests in environments that closely resemble your production environment to get accurate results.

- **Gradual load increases:** Start with a small number of users and gradually increase the load to monitor how the system responds to different levels of stress.

- **Monitor system health:** Use monitoring tools to track system health and resource utilization during testing. This will help you identify potential bottlenecks early.

- **Test different scenarios:** Run tests that simulate different types of user behavior, from simple page views to complex transactions, to get a comprehensive view of system performance.

- **Automate load tests:** Integrate performance and load tests into your CI/CD pipeline to automatically run tests with each code change. This ensures that performance regressions are caught early in the development process.

In conclusion, performance and load testing are crucial for ensuring that an application can handle its expected user load while maintaining high levels of performance. By using the right tools and following best practices, developers and QA teams can uncover potential issues early, optimize their systems, and ensure that their applications deliver a smooth user experience, even under high traffic. Whether you are using Apache JMeter, Gatling, or any of the other tools mentioned, the goal remains the same: to ensure your system can scale, perform efficiently, and handle user demands without failure.

Performance and load testing become particularly critical for applications that experience significant traffic fluctuations or must maintain responsiveness under heavy load.

Consider these illustrative scenarios.

For sports content streaming platforms during high-profile events like international cricket tournaments, performance testing is essential to ensure service continuity. Engineers might design tests that:

- Simulate one million concurrent users accessing video streams simultaneously.

- Model realistic viewing patterns with users joining, leaving, and changing video quality settings.

- Replicate geographic distribution of access across different server regions.

- Introduce network variability to test adaptive streaming capabilities.

- Measure server response times, stream initialization delays, and buffering frequency.

These tests help identify potential bottlenecks before they impact real viewers during high-stakes broadcast events.

Similarly, e-commerce platforms preparing for major shopping events conduct extensive load testing. For anticipated flash sales with limited-inventory premium products, tests might simulate:

- 500,000 concurrent users attempting to complete purchases within a narrow time window.

- Intensive database read/write operations as inventory levels update in real-time.

- Payment processing system capacity with transaction spikes 20-30 times normal volume.

- Shopping cart reservation mechanisms under extreme contention conditions.

- Failover capabilities if primary systems reach capacity thresholds.

The insights gained from these tests allow organizations to proactively address performance limitations, implement necessary infrastructure scaling, optimize database queries, and enhance caching strategies. This preparation ensures that systems remain responsive and reliable during peak usage periods, protecting both user experience and business revenue. The fundamental principle is that it is far better to discover system limitations through controlled testing than to have them revealed through service failures during critical business operations.

API and contract testing

Application programming interfaces (**APIs**) serve as the backbone of modern software systems, enabling different applications to communicate and share data. As systems become more complex and interconnected, ensuring that APIs function as expected is critical to maintaining system stability and reliability. API testing ensures that the APIs meet the required functionality, performance, security, and reliability standards. However, ensuring that APIs interact correctly with one another across different services or applications requires a slightly different approach; contract testing. This section explores both API testing and contract testing, emphasizing their importance in modern software development and the best practices for implementing them.

API testing is the process of validating the functionality, reliability, performance, and security of APIs. Unlike traditional UI testing, which tests the user interface, API testing focuses on ensuring that APIs can handle expected requests, return appropriate responses, and manage error conditions. The goal is to ensure that the API behaves as expected under various conditions, including edge cases and error scenarios.

API testing can cover several areas such as:

- **Functional testing:** Verifying that the API performs as expected. For example, if the API is supposed to return user data, functional testing ensures that it correctly retrieves the data based on given parameters.

- **Security testing:** Ensuring that the API is protected from unauthorized access, data leaks, or other security vulnerabilities. This includes testing authentication, authorization, encryption, and data integrity.

- **Performance testing:** Assessing how the API performs under load and stress. This includes testing the API's response times, throughput, and scalability when handling multiple requests simultaneously.

- **Error handling testing:** Ensuring the API returns the correct error codes and messages when invalid input is provided or when something goes wrong. This helps to confirm that the API handles unexpected situations gracefully.

While API testing focuses on the functionality of individual APIs, contract testing ensures that APIs interact correctly with other services within a system. It focuses on verifying that the communication between two parties (such as a consumer and a provider) adheres to an agreed-upon contract. This contract typically defines the expectations for the API, including the format of requests and responses, validation rules, and error handling.

The consumer-provider contract specifies what the consumer (the application making the API call) expects from the provider (the application exposing the API). For instance, if the consumer sends a specific request with parameters, the contract dictates that the provider must return a specific type of response. Contract testing ensures that changes to the provider's API do not break the consumer's expectations and that both sides remain compatible.

The key aspects of contract testing are as follows:

- **Consumer-driven contracts:** In consumer-driven contract testing, the consumer defines the contract by specifying the expectations (e.g., data format, response codes). The provider then ensures the API complies with these expectations.

- **Provider-driven contracts:** In provider-driven contract testing, the provider defines the contract and ensures the consumer's requests are met with the correct responses.

- **Pact testing:** Pact is a popular tool for implementing contract testing. It supports both consumer-driven and provider-driven contract testing, enabling teams to ensure that their APIs are always compatible.

As microservices architecture becomes increasingly popular, systems often rely on numerous APIs to communicate. In this setup, different services may evolve at different rates, and changes in one service can unintentionally break interactions with others. Contract testing minimizes these risks by ensuring that services can evolve independently while remaining compatible.

For instance, if a new version of an API is released, contract testing ensures that existing consumers can still interact with it without encountering errors, even if the API has changed. Without contract testing, breaking changes in an API could lead to unexpected system failures and costly downtime.

API and contract testing workflow

The overall workflow for API and contract testing is as follows:

- **Define the API contract:** For contract testing to be effective, the first step is to define the contract. This could be done using API documentation tools such as OpenAPI (formerly Swagger), which provides a formal specification of API endpoints, request/response formats, and error codes.

- **Write consumer tests:** The consumer writes tests to ensure that the provider's API will meet their expectations. This includes verifying that the response data matches the expected format, that the correct status codes are returned, and that any other requirements are met.

- **Write provider tests:** The provider writes tests to validate that it is fulfilling the consumer's contract. The provider must ensure that any updates or changes to the API do not break the existing contract.

- **Run the contract tests:** The contract tests are executed, often in a CI/CD pipeline, to automatically verify that the contract holds true. This includes validating the API responses during runtime and ensuring that both the consumer and provider are aligned.

- **Automate contract verification:** Automating contract tests ensures that any future changes to the API or the way it is consumed will be caught early. This helps teams maintain API stability and prevents disruptions in service.

API and contract testing are essential to ensuring that modern distributed systems are stable, scalable, and resilient. While API testing ensures that individual APIs function as expected, contract testing ensures that APIs work correctly when integrated into larger systems. By adopting both API and contract testing as part of your development and testing processes, you can ensure seamless communication between services, prevent integration issues, and maintain high-quality, reliable software. With tools like Postman, Pact, and RestAssured, teams can effectively validate their APIs and contracts, helping to deliver robust and compatible software systems that meet the needs of their users.

To illustrate the practical value of API and contract testing, consider these real-world implementations.

A weather information application might rely on external meteorological data services to provide forecasts to its users. The API contract would explicitly define expectations such as:

- When requesting current conditions for *New York City* using the endpoint `/api/v2/current/location?city=New%20York%20City`, the service must return a standardized JSON response containing temperature (in both Celsius and Fahrenheit), humidity percentage, wind speed and direction, barometric pressure, and precipitation probability.

- The response must include a timestamp indicating when the data was collected.

- Error conditions must return appropriate HTTP status codes with descriptive error messages.

Contract tests would verify these expectations are consistently met, ensuring the application can reliably parse and display weather information.

For financial technology applications integrating with payment processing services like digital wallets or credit card processors, contract testing becomes even more critical. When a user completes a purchase:

- The application sends transaction details in a precisely formatted request.

- The payment provider processes the transaction and returns a response with approval status, transaction identifier, and authorization codes.

- The application updates order status based on this response.

If the payment processor modifies their API response structure without notice—perhaps changing field names, adding required parameters, or altering data formats—applications without robust contract testing might fail catastrophically during live transactions. Contract tests would identify such compatibility issues during development or testing phases, allowing for coordinated updates before customer-facing functions are affected.

This approach resembles a formal service level agreement between systems, where both the provider and consumer have clear, verifiable expectations about their interactions. By regularly validating these contracts through automated testing, organizations maintain reliable integration points even as individual services evolve independently. This becomes increasingly valuable in microservice architectures, where dozens or hundreds of services must maintain compatible communication patterns despite being developed and deployed by different teams on different schedules.

UI testing with Selenium or Cypress

User interface (UI) testing is an essential practice to ensure that web applications function as expected from an end-user perspective. These tests validate the visual components of an application, like buttons, forms, and navigation menus, to ensure they are responsive, interactive, and provide a smooth user experience. Selenium and Cypress are two of the most popular tools used for automating UI testing, each offering distinct features and advantages for testing web applications.

Selenium is a widely used, open-source framework for automating web browsers. It supports multiple programming languages, such as Java, Python, C#, and JavaScript, making it a flexible choice for teams with varying tech stacks. Selenium allows testers to simulate real user interactions with web applications, such as clicking buttons, filling out forms, and navigating through different pages.

Some key features include:

- **Cross-browser compatibility:** Selenium supports all major browsers, like Chrome, Firefox, Safari, and Internet Explorer.

- **Multiple programming language support:** Selenium WebDriver enables testing in various languages, making it versatile.

- **Remote testing:** It can be used with Selenium Grid to perform parallel testing across multiple machines and browsers, speeding up the testing process.

Cypress is a modern JavaScript-based end-to-end testing framework designed for web applications. It operates directly inside the browser, providing faster and more reliable testing compared to traditional Selenium. Cypress is highly developer-friendly, with an intuitive API, real-time browser preview, and excellent debugging capabilities.

Some key features include:

- **Fast and reliable:** Cypress runs tests in the same execution loop as the application, making it faster and more reliable than Selenium.

- **Real-time browser preview:** Provides a visual representation of the tests in action, making it easier to debug and understand the test flow.

- **Built-in waits:** Cypress automatically waits for elements to be visible, reducing the need for manual wait times or sleeps in test scripts.

- **Automatic retry:** Tests are automatically retried on failure to handle dynamic content loading more effectively.

UI testing with tools like Selenium and Cypress plays a crucial role in ensuring that web applications provide a seamless and bug-free user experience. While Selenium offers flexibility across various browsers and programming languages, Cypress delivers a more modern, faster, and developer-friendly testing experience for JavaScript applications. Both tools are valuable for automating repetitive UI tests, catching regressions, and enhancing software quality, making them indispensable parts of a testing strategy for modern web applications.

Test data management

Test data management (TDM) is a critical aspect of the software testing process. It involves the planning, creation, storage, maintenance, and utilization of data required for testing applications. Properly managed test data ensures that tests are reliable, repeatable, and cover a wide range of scenarios, helping to identify defects and ensure the application works as expected. Inconsistent, incomplete, or outdated test data can lead to inaccurate test results, missed defects, and unreliable software releases.

Effective test data management is essential in any testing environment, particularly as applications scale and become more complex. This section explores the importance of test data management, strategies for handling test data, and tools that can help ensure that the right data is available for testing purposes.

The importance of TDM is explained as follows:

- **Accurate test results:** Proper test data ensures that tests produce meaningful, accurate results. With the right data, tests can simulate real-world conditions and catch potential bugs that may not be discovered with incorrect or artificial data.

- **Testing edge cases:** Effective TDM enables testers to create data that covers a wide range of scenarios, including edge cases that may otherwise be overlooked. This can include invalid data, boundary values, or extreme scenarios, which are crucial for identifying issues that might arise under unusual conditions.

- **Data privacy and compliance:** In many industries, applications deal with sensitive information (e.g., financial data and personal health information). Proper test data management ensures that testing does not inadvertently expose sensitive data to unauthorized users or violate data protection regulations, such as GDPR or HIPAA.

- **Efficiency in testing:** With proper TDM, testers can quickly access relevant datasets without having to manually create or manipulate data before each test cycle. This improves testing speed, consistency, and repeatability.

Some of the key strategies for an effective TDM are:

- **Data anonymization:** To protect sensitive information while still using realistic data, anonymization techniques can be applied. Anonymizing personal details, such as names or credit card numbers, ensures that testers can still work with valid, real-world data without compromising privacy.

- **Data subsetting:** Rather than using a full production database for testing, data subsetting involves selecting a representative sample of data that retains the necessary attributes for testing. This reduces storage requirements and minimizes the risk of handling unnecessary or irrelevant data.

- **Synthetic data generation:** In cases where real data is unavailable or impractical to use, synthetic data generation can be an effective solution. This involves creating artificial data that mimics real-world scenarios. Tools like Faker or Mockaroo allow testers to generate data that is both realistic and diverse, providing a broad range of test cases.

- **Versioning and snapshots:** Maintaining different versions or snapshots of test data is essential for tracking changes in the application. This allows testers to revert to specific states of data (e.g., prior to a software update) to ensure that tests can be executed consistently.

- **Test data provisioning:** Automating the process of creating, updating, and destroying test data ensures that the right data is available for each test cycle. This includes automating data setup, tearing down the data after testing, and refreshing data as needed to ensure tests are run with the most current information.

- **Data masking:** Data masking is the process of replacing sensitive data with fake but realistic data. For example, if an application needs to be tested with customer information, the customer names, addresses, and other personal details can be replaced with fictitious but structurally similar data. This allows for realistic testing while ensuring privacy.

TDM is a vital part of the testing process, ensuring that tests are accurate, repeatable, and capable of covering a wide range of scenarios. By leveraging strategies like data anonymization, subsetting, synthetic data generation, and automated provisioning, teams can ensure that they are working with relevant and secure test data while avoiding issues related to privacy and data integrity. With the right tools and practices in place, effective test data management can significantly improve the quality of software applications and streamline the testing process.

TDM approaches become more tangible when examined through specific application contexts.

In retail e-commerce environments, comprehensive testing requires diverse customer profiles and purchasing patterns. TDM strategies would generate synthetic consumer data such as:

- Customer profiles with realistic but fictional personal details: John Doe, residing at 123 Evergreen Terrace, Springfield, with email address **johndoe@testmail. example**.

- Payment instruments using valid-format but non-functional credit card numbers (for example, 4242 4242 4242 4242—a test number that passes validation algorithms but cannot process actual transactions).

- Order histories reflecting varied purchasing patterns across different product categories.

- Loyalty program statuses with different tier levels and reward point accumulations.

- Address variations covering different regions, international formats, and edge cases like territories or military addresses.

This synthetic data preserves the structural characteristics and relationships of production data while containing no actual customer information, eliminating privacy concerns during testing activities.

Healthcare information systems face even more stringent data management challenges due to regulatory requirements regarding patient confidentiality. Test data management in this context might involve:

- Creating entirely synthetic patient profiles with medically realistic but fictional medical histories.

- Generating laboratory results within appropriate reference ranges for various medical conditions.

- Simulating treatment plans and medication regimens that reflect actual clinical practices.

- Producing appointment schedules with realistic distribution patterns across medical specialties.

- Developing insurance coverage scenarios representing various payer arrangements and benefit structures.

These approaches allow thorough testing of healthcare system functionality—including complex scenarios like insurance verification, clinical decision support, and regulatory compliance reporting, without exposing actual patient health information to testing environments.

TDM can be conceptualized as creating a parallel universe of data that behaves statistically and functionally like production data while containing no actual sensitive information. Like professional actors portraying characters in a training simulation, this synthetic data allows teams to rigorously test system behavior under realistic conditions without risking privacy violations or data exposure.

Maintaining test suites in CI/CD pipelines

Maintaining test suites in CI/CD pipelines is a key aspect of ensuring the ongoing quality and stability of an application throughout its development lifecycle. CI and CD emphasize automated testing as a vital step before changes are merged and deployed. A test suite that runs efficiently in these pipelines is crucial for catching regressions early and maintaining the overall health of the application. However, as projects evolve and new features are added, test suites can become bloated, slow, and difficult to manage. Therefore, regular maintenance and optimization of these test suites are essential to keep the CI/CD process smooth and efficient.

The first step in maintaining test suites is organizing them properly. Test suites should be categorized based on the types of tests they include unit tests, integration tests, end-to-end tests, and UI tests. Unit tests should be quick and lightweight, focusing on individual components or functions, and are best run frequently in the CI pipeline. Integration tests validate the interaction between components, while end-to-end and UI tests ensure the application functions as a whole. Proper categorization allows teams to determine which tests should be run at each stage of the pipeline. For instance, running unit tests in every commit ensures rapid feedback, while more time-consuming end-to-end tests can be scheduled less frequently, such as on a nightly basis.

Next, it is important to ensure that the test suite remains fast and efficient as the project grows. Over time, the number of tests increases, and without proper maintenance, the test suite can become slow, causing delays in the pipeline and potentially discouraging developers from running tests frequently. This can be mitigated by identifying redundant, obsolete, or flaky tests that contribute little to the overall quality assurance process.

Removing or refactoring these tests helps reduce execution time and improves the reliability of the test suite. Additionally, parallelizing test execution or using cloud-based testing platforms can significantly speed up the process, allowing multiple tests to run simultaneously.

Another critical aspect of maintaining test suites is ensuring that tests are comprehensive and up to date. As new features are added, corresponding tests need to be written and integrated into the test suite. This means that test suites should evolve alongside the application. Regularly reviewing and updating test cases is essential for covering new code paths, ensuring that old tests still align with the current application functionality, and removing any tests that no longer apply. Keeping tests updated helps prevent gaps in coverage, which could lead to defects being missed or unexpected behaviors going unnoticed.

Monitoring test suite health is another vital practice for maintaining quality in CI/CD pipelines. It is important to track key metrics such as test execution time, failure rates, and the percentage of passing tests. Consistently high failure rates can indicate issues with the tests themselves, such as flaky tests or incorrect assumptions, while slow tests could point to inefficiencies in the testing process. Analyzing these metrics helps identify areas for improvement, such as optimizing specific tests, reducing unnecessary complexity, or introducing mock services to speed up tests involving external dependencies.

Maintaining test suites in CI/CD pipelines is an ongoing effort that requires consistent attention and optimization. By organizing tests effectively, removing redundancies, updating tests to reflect changes in the application, and monitoring test health, teams can ensure that their test suites remain a valuable asset to the development process. An efficient and well-maintained test suite not only speeds up the CI/CD pipeline but also improves the reliability of the software, ensuring that bugs are caught early and that high-quality releases are deployed to production.

Leading technology organizations have established sophisticated practices for maintaining test suites within their continuous integration and delivery pipelines, offering valuable lessons for implementation.

Major internet services companies have developed sophisticated test execution strategies that balance thoroughness with efficiency:

- Every code submission triggers the execution of thousands of unit tests that must complete successfully before the code can be considered for integration.

- More comprehensive integration test suites execute on scheduled intervals (often nightly) to validate system-wide compatibility.

- Resource-intensive end-to-end tests may run less frequently but must pass before code reaches production environments.

- Performance-critical components undergo specialized benchmark testing against established baseline metrics.

- Test results feed into developer dashboards providing immediate visibility into quality metrics.

These organizations implement multi-level quality gates where:

- Tests are categorized by criticality, with the most essential tests acting as absolute barriers to progression.

- Development teams receive automated notifications when their changes cause test failures.

- Historical test performance data identifies flaky tests that require remediation.

- Test execution metrics highlight areas where test optimization could improve pipeline efficiency.

The approach transforms test automation from a passive quality verification tool into an active gatekeeper that protects code integrity. Like a sophisticated security system that prevents unauthorized access, well-maintained test suites prevent problematic code from propagating through the delivery pipeline. This preventative approach significantly reduces the likelihood of defects reaching production environments, ultimately improving both development efficiency and software reliability.

Organizations that excel at continuous testing typically dedicate specific resources to test suite maintenance rather than treating it as an occasional task. Specialized roles or rotating responsibilities ensure that test assets receive ongoing attention, preventing the gradual deterioration that occurs when maintenance is neglected. This investment reflects the understanding that effective test automation represents a valuable organizational asset that requires proper stewardship to maintain its value.

Code coverage analysis and reporting

Code coverage analysis is a crucial practice in software development that helps measure how much of the application's source code is covered by automated tests. The goal of code coverage is not just to track the percentage of code tested but to ensure that the tests exercise all the important parts of the code, including edge cases, business logic, and error handling. In CI/CD pipelines, code coverage analysis serves as an early indicator of test effectiveness, helping developers and testers identify areas that may lack sufficient test coverage. However, achieving high code coverage should not be the sole objective; it is more important to ensure that the right parts of the code are tested, as high coverage without meaningful tests can lead to false confidence.

To effectively measure code coverage, it is essential to use coverage tools that integrate with the CI/CD pipeline. Tools like Jacoco, Istanbul, and Cobertura allow for the generation of detailed reports that show which lines, functions, or branches of the code have been tested. These tools track the execution of tests and provide a visual representation of coverage, highlighting areas that may require additional testing. The integration of such tools within the CI/CD pipeline ensures that coverage is continuously monitored and that developers receive feedback on their code coverage with every commit or pull request, prompting them to write additional tests when necessary.

A key aspect of code coverage analysis is the balance between quantity and quality. While achieving high code coverage (e.g., 90%) may seem desirable, it does not guarantee that the software is bug-free. A 100% code coverage figure might be misleading if the tests only cover trivial code paths, leaving critical or complex areas untested. Instead of focusing solely on the coverage percentage, teams should prioritize testing core application functionality, business logic, and integration points that are crucial to the software's success. Additionally, it is important to identify and measure different types of coverage, such as line coverage, branch coverage, and path coverage, to get a more holistic view of the testing effort.

Once the coverage data is collected, generating and analyzing reports becomes the next crucial step. Code coverage reports provide visibility into which parts of the code are well-tested and which areas need improvement. These reports can be easily integrated into the CI/CD pipeline, providing developers with immediate feedback on their commits. Automated reports ensure that testing is always in sync with code changes and prevent situations where critical parts of the application go untested. For teams working on large projects, having a code coverage report accessible in the form of a dashboard helps everyone stay informed and take proactive steps to address gaps in coverage.

While code coverage analysis is valuable, it should not be viewed as a goal in itself. It is important to continuously review and evaluate the usefulness of the coverage data. Coverage tools can sometimes give a false sense of security, as they cannot measure the quality of tests. A test may cover a piece of code but fail to properly assert the expected behavior. To address this, it is important to supplement code coverage with other quality metrics, such as test effectiveness, bug rate, and customer feedback. Additionally, adopting best practices like writing meaningful tests, using mocks and stubs for external dependencies, and performing code reviews ensures that tests are not just covering code but are also validating the software's functionality.

In conclusion, code coverage analysis and reporting are indispensable tools for maintaining software quality within a CI/CD pipeline. By integrating code coverage tools, focusing on meaningful tests, and continuously analyzing coverage reports, teams can ensure their application is well-tested and resilient. However, it is essential to remember that code coverage is only one part of the testing puzzle. A comprehensive approach that combines high-quality tests, efficient test design, and constant monitoring will lead to a more stable, reliable, and maintainable software product.

Code coverage analysis becomes particularly meaningful when applied to concrete development scenarios.

In financial services applications handling critical operations such as funds transfer or loan origination, code coverage analysis provides essential quality insights:

- Initial analysis might reveal that only 40% of the codebase is exercised by existing tests.

- Deeper investigation could show that while basic happy path functionality is tested, error handling code paths remain completely unverified.

- Coverage reports might highlight that certain regulatory compliance validations lack adequate test coverage.

- After implementing additional tests based on these findings, coverage metrics might improve to 85-90%, with critical paths achieving near-complete coverage.

This progression represents a significant risk reduction, as untested code represents potential failure points during operation. However, coverage metrics must be interpreted thoughtfully rather than targeting arbitrary percentage goals. Coverage analysis that shows 100% of the authorization module is tested but only 20% of the error recovery functionality suggests a concerning imbalance in testing priorities.

The value of code coverage extends beyond simple percentages when teams use it to improve testing strategy. When coverage tools highlight specific untested code paths, testers can analyze whether these represent:

- Error handling logic that should be verified for proper exception management.

- Boundary conditions that might expose edge-case behaviors.

- Defensive programming checks that validate input parameters.

- Optimization paths that activate under specific performance conditions.

- Legacy code that might no longer be relevant and could be refactored away.

This targeted approach to coverage analysis helps teams develop more effective test strategies focused on risk and business importance rather than arbitrary coverage targets.

Code coverage is conceptually similar to verifying building safety, you want to ensure that critical structural elements and safety systems have been thoroughly inspected before occupancy. While inspecting 100% of every element in the building might be impractical, ensuring comprehensive inspection of all foundational structures, emergency systems, and high-occupancy areas is essential. Similarly, in software development, focusing coverage efforts on core functionality, security-sensitive components, and frequently executed code paths provides the most effective quality assurance.

Conclusion

Continuous testing and quality assurance are integral to delivering reliable, high-quality software. By embracing automated testing strategies, maintaining robust test suites, and leveraging best practices in CI/CD pipelines, teams can catch defects early, ensure stability, and improve software performance. Through methodologies like TDD and BDD, and tools for code coverage, API, and UI testing, developers are empowered to create resilient applications. With consistent monitoring and refinement, CT becomes a driving force behind continuous improvement and exceptional software quality.

In the next chapter, building upon the quality assurance foundations established, we will explore **site reliability engineering** (**SRE**). This discipline bridges the gap between development and operations to create more reliable software systems. The next chapter will introduce core SRE principles and their relationship with DevOps practices, explaining essential concepts such as **service level indicators** (**SLIs**), **service level objectives** (**SLOs**), and error budgets. We will learn strategies for automating toil, implementing effective incident management processes, and conducting meaningful postmortems. The chapter will also cover practical approaches to chaos engineering for building resilience, disaster recovery planning, scaling for performance, and establishing robust observability frameworks. By connecting testing practices with SRE methodologies, we will understand how to build, deploy, and maintain highly reliable software systems at scale.

Join our Discord space

Join our Discord workspace for latest updates, offers, tech happenings around the world, new releases, and sessions with the authors:

https://discord.bpbonline.com

CHAPTER 13
Site Reliability Engineering

Introduction

Today's software systems must be highly dependable, scalable, and efficient while adapting to rapid development cycles. **Site reliability engineering** (SRE) bridges the gap between operations and software development, focusing on automation, reliability optimization, and service maintenance within defined boundaries.

Pioneered initially at *Google*, SRE has spread globally, introducing metrics like SLIs, SLOs, and error budgets that help teams balance uptime, reliability, and innovation, a difficult balance in traditional operations. By integrating software engineering with operational components, including monitoring, incident management, and capacity planning, SRE transforms how organizations maintain digital services.

In today's digital economy, downtime directly impacts financial outcomes and user satisfaction. SRE treats reliability as a core product feature rather than an afterthought. Instead of manual interventions, SREs develop automated solutions that improve system resilience, shifting from reactive to proactive engineering.

The structured measurement approach of SRE provides objective data for cross-team reliability discussions. Well-defined incident response strategies and blameless postmortems transform failures into learning opportunities. Meanwhile, practices like chaos engineering proactively test system resilience by introducing controlled failures and building systems that withstand unexpected challenges.

This chapter thoroughly examines these concepts, offering hands-on exercises to implement SRE principles in real-world scenarios.

Structure

This chapter covers the following topics:

- Understanding SRE and its relationship with DevOps
- SLIs, SLOs, and error budgets
- Incident management and postmortems
- Service-level objectives and reliability targets
- Chaos engineering for resilience
- Disaster recovery and backup strategies
- Scaling and performance optimization
- Observability and SRE tools
- Security in SRE practices

Objectives

This chapter aims to equip readers with a comprehensive understanding of SRE principles and practices. Upon completion, learners can implement SLIs, SLOs, and error budgets to objectively measure and manage system reliability. Students will develop skills to establish effective incident management processes, conduct blameless postmortems, and extract valuable insights from failure scenarios. The chapter enables participants to define appropriate service-level objectives aligned with business needs and user expectations while learning to apply chaos engineering techniques to test system resilience proactively.

Learners will gain proficiency in designing robust disaster recovery and backup strategies with appropriate RTOs and RPOs for various business contexts. The chapter provides knowledge for implementing scaling solutions and performance optimization techniques to maintain system efficiency under varying loads. Participants will learn to build comprehensive observability frameworks using metrics, logs, and traces to gain actionable insights into system behavior. Finally, readers will understand how to integrate security practices within SRE workflows, ensuring systems remain reliable and protected against evolving threats.

Understanding SRE and its relationship with DevOps

SRE emerged at large tech companies when engineers got tired of fighting the same system problems repeatedly. Instead of constantly reacting to issues, SRE teams apply software engineering principles to operations, building tools, and automation to manage systems, handle incidents, and maintain high availability.

The SRE philosophy centers around several practical principles:

- Eliminating toil, those repetitive, manual tasks that drain time and energy. If a task has been done manually three times, it is a candidate for automation.

- Defining reliability with actual metrics using **service level indicators** (**SLIs**), **service level objectives** (**SLOs**), and error budgets. These transform vague reliability discussions into data-driven conversations. Accepting that 100% uptime is unrealistic. SRE acknowledges that failures happen and works with error budgets, allowing teams to take calculated risks while maintaining service reliability.

- Automating operations wherever possible, deployments, monitoring, scaling, and incident response processes become code rather than manual procedures. Learning systematically from failures. Incidents are not opportunities to assign blame but chances to improve systems and processes through structured postmortems.

SRE vs. DevOps

The relationship between SRE and DevOps often causes confusion. Both aim to improve collaboration and system reliability; however, they approach these goals differently:

- DevOps represents a broader cultural shift breaking down barriers between development and operations teams. SRE offers a specific engineering discipline focused on reliability and automation.

- DevOps teams typically concentrate on accelerating software delivery through continuous integration and deployment. SRE teams prioritize measuring and maintaining reliability metrics and system performance.

- In DevOps environments, reliability practices can vary significantly between teams. SRE brings consistency through standardized SLOs and error budgets.

- When incidents occur, DevOps response processes may differ across organizations. SRE implements structured incident management with clear escalation paths and blameless postmortems.

Many successful organizations implement both approaches, using DevOps principles to improve collaboration and speed while applying SRE practices to ensure systems remain reliable as they scale.

Figure 13.1 showcases the DevOps vs SRE approach, and this combination helps strike the critical balance between moving quickly and maintaining stability:

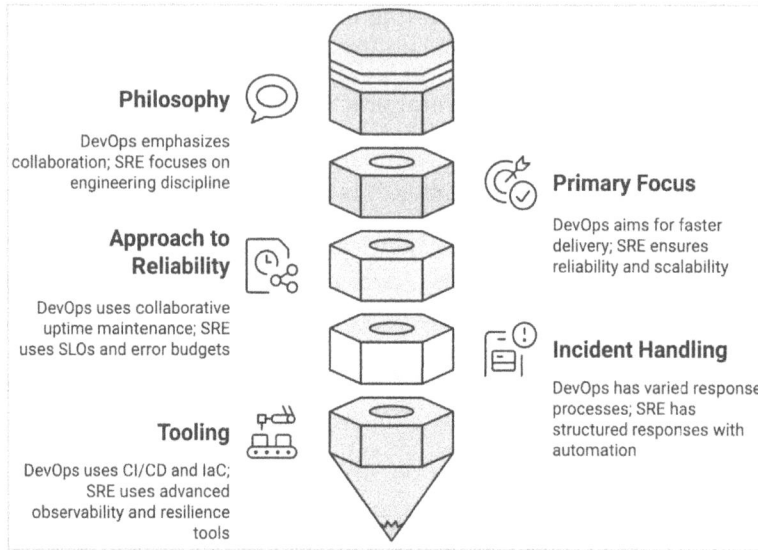

Figure 13.1: SRE vs. DevOps

To understand the practical impact of SRE principles, consider how major technology companies implement them in production environments. Google Search, where SRE originated, maintains extraordinary reliability with 99.999% uptime by implementing sophisticated automation for failure detection and recovery. Their systems can automatically redirect traffic, apply live configuration changes, and perform Rolling Updates without users noticing any impact. This level of reliability engineering enables Google to handle billions of search queries daily while continuously deploying improvements.

Similarly, e-commerce platforms like *Shopify* face extreme reliability challenges during peak shopping events such as *Black Friday*, when transaction volumes can increase tenfold within minutes. Their SRE teams employ feature flags and gradual rollouts to maintain platform stability during these high-stakes periods. By implementing precise reliability measurements and automated safeguards, they can confidently deploy new features while ensuring the shopping experience remains smooth even under unprecedented load.

These real-world implementations demonstrate how SRE transcends traditional operational approaches by embedding reliability as a fundamental engineering discipline rather than a reactive maintenance activity. The systematic measurement, automation, and incident response methodologies pioneered by SRE teams at these organizations have established new standards for operational excellence across the technology industry.

SLIs, SLOs, and error budgets

In the world of site reliability engineering, reliability is not a vague aspiration but a precisely defined and measured attribute. This transformation from subjective to objective assessment begins with **service level indicators** (**SLIs**), which serve as the foundation for a data-driven approach to reliability management. SLIs are carefully selected metrics that directly reflect the user experience, capturing what truly matters to those interacting with your systems.

When choosing SLIs, engineers focus on aspects like:

- **Availability:** Is the service responding?
- **Latency:** How quickly does it respond?
- **Throughput:** How many operations can it handle?
- **Error rates:** How often does it fail?

These measurements provide the raw data that inform all reliability decisions and improvements.

Once meaningful SLIs are established, organizations define **service level objectives (SLOs)** as target values for these indicators. SLOs represent the line between happy and unhappy users, the threshold at which reliability problems begin to negatively impact the user experience or business outcomes. For instance, if experience shows that users become frustrated when page load times exceed 300 milliseconds, an SLO might specify that 95% of page loads must be completed within that timeframe. Crucially, SLOs are not arbitrarily set targets but carefully considered thresholds that balance user expectations with technical and economic realities. They acknowledge that pursuing 100% reliability is neither practical nor necessary, instead focusing on achieving reliable enough service that keeps users satisfied.

While SLOs define acceptable performance, error budgets translate these objectives into a practical framework for managing risk and innovation. An error budget represents the allowed amount of failure within the SLO, if your SLO specifies 99.9% availability, your error budget is the remaining 0.1% of allowed downtime. This simple but powerful concept transforms reliability from a binary always working/sometimes failing proposition into a nuanced resource that can be strategically allocated. When a service operates well within its SLO, the unused error budget represents an opportunity to move faster, take calculated risks, and implement new features. Conversely, when a service approaches or exceeds its error budget, teams must prioritize reliability improvements over new feature development.

Error budgets fundamentally change organizational dynamics by aligning incentives between development teams (who typically prioritize innovation and new features) and operations teams (who traditionally focus on stability and uptime). Without error budgets, this tension often creates a counterproductive dynamic where operations teams are incentivized to resist all changes while development teams push for rapid releases regardless of reliability impacts. With error budgets, both teams work toward a shared understanding: development can move as fast as they want if the service remains within its error budget, while operations have concrete data to justify slowing down when reliability metrics indicate problems. This alignment transforms what was once an emotional debate into a data-driven discussion.

The implementation of error budgets requires not just technical infrastructure but cultural change. Organizations must develop processes for monitoring error budget consumption, establishing clear policies for what happens when budgets are depleted, and creating feedback loops that inform future planning. For example, many organizations implement budget burn rate alerts that notify teams when error budgets are being consumed unusually quickly, allowing for early intervention before problems affect too many users. Similarly, teams develop error budget policies that explicitly define the actions to take when a service exhausts its budget, typically shifting focus from feature development to reliability improvements until the service returns to acceptable performance levels.

Advanced organizations use error budgets not just reactively but proactively, incorporating them into planning and architecture decisions. Development teams might reserve portions of the error budget for planned deployments, ensuring they have sufficient margin for the inevitable issues that accompany significant changes. Architects might analyze error budget consumption patterns to identify components that consistently drain the budget, prioritizing redesigns or replacements for these reliability bottlenecks. Product managers learn to factor reliability costs into feature planning, recognizing that complex features that threaten reliability targets may require additional engineering investment or phased deployments to stay within budget constraints.

Through the systematic implementation of SLIs, SLOs, and error budgets, organizations transform reliability from a wishful aspiration to a managed resource. This framework provides a common language for discussing reliability, clear metrics for measuring it, and practical mechanisms for balancing it against other business priorities. Teams move from reactive firefighting to proactive management, from subjective debates to data-driven decisions, and from siloed responsibilities to shared ownership of both innovation and stability. The result is not just more reliable systems but more effective organizations, capable of delivering both the rapid innovation that drives business growth and the consistent reliability that keeps users satisfied and loyal.

To illustrate how these concepts operate in practice, consider *Netflix's* video streaming service. Their engineering teams define specific Service Level Indicators that directly reflect user experience, such as percentage of successful video playback starts within 2 seconds. Based on user research and business requirements, they establish a SLO that 99.9% of playback attempts should meet this threshold. This creates an error budget of 0.1%, approximately 43 minutes of degraded performance per month.

This error budget serves multiple critical functions at Netflix. When considering the rollout of a new video codec like AV1 that offers better compression but might initially cause playback issues for some users, engineering teams can make data-driven decisions about deployment speed. If the service is performing well within its SLO, they might accelerate the rollout, using a portion of the error budget to gather real-world performance data. Conversely, if recent infrastructure changes have consumed most of the error budget, they might delay the codec deployment until reliability improves.

Similarly, Google's Gmail service targets 99.99% successful message delivery for both inbound and outbound email traffic. This precise reliability target allows their engineers to balance innovation with stability in a service used by billions of users daily. When deploying new spam detection algorithms or infrastructure changes, teams monitor error budget consumption rates to ensure user experience remains within acceptable parameters.

These examples demonstrate how SLIs, SLOs, and error budgets transform abstract reliability concepts into practical engineering tools that guide decision-making, align incentives across teams, and maintain focus on user experience across complex distributed systems.

Automating toil and reducing manual interventions

Anyone who has spent time in operations knows the feeling, that recurring task you have done a hundred times, that middle-of-the-night alert that always needs the same fix, that deployment process with 27 tedious steps. This is what SRE calls **toil**, repetitive manual work that adds no lasting value but somehow consumes most of your day.

Toil is the enemy of reliability and innovation. It is an operational task that is manual, repetitive, automatable, and scales linearly with service growth. The more your systems grow, the more toil grows with them. When engineers spend their days fighting fires instead of preventing them, both morale and system reliability suffer.

The impact of toil extends beyond just wasted time. Manual processes introduce human error, forgetting steps, making typos, or missing critical details when you are exhausted at 3 AM. High-toil environments lead to burnout as engineers feel trapped in an endless cycle of reactive work. Most SRE teams aim to cap toil at 50% of their time, ensuring enough bandwidth for meaningful improvements.

Effective toil reduction starts with automating incident response. Instead of relying on humans to detect and fix every issue, modern SRE teams implement automated alerting that cuts through the noise, self-healing mechanisms that resolve common problems without human intervention, and runbook automation that executes standard procedures consistently. These systems do not eliminate the need for human judgment, but they handle routine cases automatically and provide engineers with better data when human expertise is required.

Deployments represent another major source of toil and risk. Manual deployments are error-prone and stressful, but CI/CD pipelines automate the entire process from code commit to production release. Canary deployments and feature flags reduce risk by gradually rolling out changes to small subsets of users, while automated rollback mechanisms ensure quick recovery when issues arise. The result is not just less toil but safer, more frequent deployments.

Infrastructure management transforms dramatically when automation replaces manual setup. **Infrastructure as code (IaC)** tools like Terraform turn server provisioning, network configuration, and security setup into version-controlled code rather than manual point-and-click operations. Kubernetes Operators extend this automation to application management, handling complex deployment patterns, scaling, and failover without human involvement. These approaches eliminate configuration drift and enable an infrastructure that scales automatically with demand.

Routine maintenance tasks form another category of toil that often flies under the radar until it consumes entire teams. Log rotation, database backups, certificate renewals, and security patching are necessary but tedious. By automating these processes with tooling like ELK Stack for logs, automated backup solutions, and patch management systems, teams can ensure these critical tasks happen consistently without manual effort. This automation not only saves time but improves security and compliance by eliminating gaps in maintenance.

ChatOps represents a particularly human-friendly form of automation, integrating operational tools into communication platforms like Slack or Microsoft Teams. Engineers can deploy code, check system health, or manage incidents without leaving their chat interface. This approach makes automation more accessible and collaborative, allowing teams to execute and observe operational tasks together.

Successful toil reduction is not a one-time project but an ongoing commitment. Teams should measure their progress by tracking the percentage of time spent on toil, incident resolution speed, deployment frequency, and error rates. The ultimate metric, though, is how much more time engineers can devote to meaningful improvements rather than repetitive maintenance.

By systematically identifying and automating toil, SRE teams transform their operational model from reactive firefighting to proactive engineering. This shift does not just make engineers happier; it results in more reliable systems, faster innovation, and infrastructure that scales without proportional increases in operational overhead.

Leading technology organizations have implemented impressive automation systems that demonstrate the transformative impact of eliminating toil. *Facebook* (now *Meta*) has developed sophisticated auto-remediation systems that handle database failures without human intervention. Their database repair bots can detect replication issues, inconsistencies, or performance degradation and automatically initiate corrective actions. Their Cassandra clusters incorporate self-healing mechanisms that can rebalance data, replace failing nodes, and optimize performance parameters without administrator involvement. These automation systems allow Facebook to maintain tens of thousands of database instances with a relatively small engineering team.

Airbnb presents another compelling example of toil reduction through deployment automation. Their engineering teams deploy hundreds of microservices daily through GitOps-based continuous delivery pipelines powered by Kubernetes and Argo CD. This automation handles complex deployment patterns like Canary releases and Blue/Green deployments, automatically performing health checks and rolling back changes that fail verification. What previously required careful coordination across multiple teams and hours of manual work now happens automatically, allowing engineers to focus on developing new features rather than managing deployment procedures.

The impact of these automation initiatives extends beyond just efficiency. By removing human operators from routine procedures, these organizations have significantly reduced the incidence of configuration errors, eliminated deployment inconsistencies between environments, and dramatically shortened their mean time to recovery during incidents. These outcomes demonstrate that reducing toil is not merely about making engineers' lives easier though that is a valuable benefit, but fundamentally about building more reliable, consistent, and resilient systems.

Incident management and postmortems

When systems fail, and they inevitably will, the difference between chaos and resilience lies in how teams respond. Effective incident management is not just about restoring service quickly; it is about coordinated response, clear communication, and systematic learning from each failure. In high-performing organizations, incidents are not dreaded disasters but valuable opportunities to strengthen systems and teams.

The incident lifecycle begins with detection, identifying problems before users report them. While traditional monitoring focuses on system metrics like CPU and memory usage, modern observability practices emphasize user-impacting symptoms. The goal is early detection of service degradation through proactive alerting that triggers response before minor issues cascade into major outages. Teams implement comprehensive monitoring covering the four golden signals (latency, traffic, errors, and saturation) along with synthetic testing that simulates user interactions to catch problems that might not trigger threshold-based alerts.

When an incident occurs, the response phase activates with a clearly defined process that eliminates confusion during high-stress situations. Successful incident response hinges on established roles, typically including an incident commander who coordinates overall response, subject matter experts who investigate and implement fixes, and communications leads who keep stakeholders informed. Rather than everyone jumping in to troubleshoot simultaneously, this structure ensures coordinated action and prevents duplicate or conflicting efforts. The response team follows predefined playbooks for common scenarios while maintaining flexibility for novel situations, focusing first on mitigation (reducing user impact) before moving to full resolution.

Communication during incidents is just as important as technical troubleshooting. Internal status updates keep team members aligned, while external communications manage customer expectations. Clear, honest status pages and updates build trust even during outages; users can tolerate downtime but become frustrated by vague or misleading information. The best incident communications avoid technical jargon, provide estimated resolution times, when possible, acknowledge impact without minimizing it, and offer workarounds when available. Regular updates, even when there is little progress to report, demonstrate transparency and active engagement.

After service is restored, the most valuable phase begins learning through structured postmortems. Unlike traditional blame-oriented investigations, effective postmortems operate under a blameless principle that focuses on systemic issues rather than individual mistakes. This approach recognizes that human errors are symptoms of system problems, not root causes. Engineers speak candidly about what happened without fear of punishment, enabling deeper insights into why seemingly reasonable actions led to unexpected outcomes. This psychological safety transforms postmortems from feared interrogations into collaborative learning opportunities.

The postmortem document serves as an organizational memory, capturing not just what happened but why it happened and how to prevent recurrence. A thorough postmortem includes a timeline of events, the incident's impact, contributing factors, and both immediate fixes and longer-term improvements. The analysis digs beyond superficial causes to identify underlying systemic issues, not just the server crashed but why the monitoring did not catch early warning signs or why the architecture could not tolerate that specific failure. Each postmortem generates actionable items that are prioritized alongside feature work, ensuring that reliability improvements do not get indefinitely postponed.

Organizations that excel at incident management close the loop by feeding lessons back into their systems and processes. They update runbooks with new troubleshooting techniques, enhance monitoring based on detection gaps, modify architecture to eliminate discovered fragilities, and revisit on-call training to prepare for similar scenarios. This continuous improvement cycle transforms each incident from an isolated event into a catalyst for evolution. Over time, incidents may still occur, but their frequency, duration, and impact steadily decrease as the system's resilience grows.

The true measure of incident management maturity is not the absence of failures, it is how effectively teams respond to and learn from them. When incidents are handled with clear processes, transparent communication, and genuine curiosity about systemic weaknesses, they become powerful drivers of reliability rather than dreaded disruptions. In this way, even the most challenging outages contribute to building more robust systems and more capable teams.

These principles come alive in the incident management practices of major technology companies. *Twitter* (now *X*) has developed a sophisticated incident response system that creates dedicated incident channels in Slack automatically when alerts trigger critical thresholds. These channels immediately notify the appropriate subject matter experts, populate with relevant system dashboards, and maintain a chronological record of the incident as it unfolds. This structured approach ensures that even complex incidents with multiple contributing factors receive coordinated responses with clear ownership and communication channels.

GitHub takes transparency in incident management to another level by publicly sharing detailed postmortem reports for significant service disruptions. These blameless postmortems explain what happened, why it happened, how it was fixed, and most importantly what systemic improvements will prevent similar issues in the future. This practice not only builds trust with users affected by incidents but also contributes to industry-wide learning about complex system failures and resilience patterns.

The effectiveness of these approaches is evident in the declining impact of incidents over time. Organizations with mature incident management practices typically see significant reductions in both incident frequency and mean time to resolution. More importantly, they experience fewer recurring incidents of the same type, demonstrating that their learning mechanisms and systemic improvements are effectively addressing root causes rather than merely treating symptoms. This evolution from reactive firefighting to proactive resilience engineering represents the ultimate goal of structured incident management and blameless postmortem practices.

Service-level objectives and reliability targets

Reliability is too important to be left to intuition or best efforts. Without clear targets, teams oscillate between overengineering systems to impossible perfection and underinvesting in critical reliability needs. SLOs provide the framework that transforms reliability from a vague aspiration to a measurable, manageable attribute of systems.

The journey toward meaningful reliability targets begins with understanding what users care about. While engineers might focus on CPU utilization or memory consumption, users experience systems through metrics like page load times, successful transactions, or video streaming quality. These user-centric measurements form the foundation of SLIs, the specific metrics that reflect service health from the user's perspective. Well-chosen SLIs capture the essential aspects of service quality, focusing on dimensions like availability, latency, throughput, and error rates that directly impact user experience.

With meaningful SLIs established, teams can define SLOs, and target values for those indicators that represent the line between satisfied and frustrated users. The most powerful insight of the SLO approach is that 100% perfection is neither necessary nor economically sensible. Instead, SLOs acknowledge that users typically cannot perceive the difference between 99.9% and 100% reliability, but the cost difference between these targets can be enormous. This recognition allows engineering teams to make rational trade-offs, investing in reliability improvements only when they meaningfully impact user experience.

Setting appropriate SLO targets requires balancing multiple perspectives. Historical performance data shows what the system has delivered. User research reveals what level of performance satisfies customers. Business requirements define minimum acceptable reliability for competitive positioning and revenue protection. Engineering analysis estimates the effort required to achieve different reliability tiers. By synthesizing these inputs, teams arrive at SLO targets that are ambitious enough to ensure a good user experience but realistic enough to be achievable without excessive cost.

SLOs gain their real power when transformed into error budgets, which allows for an amount of unreliability within the SLO target. If a service aims for 99.9% availability, the error budget represents the remaining 0.1% of allowed downtime (about 43 minutes per month). This budget becomes a concrete resource that engineering teams can strategically spend on activities that might impact reliability, such as deployments, experiments, or infrastructure changes. When the error budget is healthy, teams can move quickly and take calculated risks. When the budget approaches depletion, they prioritize stability over speed, deferring non-critical changes until reliability improves.

This error budget approach fundamentally changes engineering team dynamics. Without SLOs, reliability discussions often become emotional debates between operations teams (stereotypically resistance to change) and development teams (stereotypically pushing for faster feature delivery). With SLOs and error budgets, these discussions transform into data-driven decisions. Development teams gain autonomy to release as frequently as possible, provided they stay within budget. Operations teams gain objective criteria for when to slow down. Both align around a shared understanding of acceptable reliability that balances user needs with business priorities.

Implementing SLOs requires both technical infrastructure and organizational processes. Monitoring systems must collect and analyze SLI data accurately. Dashboards need to display current performance against objectives clearly. Alert systems should warn when error budgets are being consumed unusually quickly. Perhaps most importantly, teams need explicit policies defining actions to take when error budgets are exhausted, typically shifting resources from feature development to reliability improvements until service health is restored.

Organizations that embrace the SLO approach discover that it transforms how they measure reliability and how they think about it. Product discussions naturally incorporate reliability considerations alongside feature planning. Architecture decisions weigh reliability implications against performance or cost factors. And release processes evolve to protect user experience while maximizing development velocity. The result is a balanced approach where reliability becomes a strategic asset rather than an afterthought or an obsession, precisely targeted at the level that delivers value without wasteful overinvestment.

These reliability engineering principles have been adopted by cloud service providers and enterprise software companies to deliver consistent experiences at massive scale. Amazon Web Services, for example, designs its EC2 compute service with a 99.99% availability SLO per region. To achieve this ambitious target, they architect their infrastructure with redundant availability zones within each region, each with independent power, cooling, and network connectivity. This architectural approach enables AWS to maintain high availability even when entire data centers experience failures, providing a foundation of reliability that thousands of businesses depend on daily.

Salesforce applies similar principles to its global customer relationship management platform but focuses on different reliability dimensions. Their enterprise customers depend on consistent API performance across diverse geographic regions and varying load conditions. By establishing precise SLOs for API request latencies, Salesforce engineering teams can make data-driven decisions about capacity planning, load balancing, and application optimizations. These reliability targets inform architectural choices such as database sharding strategies, edge caching implementations, and global traffic routing policies.

What distinguishes these organizations is not just having reliability targets, but their systematic processes for continuously validating and refining them. They regularly analyze customer support data, user behavior patterns, and competitive benchmarks to ensure their SLOs accurately reflect evolving user expectations. This ongoing refinement ensures that engineering investments are precisely aligned with actual business requirements rather than arbitrary perfection or industry conventions. The result is reliability engineering that delivers maximum business value while efficiently utilizing engineering resources.

Chaos engineering for resilience

Modern distributed systems are complex, dynamic, and inherently unpredictable. Failures are not a question of if but when. Chaos engineering provides a systematic approach to resilience by proactively injecting controlled failures to uncover weaknesses before they impact users. Unlike traditional testing, which validates expected behavior under known conditions, chaos engineering simulates real-world disruptions, network failures, infrastructure outages, and dependency failures to ensure systems can withstand and recover from unexpected events.

The foundation of chaos engineering lies in well-defined principles:

- **Hypothesis-driven experimentation:** Instead of blindly breaking things, teams start with an assumption about system behavior under failure conditions. For instance, if one database replica becomes unreachable, the application should continue serving requests with minimal impact.

- **Minimizing blast radius:** Chaos experiments are designed to limit potential damage. Initial tests start in staging environments or with a small percentage of live traffic before scaling to broader experiments in production.

- **Automated and continuous execution:** Resilience is not a one-time goal but a continuous process. Leading teams integrate chaos tests into CI/CD pipelines to catch regressions early and prevent reliability drift.

- **Observability-driven analysis:** Effective chaos testing requires robust observability. Engineers analyze logs, metrics, traces, and alerts to understand system behavior, identify weaknesses, and validate recovery mechanisms.

A structured approach to chaos engineering follows a cycle of planning, execution, and refinement:

1. **Define the steady state:** Establish baseline performance indicators using SLIs such as latency, availability, and throughput. This defines normal system behavior.

2. **Identify weaknesses and failure modes:** Analyze past incidents, conduct dependency mapping, and evaluate single points of failure. Common targets include:

    a. Database failures (e.g., replica unavailability, slow queries)

    b. Network disruptions (e.g., packet loss, latency spikes)

    c. Infrastructure outages (e.g., node failures, auto-scaling misconfigurations)

    d. Application crashes (e.g., memory leaks, unexpected exceptions)

3. **Design controlled experiments:** Use tools like Chaos Monkey (random instance termination), Gremlin (network and infrastructure failures), and LitmusChaos (Kubernetes-native failure injection) to simulate real-world scenarios.

4. **Monitor system response:** Track performance degradation, error rates, failover mechanisms, and recovery times. Correlate results with SLIs and error budgets.

5. **Refine system design:** Use experiment insights to improve reliability, whether by enhancing auto-scaling policies, optimizing circuit breakers, or reinforcing redundancy strategies.

For mission-critical services, chaos tests extend beyond pre-production environments. Netflix, Google, and *Amazon* routinely run experiments in live systems using Canary deployments, feature flagging, and progressive rollouts to reduce risk while ensuring real-world validation. Dark launching, releasing features in a disabled state for controlled testing, further helps validate resilience before exposing users to potential disruptions.

Chaos engineering is not about breaking things for the sake of it. It is about ensuring failures happen on your terms, not unexpectedly in production. By embracing controlled failure, organizations build confidence in their systems, strengthen recovery mechanisms, and transform reliability from reactive firefighting to proactive engineering.

Netflix pioneered practical chaos engineering through its Chaos Monkey tool, which randomly terminates virtual machine instances in production environments to verify that applications continue functioning correctly despite unexpected infrastructure failures. This seemingly radical approach, deliberately causing failures in production systems, has proven remarkably effective at uncovering hidden dependencies and strengthening resilience. By regularly exercising their failure handling mechanisms, Netflix ensures that actual unplanned outages have minimal impact on streaming services used by millions of customers worldwide.

Major retailers have adapted these principles to their business contexts. Target's e-commerce platform conducts controlled chaos experiments during overnight hours when traffic volumes are lowest. These experiments simulate various backend failures, such as database latency spikes, caching service disruptions, or payment processing delays. By testing these scenarios systematically during low-risk periods, Target's engineering teams can validate that monitoring systems detect problems correctly, recovery mechanisms function as designed, and user experience degradation remains within acceptable limits even during partial system failures.

The sophistication of chaos engineering has evolved significantly beyond random instance termination. Modern chaos engineering platforms can simulate complex failure scenarios such as region-wide service degradation, network partitioning, resource exhaustion, and dependency failures with precise control over timing and scope. These capabilities allow organizations to test complex recovery mechanisms such as automated failover, traffic rerouting, and graceful degradation patterns. The most advanced practitioners integrate chaos experiments directly into their continuous integration pipelines, ensuring that resilience is continuously verified rather than periodically tested.

This proactive approach to resilience fundamentally changes how organizations think about reliability. Rather than hoping systems will handle unexpected conditions correctly, chaos engineering provides empirical evidence of resilience capabilities. The confidence gained through controlled experimentation enables faster innovation, as teams can move quickly knowing their safety mechanisms have been thoroughly validated under realistic failure conditions.

Disaster recovery and backup strategies

No system is immune to failure. Whether due to hardware failures, cyberattacks, misconfigurations, or natural disasters, service disruptions are inevitable. **Disaster recovery (DR)** and backup strategies ensure that organizations can recover quickly, minimize data loss, and maintain business continuity when failures occur. A well-designed disaster recovery plan is not just about having backups; it is about ensuring that recovery is fast, reliable, and tested regularly.

Effective DR strategies are built around three key metrics:

- **Recovery time objective (RTO):** The maximum acceptable downtime before business operations is critically impacted. A low RTO (e.g., minutes) requires high-availability systems, while a higher RTO (e.g., hours) allows for more cost-effective recovery methods.

- **Recovery point objective (RPO):** The maximum acceptable data loss measured in time. If an RPO is 10 minutes, backups must be frequent enough to ensure that no more than 10 minutes of data is lost in the event of failure.

- **Failover vs. failback:** Failover is the process of switching to a secondary system when the primary one fails. Failback is the process of restoring operations to the original system after recovery.

Backup strategies

Backups are the foundation of disaster recovery, ensuring data is preserved and can be restored when needed. The most effective backup strategies follow the 3-2-1 rule:

- 3 copies of data (one primary, two backups)
- 2 different storage types (e.g., disk and cloud)
- 1 backup stored offsite (e.g., geographically separate data center)

Backup types also vary depending on business needs:

- **Full backups:** A complete copy of all data. Reliable but time-consuming and storage-heavy.

- **Incremental backups:** Captures only data that has changed since the last backup. It is efficient but requires multiple backup sets for full recovery.

- **Differential backups:** Captures all changes since the last full backup. They are faster to restore than incremental backups but use more storage.

- **Snapshot backups:** Instantaneous copies of system states, often used for virtual machines and cloud storage.

Disaster recovery architectures

Organizations design disaster recovery plans based on business impact and cost considerations.

Common DR architectures include:

- **Cold Standby (High RTO, High RPO, Low Cost):**
  - o Data is backed up offsite, but no active infrastructure is maintained.
  - o Recovery requires provisioning new servers and restoring data, leading to long downtime.
  - o Suitable for non-critical systems with flexible downtime tolerance.

- **Warm Standby (Medium RTO, Medium RPO, Moderate Cost):**
  - o A scaled-down version of production runs in a secondary data center or cloud region.
  - o Services can be restored relatively quickly by scaling up infrastructure.
  - o Balances cost with recovery speed, commonly used in mid-sized organizations.

- **Hot Standby (Active-Passive) (Low RTO, Low RPO, High Cost):**
  - o A fully functional secondary system is running but not handling traffic.
  - o Failover is quick and usually automated via DNS failover, load balancers, or replication mechanisms.

o   Used for critical systems requiring high availability.

- **Active-Active Failover (Near-Zero RTO, Near-Zero RPO, Very High Cost):**

  o   Multiple geographically distributed systems operate simultaneously.

  o   Traffic is dynamically routed between locations to handle failures seamlessly.

  o   Requires global load balancing, database replication, and real-time data synchronization.

  o   Ideal for large-scale cloud-based architectures like those of Google and AWS.

Testing and validating disaster recovery plans

A disaster recovery plan is only as good as its last test. Organizations should perform regular DR drills, including:

- **Tabletop exercises:** Simulated discussions where teams walk through disaster scenarios and response steps.

- **Partial failover tests:** Redirecting a portion of traffic to the backup site to validate readiness.

- **Full failover drills:** Temporarily switching all operations to the secondary system to verify end-to-end recovery.

- **Data restoration tests:** Ensuring backup integrity by restoring and validating data on a test system.

Leading technology companies implement disaster recovery strategies tailored to their specific business requirements and infrastructure architectures. *Dropbox*, for example, developed a custom storage system called **Magic Pocket** that uses sharded block storage with cross-region redundancy to ensure data durability even during major infrastructure failures. This proprietary system stores multiple copies of data across geographically distributed facilities, with sophisticated integrity verification mechanisms that continuously validate data consistency and repair any detected corruption automatically.

Design software company *Canva* takes a cloud-native approach to disaster recovery, implementing comprehensive backup strategies across multiple AWS regions. Their architecture ensures that user data and design assets remain available even if an entire cloud region becomes unavailable. By implementing consistent backup procedures with automated validation and periodic recovery testing, they maintain confidence in their ability to restore services within their defined RTO and RPO targets even during significant disruption scenarios

What distinguishes sophisticated DR implementations is their integration with broader business continuity planning. Recovery mechanisms are designed not just for technical resilience but aligned with business priorities, ensuring that the most critical services receive the highest levels of protection and recovery priority. These organizations regularly conduct comprehensive disaster simulations that involve both technical teams and business stakeholders, testing not only system recovery but also communication procedures, decision-making processes, and coordination across departments.

The evolution of disaster recovery has been accelerated by infrastructure-as-code practices, which enable recovery procedures to be defined as executable code rather than manual documentation. This approach ensures that recovery processes remain current as systems evolve and can be tested regularly without extensive manual effort. By bringing software engineering practices to disaster recovery, organizations can achieve higher confidence in their recovery capabilities while simultaneously reducing the operational burden of maintaining these critical safety mechanisms.

Scaling and performance optimization

A system that works well today may not work well tomorrow. As user demand grows, infrastructure must scale efficiently while maintaining performance, reliability, and cost-effectiveness. Scaling and performance optimization are not just about adding more resources; they require thoughtful architecture, efficient resource management, and proactive tuning to ensure smooth operation under varying loads.

Scaling comes in two primary forms: vertical scaling (scaling up) and horizontal scaling (scaling out). Vertical scaling involves increasing the resources of a single machine, adding more CPU, memory, or disk capacity. While this approach can provide immediate benefits, it has physical and cost limitations, making it unsuitable for long-term scalability. Horizontal scaling, in contrast, distributes workloads across multiple machines, allowing systems to handle increased demand dynamically. This method is the foundation of modern cloud-native architectures, enabling services to scale elastically in response to real-time traffic fluctuations.

Effective scaling is not just about adding more servers, it requires intelligent load balancing to distribute traffic efficiently. Load balancers prevent any single server from becoming overwhelmed and allow requests to be routed based on factors such as latency, geographic location, or health status. Advanced load balancing techniques, such as weighted round-robin, least connections, and consistent hashing, help optimize request distribution, ensuring that no single node becomes a bottleneck.

Database performance is often a critical factor in scalability. As systems grow, database queries that work efficiently with small datasets may become slow and unmanageable. Optimization techniques such as indexing, query caching, and partitioning help reduce response times while reading replicas, and sharding strategies allow databases to scale horizontally by distributing data across multiple nodes. NoSQL databases like Cassandra or DynamoDB further enhance scalability by offering distributed, fault-tolerant storage designed to handle large volumes of data with high availability.

Beyond infrastructure, application-level optimizations play a crucial role in scaling. Inefficient code, unnecessary computations, and excessive API calls can degrade performance regardless of hardware resources. Profiling and benchmarking tools like Flamegraphs, Prometheus, and Jaeger help identify performance bottlenecks, allowing teams to optimize execution paths and reduce latency. Techniques such as lazy loading, asynchronous processing, and event-driven architectures improve responsiveness by ensuring that resources are used efficiently.

Caching is another powerful strategy for performance optimization. Frequently accessed data, such as API responses or database queries, can be stored in in-memory caches like Redis or Memcached to reduce repetitive computations and database load. **Content delivery networks (CDNs)** further optimize performance by caching static assets closer to users, reducing latency, and offloading traffic from origin servers.

Autoscaling ensures that resources dynamically adjust to demand, preventing over-provisioning during low-traffic periods and under-provisioning during spikes. Cloud providers like AWS, Google Cloud, and Azure offer autoscaling groups that automatically add or remove instances based on CPU usage, request rates, or custom-defined metrics. Container orchestration platforms like Kubernetes take this further with horizontal pod autoscaling, adjusting the number of running containers based on workload intensity.

However, scaling is not just about handling load; it also involves maintaining efficiency and cost control. Blindly adding resources without optimization can lead to excessive costs with diminishing returns. Performance monitoring tools like Datadog, New Relic, and Grafana provide real-time insights into system health, enabling data-driven scaling decisions. Capacity planning, predictive analytics, and historical performance trends help anticipate future needs, ensuring that scaling strategies remain proactive rather than reactive.

Ultimately, scaling and performance optimization require a balanced approach, investing in resilient architectures, optimizing code and infrastructure, and continuously monitoring and adapting to real-world conditions. When done right, scaling transforms reliability from a challenge into a competitive advantage, ensuring systems remain performant, cost-efficient, and ready for whatever the future brings.

Major social media and content platforms demonstrate sophisticated scaling and performance optimization strategies in their production environments. *Instagram* successfully migrated to AWS using Kubernetes orchestration to achieve elastic scaling based on demand patterns. Their infrastructure automatically scales to accommodate traffic surges when new features like *Instagram Reels* are launched or during peak usage periods. This dynamic scaling capability allows Instagram to efficiently handle billions of interactions daily while maintaining responsive performance for users worldwide.

YouTube has implemented an extensive edge caching infrastructure through Google's global CDN to optimize video delivery performance. This sophisticated caching architecture places frequently requested content physically closer to users, dramatically reducing load times and minimizing bandwidth costs. During viral events when millions of viewers simultaneously access the same content, these edge caches prevent origin servers from becoming overwhelmed, ensuring smooth playback even under extraordinary demand.

What distinguishes truly advanced scaling implementations is their predictive rather than merely reactive nature. By analyzing historical traffic patterns, user growth trends, and upcoming feature releases, engineering teams can anticipate capacity requirements before they materialize. This foresight enables proactive infrastructure provisioning, database schema optimizations, and caching strategy adjustments that prevent performance degradation rather than responding to it after users are affected.

The most sophisticated organizations implement performance optimization as a continuous process rather than a periodic project. They instrument critical code paths with detailed telemetry, establish automated performance testing in CI/CD pipelines, and continuously monitor key performance indicators against defined baselines. This disciplined approach ensures that performance improvements accumulate over time while preventing gradual degradation that might otherwise go unnoticed until it reaches critical levels. The cumulative effect is systems that remain responsive and efficient despite growing complexity and user demand.

Observability and SRE tools

In SRE, observability is the foundation for understanding system health, diagnosing issues, and ensuring reliability. While traditional monitoring provides predefined metrics and alerts, observability takes a broader approach, offering deep insights into system behavior through logs, metrics, and traces. An observable system allows engineers to ask open-ended questions, debug unexpected failures, and continuously improve reliability.

Observability is built on three core pillars: metrics, logs, and traces. Metrics provide real-time numerical data on system performance, such as CPU usage, request latency, and error rates. Logs capture detailed event records, helping teams investigate failures and track historical patterns. Traces track requests as they move through distributed systems, enabling engineers to pinpoint bottlenecks and latency issues. When combined, these elements provide a holistic view of system health, helping teams proactively detect anomalies and prevent outages.

A strong observability stack includes tools that specialize in each of these areas. Prometheus is a leading tool for collecting and analyzing metrics, offering powerful querying capabilities and real-time alerting. Grafana provides rich visualization dashboards, helping teams make sense of complex performance data. **Elasticsearch, Logstash, Kibana (ELK)** Stack and Splunk handle large-scale log aggregation and analysis, enabling deep forensic investigations. Jaeger and OpenTelemetry are widely used for distributed tracing, helping teams debug microservices and optimize request flows.

Beyond individual tools, modern observability platforms such as Datadog, New Relic, and Honeycomb offer unified solutions, integrating metrics, logs, and traces into a single pane of glass. These platforms leverage AI-driven anomaly detection, automated correlation, and predictive analytics to help teams identify issues before they impact users.

For SRE teams, observability is not just about collecting data, it is about making it actionable. SLIs and SLOs help define acceptable performance levels, ensuring teams prioritize reliability improvements based on real user impact. Automated alerting and incident response tools like PagerDuty, Opsgenie, and VictorOps ensure the right engineers are notified when issues arise, reducing response times and improving incident resolution.

By integrating observability into daily workflows, SRE teams shift from reactive firefighting to proactive reliability engineering. Insights gained from observability drive better capacity planning, more efficient debugging, and continuous reliability improvements. In a world of increasingly complex, distributed systems, observability is not just an operational necessity, it is a strategic advantage that enables teams to build, maintain, and scale resilient services.

Some of the most impressive observability implementations can be found in transportation and delivery platforms operating at massive scale. *Uber* developed its proprietary M3 metrics system to handle the extraordinary monitoring requirements of their global operations. This system scales to collect, store, and analyze billions of data points every minute across their complex microservice architecture. This comprehensive observability enables Uber's engineering teams to identify performance anomalies, troubleshoot complex interactions between services, and optimize resource utilization across their global infrastructure.

Food delivery platform *DoorDash* leverages Datadog's observability platform to provide cross-team visibility into service health. Their implementation correlates metrics, logs, and traces to create a unified view of system performance that supports both real-time incident response and longer-term optimization efforts. This integrated approach to observability enables DoorDash's engineering teams to maintain reliable service during peak order times while continuously improving platform efficiency.

The most sophisticated observability implementations go beyond technical metrics to incorporate business-level indicators. By correlating system performance data with business outcomes like conversion rates, order completion percentages, or user engagement metrics, these organizations gain insights into the actual impact of technical performance on business results. This alignment enables more informed prioritization of engineering investments, focusing efforts on the technical improvements that deliver the greatest business value.

Advanced organizations are also leveraging artificial intelligence and machine learning to enhance observability capabilities. Anomaly detection algorithms identify unusual patterns that might indicate emerging problems before they trigger traditional threshold-based alerts. Correlation engines automatically group related symptoms to reduce alert noise and help engineers identify root causes more quickly. These capabilities transform observability from a passive monitoring function into an active system that helps predict and prevent potential issues before they impact users.

Security in SRE practices

Security is an integral part of SRE, ensuring that systems remain not only available and performant but also protected against threats. In an era of increasing cyberattacks and compliance demands, reliability cannot be achieved without strong security practices. SRE teams play a crucial role in embedding security into infrastructure, automation, and operational workflows, aligning reliability goals with security best practices.

A core principle of security in SRE is shift-left security, integrating security checks early in the development and deployment process rather than treating them as an afterthought. This includes automated security scanning in CI/CD pipelines, enforcing secure coding standards, and implementing IaC security best practices. Tools like Trivy, Checkov, and Snyk help identify vulnerabilities in container images and cloud configurations before they reach production.

Another fundamental aspect is the least privileged access and zero trust architecture. SRE teams must enforce strict access controls, ensuring that services and engineers only have the minimal permissions necessary to perform their tasks. **Role-based access control (RBAC)** and **attribute-based access control (ABAC)** mechanisms in Kubernetes and cloud environments prevent unauthorized access. Additionally, secrets management tools like HashiCorp Vault, AWS Secrets Manager, and Azure Key Vault ensure that sensitive credentials, API keys, and encryption keys are securely stored and rotated.

Observability and security go hand in hand. SIEM systems such as Splunk, ELK Stack, and Google Chronicle enable real-time threat detection by analyzing logs, metrics, and traces for suspicious activities. SRE teams leverage **intrusion detection systems (IDS)** like Suricata and Wazuh, along with runtime security tools like Falco, to monitor for anomalies in containerized and cloud-native environments. By correlating observability data with security signals, teams can quickly detect and respond to security incidents.

Automated compliance and policy enforcement are also critical in SRE security. Organizations must adhere to regulations like GDPR, HIPAA, and SOC 2, and automated tools like **Open Policy Agent (OPA)** and AWS Config help enforce security policies across infrastructure. Additionally, immutable infrastructure and container security, where deployments are rebuilt rather than patched, reduce attack surfaces and improve consistency.

Incident response and postmortems in SRE extend beyond system failures to include security breaches. Runbooks and playbooks for security incidents, coupled with chaos engineering for security (chaos security drills and tabletop exercises), ensure teams are prepared to handle breaches effectively. Forensic tools like Velociraptor and TheHive help investigate and mitigate security incidents, while blameless postmortems improve future security posture.

By integrating security into the core of SRE practices, organizations can build resilient systems that are reliable and secure by design. Security in SRE is not about adding friction to development but about enabling teams to move fast while staying protected, embedding security as a shared responsibility across engineering and operations.

Leading e-commerce and entertainment companies demonstrate how security can be seamlessly integrated into SRE practices. Shopify employs automated secrets detection in their GitHub repositories using GitHub Advanced Security to prevent accidental exposure of sensitive credentials. This automated scanning occurs during the development process, identifying potential security risks such as hardcoded API keys, access tokens, or encryption keys before they reach production environments. By embedding these security controls directly into developer workflows, Shopify maintains strong security posture without impeding the rapid development cycles essential to their business.

Netflix has developed sophisticated tooling for continuous auditing of AWS **identity and access management (IAM)** policies across their cloud infrastructure. These custom tools automatically verify that access permissions follow least-privilege principles, detect policy drift that might introduce security vulnerabilities, and ensure that temporary access grants are properly revoked when no longer needed. This approach to automated security governance allows Netflix to maintain strict access controls while operating at tremendous scale across thousands of AWS accounts.

The most mature implementations of security within SRE frameworks treat security validation as another form of automated testing. Security scans for vulnerabilities, compliance checks, and penetration testing are integrated into CI/CD pipelines alongside functional tests, ensuring that security requirements receive the same continuous verification as other system properties. This shift-left approach to security testing identifies potential issues early in the development lifecycle when they are less costly to remediate.

Organizations at the forefront of security integration also implement security chaos engineering, deliberately introducing controlled security failures to test detection and response capabilities. These exercises might include deploying applications with known vulnerabilities in isolated environments, simulating credential theft, or executing unusual access patterns that might indicate compromise. By regularly exercising security monitoring and response processes, these organizations build confidence in their ability to detect and contain security incidents effectively, transforming security from a theoretical concern into a practically validated capability.

Conclusion

SRE represents a transformative approach that applies software engineering principles to operations, creating reliable, scalable systems through data-driven decisions. By implementing SLIs, SLOs, and error budgets, teams establish objective reliability targets that balance innovation with stability. Automation reduces toil, freeing engineers to focus on strategic improvements rather than repetitive tasks. When incidents occur, structured management processes and blameless postmortems transform failures into learning opportunities. Practices like chaos engineering proactively strengthen system resilience, while comprehensive disaster recovery strategies ensure rapid recovery when failures occur. Effective observability provides deep insights into system behavior, enabling proactive issue detection while integrated security practices protect systems from evolving threats. Ultimately, SRE fosters a culture where reliability becomes a shared responsibility and a continuous improvement mindset, delivering consistent performance in increasingly complex technological landscapes.

In the next chapter, we will explore how automation serves as the foundation of effective DevOps practices. Readers will discover powerful scripting techniques using Bash, Python, and Go to programmatically manage systems. We will examine cloud infrastructure automation through APIs, event-driven automation with webhooks, and emerging serverless frameworks. Practical applications include automated incident response, complex workflow orchestration with Jenkins pipelines, and advanced infrastructure automation beyond basic IaC. The concepts of self-healing systems and automated compliance will round out the chapter, providing readers with comprehensive techniques to reduce manual intervention and increase consistency across the entire software delivery lifecycle.

Join our Discord space

Join our Discord workspace for latest updates, offers, tech happenings around the world, new releases, and sessions with the authors:

https://discord.bpbonline.com

CHAPTER 14

Advanced DevOps Automation

Introduction

Scaling DevOps is not just about running more deployments or managing larger infrastructure; it is about making automation work at every level, ensuring reliability, efficiency, and speed without introducing chaos. As organizations grow, their DevOps strategies must evolve from basic CI/CD pipelines to advanced patterns like event-driven automation, GitOps, and self-healing systems. This chapter explores how to take DevOps automation to the next level, focusing on scripting, API-driven automation, serverless approaches, and intelligent remediation techniques.

At its core, DevOps is about eliminating manual, repetitive tasks and turning them into automated, self-sustaining workflows. Whether provisioning infrastructure, triggering deployments, or responding to incidents, automation should be built in such a way that it scales seamlessly.

The impact of advanced DevOps automation is perhaps best illustrated by examining how industry leaders implement these practices at massive scale. Netflix, for instance, manages over 200 million global subscribers while executing more than 1,000 production deployments daily through their sophisticated Spinnaker continuous delivery platform. This level of automation enables them to release new features continuously while maintaining exceptional service reliability.

Similarly, *Uber* orchestrates the deployment and management of over 4,000 microservices across their hybrid cloud infrastructure multiple times daily. Their deployment automation enables them to process millions of ride requests per minute while continuously improving their platform. These organizations demonstrate that advanced automation isn't merely a convenience, it is a fundamental requirement for operating at scale in today's technology landscape.

When properly implemented, these automation practices eliminate manual bottlenecks, reduce human error, and create self-optimizing systems that adapt to changing conditions without constant intervention. The difference between basic and advanced DevOps automation often determines whether an organization can scale efficiently or becomes overwhelmed by operational complexity as it grows.

This chapter will guide you through automating everything, from scripts and APIs to workflows and compliance so that DevOps becomes a force multiplier rather than a bottleneck.

Structure

The chapter covers the following topics:

- Scripting for automation using Bash, Python, Go
- Automating cloud infrastructure with APIs
- Event-driven automation with webhooks
- Serverless automation frameworks
- Automating incident response and remediation
- Workflow automation with Jenkins Pipelines
- Infrastructure automation beyond IaC
- Self-healing systems
- Automating compliance and auditing

Objectives

By the end of this chapter, you will have a strong understanding of how to automate various aspects of DevOps at scale. You will learn how to write effective scripts in Bash, Python, and Go to automate everyday DevOps tasks, integrate cloud APIs for seamless infrastructure management, and build event-driven workflows using webhooks. You will also explore serverless automation frameworks that reduce operational overhead and implement automated incident response mechanisms to improve system reliability. Additionally, you will gain insights into workflow automation with Jenkins pipelines, advanced infrastructure automation techniques beyond traditional IaC, and the principles of building self-healing systems that recover from failures without human intervention. Finally, you will understand how to automate compliance and auditing to ensure security and governance standards are continuously met. This chapter is designed to be highly practical, equipping you with the knowledge and hands-on experience needed to implement automation at every level of your DevOps ecosystem.

Scripting for automation using Bash, Python, Go

Automation is the backbone of DevOps, and scripting is the most fundamental way to achieve it. Whether it is provisioning infrastructure, deploying applications, or automating system maintenance, scripting languages like Bash, Python, and Go play a crucial role in making DevOps workflows efficient, repeatable, and scalable. Scripting is also crucial in DevOps because manual tasks introduce errors, inefficiencies, and bottlenecks. Scripts help in:

- Automating repetitive tasks (e.g., log rotation, backups, deployments).
- Enforcing consistency across environments.
- Reducing the time required for infrastructure provisioning.
- Enabling faster response to incidents and system changes.
- Integrating with APIs, cloud platforms, and CI/CD pipelines.

To appreciate the impact of scripting in real-world DevOps environments, consider how major technology organizations leverage these languages at scale. *Google* relies extensively on Bash scripts to automate daily backup rotation and maintenance tasks across thousands of Linux servers. These scripts handle log rotation, data archiving, and system cleanup operations, eliminating countless hours of manual intervention while ensuring consistent operations across their vast infrastructure.

Reddit's infrastructure team uses Python with the Fabric library to orchestrate remote command execution across their Amazon EC2 fleet. These scripts enable simultaneous configuration updates, service deployments, and health checks across hundreds of instances, with proper error handling and rollback capabilities built in. This automation allows a relatively small team to manage an infrastructure serving billions of monthly page views.

For performance-critical automation, organizations increasingly turn to Go. Kubernetes itself, the foundation of modern container orchestration, is written in Go, with controllers that handle cluster scaling, node lifecycle management, and self-healing operations. GitHub's internal DevOps tooling, built primarily in Go, provisions and manages up to 5,000 virtual machines monthly with minimal human oversight, demonstrating the language's effectiveness for high-performance automation tasks.

These examples illustrate how the choice of scripting language depends not just on technical requirements but on organizational context, performance needs, and integration requirements. Effective DevOps teams develop proficiency across multiple languages, selecting the right tool for each automation challenge.

Different scripting languages serve different purposes.

Let us explore Bash, Python, and Go and how they fit into DevOps automation.

Bash Shell

Bourne Again Shell (**Bash**) is the default scripting language for most Unix-based systems. It is ideal for automating system administration tasks, configuring environments, and executing commands efficiently. Some common use cases are:

- Automating deployments and system maintenance.

- Managing files, logs, and user permissions.

- Running scheduled jobs (cron jobs) for backups and monitoring.

For example, you can use a simple bash script as follows to automate log cleanup as follows:

```bash
#!/bin/bash
LOG_DIR="/var/log/myapp"
find $LOG_DIR -type f -name "*.log" -mtime +7 -exec rm -f {} \;
echo "Old logs deleted successfully."
```

Python

Python is widely used in DevOps due to its readability, extensive libraries, and API integration capabilities. It is perfect for automating cloud infrastructure, configuration management, and data processing. Some common use cases are:

- API automation (e.g., AWS, Azure, Kubernetes).

- Configuration management (e.g., Ansible, Terraform).

- Log parsing, monitoring, and reporting.

For example, fetching **ec2** instances from AWS via Python **boto3**:

```python
import boto3

ec2 = boto3.client('ec2')

def list_instances():
    instances = ec2.describe_instances()
    for reservation in instances['Reservations']:
```

```
    for instance in reservation['Instances']:
        print(f"Instance ID: {instance['InstanceId']}, State: {in-
stance['State']['Name']}")


list_instances()
```

Golang

Golang (**Go**) is gaining popularity in DevOps due to its speed, concurrency, and cross-platform compatibility. Many modern DevOps tools (e.g., Terraform, Kubernetes) are written in Go, making it a great choice for automation at scale. Some common use cases are:

- Building high-performance automation tools.

- Writing efficient cloud-native applications.

- Developing CLI tools for DevOps workflows.

For example, you can write a simple go CLI to ping a server:

```go
package main

import (
 "fmt"
 "net/http"
)

func main() {
 url := "https://example.com"
 resp, err := http.Get(url)
 if err != nil {
  fmt.Println("Server is unreachable.")
  return
 }
 fmt.Println("Server responded with status:", resp.Status)
}
```

Scripting is a fundamental skill in DevOps that enables automation across infrastructure, deployments, and incident response. Bash is a powerful tool for system-level automation, making it ideal for managing files, configuring environments, and executing commands efficiently. Python stands out as the most versatile scripting language, widely used for API automation, cloud infrastructure management, and data processing due to its extensive libraries and readability. Go, on the other hand, is designed for high-performance automation and is particularly useful for building efficient CLI tools and cloud-native applications. While Bash is best suited for quick system tasks, Python excels in cloud automation and Go provides the performance required for large-scale automation. Understanding the strengths of each language allows DevOps engineers to choose the right tool for the right job, ensuring scalable, efficient, and maintainable automation workflows.

Automating cloud infrastructure with APIs

Cloud infrastructure automation is a core principle of modern DevOps, enabling teams to provision, configure, and manage resources dynamically without manual intervention. **Application programming interfaces** (**APIs**) are the backbone of this automation, providing programmatic access to cloud services from providers like AWS, Azure, and Google Cloud. By leveraging APIs, DevOps engineers can build scripts, workflows, and tools to deploy infrastructure, scale resources, and enforce governance at scale. The main reason on why you should use APIs for infrastructure automation stems from the fact that manually managing cloud infrastructure is slow, error-prone, and non-scalable. APIs solve these challenges by enabling:

- **Consistency:** Automate infrastructure provisioning to ensure identical environments.

- **Speed:** Deploy and update resources instantly without manual steps.

- **Scalability:** Dynamically scale compute, storage, and networking based on demand.

- **Integration:** Connect cloud services with CI/CD pipelines and monitoring systems.

- **Security and governance:** Enforce security policies, compliance, and access controls programmatically.

With APIs, infrastructure management moves from UI-based manual operations to code-driven automation, ensuring reliability and repeatability.

Cloud providers expose APIs through **Representational State Transfer** (**REST**) or **software development kits** (**SDKs**) that enable developers to programmatically control and manage cloud infrastructure. These interfaces serve as the foundation for cloud automation and infrastructure as code:

- **AWS API:** Accessible through multiple tools including Boto3 Python SDK for application integration, AWS CLI for command-line operations, and Terraform for declarative infrastructure provisioning

- **Azure API:** Available via the Azure SDK (supporting multiple programming languages), Azure CLI for administrative tasks, ARM Templates for JSON-based infrastructure definitions, and Bicep as a more readable alternative to ARM

- **Google Cloud API:** Programmable through the gcloud CLI for administrative operations, Terraform for cross-platform infrastructure management, and comprehensive language-specific SDKs including the Python SDK

These APIs provide comprehensive operations for the complete lifecycle management of cloud resources, creating, configuring, updating, monitoring, and removing components such as virtual machines, storage systems, networking infrastructure, and security controls. By leveraging these APIs, organizations can implement fully automated, consistent, and repeatable cloud environments.

Automating AWS infrastructure with APIs

AWS provides multiple ways to interact with its services programmatically. The most common methods are AWS CLI, Boto3 (Python SDK), and Terraform, each offering different approaches to cloud automation and management.

For example, the following command will create an EC2 instance using AWS CLI:

```
aws ec2 run-instances --image-id ami-0abcdef1234567890 \
  --count 1 --instance-type t2.micro \
  --key-name my-key \
  --security-group-ids sg-12345678 \
  --subnet-id subnet-87654321
```

The command above creates a new EC2 instance using a specified **Amazon Machine Image (AMI)** identified by ami-0abcdef1234567890. It configures a **t2.micro** instance type with a specific key pair (my-key), security group (sg-12345678), and subnet (subnet-87654321). This automation eliminates the need to use the AWS console, enabling infrastructure provisioning through scripts and automation tools. For security best practices, AWS IAM roles should be used to grant the necessary permissions to execute these commands.

Similarly, you can use the Python **boto3** script to create an EC2 instance as follows:

```
import boto3

ec2 = boto3.client('ec2')
response = ec2.run_instances(
    ImageId='ami-0abcdef1234567890',
    InstanceType='t2.micro',
    MinCount=1,
    MaxCount=1,
    KeyName='my-key',
    SecurityGroupIds=['sg-12345678'],
    SubnetId='subnet-87654321'
```

```
)
```

```
print("EC2 Instance Launched:", response['Instances'][0]['InstanceId'])
```

This Python code leverages Boto3, the AWS SDK for Python, to accomplish the same EC2 instance creation. After importing the Boto3 library, it initializes an EC2 client and calls the **run_instances** method with parameters matching those used in the CLI example. The code then extracts and prints the newly created instance ID from the response object. This approach integrates AWS resource management directly into Python applications, enabling more complex workflows and conditional logic around infrastructure provisioning. The SDK approach is particularly valuable for creating custom tools or embedding AWS operations into larger applications.

These approaches demonstrate the flexibility of AWS's API ecosystem, allowing DevOps engineers and developers to choose command line tools for quick operations or SDK integration for more complex application workflows. Both methods accomplish the same infrastructure provisioning while serving different automation needs and development preferences.

In conclusion the cloud APIs represent the foundation of modern infrastructure automation, enabling organizations to programmatically control cloud resources without manual intervention. Whether using command-line interfaces, language-specific SDKs, or IaC tools, these APIs provide consistent, repeatable methods for resource provisioning and management. The ability to integrate cloud operations into scripts and automation pipelines not only accelerates deployment but also reduces configuration errors and enforces standardization.

Leading technology organizations demonstrate the transformative impact of API-driven infrastructure automation. Airbnb manages an extensive cloud footprint of over 1,500 AWS accounts using a combination of AWS Control Tower APIs and Terraform. Their infrastructure automation enables them to maintain consistent security policies, compliance standards, and operational practices across this complex environment while supporting millions of daily bookings.

Adobe leverages Azure DevOps Pipelines to orchestrate hundreds of builds and deployments daily using the **Azure Resource Manager** (**ARM**) API. This automation allows them to maintain their Creative Cloud services with consistent, repeatable deployments across global regions, ensuring that customers worldwide receive identical experiences regardless of location.

Perhaps one of the most impressive examples of API-driven cloud automation comes from Capital One's *Cloud Custodian* project, which manages compliance policies across approximately 25,000 AWS accounts. This open-source tool uses AWS APIs to continuously monitor resource configurations, automatically remediate non-compliant resources, and generate comprehensive audit reports. By encoding hundreds of security and compliance policies as code, Cloud Custodian eliminates what would otherwise require an army of operators manually reviewing cloud resources.

These implementations demonstrate how API-based automation transforms from simple scripting to sophisticated governance and operational frameworks that can scale across thousands of accounts and millions of resources while maintaining security, compliance, and operational excellence.

By exposing cloud functionality through well-documented interfaces, these APIs enable DevOps practices like **continuous integration/continuous deployment (CI/CD)**, infrastructure as code, and self-service platforms. Organizations can implement safeguards, approval workflows, and compliance checks around these API calls to ensure governance while maintaining agility. As cloud environments grow in complexity, leveraging these programmatic interfaces becomes increasingly important for maintaining operational efficiency and scalability.

Event-driven automation with webhooks

Traditional automation relies on scheduled scripts or manual triggers, but event-driven automation takes it a step further by responding instantly to changes in systems, applications, or infrastructure. Webhooks are a key enabler of event-driven automation, allowing services to communicate in real-time without continuous polling or manual intervention.

By leveraging webhooks, DevOps teams can automate deployments, incident responses, notifications, and infrastructure changes based on specific triggers, improving efficiency, reducing latency, and ensuring faster response times to critical events.

Understanding webhooks

Webhooks represent a foundational technology in modern system integration, offering an elegant solution to the challenge of real-time data exchange between disparate systems. At their core, webhooks function as automated messengers that deliver information precisely when it matters most. When a specific event occurs within a source system, it automatically sends an HTTP request, typically a POST request containing relevant data, to a predetermined URL endpoint on the receiving system. This simple yet powerful mechanism creates an efficient bridge between applications, enabling them to communicate and respond to events as they happen.

Unlike traditional API integration patterns that rely on polling, where the receiving system must repeatedly check for updates, webhooks employ a push-based architecture that fundamentally transforms system communication. This distinction is critical in resource-constrained environments where efficiency is paramount. With polling, systems waste computational resources and network bandwidth by continually requesting data that often has not changed. In contrast, webhooks conserve these valuable resources by remaining dormant until triggered by meaningful events, at which point they spring into action to deliver precisely the information that matters.

The event-driven nature of webhooks makes them particularly valuable in complex, distributed architectures. When a code repository receives a new commit, when a payment is processed, or when a monitoring threshold is breached, webhooks can instantly propagate this information to all systems that need to know, without delay or unnecessary overhead. This immediate notification ensures that downstream systems can react promptly to changing conditions, maintaining synchronization across the technology ecosystem.

The key characteristics of webhooks are:

- **Event-driven architecture:** Webhooks operate on a trigger-based model, activating only when specific events occur rather than requiring constant polling. This significantly reduces unnecessary system calls and resource consumption.

- **Real-time communication:** By delivering notifications immediately upon event occurrence, webhooks eliminate the latency inherent in scheduled jobs or polling intervals, enabling instant system responses.

- **Lightweight implementation:** Webhooks utilize standard HTTP requests with simple payloads, making them easy to implement across virtually any programming language or platform without specialized libraries.

- **Push-based mechanism:** Unlike pull-based APIs, webhooks push data to receiving systems, inverting the traditional request-response pattern and enabling more efficient data distribution.

- **Stateless operation:** Each webhook request is independent and self-contained, requiring no session management or persistent connections between systems.

- **Flexible payload format:** Webhooks typically transmit data in JSON or XML formats, allowing for structured information exchange that can be easily parsed and processed.

- **Reduced network traffic:** By eliminating continuous polling, webhooks dramatically decrease network overhead, particularly valuable in distributed systems with numerous integration points.

- **Scalable integration:** Webhooks can fan out from a single event source to multiple destination systems, enabling one-to-many notification patterns that scale efficiently.

The practical application of webhooks in DevOps environments spans numerous critical operational areas, with CI/CD pipelines representing one of the most transformative implementations. When developers commit code changes to version control systems like GitHub, GitLab, or Bitbucket, webhooks trigger automated build processes, test executions, and deployment workflows without manual intervention. This automation eliminates bottlenecks in the software delivery lifecycle, enabling organizations to deploy changes more frequently and with greater confidence. For instance, a webhook from GitHub can instantly notify Jenkins or CircleCI to initiate a build process, run comprehensive test suites, and deploy to staging environments, all within minutes of the code being committed.

Incident management represents another domain where webhooks deliver exceptional value. Modern monitoring and observability platforms like Prometheus, Datadog, or New Relic can detect anomalies or threshold violations and trigger webhooks that automatically create detailed tickets in service management systems such as Jira, ServiceNow, or PagerDuty. These tickets can include comprehensive diagnostic information captured at the moment of detection, ensuring that response teams have immediate access to the context they need. This integration dramatically reduces **mean time to detection (MTTD)** and **mean time to resolution (MTTR)**, minimizing service disruptions and their business impact.

The integration of webhooks with team communication platforms has given rise to the practice known as ChatOps, where operational events flow directly into collaboration spaces. When critical systems generate alerts, webhooks can instantly deliver notifications to Slack channels, Microsoft Teams rooms, or Discord servers, complete with relevant metrics, logs, and actionable links. This approach ensures that the right people receive timely information in their primary workspace, enhancing team awareness and accelerating collaborative problem-solving. Many organizations extend this pattern by enabling interactive responses directly within these platforms, allowing teams to acknowledge alerts, escalate issues, or even execute remediation commands without switching contexts.

Perhaps one of the most sophisticated applications of webhooks lies in dynamic infrastructure scaling. Monitoring systems that track application performance metrics can trigger webhooks when resource utilization approaches defined thresholds. These webhooks can then initiate API calls to cloud providers like AWS, Azure, or Google Cloud, automatically provisioning additional resources or scaling down during periods of lower demand. This automated elasticity ensures optimal performance during peak usage while controlling costs during quieter periods. For example, a webhook triggered when CPU utilization exceeds 70% might call the AWS Auto Scaling API to add additional EC2 instances, ensuring application responsiveness without requiring constant human monitoring.

Webhook working

Webhooks enable systems to communicate automatically when events occur:

- **Event occurs:** A system detects a change (commit, deployment, failure).

- **Webhook sends data:** An HTTP request with payload is sent to a predefined URL.

- **Listener processes event:** A server receives the webhook and identifies required actions.

- **Automation executes:** Actions like deployments or notifications run based on the data.

For example, automated deployment where the following sequence of action happens:

1. Developer pushes code to GitHub.

2. GitHub webhook notifies Jenkins server.

3. Jenkins receives webhook, pulls code, and runs tests.

4. On successful tests, Jenkins deploys to production.

Webhooks can be used with monitoring tools (Prometheus, Datadog, AWS CloudWatch) to automatically handle incidents. For example, automating Slack Alerts from Prometheus Alerts:

1. Prometheus AlertManager detects a system issue.

2. It sends a webhook to a Slack bot.

3. The bot posts an alert message in Slack.

4. If critical, a Jira ticket is automatically created for engineers.

The following is a webhook example from Prometheus AlertManager:

```
{
  «status»: "firing",
  "alerts": [
    {
      «labels»: {
        «alertname": "HighCPUUsage",
        "instance": "server1",
        "severity": "critical"
      },
      «annotations»: {
        «summary": "CPU usage exceeded 90% on server1"
      }
    }
  ]
}
```

Similarly, you can automate Slack alerts with Python webhook listener:

```
from flask import Flask, request
import requests

app = Flask(__name__)
```

```
SLACK_WEBHOOK_URL = "https://hooks.slack.com/services/your/slack/webhook"

@app.route('/webhook', methods=['POST'])
def webhook_listener():
    data = request.json
    alert_message = f"{data['alerts'][0]['annotations']['summary']}"

    requests.post(SLACK_WEBHOOK_URL, json={"text": alert_message})
    return "Alert received", 200

if __name__ == '__main__':
    app.run(port=5000)
```

So, if you put the two examples together:

- A Flask-based webhook listens for Prometheus alerts.

- When triggered, it posts an alert to Slack automatically.

- This eliminates manual alert checking, ensuring real-time incident response.

Hence, webhooks are a powerful tool for event-driven automation in DevOps, enabling instant responses to system events. Instead of relying on manual triggers or scheduled tasks, webhooks push real-time data to automation systems, improving efficiency and scalability. GitHub webhooks automate CI/CD pipelines, Prometheus webhooks enable real-time incident management, and cloud provider webhooks facilitate auto-scaling based on demand. By integrating webhooks with tools like Jenkins, Slack, AWS Lambda, and Python-based listeners, DevOps teams can build highly responsive, automated workflows, minimizing delays and eliminating repetitive manual tasks.

Financial services company Intuit demonstrates the power of event-driven automation through their GitOps deployment model. When developers commit code to GitHub repositories, webhooks automatically trigger Argo CD to synchronize and deploy applications across their Kubernetes clusters. This webhook-driven pipeline ensures that their cloud-native applications remain consistent with their declared state in version control, eliminating deployment delays and configuration drift across their complex microservices architecture.

Payment processor Stripe integrates webhooks from their Datadog monitoring platform directly into their infrastructure automation system. When anomalies are detected in service performance metrics, these webhooks trigger automatic scaling operations for the affected microservices, often resolving potential issues before they impact customers. This closed-loop system responds to changing conditions faster than human operators ever could, maintaining consistent performance during transaction volume spikes.

The scale of webhook-driven automation can be staggering. E-commerce platform Shopify processes over one billion webhook events daily across 175 countries, coordinating payments, inventory updates, shipping notifications, and third-party integrations. Their webhook infrastructure forms the backbone of an event-driven ecosystem that connects merchants, customers, and partners with near real-time data synchronization.

These examples illustrate how webhook-driven automation extends beyond simple notifications to create interconnected systems that respond instantaneously to events, enabling organizations to build responsive, resilient infrastructure that adapts to changing conditions without manual intervention.

Serverless automation frameworks

Serverless automation eliminates the need for managing infrastructure, allowing developers to focus purely on writing code. Serverless automation frameworks enable DevOps teams to automate deployments, infrastructure provisioning, and event-driven workflows without maintaining servers. These frameworks leverage cloud-based **function as a service** (**FaaS**) offerings like AWS Lambda, Google Cloud Functions, and Azure Functions, ensuring cost efficiency and scalability.

Some popular serverless frameworks are:

- **AWS Serverless Application Model (SAM):** AWS-native framework for defining and deploying serverless apps using CloudFormation.

- **Google Cloud Functions framework:** Google's tool for building and testing serverless functions locally before deploying.

- **Azure Functions core tools:** CLI-based tool for developing, testing, and deploying Azure Functions.

- **Pulumi:** Infrastructure-as-code framework that supports serverless deployments in multiple languages.

Serverless computing fundamentally shifts the infrastructure responsibility from developers to cloud providers, operating on these key principles:

- **Event-driven execution:** Code runs only in response to specific triggers or events

- **Zero infrastructure management:** Developers deploy code without provisioning or maintaining servers

- **Automatic scaling:** Resources scale instantly from zero to peak demand and back

- **Consumption-based pricing:** You pay only for actual compute time used, not idle capacity

Let us take an example to understand the serverless compute scenario better. Imagine a scenario where CPU usage on an EC2 instance exceeds 80%, and we need to automatically launch a new instance. This can be automated using AWS Lambda. So, the workflow can look like:

- AWS CloudWatch detects high CPU usage and triggers an event.

- AWS Lambda function receives the event and launches a new EC2 instance.

- The system automatically scales without human intervention.

The following code is an example of the AWS Python lambda function for autoscaling:

```
import boto3

def lambda_handler(event, context):
    ec2 = boto3.client('ec2')

    response = ec2.run_instances(
        ImageId='ami-0abcdef1234567890',
        InstanceType='t2.micro',
        MinCount=1,
        MaxCount=1
    )

    instance_id = response['Instances'][0]['InstanceId']
    print(f"New EC2 Instance Launched: {instance_id}")
    return {"status": "success", "instance_id": instance_id}
```

In conclusion, Serverless automation frameworks provide a lightweight, cost-efficient, and scalable way to handle automation tasks without managing infrastructure. They enable event-driven workflows, making them ideal for auto-scaling, CI/CD pipelines, and cloud automation. By leveraging tools like AWS Lambda, Google Cloud Functions, and Azure Functions, DevOps teams can build efficient self-healing, scalable systems that reduce operational overhead and accelerate software delivery.

The travel technology company Expedia provides a compelling example of serverless automation at scale. Their platform executes approximately 15 billion AWS Lambda invocations monthly to handle pricing calculations, booking workflows, and customer notifications. This serverless approach enables them to handle dramatic fluctuations in travel search and booking volume without maintaining a massive fleet of continuously running servers, significantly reducing infrastructure costs while maintaining consistent performance.

Streaming music provider Spotify leverages Google Cloud Functions to power real-time song recommendation updates based on user behavior events. When listeners interact with songs through plays, skips, or likes, these events trigger serverless functions that update personalization algorithms instantly. This architecture allows *Spotify* to process billions of events daily while only paying for the precise computation time needed to handle each user interaction.

Even physical products benefit from serverless automation. *Coca-Cola's* Freestyle beverage machines, IoT devices found in restaurants worldwide, use AWS Lambda functions to process millions of drink orders, capture consumption analytics, and manage recipe updates. This serverless approach allows each machine to operate independently while maintaining a lightweight connection to the cloud for updates and analytics.

These implementations showcase how serverless automation enables organizations to build highly responsive, cost-efficient systems that scale automatically with demand. By eliminating server provisioning, capacity planning, and maintenance, teams can focus on building business logic rather than managing infrastructure, accelerating innovation while reducing operational complexity.

Automating incident response and remediation

Automating incident response and remediation accelerates issue resolution and minimizes downtime by executing predefined actions when problems occur. This approach transforms reactive support into proactive protection.

The key components are:

- **Event detection:** Monitoring systems identify anomalies or failures through logs, metrics, and threshold breaches.

- **Automated triage:** Classify incidents by severity, impact, and required response.

- **Orchestrated response:** Trigger appropriate remediation workflows based on incident type.

- **Self-healing actions:** Execute predefined recovery procedures without human intervention.

- **Notification system:** Alert relevant stakeholders with context-rich information.

With automating incident response, you will be able to also do the following:

- **Faster detection and resolution:** Automated monitoring tools can detect issues and trigger remediation actions instantly.

- **Reduced human error:** Automation eliminates manual mistakes and inconsistencies in incident handling.

- **Scalability:** Automated systems can handle multiple incidents simultaneously, reducing operational overhead.

- **Improved compliance:** Automated auditing and logging ensure adherence to security and compliance policies.

- **Proactive remediation:** Automation can fix issues before they impact end users.

To understand this better, consider a common scenario: an e-commerce platform experiences sudden database performance degradation during peak shopping hours. The system monitoring detects high CPU utilization on the primary database instance.

Without automation, this scenario typically unfolds like this: An engineer receives an alert, logs into monitoring systems, identifies the database issue, creates a backup, manually scales the database, and notifies stakeholders, a process that might take 30-45 minutes.

With the automated approach shown in the following code, the entire remediation cycle executes within seconds. The system detects high CPU utilization, and triggers the Lambda function, which automatically:

- Creates a safety snapshot for rollback if needed.

- Identifies the current instance size and determines an appropriate upgrade.

- Immediately scales up the database instance.

- Notifies the operations team with detailed information.

```python
import boto3
import json
import logging
# Configure Logging
logging.basicConfig(level=logging.INFO)
logger = logging.getLogger()
# Initialize AWS clients
rds = boto3.client('rds')
sns = boto3.client('sns')
def lambda_handler(event, context):
    # Extract DB instance information from CloudWatch alarm
    alarm_data = json.loads(event['Records'][0]['Sns']['Message'])
    db_instance = alarm_data['Trigger']['Dimensions'][0]['value']
    logger.info(f"Remediating performance issues for {db_instance}")

    # Create snapshot before remediation
    snapshot_id = f"{db_instance}-auto-snapshot-{context.aws_request_id[:8]}"
    rds.create_db_snapshot(DBInstanceIdentifier=db_instance, DBSnapshotIdentifier=snapshot_id)
    logger.info(f"Created safety snapshot: {snapshot_id}")

    # Apply remediation: Scale up the instance
```

```
    response = rds.describe_db_instances(DBInstanceIdentifier=db_
instance)
    current_type = response['DBInstances'][0]['DBInstanceClass']

    # Determine new instance size
    instance_tiers = {
        'db.t3.medium': 'db.t3.large',
        'db.t3.large': 'db.r5.large',
        'db.r5.large': 'db.r5.xlarge'
    }
    new_type = instance_tiers.get(current_type, 'db.r5.large')

    # Apply the scaling operation
    rds.modify_db_instance(
        DBInstanceIdentifier=db_instance,
        DBInstanceClass=new_type,
        ApplyImmediately=True
    )
    logger.info(f"Scaled instance from {current_type} to {new_
type}")

    # Notify team
    sns.publish(
        TopicArn="arn:aws:sns:us-east-1:123456789012:db-incidents",
        Subject=f"DB Remediation: {db_instance}",
        Message=f"Automated remediation applied to {db_
instance}. Scaled from {current_type} to {new_type}."
    )

    return {
        'statusCode': 200,
        'body': json.dumps('Remediation completed successfully')
    }
```

The customer experience goes from a prolonged slowdown to a brief performance blip that resolves before most users even notice an issue.

Effective incident response automation is not just about individual scripts, it is about creating a cohesive framework. Organizations should inventory their most common incidents, map standard response procedures, and gradually automate each workflow.

The approach should be progressive: start with low-risk, high-frequency incidents before tackling more complex scenarios.

Automated remediation should also include:

- Clean rollback mechanisms if automated fixes fail.
- Audit trails capturing all automated actions.
- Regular testing through chaos engineering exercises.
- Continuous refinement based on effectiveness metrics.

In conclusion, the move from manual to automated incident response represents a fundamental shift in operational maturity. Organizations that successfully implement these practices see dramatic improvements in reliability metrics: reduced MTTR, decreased incident frequency, and diminished service impact. Perhaps most importantly, automated remediation frees technical teams from repetitive toil, allowing them to focus on innovation rather than firefighting. In today's competitive landscape, this capability is not just an operational advantage, it is becoming a business necessity.

Cloud storage provider *Dropbox* demonstrates the power of automated incident response through their self-remediation systems. When their monitoring detects I/O latency exceeding defined thresholds on storage nodes, Lambda functions automatically initiate storage tier scaling operations to alleviate the bottleneck. This automation responds to performance degradation within seconds, often resolving issues before users experience any noticeable impact and eliminating what would otherwise require manual intervention by storage engineers.

Professional networking platform LinkedIn has transformed incident management through comprehensive SRE runbook automation. Their system maintains an extensive library of predefined playbooks that execute automatically for approximately 70% of known incident types. When their monitoring platform detects specific failure patterns, it automatically triggers the appropriate remediation workflow, which might include service restarts, traffic rerouting, or resource scaling. This approach has dramatically reduced their **mean time to recovery (MTTR)** while allowing their engineering teams to focus on innovation rather than repetitive troubleshooting.

The impact of incident automation extends beyond individual organizations. According to operational metrics, PagerDuty customers typically reduce their MTTR by an average of 60% after implementing automated incident response workflows. This improvement directly translates to increased system availability, enhanced user experience, and reduced operational burden on technical teams.

These examples illustrate how automated incident response transforms the fundamental nature of operations from reactive firefighting to proactive system design. By investing in automation that addresses common failure modes, organizations can achieve higher reliability with smaller operations teams, creating a virtuous cycle where engineers spend more time improving systems and less time manually recovering from incidents.

Workflow automation with Jenkins Pipelines

Jenkins Pipelines transform software delivery by codifying build, test, and deployment processes into automated workflows. This approach brings consistency, visibility, and reliability to the development lifecycle. Traditional Jenkins jobs relied on manual configuration through the UI, creating maintenance challenges and hindering version control. Jenkins Pipelines solves this by defining entire workflows in code using a domain-specific language called Jenkinsfile.

The following is an example of a Jenkins workflow file:

```
pipeline {
    agent any

    tools {
        maven 'Maven 3.8.6'
        jdk 'JDK 17'
    }

    stages {
        stage('Checkout') {
            steps {
                checkout scm
            }
        }

        stage('Build') {
            steps {
                sh 'mvn clean compile'
            }
        }

        stage('Test') {
            steps {
                sh 'mvn test'
                junit '**/target/surefire-reports/*.xml'
            }
        }

        stage('Package') {
```

```
            steps {
                sh 'mvn package -DskipTests'
                archiveArtifacts artifacts: 'target/*.
jar', fingerprint: true
            }
        }

        stage('Deploy to Dev') {
            when {
                branch 'develop'
            }
            steps {
                sh './scripts/deploy.sh dev'
            }
        }

        stage('Deploy to Production') {
            when {
                branch 'main'
            }
            steps {
                timeout(time: 1, unit: 'DAYS') {
                    input message: 'Approve production deployment?'
                }
                sh './scripts/deploy.sh prod'
            }
        }
    }

    post {
        always {
            cleanWs()
            emailext body: 'Build status: ${BUILD_STATUS}',
                    subject: 'Build Notification: ${PROJECT_
NAME} - ${BUILD_NUMBER}',
                    to: 'team@example.com'
        }
    }
}
```

The pipeline aforementioned demonstrates how Jenkins orchestrates the entire application lifecycle. When a developer pushes code, Jenkins automatically goes through the following steps:

1. Retrieves the latest code from version control.

2. Compiles the application using Maven.

3. Runs automated tests and collects results.

4. Packages the application into a deployable artifact.

5. Deploys to the development environment for branch-specific changes.

6. Requests human approval before production deployment.

7. Notifies the team of build results.

What previously required multiple manual steps now executes consistently with a single commit, reducing delivery time from hours to minutes.

Jenkins Pipelines transform organizations by codifying deployment knowledge into repeatable, automated processes. This approach not only accelerates delivery but also enhances quality by ensuring consistent testing and deployment. As development teams grow and applications become more complex, pipeline-based workflows become essential infrastructure, turning manual, error-prone deployments into reliable, efficient operations that support rapid innovation.

Hyperconverged infrastructure provider Nutanix demonstrates the power of pipeline automation through their extensive Jenkins implementation. Their engineering teams use parallelized Jenkins pipelines to orchestrate releases for over 100 microservices, coordinating complex dependencies, integration tests, and deployment sequences. This pipeline-based approach enables them to maintain a rapid release cadence while ensuring comprehensive testing and validation across their entire platform.

Retail giant *Walmart Global Tech* relies on Jenkins to manage an extraordinary workload of over 2,000 jobs per hour for their retail and e-commerce systems. These pipelines coordinate everything from inventory updates and price changes to website deployments and mobile application releases. By codifying these workflows in Jenkins, Walmart maintains consistent operations across thousands of stores and multiple digital platforms with minimal manual intervention.

Media organization BBC has transformed their content delivery through Jenkins pipelines that manage approximately 30,000 production deployments annually. These pipelines handle the complex process of encoding, transcoding, and distributing media assets across multiple platforms while maintaining strict compliance with broadcasting standards. This automation allows the BBC to deliver content to global audiences with unprecedented speed and reliability.

These implementations demonstrate how pipeline-based automation enables organizations to coordinate increasingly complex software delivery processes at scale. By expressing these workflows as code, teams create repeatable, auditable processes that maintain consistency while adapting to evolving business and technical requirements. The resulting acceleration in delivery velocity provides a significant competitive advantage in industries where rapid innovation is essential.

Infrastructure automation beyond IaC

Infrastructure as code (**IaC**) revolutionized resource provisioning, but modern infrastructure automation extends significantly beyond static templates. These advanced approaches enable a dynamic, intelligent infrastructure that adapts to changing needs.

Today's infrastructure can observe, learn, and adapt without human intervention. These systems use operational data to trigger automated adjustments:

- Anomaly-driven scaling moves beyond simple threshold-based rules. For example, an e-commerce platform might automatically detect unusual traffic patterns three weeks before Black Friday, analyzing historical data and current trends to preemptively scale infrastructure before traditional monitoring would trigger alerts.

- Performance-optimized provisioning continuously evaluates workload characteristics to adjust resources. A data processing pipeline might automatically switch from compute-optimized to memory-optimized instances when it detects that jobs have become more memory-intensive over time, without requiring DevOps teams to manually analyze and implement changes.

- Cost-aware infrastructure intelligently optimizes spending. A development environment might automatically downgrade database instances during weekends and evenings when developer activity is minimal, then restore capacity before the workday begins, reducing costs by up to 65% while maintaining consistent performance during work hours.

Streaming giant *Netflix* exemplifies advanced infrastructure automation through their Auto-Tuning Platform. This system employs machine learning models to optimize AWS instance type selection dynamically based on streaming load patterns, content characteristics, and cost parameters. Rather than relying on static instance type selections, the platform continuously evaluates workload performance and automatically adjusts infrastructure configurations to optimize both performance and cost, saving millions in infrastructure expenses while maintaining optimal viewer experiences.

Travel platform Booking.com operates self-optimizing Kubernetes clusters that continuously rebalance resources and implement predictive auto-scaling without manual intervention. Their system analyzes historical traffic patterns, current resource utilization, and upcoming events (such as holidays or promotions) to proactively adjust cluster capacity before demand spikes occur. This automated approach ensures consistent performance during peak travel seasons while minimizing unnecessary resource allocation during quieter periods.

Google Cloud Platform's *Autopilot Mode* represents the industry trend toward fully managed infrastructure that self-optimizes. This system automatically adjusts GKE node pools based on sophisticated resource usage forecasts, eliminating the need for manual capacity planning or scaling operations. The system continuously evaluates workload characteristics and adjusts node types, sizes, and quantities to maintain optimal performance while controlling costs.

These examples illustrate the evolution from static infrastructure definitions to truly intelligent, adaptive systems that autonomously optimize themselves based on changing conditions. By embedding intelligence into infrastructure management, organizations reduce operational overhead while simultaneously improving performance, reliability, and cost efficiency, a combination that creates significant competitive advantage in technology-intensive industries.

Autonomous operations

The next evolution moves beyond reactive automation to proactive infrastructure management:

- Continuous optimization engines regularly evaluate infrastructure and reconfigure it based on actual usage. Unlike traditional right-sizing exercises that occur quarterly, these systems might identify that a production database is consistently using only 30% of provisioned IOPS and automatically adjust storage tiers, generating significant savings without performance impact.

- Automated A/B infrastructure testing applies web development concepts to infrastructure. When deploying a new service architecture, the system automatically provisions both the current and new designs, routes a percentage of traffic to each, and evaluates metrics like response time, error rates, and resource efficiency before deciding which configuration to fully adopt.

- Self-healing architectures go beyond simple restarts. When a microservice experiences repeated memory leaks, the system might automatically deploy an instrumented version that collects diagnostic data, identifies the issue, and applies targeted remediations without declaring a full outage or requiring developer intervention.

Policy-driven management

Modern infrastructure automation introduces sophisticated policy-driven approaches:

- **Automatic compliance enforcement** continuously validates infrastructure against regulatory and security requirements. When healthcare systems deploy new virtual machines, governance engines automatically verify encryption settings, network isolation, and access controls, remediate non-compliant configurations, and generate audit trails, all before protected health information is processed.

- **Configuration drift management** detects unauthorized changes and maintains approved states. If a database administrator manually modifies security groups on a production database to troubleshoot an issue but forgets to revert the change, the system automatically detects this drift, evaluates it against security policies, and either reverts the change or initiates an approval workflow.

- **Resource lifecycle policies** enforce standardized management across environments. Development instances can be configured to automatically hibernate after four hours of inactivity and terminate after two weeks without use, while production resources follow different policies, eliminating the orphaned resource problem that plagues many cloud environments.

Intelligence-embedded infrastructure

AI-powered infrastructure represents the cutting edge of autonomous systems:

- Predictive maintenance forecasts failures before they occur. Network infrastructure might analyze packet loss patterns, throughput variations, and historical data to determine that a specific router is likely to fail within the next 72 hours, automatically rerouting traffic and dispatching replacement hardware before users experience disruption.

- Workload behavior modeling learns application patterns to optimize configurations. A system might observe that a particular microservice consistently experiences memory pressure during month-end processing, automatically adjusting resource allocations on a schedule without requiring the development team to manually account for these cyclical demands.

- Autonomous security adaptation responds to emerging threats. When unusual access patterns are detected across multiple systems, security infrastructure can automatically implement progressive access restrictions, adjust monitoring thresholds, and deploy targeted protections based on specific threat characteristics, all before a human security analyst would typically receive an alert.

Modern infrastructure automation has evolved from static templates to intelligent systems that make autonomous decisions based on operational data, compliance policies, and predictive analytics. This shift moves operations teams from reactive provisioning to focusing on defining high-level policies and business objectives. Organizations that embrace these advanced automation approaches gain not only operational efficiency but also enhanced resilience, improved security posture, and optimized resource utilization, creating competitive advantage through infrastructure that adapts to business needs without constant human intervention.

Self-healing systems

Self-healing systems represent the pinnacle of operational automation, infrastructure, and applications designed to detect, diagnose, and recover from failures without human intervention. These systems continuously monitor their own health and automatically remediate issues, dramatically reducing downtime and operational overhead.

Anatomy of self-healing

At their core, self-healing systems incorporate several critical capabilities working in concert:

- Comprehensive health monitoring establishes baseline behavior and identifies anomalies across all system components. Rather than simple binary up/down checks, advanced monitoring evaluates performance characteristics, error rates, resource utilization, and user experience metrics to detect subtle degradations before they cause outages.

- Automated diagnosis engines determine root causes by correlating events across system boundaries. When a web application experiences increased response times, the diagnosis system might automatically discover that the issue stems from database query performance rather than application code or network congestion.

- Intelligent remediation workflows apply the appropriate fix based on the specific failure mode. These workflows range from simple actions like restarting services to complex procedures such as database failovers, traffic rerouting, or dynamic reconfiguration.

E-commerce platform *Shopify* demonstrates sophisticated self-healing capabilities in their Kubernetes infrastructure, which manages over 50,000 pods across their global deployment. Their system implements comprehensive health checks, readiness probes, and multi-level auto-scaling policies that collectively ensure application resilience even during extreme traffic events like Black Friday. When anomalies are detected, the platform automatically adjusts resource allocation, replaces failing components, and reroutes traffic, often resolving potential issues before they impact merchants or customers.

Enterprise software provider Salesforce has implemented advanced self-healing for their microservices architecture. When their monitoring detects deployment failures or service degradation, the system automatically initiates a sophisticated remediation workflow that may include dynamic rollback to previous versions, gradual traffic shifting, and automated debugging to identify root causes. This self-healing capability enables them to maintain 99.9%+ availability across their complex, interdependent services.

The technical implementation of self-healing systems often leverages powerful platform capabilities like the Kubernetes **Horizontal Pod Autoscaler (HPA)**, which can detect and respond to resource utilization spikes within 30 seconds. During sudden traffic increases, these mechanisms automatically scale the affected services, maintaining performance while preventing cascading failures that might otherwise impact the entire system.

These examples illustrate how self-healing has evolved from simple restart mechanisms to sophisticated, multi-layered resilience strategies. By combining proactive monitoring, intelligent remediation, and graceful degradation capabilities, organizations can build systems that not only recover from failures but adapt to them, learning and improving with each incident rather than merely returning to the previous state.

Self-healing in action

Consider how self-healing operates across different system layers:

- At the infrastructure level, when a cloud instance experiences hardware degradation, the system automatically detaches affected storage volumes, launches replacement instances, reconnects persistent resources, and updates load balancers, all before users notice any impact.

- At the application level, when a microservice begins returning errors, the system might automatically roll back to the previous deployment, reroute traffic to healthy instances, scale up additional containers, or adjust retry policies in dependent services to maintain overall system integrity.

- At the data level, when database replication falls behind schedule, automated remediation might dynamically allocate additional network resources, temporarily reduce read load on the primary instance, or initiate specialized catch-up procedures to restore synchronization without manual intervention.

Designing truly self-healing systems requires several fundamental components:

- Health assessment frameworks that go beyond simple health checks to establish comprehensive views of the system state. These frameworks collect telemetry from all components and apply contextual awareness to differentiate between normal variations and actual problems.

- Circuit breakers and bulkheads that contain failures before they cascade through the system. When an API experiences degradation, circuit breakers automatically stop sending requests to failing endpoints and redirect traffic to alternate resources or gracefully degrade functionality.

- State reconciliation loops that continuously compare the actual system state with the desired state and make adjustments as needed. Kubernetes exemplifies this approach by constantly monitoring deployment specifications and automatically taking actions to align the running environment with declared intentions.

- Automated rollback mechanisms that quickly restore working configurations when updates cause problems. Modern deployment pipelines incorporate automatic verification of key metrics after releases and trigger immediate rollbacks when critical indicators deteriorate.

Self-healing systems represent a fundamental shift from reactive incident response to proactive system resilience. By automating the detection, diagnosis, and remediation of failures, these systems dramatically reduce mean time to recovery while freeing technical teams from routine troubleshooting. As applications grow more complex and distributed, self-healing capabilities become essential rather than optional, transforming fragile services into resilient platforms that maintain availability even under adverse conditions. Organizations that master self-healing architectures gain not only operational efficiency but also enhanced customer experience through consistently reliable services.

Automating compliance and auditing

Compliance and auditing are essential in DevOps to ensure security, regulatory adherence, and operational consistency. Manual compliance checks are slow, error-prone, and difficult to scale, making automation a critical component of modern compliance strategies. By integrating policy enforcement, security scanning, and automated audits into CI/CD pipelines, organizations can ensure continuous compliance without slowing down development.

Automating this also matters because of the following reasons:

- **Continuous compliance:** Policies are enforced automatically instead of periodic manual reviews.

- **Reduced risk:** Automated security and compliance checks prevent misconfigurations and vulnerabilities.

- **Audit readiness:** Real-time logging and automated reporting ensure compliance with frameworks like ISO 27001, SOC 2, HIPAA, PCI-DSS, and GDPR.

- **Scalability:** Compliance automation works across multiple environments without human intervention.

- **Faster development:** Developers can ship code faster, knowing that compliance checks are handled automatically.

You can use the following compliance automation tooling as well to make your systems always in the best state:

- **IaC compliance:** Tools like Checkov, Terraform Sentinel, and **Open Policy Agent** (**OPA**) enforce security policies in IaC scripts.

- **Automated security scanning:** Trivy, Aqua Security, and Snyk scan container images, dependencies, and infrastructure for vulnerabilities.

- **Access control and IAM audits:** Automated policies in AWS IAM Access Analyzer, Google Cloud Policy Intelligence, and Azure Policy detect misconfigurations.

- **Audit logging and monitoring:** SIEM tools like Splunk, ELK Stack, and AWS CloudTrail automatically collect and analyze logs for compliance violations.

- **Policy as code (PaC):** Tools like Kyverno and OPA Gatekeeper enforce security and compliance policies as code.

Moreover, you can also use some advanced compliance automation techniques as:

- **CI/CD compliance gates:** Integration of security scans in Jenkins, GitHub Actions, GitLab CI, or Azure DevOps.

- **Automated compliance reports:** Regular compliance audits with AWS Audit Manager, GCP Security Command Center, or Azure Compliance Manager.

- **Self-healing security policies:** Auto-remediation of misconfigurations using AWS Config Rules, Terraform Sentinel, and Azure Policy.

- **Cloud-native policy enforcement:** Kubernetes admission controllers (OPA, Kyverno) ensure workloads follow security best practices.

Automating compliance and auditing ensures continuous security, governance, and regulatory adherence without slowing down development. By leveraging policy-as-code, automated scanning, security monitoring, and compliance reporting, organizations can maintain secure, audit-ready, and compliant cloud environments. This proactive approach not only reduces security risks but also helps teams focus on innovation while staying compliant.

GitHub demonstrates the impact of automated compliance through their Advanced Security platform, which continuously scans over 60 million repositories for secret leaks, vulnerable dependencies, and security issues. This automation identifies potential compliance violations and security risks at the earliest possible stage, during development, enabling teams to address issues before they reach production environments. By integrating these checks directly into developer workflows, GitHub has transformed security compliance from a bottleneck into a seamless part of the development process.

Communications platform Twilio employs a sophisticated Compliance Bot that automatically remediates security misconfigurations within minutes of detection. When the system identifies policy violations such as overly permissive security groups, public storage buckets, or unencrypted databases, it automatically implements approved remediations without human intervention. This automated approach ensures continuous compliance with security standards while minimizing the operational burden on engineering teams.

The scale of automated compliance operations can be staggering. AWS Config evaluates over 2 billion resource configurations monthly across customer environments, automatically assessing each against defined compliance rules and security best practices. This continuous evaluation provides organizations with real-time visibility into their compliance posture and automatic remediation of common issues, transforming what would otherwise require enormous manual effort into an automated, continuous process.

These implementations showcase how compliance automation has evolved from periodic manual audits to continuous, programmatic evaluation and enforcement. By codifying compliance requirements and integrating them directly into infrastructure and development workflows, organizations maintain stronger security postures with less manual effort, enabling faster innovation without compromising governance standards.

Conclusion

In this chapter, we explored advanced automation techniques that help scale DevOps practices efficiently. We started with scripting fundamentals using Bash, Python, and Go to automate repetitive tasks, then moved on to cloud infrastructure automation using APIs. We saw how event-driven automation with webhooks enables real-time responses to system changes, and how serverless automation frameworks simplify execution without managing infrastructure.

We then looked into incident response automation, demonstrating how self-healing systems detect, diagnose, and resolve failures automatically. Finally, we covered compliance and auditing automation, ensuring continuous security and governance enforcement without slowing down development. These approaches eliminate manual inefficiencies, reduce downtime, and enhance security, allowing DevOps teams to focus on innovation instead of firefighting operational issues.

As DevOps continues to evolve, emerging technologies are reshaping how we build, deploy, and manage systems.

In the next chapter, we will explore the future of DevOps, covering trends like AI-driven automation, GitOps, edge computing, NoOps, and quantum computing. We will examine how these advancements influence infrastructure management, software delivery, and operational efficiency, providing insights into the next wave of DevOps transformation.

Join our Discord space

Join our Discord workspace for latest updates, offers, tech happenings around the world, new releases, and sessions with the authors:

https://discord.bpbonline.com

CHAPTER 15
Platform Engineering

Introduction

The DevOps landscape is continuously evolving, with new paradigms and technologies reshaping how teams build, deploy, and operate software. Platform engineering is the next step in this evolution, focusing on creating self-service developer platforms that abstract complexities while enabling rapid innovation. Instead of every team reinventing infrastructure, security, and deployment strategies, platform engineering provides reusable, scalable solutions that empower developers to focus on building features rather than managing infrastructure.

This chapter explores the cutting-edge trends influencing modern DevOps practices. From AI-driven automation and GitOps to NoOps and quantum computing, we will examine how these advancements redefine software delivery, infrastructure management, and operational efficiency. As organizations move toward serverless, low-code, and sustainable development practices, the role of DevOps professionals is also shifting. By understanding these trends, engineers can stay ahead of the curve and actively shape the future of DevOps.

This chapter explains these emerging trends through real-world examples, case studies, and thought-provoking insights. It also challenges you to think critically about how they will impact your own development workflows and infrastructure strategies.

The practical impact of platform engineering is vividly demonstrated by organizations that have successfully implemented these principles at scale. Netflix's internal platform, aptly named *Paved Road*, serves as a compelling example of how Platform Engineering transforms software delivery. This comprehensive developer ecosystem enables thousands of engineers to deploy microservices using standardized pipelines, monitoring templates, and infrastructure patterns. By providing these curated paths, *Netflix* dramatically reduces the cognitive load on developers while ensuring consistent quality, security, and operational excellence across their vast technology landscape.

Shopify presents another instructive case study in Platform Engineering excellence. Their platform teams manage over 50,000 Kubernetes pods through GitOps workflows powered by Argo CD, enabling them to maintain reliability during peak shopping events like *Black Friday* when transaction volumes increase tenfold within minutes. This sophisticated platform abstracts away the underlying complexity of container orchestration, allowing Shopify's product engineers to focus on creating business value rather than managing infrastructure.

These industry leaders demonstrate that platform engineering is not merely about providing tools but about creating thoughtfully designed, developer-centric experiences that make the right way the easy way. As we explore the emerging trends reshaping DevOps and platform engineering throughout this chapter, these real-world applications will help illustrate how theoretical concepts translate into transformative business outcomes.

Structure

This chapter will cover the following topics:

- AI and machine learning in DevOps
- GitOps for infrastructure management
- Edge computing and DevOps
- NoOps the future of operations
- Serverless architectures and DevOps
- Low-code and no-code platforms
- Quantum computing and DevOps
- DevOps and sustainability
- Future roles in DevOps

Objectives

By the end of this chapter, you will understand the key advancements shaping the future of DevOps and platform engineering. You will learn how AI and GitOps are transforming infrastructure automation, how edge computing is changing deployment models, and why NoOps and serverless architectures are redefining operational roles. This chapter will also introduce you to the growing impact of low-code development, the potential of quantum computing, and the increasing importance of sustainability in DevOps. More importantly, you will gain the ability to critically assess these trends, understand their real-world applications, and position yourself effectively for the future of software engineering.

AI and machine learning in DevOps

The world of DevOps is changing fast, and **artificial intelligence (AI)** and **machine learning (ML)** are playing a big role in this transformation. Traditionally, DevOps relied heavily on human engineers to monitor systems, troubleshoot issues, and optimize performance. But as software development speeds up and infrastructure scales dynamically, manual processes are no longer enough. AI and ML bring intelligence to DevOps workflows, helping teams predict failures before they happen, automate repetitive tasks, and make better decisions based on data.

Let us examine how AI and ML are reshaping DevOps and what this means for the future of software delivery.

AI-powered monitoring and incident response

Imagine you are running a large-scale web application serving millions of users. A sudden spike in traffic could overload your servers, causing downtime. Traditionally, engineers would rely on dashboards and alerts to catch these issues, but by the time they act, the damage is already done.

This is where AI-powered monitoring tools like Datadog, Dynatrace, and New Relic come in. These tools collect logs and metrics and analyze them in real-time using machine learning.

Here is what they can do:

- **Anomaly detection:** AI models learn the normal behavior of your system (CPU usage, memory consumption, network traffic) and can spot deviations instantly. If your database suddenly starts slowing down, the system raises an early warning before users notice a problem.

- **Automated root cause analysis:** Instead of digging through endless logs, AI correlates logs, traces, and metrics to pinpoint the cause of an issue, whether it is a buggy deployment, a memory leak, or an overloaded service.

- **Self-healing systems:** Some platforms use AI to take automatic action, like rolling back a failed deployment, restarting a crashed service, or rerouting traffic away from a failing node. This means fewer late-night emergency calls for engineers.

Predictive analytics

One of the biggest challenges in DevOps is managing infrastructure efficiently. Allocating too many resources wastes money, while allocating too few slows down or crashes applications. AI helps teams predict future needs and adjust resources dynamically.

Cloud platforms like AWS, Azure, and Google Cloud now offer AI-powered autoscaling. Here is how it works:

- Instead of scaling servers based on fixed rules, AI analyzes past traffic patterns and forecasts future demand.

- If your system sees more users logging in every morning at 9 AM, AI learns this trend and automatically scales up servers before the traffic spike hits.

- If your application suddenly starts consuming more memory due to a software update, AI can recommend optimization strategies or scale resources accordingly.

This kind of predictive scaling leads to cost savings, better performance, and fewer unexpected outages.

AI-enhanced CI/CD pipelines

CI/CD is the backbone of modern software delivery. However, not every change should be deployed instantly; some changes introduce bugs or security risks.

AI makes CI/CD pipelines smarter by:

- **Prioritizing tests efficiently:** Instead of running a full test suite every time, AI selects the most relevant tests based on code changes, saving time without compromising quality.

- **Automated code reviews:** Tools like DeepCode and Codacy scan pull requests for security vulnerabilities, coding errors, and performance issues, giving developers instant feedback before merging.

- **Predicting deployment failures:** AI models analyze past deployments and estimate the risk of a new release causing issues. If a deployment is likely to fail, the system can alert engineers or even delay the rollout until further validation.

By making CI/CD pipelines more intelligent, AI helps teams release software faster and with fewer errors.

AI for security

Security is a critical concern in DevOps, and AI is becoming a powerful weapon against cyber threats. Traditional security monitoring relies on predefined rules, like blocking a specific IP address after multiple failed login attempts. However, attackers are constantly evolving, and static rules do not always catch new threats.

AI-driven security tools (like Darktrace, Microsoft Defender, and CrowdStrike) analyze network traffic, user behavior, and system logs in real-time.

They can do the following:

- **Detect unusual behavior:** If an AI system notices a server making suspicious outbound connections at 3 AM, it flags it as a potential attack.

- **Identify insider threats:** AI can track user behavior and detect anomalies, such as a developer suddenly accessing sensitive production systems they have never touched before.

- **Automate compliance checks:** AI continuously scans infrastructure for security misconfigurations (e.g., open ports, weak encryption) and provides remediation suggestions.

With AI-enhanced security, teams can catch threats earlier and respond faster, reducing the risk of breaches and downtime.

AI-powered chatbots and assistants

Would it not be great if you could ask an AI assistant, *Why is my Kubernetes cluster running slow?* and get an instant answer? That is precisely what AI-powered chatbots and virtual assistants do.

- Microsoft Copilot, AWS Q, and Google Bard are being integrated into DevOps workflows to assist engineers.

- These AI assistants can answer questions, fetch logs, suggest fixes, and even trigger automated workflows, all through a simple chat interface.

- Some teams use AI-powered bots in Slack or Microsoft Teams to provide real-time system health updates and take action based on commands.

This reduces engineers' time digging through dashboards and allows them to focus on solving real problems instead of searching for data.

Future of AI in DevOps

AI and ML are not just trends; they are shaping the future of DevOps. However, let us understand what the future look like:

- **AI-generated IaC:** Instead of manually writing Terraform or Kubernetes YAML files, AI could generate optimal configurations based on high-level requirements.

- **Fully autonomous DevOps Pipelines:** In the future, AI may handle everything from writing code to testing, deploying, and monitoring, with human engineers acting as supervisors.

- **AI-driven software architecture optimization:** AI could analyze system performance and suggest better architectures, helping teams improve efficiency and scalability without trial and error.

However, AI is not a replacement for human engineers. It is a tool that augments our abilities, automating repetitive tasks while allowing DevOps professionals to focus on innovation and problem-solving.

AI and ML are revolutionizing the way we build, deploy, and manage software. From predictive analytics to intelligent automation, AI is helping DevOps teams work faster, smarter, and more efficiently.

However, adopting AI in DevOps is not just about using fancy tools, it is about changing the way we think about operations:

- Instead of reacting to incidents, we can predict and prevent them.

- Instead of manually fine-tuning infrastructure, we can let AI optimize it dynamically.

- Instead of being overwhelmed by data, we can use AI to extract meaningful insights in real time.

The transformative potential of AI in DevOps is already being realized across multiple industries. Uber's sophisticated Michelangelo Machine Learning Platform exemplifies this integration, powering critical operational functions including ride demand predictions, dynamic fare calculations, and intelligent system auto-scaling based on anticipated user patterns. This platform does not merely analyze data, it actively orchestrates infrastructure decisions that would previously require human judgment and intervention.

Google's AutoML for cloud operations demonstrates another dimension of AI's impact, using advanced predictive models to identify potential server failures before they occur. By analyzing patterns across thousands of system metrics, these models can detect subtle anomalies that would be impossible for human operators to identify, enabling preemptive remediation before users experience any impact.

The tangible benefits of these approaches are significant. Financial services organizations implementing IBM's Watson AIOps have reported a 35% reduction in **mean time to remediate** (**MTTR**) across their technology portfolios. This improvement translates directly to enhanced service reliability, reduced operational costs, and improved customer experience.

Leading organizations are leveraging specialized tools in this space, including Datadog's AIOps capabilities for anomaly detection, Moogsoft for event correlation and incident prediction, and Splunk ITSI for service intelligence. As these technologies continue to mature, the boundary between human and machine decision-making in operations will increasingly blur, with AI handling routine analysis and humans focusing on strategic improvements and novel challenges.

GitOps for infrastructure management

Infrastructure management has always been a complex, time-consuming task. In traditional DevOps, teams relied on manual configurations, imperative scripts, and ad-hoc changes, often leading to inconsistencies, drift, and operational headaches. GitOps changes this by treating IaC and automating deployments through version control systems like Git. But GitOps is more than just an infrastructure automation technique, it is a core enabler of Platform Engineering.

Platform engineering is about creating a developer-centric ecosystem where infrastructure and application environments are self-service, scalable, and reliable. GitOps ensures that infrastructure remains consistent, version-controlled, and fully automated, reducing friction for developers while improving operational stability.

Let us dive into how GitOps transforms infrastructure management and its critical role in platform engineering.

GitOps

GitOps is an operational model where Git is the single source of truth for both infrastructure and application deployments. Any change to infrastructure, whether it is provisioning a new database, updating Kubernetes configurations, or scaling services, is made via Git pull requests and automatically applied through automated pipelines.

The key principles of GitOps are:

- **Declarative infrastructure:** Infrastructure is defined in code (e.g., Kubernetes manifests, Terraform files, Helm charts).

- **Version-controlled changes:** Every infrastructure change is committed to Git, providing a clear history and audit trail.

- **Automated synchronization:** A GitOps agent (like Argo CD or Flux) continuously ensures that the live infrastructure matches the desired state in Git.

- **Rollback and recovery:** If something goes wrong, reverting to a previous stable state is as simple as rolling back a Git commit.

This methodology aligns perfectly with platform engineering because it allows teams to automate infrastructure provisioning and maintenance, reducing manual intervention and ensuring consistency across environments.

GitOps and platform engineering

Platform engineering is about providing self-service platforms for developers to deploy and manage applications without needing to interact directly with the infrastructure. GitOps is a key component in this because it abstracts complexity and makes infrastructure changes seamless. GitOps empowers platform engineering as follows:

- **Self-service infrastructure:** Developers do not need to wait for operations teams to provision resources. They simply commit a change to a Git repository, and the platform automatically applies it.

- **Standardized environments:** Infrastructure is defined as code, ensuring that all environments (dev, staging, production) remain consistent and aligned with compliance policies.

- **Faster deployments with fewer errors:** Changes go through Git-based workflows, including peer reviews and automated testing, reducing misconfigurations and human errors.

- **Security and compliance built-in:** Since every infrastructure change is logged in Git, it provides an immutable audit trail, critical for regulatory compliance and security.

By implementing GitOps, platform engineering teams eliminate the need for manual intervention, allowing developers to focus on writing code while infrastructure teams ensure the platform remains reliable, scalable, and secure.

GitOps workflow

A GitOps workflow typically looks like the following:

- **Developer requests a change:** A developer or infrastructure engineer makes a change to an IaC file (e.g., a Kubernetes YAML file or a Terraform module) in a Git repository.

- **Pull request and review:** The change is submitted as a pull request (PR), reviewed by peers, and subjected to automated tests (such as linting, security scans, or validation checks).

- **Merge and apply:** Once approved, the change is merged into the main branch. A GitOps tool (like Argo CD or Flux) detects the change and automatically applies it to the live infrastructure.

- **Continuous reconciliation:** The GitOps agent continuously monitors the live environment and reconciles any drift. If someone manually changes infrastructure outside Git, GitOps detects it and corrects it, ensuring consistency.

- **Rollback if needed:** If something breaks, rolling back is as simple as reverting the last Git commit. The GitOps agent will automatically restore the previous state.

GitOps is particularly powerful in Kubernetes environments because Kubernetes itself is declarative. Popular tools like Argo CD, Flux, and Jenkins integrate seamlessly with Kubernetes to manage deployments, scaling, and configuration updates. As organizations scale, managing infrastructure across multiple Kubernetes clusters or cloud providers becomes a challenge. GitOps extends beyond single-cluster setups to multi-cluster and multi-cloud environments, ensuring:

- **Centralized management:** A single Git repository can control infrastructure across AWS, Azure, and Google Cloud.

- **Policy enforcement:** GitOps tools enforce policies across all clusters, ensuring compliance and security.

- **Cross-cluster deployments:** Workloads can be deployed across multiple regions automatically.

Platform engineering teams leverage this to build scalable, hybrid-cloud platforms, giving developers the flexibility to deploy anywhere without worrying about the underlying infrastructure.

Challenges and best practices for GitOps

While GitOps offers tremendous benefits, implementing it effectively across an organization requires thoughtful planning and discipline. Organizations often encounter several challenges when scaling GitOps practices, from maintaining consistency to managing the complexity of multiple environments.

The core promise of GitOps, infrastructure defined as code with Git as the single source of truth, breaks down quickly if teams start making manual changes to environments.

To implement GitOps successfully, consider the following essential practices:

- **Enforce the No Direct Changes rule:** Implement technical guardrails that prevent manual modifications to production environments. All changes must flow through Git repositories, ensuring complete auditability and reproducibility. Some teams use admission controllers in Kubernetes to reject any resources not applied through their GitOps controllers.

- **Establish robust access controls:** Design your permission structure carefully, using branch protections and required reviews in Git alongside role-based access control in your infrastructure. A financial services client reduced security incidents by 70% after implementing a model where even senior engineers could not merge infrastructure changes without peer review.

- **Adopt mature branching strategies:** Apply software engineering best practices to your infrastructure code. Use feature branches for infrastructure changes, implement thorough code reviews, and consider environment-specific branches that reflect your promotion process from development to production.

- **Build comprehensive observability:** Monitoring becomes even more critical with GitOps. Implement systems that track not just application performance but also the reconciliation process itself. Leading organizations set up alerts for drift detection and reconciliation failures, treating them as critical incidents.

- **Integrate security throughout:** Automate security scanning of infrastructure definitions before changes reach production. This includes checking for misconfigurations, overly permissive settings, and known vulnerabilities in container images or dependencies.

The most successful GitOps implementations also invest heavily in developer experience. A retail platform team created simplified templates and abstractions that allowed application teams to define their infrastructure needs without becoming Kubernetes experts while still enforcing organizational standards through their GitOps pipeline.

GitOps represents a fundamental shift in infrastructure management that aligns perfectly with platform engineering goals. By treating infrastructure as code and leveraging Git's powerful collaboration features, organizations create the foundation for truly developer-centric platforms.

The most compelling aspect of GitOps is not the technology itself but the organizational transformation it enables. Development teams gain unprecedented autonomy, while operations teams can focus on platform improvements rather than manual deployments.

The real-world impact of GitOps is demonstrated by organizations that have implemented these principles at scale. Weaveworks' GitOps Engine powers Intuit's deployment platform, enabling them to manage over 2,000 applications across multiple Kubernetes clusters with unprecedented consistency and reliability. By centralizing their infrastructure definitions in Git repositories and automating the synchronization process, Intuit has significantly reduced deployment errors and accelerated their release cycles.

Amazon EKS users have similarly embraced GitOps principles, with large enterprises managing hundreds of microservices entirely through Git-based workflows. These organizations treat their infrastructure repositories as the single source of truth, with systems like Argo CD continuously reconciling the actual state with the desired state defined in these repositories.

The quantifiable benefits of this approach are compelling. Fidelity Investments transitioned over 500 services to GitOps-based deployment models, resulting in a remarkable 70% reduction in deployment-related errors. This improvement stems from the inherent advantages of GitOps: version-controlled infrastructure changes, mandatory peer reviews, automated validation, and a clear audit trail for every modification.

The GitOps ecosystem continues to evolve rapidly, with tools like Argo CD, FluxCD, Jenkins X, and GitHub Actions providing increasingly sophisticated capabilities for declarative infrastructure management. These platforms are extending beyond basic Kubernetes deployments to encompass database changes, network configurations, and even cloud provider settings, moving toward a future where all infrastructure components are managed through version-controlled declarations.

Edge computing and DevOps

Edge computing fundamentally transforms how we build and deploy applications by pushing computation closer to data sources and users. For platform engineers, this shift introduces a new frontier, extending developer-centric platforms beyond centralized clouds to a diverse ecosystem of edge locations. This evolution creates both unique challenges and exciting opportunities to reimagine how we build infrastructure.

The traditional cloud computing model, with its centralized data centers, has proven insufficient for applications requiring near-instantaneous response times or those generating massive data volumes.

Consider a telecommunications company that found out that its cloud-based video analytics platform could not deliver the performance needed for real-time traffic monitoring. By moving processing to edge nodes near cameras, they reduced latency from seconds to milliseconds, completely transforming the user experience.

Edge computing brings computing resources closer to where data originates, enabling:

- Ultra-low latency for time-sensitive applications like autonomous vehicles and industrial automation.

- Bandwidth optimization by processing data locally instead of transmitting everything to the cloud.

- Enhanced reliability with operations that continue even during cloud connectivity disruptions.

- Improved privacy by keeping sensitive data processing local rather than in centralized locations.

For platform engineering teams, edge computing dramatically expands the scope of what must be managed. Instead of a handful of cloud regions, platforms now extend to potentially thousands of distributed locations with varying capabilities, connectivity, and environmental conditions.

Building developer-centric edge platforms

The core challenge for platform engineers is how to extend modern platforms' self-service, developer-friendly experience to this heterogeneous edge environment. Simply applying cloud-native practices without adaptation does not work.

A manufacturing client attempted to use their standard cloud deployment pipeline for edge devices in their factories, only to discover frequent failures from network disruptions and resource constraints. Their platform team had to rethink their entire approach, creating an edge-aware platform that could handle these unique challenges.

Successful edge platforms typically address several key areas.

Deployment and configuration management

Traditional CI/CD pipelines assume consistent, always-connected environments. Edge environments require more resilient approaches:

- GitOps with store-and-forward capabilities that can queue changes during disconnected periods.

- Lightweight container orchestration using specialized Kubernetes distributions like K3s or MicroK8s.

- Progressive deployment patterns with canary testing and automatic rollbacks to prevent widespread outages.

- Differential updates that minimize bandwidth usage by sending only changed components.

Resource optimization

Edge nodes often have limited computing capabilities compared to cloud environments:

- Workload-specific hardware acceleration using GPUs, TPUs, or FPGAs for AI/ML processing.

- Intelligent workload placement that balances processing between edge nodes and the cloud.

- Efficient containerization with minimized images specifically optimized for edge deployment.

- Dynamic resource allocation that adapts to changing conditions and priorities.

An energy company deployed edge computing across hundreds of remote substations with limited computing resources. Their platform team created standardized hardware profiles and workload templates that developers could target without needing to understand the underlying constraints. The platform automatically optimized each deployment based on available resources and application priorities.

Observability at scale

Monitoring distributed edge deployments presents unique challenges:

- Hierarchical monitoring architectures that aggregate data at multiple levels.

- Local buffering and selective transmission of telemetry data to manage bandwidth constraints.

- Edge-based anomaly detection that can identify issues without cloud connectivity.

- Automated remediation capabilities that can address common problems locally.

A healthcare organization we consulted with implemented an observability system for their edge-based patient monitoring platform that could detect and address issues locally while smartly prioritizing which telemetry data to send to their central operations. Critical alerts were pushed immediately, while routine metrics were batched and compressed to conserve bandwidth.

Security and compliance

Edge environments often exist outside traditional security perimeters:

- Zero Trust security models that assume no implicit trust between components.

- Automated certificate management for secure communication between edge nodes and the cloud.

- Secure hardware enclaves that protect sensitive data even on physically accessible devices.

- Consistent policy enforcement across the entire platform footprint.

A financial services company extended its platform to include ATMs and point-of-sale systems. The platform team implemented a comprehensive security framework that included secure boot processes, encrypted storage, and continuous verification of software integrity. This approach allowed the company to meet regulatory requirements while still enabling rapid deployment of new features.

The most successful edge platforms share a common characteristic: they abstract complexity without hiding it completely. Developers need to understand the unique characteristics of edge environments but should not have to become experts in distributed systems to deploy applications.

A smart city initiative we worked on demonstrates this balance. The platform engineering team created a unified development experience where application teams could build once and deploy across cloud and edge environments.

The platform handled the underlying complexities:

- Automatically optimizing container images for resource-constrained edge devices.

- Managing intermittent connectivity with store-and-forward deployment mechanisms.

- Providing consistent observability across all environments.

- Enforcing security policies appropriate to each deployment target.

This approach enabled developers to focus on building innovative applications while the platform handled the complexities of the distributed infrastructure. Traffic management applications could process video streams locally at the edge while sending aggregated data to the cloud for long-term analysis and planning.

As edge computing continues to evolve, platform engineering teams are exploring new frontiers:

- Mesh architectures that enable edge nodes to collaborate directly without cloud mediation.

- Edge-native development frameworks that help developers build applications optimized for distributed environments.

- AI-augmented operations that use machine learning to manage increasingly complex edge deployments.

- Cross-vendor edge standardization that simplifies deploying to heterogeneous edge environments.

The most forward-thinking organizations are already building unified platforms that span from cloud to edge, providing consistent developer experiences regardless of where workloads run. This approach does not just solve today's edge challenges, it creates a foundation for whatever comes next in our increasingly distributed computing landscape.

By embracing these principles and approaches, platform engineers can extend developer-centric ecosystems all the way to the edge, enabling innovation while maintaining the reliability, security, and operational excellence that organizations require.

The practical implementations of edge computing are reshaping how platform teams design and deploy applications across industries. Cloudflare Workers exemplifies this transformation, serving approximately 30% of internet requests from edge locations strategically positioned for minimal latency. This distributed execution model enables applications to respond to user interactions within milliseconds rather than hundreds of milliseconds, creating fundamentally different user experiences that would not be possible with traditional cloud architectures.

Content delivery pioneers like Netflix have embraced edge computing through their Open Connect program, which positions specialized edge servers within internet service provider networks. These servers cache video content physically closer to viewers, dramatically improving streaming quality while reducing bandwidth costs across their global customer base. This approach demonstrates how edge computing can simultaneously enhance user experience and operational efficiency.

The performance improvements enabled by edge computing are substantial. Verizon's 5G Edge infrastructure has demonstrated 40% reductions in application response times for connected vehicle applications, transforming what's possible for real-time services that require instantaneous processing. This latency reduction enables entirely new categories of applications that simply wouldn't function with traditional cloud architectures.

Platform engineering teams are leveraging specialized tools to build these edge capabilities, including AWS Greengrass for extending cloud applications to local devices, Azure IoT Edge for intelligent processing at the network edge, and Akamai EdgeWorkers for running custom code at global edge locations. These tools provide the foundation for next-generation applications that blend cloud scalability with edge responsiveness, creating experiences that were not previously possible.

NoOps the future of operations

The DevOps landscape continues to evolve at a rapid pace, with automation becoming increasingly sophisticated. At the cutting edge of this evolution lies NoOps, a vision where operations become so automated that developers can focus solely on delivering value through code without worrying about operational concerns. While the name might suggest *no operations*, the reality is more nuanced, operations do not disappear but are instead transformed through platform-driven automation.

The concept of NoOps represents a natural progression in our journey from traditional operations to DevOps and now to increasingly automated approaches. We witnessed this progression firsthand at a financial services company that transformed from having 20 engineers manually deploying applications to a model where developers pushed code, and a sophisticated platform handled everything else, from testing to deployment, scaling, and monitoring. This transformation was not about eliminating their operations team but rather shifting their focus from repetitive tasks to building powerful automation.

At its core, NoOps is built on several foundational elements that work together to minimize manual operational intervention:

- **Full-stack automation** is the backbone of any NoOps environment. Everything from infrastructure provisioning to application deployment, monitoring, and even incident response becomes codified and automated. A healthcare organization we consulted with automated 95% of their operational tasks, allowing their small platform team to support hundreds of applications across multiple environments.

- **Self-healing systems** can detect and remediate issues automatically. These systems use predefined rules and increasingly sophisticated AI to identify anomalies and take corrective action without human intervention. For example, modern platforms can automatically restart failed services, scale resources based on demand, and even roll back problematic deployments.

- **Platform as a product** thinking treats internal developer platforms as products designed for developer experience. These platforms abstract away infrastructure complexity behind intuitive interfaces, making deployment and operations accessible to developers without specialized operational knowledge. A media company built a developer portal that allowed their content teams to deploy new features without understanding the underlying Kubernetes clusters or cloud infrastructure.

- **AI-augmented operations** leverage machine learning to predict potential issues before they impact users. These systems analyze patterns across metrics, logs, and events to identify anomalies that might indicate future problems. Several organizations now use AI to detect potential outages hours or even days before they occur, enabling proactive resolution.

NoOps through platform engineering

Platform engineering teams are the architects of NoOps environments, creating the self-service capabilities and automation that make operations invisible to developers. Rather than eliminating operations, platform engineering elevates it to focus on enabling developer productivity through automation.

A retail platform we worked with transformed its operations approach through platform engineering. Their journey illustrates the practical reality of moving toward NoOps:

- They started by identifying the most common operational tasks that slowed down their developers, environment provisioning, database creation, deployment pipelines, and monitoring setup.

- Their platform team built self-service capabilities that allowed developers to perform these tasks without operational involvement, using standardized templates that enforced best practices.

- They implemented GitOps for automated deployments, where code changes in version control automatically triggered testing and deployment without manual intervention.

- They integrated AI-driven monitoring tools that could detect anomalies and either resolve them automatically or provide detailed context to developers.

The results were transformative. Deployment frequency increased by 300%, while incidents decreased by 60%. Most importantly, developers spent more time on innovation and less on operational concerns

Real-world applications of NoOps

NoOps principles are already being applied in various domains, demonstrating practical benefits beyond theoretical appeal, as follows:

- **Serverless computing** represents one of the purest forms of NoOps in action. Services like AWS Lambda, Azure Functions, and Google Cloud Functions completely abstract away the underlying infrastructure. Developers simply write code, and the platform handles everything else, scaling, high availability, and infrastructure management. A media streaming service we advised reduced their operational overhead by 70% by moving to a serverless architecture for their content processing pipeline.

- **Kubernetes with GitOps** combines the power of container orchestration with automated deployment pipelines. When implemented correctly, developers never interact directly with clusters, they simply push code to Git repositories, and platforms like Argo CD or Flux automatically synchronize the desired state with the actual state of the system. This approach dramatically reduces the operational burden while improving consistency and reliability.

- **AI-driven operations** use machine learning to detect, diagnose, and remediate issues automatically. Tools like Datadog, Dynatrace, and New Relic increasingly incorporate AI to identify potential problems before they impact users. Some organizations have reduced their **mean time to resolution** (**MTTR**) by over 80% by implementing AI-driven incident response, with many routine issues being resolved before anyone receives an alert.

Challenges and limitations

Despite its promise, NoOps is not without challenges. Not all applications are suited for fully automated operations, particularly legacy systems designed for different operational models. Security and compliance requirements may necessitate human oversight in regulated industries. And the journey toward NoOps requires significant investment in platform capabilities and cultural change.

A manufacturing company we worked with discovered these challenges when attempting to implement NoOps principles. Their mix of modern microservices and legacy systems meant they could not achieve full automation overnight. Instead, they adopted a pragmatic approach: implementing NoOps for new applications while gradually modernizing legacy systems. This hybrid approach allowed them to realize benefits incrementally rather than waiting for a complete transformation.

As we look toward the future, operations will not disappear, but they will be transformed. Platform engineering teams will focus less on day-to-day operational tasks and more on building powerful abstractions and automation that enable developers. AI will play an increasingly important role in predicting and preventing issues before they impact users. And the boundary between development and operations will continue to blur as more operational concerns are addressed through code and automation.

The most successful organizations would not eliminate their operations teams but would transform them into platform engineers focused on creating developer-centric ecosystems. These platforms will make infrastructure invisible to developers, allowing them to focus on delivering business value through code. The result will be faster innovation, improved reliability, and more efficient use of technology resources.

NoOps represents not the end of operations but its evolution from manual intervention to strategic enablement through platform engineering. As automation continues to advance, the role of operations will shift toward creating and maintaining the platforms that make this automation possible, ultimately enabling developers to focus on what they do best: building innovative solutions to business problems.

Leading technology organizations are actively implementing NoOps principles to achieve unprecedented operational efficiency. Netflix's Titus Platform represents a sophisticated implementation of NoOps concepts, providing fully self-managed container orchestration that operates with minimal human intervention. This platform handles the complete lifecycle of containerized applications, from deployment to scaling to eventual decommissioning, enabling Netflix's engineering teams to focus on content delivery innovation rather than operational concerns.

Heroku pioneered many NoOps concepts through their PaaS model, where developers simply push code, and the platform autonomously handles all aspects of deployment, scaling, patching, and monitoring. This approach creates a developer experience completely abstracted from underlying infrastructure complexity, dramatically accelerating delivery cycles while maintaining operational excellence.

The progress toward NoOps is measurable. Capital One's serverless platform team reports that approximately 90% of their services now operate without routine human intervention, with automation handling everything from deployment to scaling to incident response. This shift has allowed them to reallocate significant engineering resources from operational maintenance to customer-facing innovation.

These examples highlight the essential characteristic of successful NoOps implementations: they don't eliminate operations work but rather transform it from manual intervention to strategic platform engineering. The organizations achieving the greatest success with NoOps recognize that building sophisticated self-service platforms requires significant initial investment but yields exponential returns through enhanced developer productivity and operational reliability.

Serverless architectures and DevOps

Serverless architecture represents one of the most transformative shifts in modern application development, fundamentally changing how we build, deploy, and scale applications. At its core, serverless computing allows developers to focus almost exclusively on writing code that delivers business value while cloud providers handle the underlying infrastructure management. This paradigm shift has profound implications for DevOps practices and aligns perfectly with the goals of platform engineering, simplifying the developer experience while maintaining operational excellence.

Evolution of infrastructure management

Serverless computing represents the natural progression in how we manage infrastructure, as shown:

- **Traditional infrastructure:** Physical servers in data centers requiring manual setup and maintenance.

- **Infrastructure as a service (IaaS):** Virtual machines in the cloud with automated provisioning.

- **Platform as a service (PaaS):** Managed environments handling some operational concerns.

- **Containers:** Lightweight, portable units of deployment with orchestration.

- **Serverless:** Function-based computing with no infrastructure management.

Each step in this evolution has abstracted away more infrastructure complexity, allowing developers to focus increasingly on application logic rather than operational concerns. Serverless takes this abstraction to its logical conclusion, developers simply write functions that respond to events, and the cloud provider handles everything else, from provisioning to scaling to maintenance.

This does not mean servers disappear; they are still there, but their management becomes the responsibility of the cloud provider rather than your operations team. Functions run on infrastructure that is provisioned on-demand, scaled automatically based on load, and billed only for actual execution time.

Serverless and DevOps

Serverless architecture fundamentally changes the DevOps lifecycle in several keyways:

- **Deployment simplification:** Traditional deployments involve complex orchestration of servers, networking, and storage. With serverless, deployments focus on function code and event triggers. A retail company we worked with reduced their deployment process from dozens of steps to just a few, pushing code to a repository, which triggered automatic testing and deployment of functions. This simplification dramatically reduced deployment times and eliminated many potential failure points.

- **Automatic scaling:** One of the most challenging aspects of operations is capacity planning and scaling. Serverless architectures handle this automatically, scaling from zero to thousands of instances based on demand. A media streaming service experienced a viral moment when one of its videos was shared widely on social media. Their serverless backend scaled seamlessly from handling hundreds of requests per minute to hundreds of thousands without any manual intervention or pre-planning.

- **Monitoring and observability evolution:** Serverless requires rethinking monitoring approaches. Instead of server metrics like CPU and memory, the focus shifts to function execution times, error rates, and event processing statistics. The challenge lies in correlating events across a distributed system of functions. A telecommunications company implemented distributed tracing across their serverless functions, allowing them to track requests as they flowed through multiple services and pinpoint performance bottlenecks that would have been nearly impossible to identify in traditional architectures.

- **Security transformation:** Security practices evolve significantly with serverless. The attack surface changes from server-level vulnerabilities to function configuration and code-level security. Functions operate with specific permissions using **identity and access management (IAM)** roles, creating a more granular security model. A healthcare organization implemented a principle of least privilege across its serverless functions, with each function having only the specific permissions needed for its task, dramatically reducing its potential attack surface.

Platform engineering for serverless environments

Platform engineering is crucial in making serverless architectures accessible and manageable at scale. While serverless abstracts infrastructure complexity, it introduces new challenges around function management, event coordination, and observability that platform teams must address.

A financial services company that built a comprehensive platform for serverless development will showcase the key elements of successful serverless platform engineering as follows:

- **Developer self-service portals:** They created intuitive interfaces that allowed developers to create, deploy, and manage serverless functions without deep AWS expertise. These portals provided templates for common patterns, handled configuration management, and automated the creation of supporting resources like API gateways and event sources.

- **Standardized CI/CD pipelines:** Their platform team built specialized CI/CD pipelines optimized for serverless deployment, handling function packaging, IaC deployment, and integration testing. These pipelines enforced security best practices and ensured consistent approaches across development teams.

- **Centralized observability:** They implemented unified logging, monitoring, and tracing across serverless functions, giving developers visibility into their application behavior without requiring expertise in cloud-specific monitoring tools. Dashboards provided function-specific metrics alongside business KPIs, making it easy to correlate technical performance with business outcomes.

- **Governance frameworks:** To prevent function sprawl and maintain control in a highly distributed environment, they established governance frameworks that enforced naming conventions, tagging standards, and deployment practices. These frameworks struck a balance between developer autonomy and organizational control.

The most compelling aspect of serverless architecture is not the technology itself but the organizational transformation it enables when combined with effective platform engineering.

A retail organization we worked with used serverless architecture as the foundation for their new e-commerce platform. Their platform engineering team created a comprehensive developer ecosystem that handled the complexities of serverless deployment while providing intuitive interfaces for common tasks:

- Developers could deploy new product features without understanding the underlying cloud architecture.

- Operations teams focused on platform improvements rather than day-to-day server management.

- The business gained the ability to scale automatically during peak shopping periods.

- Costs aligned directly with business activity, as they only paid for function execution during actual customer interactions.

The result was a 70% reduction in infrastructure costs, 65% faster feature delivery, and significantly improved reliability during peak shopping periods, all with a smaller operations team than their previous server-based architecture required.

While serverless can be cost-effective, it requires different approaches to cost management. Platform teams are building tools to provide cost visibility, enforce budgets, and optimize function execution to maximize value.

Serverless architecture represents not just a technological shift but a fundamental change in how we approach application development and operations. By abstracting infrastructure complexity and enabling automatic scaling, it allows organizations to focus more on delivering business value and less on operational concerns. Platform engineering makes this promise accessible at scale, providing the tools, frameworks, and practices that enable development teams to leverage serverless effectively while maintaining organizational governance and operational excellence.

The organizations that succeed with serverless will be those that recognize its value not just as a technology but as a catalyst for transforming how development and operations teams collaborate to deliver business value.

The scalability advantages of serverless architectures become particularly evident during high-demand scenarios. Walmart's e-commerce platform leveraged AWS Lambda to handle massive traffic surges during Black Friday 2022, with their serverless functions scaling seamlessly to process over 500,000 invocations per minute at peak periods. This elastic capacity enabled them to accommodate extreme traffic fluctuations without the complex capacity planning and over-provisioning that would be required with traditional architecture.

Serverless approaches extend beyond web applications to power innovative IoT solutions. Coca-Cola's Freestyle beverage machines represent a compelling example, with their entire backend infrastructure running on AWS Lambda, DynamoDB, and API Gateway. This serverless architecture allows thousands of distributed beverage dispensers to operate independently while maintaining a lightweight cloud connection for recipe updates, inventory management, and usage analytics.

The operational benefits of serverless extend to media processing workflows as well. Netflix's serverless encoding system automatically scales to process over 200,000 video files daily, adjusting capacity based on current encoding demands without requiring manual intervention. This approach enables them to optimize processing resources precisely when needed while maintaining near-zero costs during periods of inactivity.

These implementations demonstrate that serverless architectures aren't merely conceptual alternatives but proven approaches for handling real-world, large-scale workloads. By abstracting infrastructure management and providing true consumption-based pricing, serverless enables organizations to focus engineering resources on business differentiation rather than infrastructure maintenance. The most successful implementations combine serverless with effective platform engineering, creating developer-friendly interfaces that make serverless capabilities accessible without requiring specialized cloud expertise.

Low-code and no-code platforms

Low-code and no-code platforms simplify and accelerate software development by reducing the need for extensive coding. They empower developers, business users, and operations teams with visual interfaces, drag-and-drop components, and automation tools. These platforms play a crucial role in platform engineering, enabling self-service ecosystems and bridging the gap between development and operations.

Here is a breakdown of their key aspects:

- **What are low-code and no-code platforms:**
    - Low-code platforms cater to developers by offering pre-built components and automation tools, requiring minimal hand-coding.
    - No-code platforms target business users, enabling application creation through drag-and-drop interfaces without programming knowledge.
- **Examples of low-code and no-code platforms:**
    - **Low-code**:
        - **OutSystems and Mendix**: Full-stack low-code development with backend, frontend, and database integration.
        - **Microsoft Power Apps**: Business application development with minimal coding.
        - **Retool**: Rapid internal tool development with database connectivity.
    - **No-code**:
        - **Zapier and Integromat**: Automate workflows by connecting applications without scripting.
        - **Bubble and Adalo**: Build web and mobile apps without coding.
        - **Airtable**: No-code database that replaces spreadsheets with API integrations.
    - **Role in platform engineering**:
        - **Speeds up development**: Applications can be built in days instead of weeks using pre-built modules.

- **Empowers non-developers**: Business users can automate workflows without engineering support.

- **Enhances self-service infrastructure**: Developers can deploy test environments using low-code IaC tools without waiting for operations teams.

- **Use cases:**

  o A **SaaS developer** using Retool to build an internal system log dashboard in minutes.

  o A **marketing team** automating customer onboarding emails with Zapier.

  o A **DevOps team** defining pipelines visually using no-code GitHub Actions.

  o A **platform engineering team** creating a self-service portal for provisioning and monitoring infrastructure.

- **Limitations to consider:**

  o No-code tools lack flexibility for complex applications.

  o Proprietary low-code platforms may lead to vendor lock-in.

  o Performance issues can arise in high-scale applications.

  o Pre-built components may introduce security vulnerabilities.

- **Future of low-code and no-code:**

  o AI-powered development tools like GitHub Copilot and OpenAI's Codex will enhance low-code environments.

  o Cloud-native low-code platforms will integrate deeper with Kubernetes and serverless architectures.

  o Security-focused no-code solutions will ensure compliance and safe deployments.

Low-code and no-code platforms would not replace engineers but will enhance efficiency, accessibility, and innovation. By leveraging these tools, Platform Engineering can build self-service ecosystems, accelerating digital transformation and fostering seamless collaboration between technical and non-technical teams.

The adoption of low-code and no-code platforms is accelerating rapidly across industries as organizations seek to democratize development capabilities. Microsoft Power Platform exemplifies this trend, with over 15 million monthly active users creating business applications, automated workflows, and data visualizations with minimal traditional coding. Even large enterprises like Coca-Cola, Heathrow Airport, and Toyota have implemented Power Platform centers of excellence to govern and scale their low-code initiatives while maintaining necessary governance controls.

Internal tools development has been particularly transformed by low-code approaches. Retool, a popular low-code platform for internal applications, reports that engineering teams at companies like Amazon, DoorDash, and Brex build critical operational dashboards and administrative interfaces in days rather than weeks. These tools connect directly to production databases and APIs while implementing proper access controls and audit logging, enabling rapid development without compromising security.

The integration of these platforms with DevOps practices is creating new possibilities for operational efficiency. Salesforce's Flow automation platform processes over 2 billion workflow executions daily, many of which automate traditionally manual operational processes. This convergence of low-code accessibility with production-grade reliability represents a significant evolution in how organizations approach internal tool development.

Platform engineering teams are increasingly incorporating these low-code capabilities into their developer ecosystems, creating hybrid experiences that combine the accessibility of visual development with the power of traditional coding when needed. This approach enables a broader range of contributors to participate in the software development process while ensuring that the resulting applications meet enterprise requirements for security, scalability, and maintainability.

Quantum computing and DevOps

Quantum computing is a transformative technology with the potential to revolutionize problem-solving across industries. As it moves from theory to practical applications, platform engineering teams must adapt DevOps practices to support quantum software development. This requires integrating quantum computing with classical infrastructure, rethinking testing methodologies, and addressing unique challenges like security, monitoring, and resource management.

Here is a breakdown of the key aspects:

- **Fundamentals of quantum computing:**

  o Quantum computers use **qubits**, which leverage superposition and entanglement to perform calculations differently from classical computers.

  o Unlike classical bits (0 or 1), qubits can exist in multiple states simultaneously, allowing quantum systems to explore multiple solutions in parallel.

  o Quantum computing has applications in **cryptography**, **pharmaceuticals**, **materials science**, and **finance**, where complex problems require vast computational power.

- **Challenges for DevOps in quantum computing:**

  o **Programming models differ significantly**: Quantum development requires knowledge of quantum mechanics.

- o **Hybrid environments**: Quantum computers rely on classical systems for most functionalities.

- o **Testing complexity**: Quantum results are probabilistic, requiring statistical validation rather than traditional pass/fail tests.

- **Quantum computing development environments:**

  - o **Most quantum computing is done via cloud-based platforms**:
    - IBM Quantum, Amazon Braket, Microsoft Azure Quantum, and Google Quantum AI provide access to quantum processors and simulators.

  - o **Quantum programming languages and frameworks**:
    - Qiskit (IBM), Cirq (Google), Q# (Microsoft), PennyLane (Xanadu) offer quantum circuit development and integration tools.

- **DevOps integration for quantum computing:**

  - o **CI/CD pipelines**: Adapting DevOps workflows to quantum environments for efficient development and deployment.

  - o **Version control**: Managing quantum algorithm changes, ensuring reproducibility despite quantum uncertainties.

  - o **Simulation environments**: Testing quantum software using classical simulators before execution on real quantum hardware.

- **Monitoring and observability in quantum computing:**

  - o Quantum systems require specialized performance metrics beyond CPU and memory usage, such as:
    - **Qubit coherence time**: How long a qubit retains information.
    - **Gate fidelity**: Accuracy of quantum operations.
    - **Quantum error rates**: Likelihood of computation errors due to environmental factors.

  - o **Statistical observability techniques** are needed to analyze quantum results, detect anomalies, and optimize performance.

- **Security Considerations:**

  - o Quantum algorithms like **Shor's algorithm** threaten classical encryption; organizations must explore **quantum-safe cryptography**.

  - o **Access controls** and **data protection strategies** are crucial for shared quantum resources.

  - o Proprietary quantum algorithms require **intellectual property protection** against unauthorized use.

- **Resource and cost management:**
  - Quantum computers are **scarce and expensive**, requiring **queue management** and workload prioritization.
  - Organizations must balance **cost-efficiency** with providing access to quantum resources for research and development.
- **Future of quantum computing in DevOps and platform engineering:**
  - **Higher-level abstractions** will make quantum computing more accessible, similar to how cloud computing evolved.
  - **Automation and API-driven integrations** will enable broader adoption without requiring quantum expertise.
  - Organizations that invest in **quantum-ready platforms today** will gain a competitive edge as quantum computing matures.

The convergence of quantum computing and DevOps is both a technical challenge and a strategic opportunity. Forward-thinking platform engineers will play a crucial role in making quantum technologies practical, scalable, and accessible to development teams worldwide.

While quantum computing remains in its early stages, pioneering organizations are already establishing the DevOps practices necessary for this emerging paradigm. IBM Quantum exemplifies this forward-thinking approach, developing specialized DevOps pipelines for hybrid classical-quantum workloads that leverage Kubernetes and Red Hat OpenShift for orchestration. These pipelines enable researchers to develop, test, and deploy quantum algorithms with similar reliability and reproducibility as traditional software, despite the significant differences in underlying computing models.

Microsoft Azure Quantum provides another example of DevOps principles applied to quantum computing, offering CI/CD pipelines specifically designed for quantum algorithms. These pipelines include specialized testing frameworks that account for the probabilistic nature of quantum computation, validation tools that ensure algorithms will execute correctly on specific quantum hardware, and deployment mechanisms that manage the hybrid quantum-classical execution environment.

Early quantum computing companies are embracing DevOps practices to accelerate their research. Rigetti Computing reports that approximately 80% of their quantum experiments now run through automated DevOps pipelines, significantly improving researcher productivity and experiment reproducibility. These pipelines handle the complex preparation of quantum circuits, manage execution queues across limited quantum resources, and systematically catalog results for subsequent analysis.

These implementations, while still evolving, demonstrate how DevOps principles can be adapted for emerging computing paradigms. The organizations establishing quantum DevOps practices today are not only accelerating their current research but also building the foundations for more accessible quantum computing in the future. Platform engineering teams should monitor these developments closely, as the lessons learned from quantum DevOps may influence practices across other computing domains where deterministic outcomes cannot be guaranteed.

DevOps and sustainability

- **Environmental impact and context:**

  o Data centers now consume approximately 1-2% of global electricity, generating carbon emissions equivalent to the entire airline industry.

  o The environmental footprint of digital systems extends beyond energy usage to include hardware manufacturing impacts, resource utilization efficiency, and electronic waste management challenges.

  o As digital transformation accelerates, platform engineering teams face mounting pressure to address sustainability while maintaining performance.

- **Strategic foundations of sustainable DevOps:**

  o Platform engineering teams occupy a pivotal position in sustainability efforts as they control infrastructure decisions, deployment methodologies, and operational practices.

  o DevOps principles naturally extend to sustainability through their focus on automation, efficiency optimization, and continuous improvement cycles.

  o Environmental responsibility and technical excellence can be pursued as complementary rather than competing priorities.

- **Infrastructure optimization approaches:**

  o Strategically leverage cloud providers' green offerings: renewable energy-powered regions, comprehensive carbon footprint calculators, and detailed sustainability dashboards.

  o Develop and implement infrastructure-as-code templates that default to energy-efficient instance types and automatically scale resources based on actual demand patterns.

  o Embrace architectural approaches that maximize hardware utilization through containerization, serverless computing paradigms, and intelligent workload distribution.

- **Application efficiency enhancement:**

  o Address how inefficient code unnecessarily consumes computing resources, directly increasing energy usage and carbon emissions.

  o Establish clear performance budgets that set explicit limits on resource consumption across application components.

o   Integrate comprehensive sustainability metrics into continuous integration pipelines to identify inefficiencies early.

o   Provide developers with specialized tools to profile code for resource efficiency and frameworks implementing energy-aware design patterns.

- **Data lifecycle and storage optimization:**

o   Confront the environmental challenges posed by exponential growth in data storage requirements.

o   Implement sophisticated data lifecycle management policies that automatically identify, and transition infrequently accessed data to cold storage.

o   Deploy optimization techniques, including compression, deduplication, and efficient storage formats, to minimize physical resource requirements.

o   Balance environmental impact reduction with maintained data availability and integrity through thoughtful governance policies.

- **Comprehensive observability systems:**

o   Expand traditional monitoring beyond performance and reliability to incorporate sustainability indicators into observability frameworks.

o   Track granular metrics, including energy consumption per transaction and carbon emissions per deployment across environments.

o   Implement alerting systems that identify unexpected environmental impact spikes and create dashboards visualizing sustainability trends.

o   Establish feedback loops driving continuous improvement in environmental outcomes through data-driven insights.

- **Organizational culture and practices:**

o   Foster sustainability champions within engineering teams and create cross-functional working groups dedicated to environmental impact reduction.

o   Incorporate meaningful sustainability objectives into team performance metrics and recognition systems.

o   Organize dedicated green days focusing specifically on environmental improvements, sustainability-themed hackathons, and regular knowledge-sharing sessions.

o   Build organizational capability by making sustainability a visible priority and celebrating environmental wins.

- **Supply chain and ecosystem engagement:**

o   Recognize how technology purchasing decisions about vendors, cloud providers, and hardware have significant environmental implications.

o Establish comprehensive sustainability criteria for procurement decisions and require vendors to provide detailed carbon footprint information.

o Prioritize partnerships with organizations demonstrating strong environmental commitments and climate action plans.

o Participate actively in industry initiatives establishing sustainability standards and benchmarks for technology providers.

- **Measurement, reporting and accountability:**

o Implement robust frameworks for calculating operations' carbon footprint using standardized methodologies like the Greenhouse Gas Protocol.

o Establish clear baselines, meaningful improvement targets, and regular transparent reporting against environmental goals.

o Participate in external benchmarking initiatives comparing performance against industry peers to drive competitive improvement.

o Create transparency about the environmental impact that demonstrates organizational commitment to stakeholders.

- **Future evolution and innovation:**

o Anticipate deeper integration of DevOps and sustainability as environmental regulations become more stringent.

o Explore emerging technologies, including carbon-aware scheduling algorithms, sustainable coding languages, and advanced cooling systems.

o Leverage artificial intelligence to optimize resource allocation, predict environmental impact, and automate sustainability improvements.

Position environmental responsibility not merely as compliance but as an innovation opportunity driving both ecological and business benefits.

Industry leaders are demonstrating that sustainability and operational excellence can be complementary rather than competing priorities. Google's data center operations exemplify this synergy, with a commitment to carbon-free energy by 2030 and current operations already running on carbon-free energy for 90% of their hours in 2023. This achievement combines sophisticated energy procurement strategies with advanced workload scheduling that prioritizes regions with available renewable energy.

AWS has integrated sustainability directly into their infrastructure offerings through Graviton processors, which deliver up to 40% better energy efficiency compared to traditional x86 architectures. This improvement demonstrates how environmental considerations are increasingly influencing fundamental infrastructure decisions, with energy efficiency becoming a key metric alongside performance and cost.

The visibility of sustainability metrics is improving dramatically through specialized monitoring tools. Microsoft's sustainability dashboard provides real-time tracking of carbon footprints across all cloud regions, enabling organizations to make informed decisions about workload placement based on environmental impact. These tools are transforming sustainability from a periodic reporting exercise to an ongoing operational consideration.

Platform engineering teams are uniquely positioned to integrate these sustainability practices throughout the technology lifecycle. By building energy efficiency into infrastructure templates, implementing intelligent scheduling that considers environmental impact, and providing developers with visibility into the sustainability implications of their design choices, platform teams can make environmental responsibility an integral part of the development process rather than an afterthought.

Future roles in DevOps

The following are the emerging roles in platform engineering:

- **Evolution of the DevOps landscape:**
  - o DevOps is undergoing a profound transformation driven by AI, complex cloud ecosystems, regulatory pressures, and changing business expectations.
  - o New specializations and hybrid roles are emerging that didn't exist just a few years ago.
  - o Platform engineering continues to mature as a discipline with increasingly specialized functions.

- **AI-powered DevOps transformation:**
  - o AI operations engineers combine machine learning expertise with infrastructure and reliability engineering.
  - o These specialists design platforms for model training, manage AI application deployment, and monitor systems where infrastructure and application boundaries blur.
  - o They implement specialized CI/CD pipelines, including model validation, drift detection, and data quality assessment.
  - o Bridge the historical divide between data science and operations teams.

- **Security integration:**
  - o Security platform engineers build automated controls directly into the infrastructure.
  - o They implement security-as-code and create self-service security capabilities.
  - o Focus shifts from gatekeeping to enabling development through accessible security tools.

o   Approach protection from an engineering and automation perspective rather than a compliance-only mindset.

- **Multi-cloud management**

    o   Cloud orchestration engineers build platforms spanning multiple providers.

    o   They implement consistent governance across diverse environments and optimize workload placement.

    o   Create abstraction layers shielding application teams from underlying infrastructure differences.

    o   Help organizations avoid vendor lock-in while leveraging the unique capabilities of different platforms.

- **Developer experience focus:**

    o   Application platform engineers create higher-level abstractions, allowing developers to focus on business logic.

    o   Design self-service platforms with pre-configured, secure, and compliant environments.

    o   Measure success by developer productivity and software delivery acceleration.

    o   Prioritize user experience for technical teams using internal platforms.

- **Compliance automation:**

    o   Compliance platform engineers translate regulatory requirements into automated controls.

    o   Implement continuous compliance monitoring and automated evidence generation.

    o   Build real-time compliance dashboards and self-service regulatory guidance tools.

    o   Transform governance from manual documentation into automated, continuous activities.

- **Platform as a product:**

    o   Platform product managers approach internal platforms with product thinking.

    o   Focus on business value, stakeholder needs, and strategic alignment.

    o   Track metrics on adoption, efficiency gains, and business outcomes.

    o   Ensure technical excellence translates to tangible business results.

- **Sustainability engineering:**

  o Sustainable operations engineers optimize for energy efficiency and reduce environmental impact.

  o Implement carbon footprint monitoring and resource consumption tracking.

  o Create policies prioritizing workloads based on energy availability.

  o Align platform engineering practices with broader sustainability objectives.

- **Education and enablement:**

  o Developer productivity engineers remove friction points in development workflows.

  o Platform evangelists drive adoption through education and community-building.

  o Knowledge engineers create documentation systems and interactive learning experiences.

  o Focus on ensuring platforms are widely adopted and effectively utilized.

- **Future Outlook:**

  o Organizations will create custom role definitions reflecting specific needs rather than standardized job descriptions.

  o Successful platform engineers will develop T-shaped skill profiles combining depth and breadth.

  o Most valuable professionals will translate between technical and business languages.

  o The core mission remains to create systems that enable others to work more effectively, reliably, and securely.

These emerging roles are already taking shape in forward-thinking organizations building internal developer platforms. Spotify's Backstage, an open-source developer portal framework, has been adopted by major enterprises including Expedia, American Airlines, and Netflix to create unified interfaces for managing developer tools and services. These platforms exemplify the shift toward treating infrastructure as a product, with dedicated teams focused on developer experience and productivity.

Twilio's Internal Developer Platform showcases the scale these specialized teams can support, managing over 4,000 microservices through self-service infrastructure APIs. Their platform team has created standardized templates, automated approval workflows, and comprehensive observability solutions that enable product engineers to deploy and manage services without deep infrastructure expertise.

The organizational impact of these specialized platform roles is substantial. Salesforce's internal platform team supports more than 10,000 developers worldwide with self-service CI/CD, monitoring, and deployment workflows. This approach has dramatically accelerated their development velocity while maintaining the security and reliability standards essential for their enterprise customers.

The emergence of these roles reflects a fundamental shift in how organizations approach technology delivery. Rather than expecting every engineer to master the full stack of modern cloud infrastructure, organizations are creating specialized teams focused on building developer-centric platforms that abstract complexity without removing flexibility. The most successful platform teams approach their internal users as customers, creating intuitive, well-documented services focused on developer experience rather than merely providing access to underlying infrastructure.

Conclusion

As we conclude our exploration of platform engineering and DevOps futures, several transformative trends emerge that will reshape software delivery. The integration of AI into DevOps workflows promises not just automation but genuine intelligence that amplifies human capabilities. GitOps approaches are creating unprecedented consistency and reliability by treating infrastructure as immutable, version-controlled artifacts. Edge computing, serverless architectures, and quantum systems challenge engineers to orchestrate workloads across increasingly heterogeneous environments.

The democratization of software development through low-code and no-code platforms is extending the reach of platform engineering beyond traditional developers to business users and analysts. Environmental sustainability has evolved from a peripheral concern to a central consideration, driving resource optimization innovations that benefit organizations and the planet. These shifts are creating new specialized roles while also demanding professionals who can bridge technical and business domains.

While distinct, these trends are deeply interconnected. AI enhances sustainability through intelligent optimization. GitOps enables effective management of edge environments. Serverless architectures and low-code platforms both democratize development. These connections remind us that platform engineering is an integrated discipline that evolves continuously to address changing landscapes.

The essence of platform engineering remains constant: creating systems that enable others to work more effectively. This requires technical excellence, organizational wisdom, user empathy, and business understanding. The future belongs to engineers who balance innovation with pragmatism, automation with human-centered design, and technical depth with strategic breadth.

By embracing these emerging trends while remaining grounded in fundamental principles, platform engineers will continue transforming how organizations deliver software, advancing a technical discipline and addressing the most pressing challenges facing technology organizations today.

Join our Discord space

Join our Discord workspace for latest updates, offers, tech happenings around the world, new releases, and sessions with the authors:

https://discord.bpbonline.com

Index

www.ingramcontent.com/pod-product-compliance
Lightning Source LLC
Chambersburg PA
CBHW061742210326
41599CB00034B/6768